PLAN SEA

A Guide to a Work-Travel Life
Amazing Adventures Around the World
and Preparing for Your Own Sea Change

S. E. Ansley

GASHE

Plan Sea was written by S.E. Ansley between August 2017 and December 2020, on a trip that visited twenty-five countries.

The events and conversations in this book have been set to the best of the author's ability. Some names and details have been changed to respect the privacy of individuals.

First edition December 2020

Book design by Danielle Pettee & S.E. Ansley
Front cover photograph by Ruben Gutierrez on Unsplash
Back cover photograph by Magdalena Dziewic
All photographs inside the book by S.E. Ansley

Printed internationally by IngramSpark

ISBN 978-0-473-52319-0 (Paperback)
ISBN 978-0-473-52320-6 (Hardcover)
ISBN 978-0-473-52321-3 (eBook)
ISBN 978-0-473-52322-0 (PDF)
ISBN 978-0-473-52323-7 (AudioBook)

Published by GASHE International
www.planseabook.com

For all enquiries related to Plan Sea
please contact press@gashe.com

This book is dedicated to

My Parents

For, whatever their approach, their lessons helped
lead to my present wisdom and consciousness

And to all whom I've encountered
and loved along the way

Table of Contents

A Forewarning on Randomness (Introduction)   1

1   Quantum Life   3

2   Road to Nowhere   9

3   The Message   31

4   The Dream on Jeju Island   47

5   Fairy Tale Land   75

6   Night Train to Chiang Mai   93

7   India, Revisited   113

8   Auroville Fifty   135

9   One Hundred Day Vipassana   148

10   Living Examples of Grace   169

11   Chicken Meditation   195

12   Festivals and Hungarians   211

13   Night of the Full Blood Moon   229

14   The Baltic Trip, Part I   243

15   You Cannot Force Magic   261

16   Dobra Atmosfera   276

17   Year of the Pig   289

18   A Wedding in Sri Lanka   306

19   Himalayan Heights   323

20   Homeless Where the Heart Is   348

21   One Final Crazy Adventure   375

22   Lockdown in Paradise   395

23   Preparing for Sea Change   424

Gratitude (Special Thanks & Acknowledgements)   436

A crew of utterly unhelpful Himalayan dogs, on the return from Khir Ganga

A Forewarning on Randomness

Fittingly, on the final evening before I sent Plan Sea to print, a Jupiter-like sunset dropped towards the Arabian Sea. This writing odyssey has lasted well over three years; two years longer than anticipated. As this book – and life – progressed, I knew that Plan Sea could be so much more than travel tips.

Our planet is at a precarious crossroads. Many of us had seen it coming for a while; ultimately, we're all affected. Individually, we cannot affect much about the wider world. But we do have control over our actions, and reactions. Thus, it's essential to focus on ourselves. By finding inner peace and sharing good energy with those around us, the outside world matters less.

If humanity can unify, sacrifice some conveniences to aid the transition to a calmer, fairer and more conscious society, we have reason for optimism. It's time to break some conventions, take bold actions, and stand up for human (and animal) rights. It starts with observing what's actually happening, and questioning the truth of what we're told.

The forewarning is that this book could – and does – head anywhere. Very little was planned in advance, and most of it happened on a shoestring budget. It's the epitome of a DIY project, and was all done on the road. Some parts are raw, there may be mistakes: This is how it is. Thank you for joining these adventures with me. I hope it provides some inspiration and insight into your own life. Enjoy the journey.

Sea – December 1, 2020

The Original Opening of Plan Sea

Many mornings I wake from slumber, rub the dust from my eyes and wonder: "Where am I?" Every morning, usually a different bed, an alternate locale, a blip of temporary confusion, a contemplation of any lingering fragments of dreams, then an invigorating revelation of what's to unfold over the day ahead.

This particular morning I've woken in Bangalore, the "Silicon Valley of India". It's my sixth and final day in the city. Tonight I take an excitingly perilous night bus to Pondicherry, the gateway city to the experimental utopian community of Auroville. I've been in India three weeks, on my annual August business trip.

As of now, I've been travelling two months. It kicked off with my fortieth birthday, at a friend's longtime, self-built house atop cliffs, beside wild beaches in a remote national park, an hour south of Byron Bay, Australia. I long considered it my favourite spot in the world. The past two months I've woken up in historic old buildings in Helsinki, various indoor and outdoor consignments in Berlin, a desert in central Spain, a tent concealed behind a German roadside rest stop, a backyard in Bohemia, an overnight bus from Prague, a mysterious puddle of water in Bruges, a penthouse on an Amsterdam island, a quarry in Denmark, different rooms of the same Copenhagen house, bunkbeds in Delhi, and a friend's room in his remote village in Kerala, southern India.

This is the fourth successive year I left a comfortable Melbourne life for extended travels, spending approximately half of each year elsewhere. Circumstances suggest I've already broached the world of perpetual travel, with no further reason to return to Melbourne or Australia, at least until February and March, when my annual high school softball coaching resumes for a ninth year. It's the only time or place I absolutely have to be anywhere in the world. And even then, does one really *have* to be anywhere?

In the meantime, I live day by day, excitedly back in the moment, working hard to ensure future travels come much easier than my lifelong reality: that is, scraping by and struggling, every day. In three weeks I arrive in Seoul, Korea, to "close the circle" of a recent, riveting experience birthed in Denmark. After that, I have no plans whatsoever.

This is my life right now. It certainly is interesting, sometimes frightening and frequently exhilarating. One can, and will always, find a way.

Sea – September 2017

Chapter 1

Quantum Life

As I slowly slipped along freshly muddy Himalayan pathways, all dreams I'd harboured – of home, love, family, music, and peace to all beings – any misstep, would ensure everything plunging altogether into a raging, rocky waterfall, before gushing out to the ferocious Parvati River and, eventually, the sea. The cliff-edge foot-wide trail was further inhibited by another unhelpful mountain dog, who was perplexed at firm English commands of "Turn around!" or insistent prodding on her back. Under the mist of falling rain, the vague pathway ahead disappeared, rising up, narrower through bushes; sharp, slippery and muddy, towards a frothing waterfall. *What if I must come down?* I couldn't risk it, not with well-worn running shoes and an increasing urgency to navigate out of the anonymous mountain jungle, before drenching downpour and looming darkness.

There is no pedestal for ego with life at stake. Bravado will impress neither puzzled mountain dogs nor the swamp and forest below; perhaps nothing more than a wooden tribute in remembrance. There was no reason for added risks, particularly with more to come: on this trek and in life itself.

With a deep breath, I firmly nudged the dog around; her paws begrudgingly latched on a small ridge. I delicately tiptoed past, and made my way down. Slowly, surely, along a clearer route; a narrow bridge across another waterfall led onto the next majestic mountain. In fact, the view was even more dazzling from the opposite side, along higher cliffs. Wild marijuana plants blossomed in abundance, and the river rumbled mercifully further below, yet every slippy step remained basked in steadfast concentration.

Responsible inner voices warn us of risk and danger: from people, places or circumstances. Think back to your own particularly "lucky breaks": close calls, millimetres from disaster, encountering somebody in the nick of time, or a window that opened after all others clattered shut. Any of those manifesting would have diverted our paths, if not ended things entirely.

My probable life trajectory was not looking good. There were numerous clear occasions when I could have been arrested, imprisoned, beaten, frozen to death, or succumbed to dark forces, but extraordinary luck granted me enough chances to turn my life around. The more often we put ourselves in risky or unpleasant situations: the higher probability of bad things happening. Consequently, the inverse is also correct. Through this, we inherently hold reasonable control over our destinies.

Everything Is Possible... and Has Happened

"According to quantum theory, the universe doesn't just have a unique single history. Instead the universe has every single possible history, each with its own probability."
- Stephen Hawking, Brief Answers to the Big Questions

Quantum theory nominates, that for nothing to be possible, everything must be possible. Through this premise in the universe's creation, even the most inconceivable actuality has occurred somewhere, within infinite quantum histories. If every possibility is conceivable and has happened, then why not align ourselves along the paths that lead to our chosen destinations?

Beyond the fury and aura of the universe remains inexplicable powers. Critical interventions in the nick of time? Waking moments before nearby cars collide? An instinctive commando fall and roll away from an onrushing train? Following an inclination to move safer into the hills, hours before nationwide terrorist attacks? A final lap around a quarry, before crossing paths with a seemingly pre-destined soul?

While philosophers ruminate, scientists are expected to uncover many of the universe's remaining secrets by the end of this century. Many issues will be aided by the coming revolution of quantum computing. Researchers will be able to input all of the vastly available data about everything – even if seemingly unrelated – into quantum computers, and generate solutions. For example, scenarios that might halt climate change, inter-national drug and human trafficking, and global terrorism.

It's one matter to theorise about mind-boggling concepts, and another to experience them. Plentiful chance encounters in my lifetime manifested from improving my odds, simply by putting myself out there. Seemingly inconsequential decisions, like where to stay or chill, return home or head somewhere, uncovered magical dimensions. Frequent clues and openings are handily observable, that can assist in architecting major shifts in our lifestyles, workplaces and relationships. With even reluctant acceptance of the science of the universe, its powers and mystique are abundant everywhere, and can be applied to everything: Travel, life and dreams.

The Power and Poignancy of Flexibility

The less commitments one holds, the more open plans become. Having a fully flexible schedule, with the ability to work from anywhere, lends to further possibilities. Travel organically evolves matrices of ideas. The traditional "return ticket" takes us somewhere, perhaps stopping along the way; stay a while, then home. Finite side adventures are available from a base; however, dates and locales are set. Locked-in milestones, including festivals, weddings, conferences and visa expiry deadlines, necessitate diligent planning. They provide the inherent convenience of establishing a sequence of events that trigger the crafting of larger journeys. For instance, a recent Sri Lanka visit came from a friend's wedding invitation. When I was asked to speak at a conference in Delhi, it crafted the premise of a three-month trip. Fly into India, reach Sri Lanka for the wedding two months later, and for everything else: Go with the flow.

Way more adventurous, are one-way trips. Arrive at a locale, then figure out details accordingly. Fly into one country, out from another, shifting continents as inspired. Without return flights, devoid of commitments anywhere, and the freedom to come off one's path, even a little, the focus turns to one leg at a time. Check the vibe, and adapt as appropriate. Truly enjoy each moment; tomorrow will come. We learn that the journey is what's most important, in just about everything. Sometimes we find a place we love, and stay a while, or resolve to return. Often, there comes a clear inclination to move on.

Sometimes The Best Laid Plans... Don't Happen

All the apparent plans in the world mean nothing if circumstances prevent their happening. The actuality of this trip, that I remain upon three-plus years later, was nothing how I originally envisioned. It wasn't the one I longed for after the conclusion of last year: depressed, confused, my heart literally aching after a hospital heart attack scare, broke and broken in a cold semi-detached bungalow, forcing a "normal" routine back in grey and costly Australia.

My original travel plans were bold and, in the end, untenable. Multiple parallel realities would have enabled my debut exploration of Alice Springs and a return to southern Africa, simply if I had enough money. With even modestly extra cashflow I'd have attended the 2017 Solar Eclipse Festival in Oregon, then Burning Man. I'd undoubtedly have travelled in alternate circles, and been in a different relationship with other demands and needs. Crucially, I'd unlikely have struggled through the necessary growth and spiritual awakening that emerged early in 2018, that saved my life in many ways.

Several devastating heartbreaks, multiple near-death experiences, homeless periods, money stress and strife? I wouldn't change a thing. This is how my life played out, as it was. Our paths can be guided in unforeseen directions – even if at the time we don't know what it all means.

By living in the moment, while consistently working towards milestones in the future, life is regularly enthralling, captivating and real. It provides necessary purpose to endure. It is within reach of anybody with passion, a dream and the commitment to make things happen, irrespective of money, entitlement or experience. It requires summoning some courage to take the first steps, prepare diligently, and venture into the unknown, staying open and ready for everything.

Take Opportunities Presented

Every single decision – right, wrong, risky or seemingly inconsequential – precedes the next, and onward, ad infinitum. The nagging voice in our heads usually speaks with reason, although listening every time would itself drastically shift our course. Everything sets up for what comes next.

Clues might appear in the form of a mid-winter "Help Wanted" window sign, while living rough on the streets, freezing and starving. Frequently, there are invitations that open new creative horizons – "What might the North have to offer?" - or hunches towards unexpected relationships. The voice can be blunt: "Danger!" and should not be ignored. Our survival instincts guide us along, although ego stokes peril, rolling against chance. On the occasions we think we know better than our subconscious, these are often met with instant karma.

Sometimes it feels the universe wills us towards pre-destined directions, offering numerous detours to pursue, and yet we arrive at the same place. Constantly diminishing "luck" fuels downward spirals, saps confidence and spawns further errors. Nobody is to blame. Maybe we're not ready, or old habits rumble us away from bliss. At some point, the cycle will be broken, whether we do it ourselves, or require more drastic intervention. Awareness of – and action upon – daily clues, like a puzzle or maze, brings us closer toward our destiny. At the very least, we might blindly but assuredly stumble into transient magic and adventure, grateful for the moment, in knowing that nothing lasts forever.

We're irrepressibly lucky that any of us are alive. When we become down on life, mull The End, or lack authentic enthusiasm for anything, start with being appreciative for our little living window of time on Earth. While we're here, make the most of it. Steer towards the direction desired, and enjoy the ride. Anything can happen. Everything has.

The middle of Nowhere: A regional Burn in a Spanish desert, July 2017

Chapter 2

Road to Nowhere

Looking back to the beginning of this trip, feels as far in the past as a morning's grasping for fading remnants of dreams. Where does a journey actually begin? For, every present moment emanates from our complete and collective history of personal and societal experiences, since the beginning of Time.

For me, this was neither an easy year nor existence. 2017 unravelled indignantly, with on-the-dot-of-midnight further bullying and exclusion, from so-called "radically inclusives". I lived in an increasingly unfriendly share house, with a new housemate I didn't choose, and brooding from other co-habitants. I'd been depressed since my dramatic return from Moscow ten months earlier. Last year's epic five-month voyage spanned Cape Town, Afrikaburn, a road trip through South Africa, Zambia buses to Malawi, cancelled flights and 8+ hour layovers in both Tanzania and Ethiopia, jetlag at the Taj Mahal, a too-short Delhi business weekend, Toronto family, friends and fling, a powerful Burning Man, riveting San Francisco afterglow, and then all roads led to Red Square. A four-day triple-continental bender commenced with a trippy walk along Moscow river, a Club Propaganda all-nighter, then a classic vinyl sing-along with an acclaimed airport architect in his downtown Moscow apartment. From there, a long-haul flight via Delhi into Sydney culminated in a Dr. Love all-nighter, and I didn't sleep that entire weekend, until Monday. Then I was off to a miniature festival south of Canberra, that replaced the flooded-out Burning Seed. After a couple of days of pouring rain, everybody evacuated the makeshift venue, before further catastrophic flooding, and the party (and trip) was over.

I returned to daily drabness in concrete Melbourne and The System. I wondered how I'd afford rent and food, asking again: *What am I doing here?* I lacked spark and colour in a mono-chrome metropolis. For many months I worked my ass off for travel savings, rising before dawn most days to scoot across Melbourne to coach or umpire softball kids. To pass time before afternoon matches I'd work on mundane, underpaid web projects from expensive cafes that depleted my savings intended for prospective plans, most of which were eventually cancelled. In Australia I was not feeling lifelong love connections: Where were the girls in my dreams?

Grim moments relentlessly inspire prolific ascents. It's normal to be depressed, even meekly contemplating suicide, as I did, locked in my Brunswick West bungalow for days without light, ruminating The End. But, give it time. There's beauty in the art of sorrow. There remains much of the world's – and our lives' – mysteries to uncover.

Who could I blame for my life but myself? From the moment we're born, it's up to us to figure everything out, and make things happen. I pay a debt of gratitude to my parents for, whatever their hands-off, DIY approach, it fostered my learned life accomplishments. My parents provided comfortable and secure homes in Singapore – one of the world's cleanest and most peaceful nations – and enrolled me in the best education money could buy.

My Canadian mother – a creative and teacher – immersed my sister and I in arts, music and acting. Mum ensured I had musical equipment at my disposal, like guitars, keyboards and a four-track recorder. My New Zealander father was a devout All-Black fan, and one of the first banking executives to adopt personal computers. Dad helped me develop a sharp mind through chess, mathematics and computers, although he was barely around due to his frequent business travels. It's hard to call my dad an alcoholic, but he enjoyed drinking every day, particularly vino rouge.

Both of my parents were dramatic, living in bubbles they built for our protection, and manifested webs of lies that didn't need to be. There was a confusing practice attempt at separation when I was seven. We were pulled from flourishing Singapore school life, and thrust into Canadian winter and education. After many confused months, my parents' reunited, and we returned to Singapore. My spoiled younger sister constantly got me in trouble; she was persistently angry at everyone, despite being gifted all: movie roles, university education, two cars, her daughter was selflessly raised by our mother, her dog Lucky was saved from the kennel (unlike mine, Majerle).

After our parents formally separated when I was age ten, I had to fend for myself, battle through, try and fail. My sister and mother bonded tighter, often ignoring me together, sometimes for weeks on end. I was forced by my mother to attend weekly Roman Catholic church and catechism studies. I questioned the truth behind suspect religious messages, before the teacher forbade any further questioning. I had no male influences, other than my dad's friend Jim, who taught me baseball, but was then a heavy alcoholic.

Culture shock at age sixteen, slammed upon our relocating from conservative and well-behaved Singapore, into the vice and underground of Toronto, where I entered the brainwash of North American media and consumerism. My nice but weird Canadian family was deeply rooted in mental illness, although none of them ever realised or acknowledged it. I didn't know what to believe, living in a house of lies, a family of drama, and mainstream society clearly full of bluster and nonsense. Starving for companionship, I encountered sinister energies, and committed various regrettable acts as a delinquent teenager.

Knowing my potential, I wised up and took adult education more seriously. I wrote a book about a city of dogs (Onward Muttford), made my first real friends – Liz and Lesley – and was introduced to Toronto's pulsating underground through Martin Streek (RIP), who shared life on The Edge, 102.1 FM.

This era culminated in two years of homelessness. I was justifiably kicked out of my mother's house at nineteen, with my belongings packed into garbage bags and guitar confiscated. I laboured through a dreadful eighteen-month relationship with my first girlfriend, in a frightening, small Ontario country town. During my final nine brutal months, I shivered through a Canadian winter in a minuscule, cold concrete basement freezer room; later I fell exceptionally ill. If my girlfriend and I fought, sometimes my only meals were heating frozen pizzas for hours, with matches or candles. My relationship mercifully came to an end upon the dying wish of her father; the early-morning news was dramatically delivered by his murderer best friend.

This spawned a full year living outside on the streets. I slept under bridges and mostly on rooftops, around Burlington, Hamilton and Toronto, including through a freezing winter, with temperatures that plummeted beyond minus-thirty degrees. Cardboard boxes stuffed with newspaper, clothing and blankets afforded me sufficient warmth; multiple layers of socks, gloves and clothes protected me from unrelenting air. Most nights the Moon offered me hope, assuring that I would love again. And, somehow I survived it. I was homeless for two years, with a lost book of stories and many lucky breaks in between.

We must be ready to take opportunities presented. While shivering one night in the middle of freezing winter, I noticed a "Help Wanted" sign conveniently placed in the window of a pizza shop I'd frequently visited, and mustered the courage to ask about the job. Suddenly I had multiple daily pizza meals and pocket money. Miraculously, days later at 3000-capacity NRG/Kingdom nightclub in Burlington, I earned another job. One night their lighting tech didn't show and, as they'd known me for years, I was randomly thrust into the role.

Two jobs after nothing led to better eating and a rejuvenated mindset. I rented a room in a friend's condo for a few months, and it became the most exciting time of my life. I conducted live lights and lasers from a big stage, in front of thousands while top DJs spun; notably Fridays that were broadcast nationally on 102.1FM. I discovered the underground rave scene – one of top quality and creativity in music-mad Toronto – and also the drugs that accompanied it, that led me off track when my employment predictably ceased.

Certain friends of mine abruptly remained no longer, after they learned of my homeless status. Lonelier and destitute again, scrounging to afford raving habits, I plunged ever deeper into the rave scene's deadly underworld. Months of drama and near misses culminated in my assault on a pubic bus by a large vicious drug dealer, whose hefty sucker punch shattered my right eye socket behind sunglasses. This prompted nine months of personal rehabilitation, that I spent in veritable hiding in a Hamilton ghetto apartment, under the flat of a Satan's Choice.

I knew I could do better. My old reputation soiled me. I was tired of being a broken family outcast, destitute deviant and unsuccessful party peddler. In the dawn of the 21st century, I surprisingly celebrated the overhyped Y2K at my grandmother's house – a big first step towards healing old family wounds. I reemerged under my initials: SEA. The name became my online identity and social persona. Hence, Plan Sea deserved to be more than simple travel trips. It's about the impetus to reinvent oneself, and mustering the courage to change.

The Epic Trip Begins

When planes lift off, it feels like goodbye. Perhaps I won't return. Travel excels for peaceful inner reflection, affording plentiful time to ponder and wonder. Transit ensures countless hours waiting, contemplating, imagination, planning and dreams.

On June 13, 2017, I departed my West Brunswick bungalow, lugging two backpacks for travel, with the rest of my stuff stored in the garage. After a few days in Sydney with Burner friends J-Man and Hannah, I made my way to the tropical Gold Coast, where I hung with battle-weary Sheather for a couple of blockchain-themed nights near Mullumbimby.

My milestone fortieth birthday was graciously hosted at my favourite locale in the world. Grumpy but loveable Craig Bower's hand-built manor was perched atop sandy cliffs, between the Pacific Ocean and tropical bush of Broadwater National Park. A dozen diverse friends attended the pleasantly low-key and responsible weekend. There was relentless drama with my hot-headed short-term girlfriend, and an inexplicable racist rant from Bower, who blamed Islam for the problems of the world. On the night before my birthday, I overhead bursts of drunken, self-touting ranting from an old friend and protege, who leaked confidential company matters to outsiders. My girlfriend literally spat on me, for sharing time with everybody at my birthday, one female friend in particular. Otherwise, it was a lovely time, shared with souls who were dear to me. In the end, it became my unannounced farewell to Australia.

Following the weekend, my calmed-down girlfriend, a couple of her cool friends and I drove to Byron Bay, for a relaxing oceanside picnic in sunshine. After teary airport goodbyes, she flew home, while the rest of us drove to Brisbane. I spent an evening at a Burner friend's house, before the couple and I met up the next night. They looked after me properly, before I departed hazy-eyed to Brisbane airport ahead of a midnight flight. I was finally on my own, with time to think and reflect. Past life becomes a blur of aeroplane fuel lifting towards the heavens, and there's little we can do about anything now.

...

The first leg of my sleep-filled Finnair flight offered a morning stopover in Hong Kong, the dynamic east-Asian megacity. The spacious airport and the metropolis' distant skyscrapers reminded me that there was vastly more of this giant planet to explore. The subsequent cross-continental flight glided over desolate central Asia. Eventually, the ground below filled with the forests of eastern Europe. My first visit to Europe in fifteen years began with the plane landing shakily, hurtling down the runway... then taking off again. Winds prevented a safe landing, and required a low-flying loop to try again. On a second attempt, we successfully touched down in Helsinki.

After a modern train to a central old hostel, I wandered around the waterside Finnish capital on a rare sunny day. As night fell, I found a music bar, and splurged on a €10 beer. I woke in the middle of the night to the amazement of lingering sunlight at 1am, and only half an hour of complete darkness.

I devoured a lovely breakfast at Finland's oldest cafe, Ekberg, before returning to Helsinki's airport. This flight's delays came from storms in Germany, and we were temporarily diverted to Berlin's Schönefeld Airport. The plane sat on the tarmac for hours: some bureaucratic loophole about customs and immigration not expecting our plane to land there. Eventually we took off in torrential thunderstorms; the jet barely hovered above buildings, twisting and turning, before it landed in massive puddles at Berlin's ageing Tegel.

The daredevil delight of the Helsinki double landing, and storm-diverted flights to Berlin, posed early commentaries on my journey ahead. One: that it's going to be wild. Another: not to have preconceived expectations about anything. And, that after the past nine gruelling months, I'd earned this trip.

...

Following fairly efficient public transportation to East Berlin in sopping rain, I arrived at my hostel for the weekend: the incomparable Sandino World Improvement Network. I'd booked a space in the garden for my little green tent, but it was deplorable camping weather. Fortunately, for me, the storm prevented another guest's arrival, and I was afforded Sandino's sole spare bunk for a warm night indoors.

Delayed travels and shambolic weather kept me inside, where I soaked up Sandino's vibe. I met other guests, and further chatted with its staff: Jack from Chesterfield, his girlfriend Jill, and Clara, from Toronto. I particularly enjoyed conversations with Sandino's East German owner, Shami, who was a delightful conversationalist, despite his shy but improving English. Shami detailed his vision behind the World Improvement Network, and acknowledged our collective responsibility to help change the world. Every morning Shami and I sipped office-brewed cappuccinos with sugar and milk. I learned about Berlin realities, and exchanged tales about travels and dreams.

On Saturday, my "second" fortieth birthday, I hung with Andi: an Australian-Israeli DJ and music producer I'd randomly met in Melbourne. Andi invited me to Greenhouse Arts Factory: a creative warehouse. Later, Andi escorted me to an underground venue, then known as JK but is no longer in existence. JK was a hidden riverside industrial complex, seemingly erected out of recycled materials. Inside featured several rooms of pounding beats, while the frequencies of speakers and subwoofers artfully and uncannily simulated the swaying boats.

Andi departed while I was treated to LSD by an older soul, and I danced away for many hours. At one point I wondered if David August danced beside me. Although everything was available for me to party another day, I felt alone, tired and needing to save cash. Instead I delightfully, exhaustedly strolled back to Sandino, through laid-back Berlin on a sunny, upbeat Sunday morning.

However this actual trip differed from how I'd originally imagined it, the reality was how it was. It would take me weeks to ease into this year's travels. The impact of that first weekend in Berlin, and clearing my head simply by being somewhere different, contributed to an avalanche of inspiration.

Road Trip to Nowhere

Due to my S-Train's re-routing, then prematurely disembarking at Treptower Park, I never had a chance to make my bus' official departure time. I darted between empty taxi stands, bus stops and the station itself, to ensure just-in-time boarding of an alternative train. I raced through the halls of Sudkreuz and bolted towards indicated "Bus" signs. Thirty minutes late, I'd resigned to backup plans; as fate transpired my bus was perfectly tardy enough. Exiting the station, racing around a bend, there were no waiting buses, but one approaching: Mine! Onboard, I thanked my lucky stars.

From Dresden I rode a train to Děčín, that entered Bohemia over the picturesque Czech border. Awaiting me was Peter Czech: a celebrated New Zealand artist. We'd met at Kiwiburn in early 2017. I was impressed at Peter's "So Beautiful" video mashup of live rhythmic dancers, that deployed cameras and effects to transform nude silhouettes into vibrant art narratives. Peter owned a building in Děčín, invited me to visit and I'd suggested attending Nowhere: a Burn in a remote Spanish desert north of Barcelona.

Peter handled transportation arrangements, and rented a Skoda stationwagon for our cross-continental drive. I wrongly assumed Peter owned a car, and grossly under-calculated rental costs, petrol and tolls. This added unexpected layers of guilt, on top of my other prevalent money stress, but Peter was gracious and cool. Our marathon drive included an overnight stop at a random Germany roadside motel, before an all-day effort through France and Spain. We reached outer Barcelona at sundown, and spent an hour in a massive supermarket, scavenging for festival supplies. We arrived at the Burn's anonymous desert in the middle of the night. Exhaustedly, we slept in the parking lot, with my green tent hastily erected while Peter dozed in the car. We awoke in a desert with distant sound systems rumbling and the comforting aroma of coffee.

Of my nine Burns to date, Nowhere was the most dis-appointing. Peter paid to join a New Zealander camp; I free-camped nearby. This demonstrated the disparity of exclusivity: splitting people between sides of imaginary walls conjured by money or entitlement, even in the most well-meaning of places. I didn't cross paths with a handful of other friends who were attending, and I found individual camps - "Barrios" - unwelcoming. Barrios were generally split by language and nationality, such as Italian camps, French camps, etcetera. It was the first Burn where I neither participated nor volunteered in any way. Everything combined for incredible loneliness, with much solo time to contemplate the lows of recent life, burnt by desert sun, dust and self.

Highlights were few and far between. The desert itself was typically brutal: scorching hot and dry in the day, while contrastingly frigid at night. Encircling the desert lay small rocky mountains around a plateau, that encouraged scenic hikes. "Gas Man" was a hilariously costumed hippie superhero on a motorbike, who blasted music and doled out plentiful free shots of powerful "gas". On a couple of afternoons I serenely composed orchestral music on my laptop.

Two days before the end, thunderstorms hit Nowhere and rain bucketed down for hours. Floodwater raced through most of the festival site; fortunately we were camped at the top of an incline. I huddled in the spacious central public tent while onrushing water manifested reservoirs. I stood beside a group of pleasant French ravers and helped create buffers for the water. Streams of water became collective gushes, and everybody inside latched onto poles and each other, somehow rolling and sharing joints in between. Naked hippies ran outside in the rain, delightedly sliding in mud.

The final day, by when I'd accepted this Burn, however feral and non-fascinating, was the one I needed, I relaxed into heightened mental capacity. There's something about limited time remaining, that prompts us to make the most of our current places and situations. While most people packed, or recovered from the massive Saturday night, I wandered around in sunshine, up for practically anything.

A Dutch couple, Anders and Vanilla, and a man named Goblin introduced themselves. As free campers they shared similar sentiments about the unfriendliness of Barrios, and proposed exploring the remnants of Nowhere together. We set a fair target of acquiring leftover beverages from every camp. This translated into hours of lighthearted fun. We overindulged in available alcohol, and stumbled across magic mushrooms from a spacey French camp. The couple generously offered me a place to stay in Amsterdam, should I need one.

As the mushrooms kicked in, my inhibitions dropped. I felt authentic waves of relaxation and relief for the first time in months. It included my missing out on subtleties, but it was all short-lived, and peaked when Anders asked me, point blank, about sexual intimacy. Stunned, I couldn't respond, but with my buzz busted I no longer felt comfortable or safe. This was an evening I wanted to simply enjoy new connections.

After momentarily clearing headspace, I ambled to one of the few remaining music stages. The Dutch couple and Goblin were there; Anders was sheepish, but we amicably danced around each other for hours. I was particularly preoccupied with a vivacious topless dancer, made a few typical temporary dancefloor connections, and conversed with Goblin in broken English. Eventually the Dutch couple retreated to their campervan; they manifested a human baby from their efforts!

Characteristically, I danced through the night, moving between stages as each one closed. I held a habitual tendency of lasting to the end, following distant beats, seeking the very final dancefloor: the one that when its music stops, the party is truly over. I danced many hours: 20,000 steps in a trance. I was fully aware of particular energies trying to lure me in, but I maintained solitude. As the final drum & bass beats in the Italian Barrio subsided, underneath flickers of early sun on the desert horizon, I haggardly retreated to my tent and slept.

...

Hours later, dazed and hungover, I delicately emerged from the tent. Peter had packed everything and prepared coffee. Setting forth in the Skoda, we departed the Spanish desert and drove north. I had no fixed plans for several days, when I was to meet my English friend Alan, before our own road trip to a Scandinavian Burn called Borderland. While driving through France I contacted my father, who owned a quaint cottage in Brittany, but he wouldn't be in the country for weeks.

Accepting Peter's invitation to explore Děčín, we diverted through France. We were mutually aghast by so many expensive

French road tolls. Two other New Zealander friends of Peter were cryptocurrency traders, and they temporarily resided in his top floor studio apartment. My bed for a couple of nights was a couch in the corner. Děčín was picturesque and low-key. It broadcast a rainbow of pastels when the sun descended, and featured multiple rivers converging in a valley between volcanic mountains. Peter's gracious hospitality and the charming obscurity of Děčín lent me reasons to return.

Penthouse in Amsterdam

The second half of my European trip was shared with my worldly friend Alan. He was my campmate at Burning Man 2016, and part of our riveting post-Burn escapades in San Francisco. My night bus from Prague arrived in Bruges, the historic Belgian city. I met Alan at our hostel a short ways out of town. Bruges (silent "s") was famous from the film, "In Bruges", about two hitmen patiently waiting to enact their next execution. Bruges was a stunning old city, with its exquisite cobblestoned streets, antiquated buildings and a landmark central cathedral.

Alan and I excitedly strode to Bruges' centre, on a night of concerts and celebrations for Belgium's national holiday. In the middle stood a large music stage, with busy crowds and plentiful beer vendors touting triple strength brews. After the concert we entered a lively bar, and danced in confined spots while downing evermore triple strength beer. That's the last I remembered. Apparently I spotted a bar advertising espresso martinis and insisted on treating us, before we stumbled home.

...

I woke in a hostel bed, incredibly dehydrated and hungover in a strange wet puddle; another puddle soaked the floor around our big bottle of water. With ten minutes before checkout, I rushed to clean up as best as possible, with a splitting headache and a mental blank from last night's events. According to Alan, I bombarded into the room in the middle of night, flicked on the lights and startled the poor other roommate. Alan was unsure about the water everywhere. Excessive alcohol caused me to black out – not the only time on this journey – and my possible incontinence was alarming but unsurprising.

Our road journey from Bruges ventured through the Netherlands. As we were keen on acquiring certain high-grade Dutch botany ahead of Borderland, Amsterdam posed an ideal destination for a night or two. We swiftly discovered untenably expensive Amsterdam accommodation prices: even campsites well out of the city cost €40.

After exhausting all available options, begrudgingly, more in that I dislike asking for favours, I dispatched the Dutch Nowhere couple a casual message. A prompt answer followed up their original offer: we were welcome to stay at their vacant apartment. Super! Following directions led to KNSM-eiland, a human-made island with rows of fancy condo buildings that faced flotillas of moored house boats, and was a short cycle from Amsterdam city centre. One pleasant surprise was Nowhere's Goblin visiting for the weekend. Anders was shy but pleasant, and the unexpectedly lovely weekend began.

Their apartment was a well-decorated penthouse of the far east building on KNSM-eiland. Vanilla's flat was up for sale; it was presently filled with furniture and spotlessly clean, and it sat vacant while she lived with Anders. The lounge led to a small, windy corner balcony that afforded glorious views of downtown Amsterdam and the harbour beneath. Alan, Goblin and I each had a plush room and bed.

After our quintet's dinner beside the water, Alan and I ventured downtown. The streets were busy, particularly in the centre. Our first cannabis stop was sketchy and unmemorable. Alan and I strode to the edge of the roaring Red Light district; we lacked the nerve to enter. On a bridge that crossed a canal, a bald-headed gay man in long black clothing chatted with me. He enjoyed my rapport, enough to wink and hand me the key to his home. Repeating instructions to his apartment, he urged that I find him later, then strolled away. Alan and I bemusedly exchanged stoned, surreal glances. *What to do with this key?* We began to leave, then stopped, circled back, pieced together minimal clues, and dispatched the key in the apparent building's mailbox. Our second night was quieter: it was mostly spent in the penthouse, enjoying excellent wine with Vanilla and Goblin, while resting for Burning carnage ahead.

After the rollicking Amsterdam experience, we packed our

belongings into Alan's stationwagon and returned to the highway. Ten hours later in darkness, we arrived at Borderland, and were greeted with hugs and sweet port by the Port at the top of a dusty hill. Venturing deeper into the quarry beside the sea, we idled slowly into the centre basin, near the Clown Police station and medical Sanctuary. A hurried set up of Alan's giant tent formed our campsite, before we set off for the festival's monumental and riveting opening night.

The Sunset of Dreams

The middle of the abandoned seaside granite quarry at Boesedal Kalkbrud, site of Borderland, housed a giant pyramid that previously stored cranes. It was dark in daytime, yet vibrantly illuminated at night. Echoes reverberated around the Pyramid; bass boomed while higher frequencies fluttered up and around to the peak. The space was not utilised, other than a large, artistic swing that hung from the centre and an excellent downtempo performance on the closing weekend. The Pyramid's unique sonic qualities hinted at massive untapped creative potential. Paths from the Pyramid weaved in plentiful directions: some towards the sea; others up rocky or grassy hills. One path led through a corridor into a more remote quarry, that was reserved for the loudest soundsystems.

Littered around the central quarry stood many dozens of "theme" camps. Typical themes included interactive art, music, countless open bars (as per the Burning principle of gifting), massages, free hugs, spas, acrobatics, kids camps and more. A particularly controversial event was the Slave Market, that battled animated and anguished supporters of contrasting mindsets: Was it politically correct to satirise slavery?

Weeks at Burns transform into veritable hamlets that transcend eras. Most revellers are happy, caring, sharing and high. The multitude of diverse camps was convenient for quality all-day partying; moving from one camp to another like an endless rave. After deflating and lonely Nowhere, I increased my participation at Borderland. I gathered litter and helped camps as spontaneously required – whether lugging heavy tea carts up steep hills to cliffs, assisting with audio/visual setups or sweeping pathways after downpour. Alan had transported his massive, festival-grade soundsystem from the UK, and loaned the speakers to several camps over the week. We intended to pop up a renegade stage at an undetermined interval. As I didn't appreciate the negative connotations of "Clown Police", I served as a freelance Ranger: always alert and available.

Between exerting generous energy and partying long hours, I was increasingly fulfilled at Borderland. I met a plethora of captivating and stoic souls, including tall Nordic beauties, astonishingly giant Danish men, DJs, actors and visionaries. I nurtured regular "friends" as part of a low-key party crew. We'd hang together daily and explore, while Alan was rock-solid as a campmate and confidant. By the weekend I was entirely satisfied, had truly chilled out, and I revelled in each present moment. I followed a hunch to erect my little green tent under cliffs beside the sea, with the intent of sleeping in secluded tranquility over the weekend.

On Friday evening, Alan and I wandered around to investigate plausible locales for popping up the soundsystem. With a small bag of supplies and not much presently happening at Borderland, we moseyed through the rocky, cliff-lined corridor, towards the outer quarry with louder stages. There was one camp en route with a smoking teepee and small stage. As we passed, Alan and I noticed a clear sign beside their mailbox: "Free weed!" Underneath the sign was a medium-sized bowl filled with generous clumps of marijuana. Already well-stoned, Alan and I exchanged disbelieving smiles, toddled a little further, then trudged back to verify the sign's legitimacy. We were warmly invited by the camp's creators into their camp, that became a hot box within the teepee. Reliably, one after another, weed-enticed hippies sauntered past, read the magic sign, and joined our rapidly-sedated circle. Camp organisers hastily erected an outdoor soundsystem, and pumped out feel-good hits under the falling sun. The warmth and colours matched the jovial spirits of the fleeting group of merry-making miscreants.

As sunset conducted its concert in the sky, the camp's blaring speakers were relocated into the quarry's corridor. Two dozen dancers bounced to beats while stalling and recruiting any passerby's. There was one special girl in particular I couldn't take my eyes off: she was angelic, beaming and blissful. Then played Mamas and the Papas' classic, "California Dreamin'": the epitome of optimism, as sunset cascaded across the quarry. Everybody sang and danced in collective delight. Golden light reflected off the angel's face; I thought she was the most beautiful of all the energies at Borderland.

As night fell, each of the trapped hippies freed themselves and resumed their lives. My night became a blur, from a medley of substances, with effects transversing through euphoria, chemical enlightenment and sleep deprivation. I raged along plentiful dancefloors, indulged in deep conversations around chillout camps, and stumbled around the entirety of Borderland's quirky offerings.

Undoubtedly exhausted, late beyond night, as sound from the main quarry trickled into collectively sleepy silence, I strolled one more loop, before heading to the oceanside cliff that obscured my tent. With everything prepared for comfortable rest, I could have crashed entirely satisfied. There was the sound of small rippling waves and the wind against cliff's edge, while sunlight hinted from beyond the horizon.

Of my personal stash, only one joint remained: enough to smoke and sleep. Yet my inner voice spoke clearly: *Smoke your final joint. Take one final lap around the quarry, and see what happens.* Despite fatigue urging I take rest, my inner-adventurer acknowledged that nothing would happen by remaining, but a remote chance of *something* was assured by exploring.

I rolled my final joint, cleaned up and adorned my full white kurta outfit of a long-sleeved shirt and pants. I headed along the rocky beach towards a lifeless quarry. Almost immediately, I crossed paths with a stunning, tall Norwegian. We conversed; it was electric. Already feeling that my decision was worthwhile, I passed the now-deserted hippie trap with its empty marijuana bowl, and continued towards the outer quarry arena.

A solitary stage pumped out punishing house and techno. I gravitated towards its speakers and grooved by myself on the open air dancefloor. Soon the heavens opened, and rain fell while partiers scattered; most ducked into a nearby camp. Instead, I stood in the rain, euphoric but drenched; I revelled living in the absolute moment.

A random stranger emerged from the camp, skipping through raindrops to approach me. After a quick chat, he invited me to the warmth and dryness of his spot inside: "Joints, drinks, music." I followed him into a large tent, where twenty people rested on carpeted ground, shrouded in pillows and low-lying tables. A floor-seated DJ spun softer beats.

Upon sitting, the noble recruiter introduced his friend: The angel from sunset! I couldn't believe my fortune. As calmly and cooly as possible, I introduced myself.

"Sea." I shook hands with the angel, as we exchanged grins.

"Boogie," she warmly responded. Boogie filled my large silver cup with a drink. A feather in her long brown hair waved in the wind while her hazel eyes sparkled.

Her friend soon left, and I would have understood had Boogie similarly departed, but she remained. Her eyes twinkled during casual chats about roots, family and interests; we shared mutual musical passions. Boogie was a performing bassist, having recently played for her father's band in Hungary. When she mentioned there was a music camp at Borderland, I suggested we play together, later: anything to prolong the experience.

With Boogie it was easy and effortless to chat about anything, although I reckoned this beauty would surely ditch me. An hour later, I riskily proposed leaving together and exploring the quarry. To my astonished elation, Boogie accepted. Side by side, mutually fascinated, we idled slowly beyond the outer quarry, through the rocky corridor into the main basin of Borderland. After stopping for random beverages, we entered the dim, spacious pyramid, strolled around, and listened to the frantic pattering of intensifying rain on rooftop. We split the remainder of Boogie's uplifting treats, while rolling joints from her stash.

Unrelenting downpour coerced our sprint through falling water, towards the nearby, vacated band camp. Inside contained dozens of different instruments: keyboards, a drum kit, guitars, bass, violins, horns and more. I fingered a violin, before pressing keys on a piano; Boogie switched between a horn, guitar and bass. Alone we sat in bliss, not really jamming; chatting more than playing.

Several friendly, soft-spoken musicians filtered into the tent.

"How old is everybody here?" asked a tall man in his twenties.

"Twenty-three," Boogie replied, and my heart broke. *So young.* It felt like a punch to the gut.

My turn came: "Sixty-nine," I joked, but hurting.

A shorter man entered, and took control of what had been a laid back session. I banged along on drums as the group played simple grooves, but I lost mental momentum and was subsequently tentative. Mostly I didn't want anybody else around, but Boogie looked delighted.

Sensing an opportunity to restore our twosome, we wished everybody farewell and headed into light rain. A freak parade trumpeted along an otherwise deserted quarry pathway. Boogie and I explored much of the quarry, including atop the cliffs under which my tent rested seaside, close to the camp she shared "with friends" alongside the edge. At one of the larger camps we infiltrated a serious and tearful group session, where the instructor requested that everybody hug their partner. Boogie and I jumped into the sombre camp and enjoyed our first embrace, while astonished mourners looked on.

Feeling a need to impress, I convinced Alan to pop up the massive soundsystem, and we bundled two large speakers into his car. Soon the speakers were pumping in the outer quarry. I played a laptop DJ set, including drum & bass and Lana Del Ray's "High By The Beach". Dozens of passerby's manifested a temporary dancefloor.

While Alan continued to blast beats, Boogie and I returned to the main quarry. We were both exhausted and hungry, yet unrelenting in deep conversation and electric rapport. With the sun falling and nightfall looming, we passed several large tents; one served food. Boogie entered to muster snacks and further awakening supplies. To afford her space I turned my back, and took a few steps for a better sightline of the nearby freak and dwarf parade. I was amused at the parade's humorous costumes and clanging detuned sounds. Minutes later, I returned to the food tent and searched for Boogie, but she completely vanished. *I knew she'd ditch me.*

My heart sank. I knew from plentiful experiences that finding anybody at festivals after dark was unlikely. Fatigue, hunger and our huge age disparity brought a sense of acceptance, although I wasn't yet ready to concede. For an hour, I walked around the entire venue, near Boogie's tent up the cliff, through both quarries, then back to Alan, with whom I shared my dismay. Above all, I craved sleep. After a last detour around the clifftop, I scaled the treacherous rocky decline, zipped myself into my seaside tent, and fell into heavy slumber.

...

I awoke in my tent with the morning sun blazing. I wiped the fog from my eyes, before struck the gut wrench of loss. Slow moving, dehydrated by a chemical hangover and emotionally depleted, I exited the tent into paradise.

The final day of Borderland concluded with its only burn: a hasty one with petrol. Numerous camps initiated teardown, while many people departed entirely. That night I tried to party late into the night, but soundsystems were consistently shut down, even one in a relatively private and discrete bus.

"You don't want a complaint," warned one of the organisers, while the medieval Dane of the bus too easily complied with the demand. The party, and Borderland, were over.

I didn't see Boogie again until Monday, while Alan and I packed everything into the stationwagon. Small speakers blasted music from a nearby camp. Boogie was with a short guy who kept his back to me, albeit respectfully, while Boogie, with a feather in her brown hair, eyed me relentlessly. She and I nodded in recognition, but I didn't approach out of respect for her companion. I still hurt from losing her at sunset.

While Boogie danced nearby, Alan and I bundled our gear into the car, pondered the end of a wonderful week, and drove slowly out of the quarry. We rode along the dusty quarry path, before disappearing from Borderland like the dream it was.

Sometimes the Fantasy is Better Left Alive

In Copenhagen, Alan and I slept at an overpriced hostel, before visiting Christiania to indulge in quality green. Christiania was an autonomous community within Copenhagen, and featured an outdoor market with dozens of stalls selling high quality bud and supplies. Lovers of Sativa, Indica or hashish were readily satisfied. Hundreds of chilled-out smokers converged on stone steps, beside hectares of lush forest, a lake and creative village.

Basking in the sun with a Borderland afterglow was scintillating, whatever our fatigue and comedown.

The next morning, Alan departed on the long road home to the UK. I remained in Copenhagen for two further nights, before Delhi business plans. I rented another overpriced room, at a more modern and fancier hostel. That evening, a Burner afterparty was hosted at the Lighthouse. This was a creative community erected within the outer city's sprawling Carlsberg beer factory, and a forty minute walk from Copenhagen. Despite initial awkwardness in that I knew nobody, Burner spirit was welcoming, and I recognised various people who were now scrubbed up and donned "normal" attire. There were British actors, tall viking-like Danes and the usual diverse assortment of Burning Man-themed characters. Many sat outside around picnic tables piled with leftover bottles of alcohol, soft drinks and plates of mostly vegetarian food, while embattled bursts of sun shone through gloomy clouds.

From the outset I felt a new set of eyes on me: a brunette in pink butterfly wings. Butterfly was an Israeli-Argentinian. This was the final night before her own lengthy globetrotting, and she was to fly to Buenos Aires the next morning. The apparent boyfriend didn't look thrilled about anything, but he remained solemn and respectful. Their crew was impressed about my forthcoming trek to India and my past years of travels.

Two hours into festivities, the heavens opened and torrential rain plummeted upon the Lighthouse. In true Burner fashion, we hastily rigged temporary cover, spreading available tarp to create roofing that was tied with rope or string, and propped up with ladders. It was inelegant, but effective and unifying.

Hours after the blurry daze subsided, night fell and attendance thinned. I'd expected to return to my fancy hostel's plump bed, but a casual afterparty was brewing, at the house of an out-of-town Burner. After a flurry of intensified discussion between Israelis, Butterfly invited me to the house. Members of her crew nodded in agreement, including, eventually, the apparent boyfriend.

A dozen bedraggled Burners trudged out of the Lighthouse and hopped on a bus for several stops, before we disembarked in a suburban neighbourhood. We skipped through sleeping streets and pastel apartment blocks. The Burner's decades-old house was built out of wood and stone; it was warm with comfortable furnishings and a homely vibe. There were several bedrooms, a spacious carpeted living room with an adjacent kitchen, and sliding glass doors that led to a deck and garden.

With rooms reserved for the owner's friends I figured I'd sleep on the carpet, but all the awkwardness crystallised, as Butterfly invited me into a small candlelit bedroom, with a high queen bed that filled the space. I looked around at her crew; even the apparent boyfriend's eyes were filled with encouragement. Inside the bedroom with the door closed, Butterfly embraced me. Each movement rocked the rickety wooden house.

An auxiliary benefit was sleeping in a proper bed, and I woke inspiredly beside a relaxed and excited Butterfly, who was gathering a determined mindset for her epic voyage ahead. The innocent Wednesday turned into an awesome after-after party. It was super chilled, mostly spent on the sunny outdoor deck, with platters of premium marijuana, pitchers of streaming coffee, and leftover alcohol. Around midday, Butterfly bid emotional goodbyes to everybody, before hugging and thanking me. I felt humbled and honoured.

In the afternoon everybody departed on missions, and I sat on the living room carpet contemplating my next steps. The only other occupant was a tall, slender blonde Dane, a most dashing young woman; she was the friend of the house's owner. She hinted I could leave and I prepared to, although I remarked that I was happy to remain, stay silent and read.

The Dane was a writer and poet; she was creative, deep-thinking and resolutely independent. She'd become jaded about Danish men. After some time, she warmed to me. Ravishing her in a full body massage opened deeper connections, and we united for two wonderful days and a night. We visited a nearby supermarket, with our arms electrically linked. After cooking pasta, we enjoyed joints and drinks on a candlelit patio. I crashed in her arms, in a brighter and more spacious bedroom that featured musical instruments and a computer.

The morning spawned my own epic cross-continental travel day. With the tall blonde Dane – whose unusual name I couldn't remember – we enjoyed coffee and breakfast, before heading to my hostel. She waited in the common lounge while I hurriedly collected my belongings. I'd spent a considerable sum for two nights at this fancy place, yet spent all my time elsewhere.

Back in the lounge, the Dane and I paused before a powerful goodbye. Normally people would exchange contact details, but I offered a more adventurous proposal:

"I really like you. I hope to see you again. But, how about we leave it to fate and destiny? If it's meant to be, the universe will make it happen."

The Dane's eyes lit up, shining and almost aroused. We embraced like we'd been a couple for years, and kissed farewell.

"You don't even know my name," she purred, and I nodded disappointedly. The electric, fleeting connection headed back into her universe. I assumed I'd see her next year at Borderland.

While I waited for flights at airports, I contemplated everything from the past five weeks in Europe. How could I complain? Whatever my earlier stresses had subsided, after an enchantingly fulfilling Borderland experience, and an electric rapport with several sensational souls. Hope and inspiration filled, with India looming.

At some point during the week, Boogie and I connected online, sharing simple and polite messages. Hers read: "Thank you for the magical moments we spent together. You gave me some wonderful memories that I carry close to my heart. I'm sorry we lost touch, but sometimes the fantasy is better left alive. :) Who knows where the wind blows us..."

Sea's lime-green tent, under cliffs near the sea, at Borderland, July 2017

Chapter 3

The Message

Flush with inspiration in the wake of five riveting weeks in Europe, I arrived in Paharganj, the irrepressibly intense central Delhi neighbourhood. Following efficient Finnair flights from Copenhagen and Helsinki, plus hours of bewildered taxi driving through Delhi, my initial residence was a hastily-arranged budget hotel for the weekend of the DomainX conference and GameX cricket extravaganza.

Saturday's DomainX conference was a breeze, despite my morning's pre-presentation nerves. After the first hour's deliberations, including a traditional candle lighting ceremony and a keynote speech from ICANN, it was my turn to moderate a panel of domain experts, about the importance of domain names. With the successful session complete, I relaxed, enjoyed a luxurious buffet lunch, and exchanged business cards with eager Indian domainers and bloggers.

The first-ever GameX cricket match was competed on a steamy, balmy Sunday with temperatures approaching forty degrees. I arrived at Rohini Sports Complex in north Delhi before any other participants. A friendly group of middle-aged Indian businessmen invited me to share piping hot chai while I waited. They politely asked the typical questions, translating for their less English-capable peers.

Once both teams arrived, after an extended warmup the monumental match between Team Domainers and Team Bloggers commenced. I hadn't played a full match of cricket since I was a child, but today's game was relaxed enough. Two clearly superior players represented Team Bloggers, but our Domainers featured depth throughout the lineup, including the almighty Australian Jon Yau, founder of stockphoto.com.

Under scorching sun I took one particularly difficult catch. While batting I made increasingly strong contact, before lining a first run up the middle. Alas, a juicy ball soon followed, and my over-excited hacking resulted in popping the ball into the sky for an easy out. We narrowly lost to Team Bloggers, but everybody was a winner.

On Sunday night guests, organisers and players from DomainX and GameX reunited at fancy Lotus restaurant for VIP dinner and drinks. Long buffet tables of steaming Indian curries, rice and breads complemented fish, meat and desserts, while the open bar was convenient if not dangerous.

From the beginning of a new week in Paharganj, I checked into Hotel New Hindustan. Paharganj was controlled chaos: an authentic taste of India, that one couldn't appreciate from chaperoned limousines or five-star hotels. Narrow streets and tighter alleyways were thick with pedestrians, beeping scooters and bicycles pulling carts of vegetables. Street dogs languished between missions, pondering cows stood where they pleased, and colossal layers of scents of spices, sewage and petrol wafted across the pavement. There was always the chatter of voices; horns incessantly honked, dogs barked, children played or cried, merchants touted their wares, music distortedly blared from tinny speakers, and sirens occasionally wailed. At night, streets and rooftop restaurants illuminated from strings of pulsating lights. All of this energy was concentrated within a small cluster of streets that converged at a central hub, with a panorama of five-storey buildings, shops, and Nepalese or Tibetan rooftop restaurants. The food was fragrant and delectable, while the eateries offered epic views of the madness below.

At Hotel New Hindustan, I connected with several intriguing energies: a young Swede in his twenties, a young Dutch woman and a twenty-year-old Romanian girl. The hostel featured a diverse assortment of guests, locals, and the generous owners of the hotel themselves, who graciously treated me to a lavish evening on my final day. My adventures with the Swede included dodging red-eyed street peddlers, who awkwardly but insistently attempted to sell us hash from shadowy alleys. We detoured for an unwitting drink at an 80s-style Delhi drag bar, where we were certainly popular. Selfies were taken by and with all sorts of questionable characters and orientations. We finished our drinks, and – to the disappointment of several smiling men – discretely departed. To avoid the persistent hashish-touting beggar, we took a random turn and eventually discovered a lovely restaurant, with great food, attentive service and passionate serenades by the in-house guitarist.

Waking in my bunkbed in the daze of a new day, freeing my phone from airplane mode resulted in typical superfluous notifications flooding my screen. One message stood out: Boogie, the lost angel at Borderland. Boogie had taken the time to compose a long and thoughtful message, including:

"I wanted to write you these days so many times, because you sneaked into my dreams way too often. Did you cast some magical voodoo on me?! It definitely worked! I have my ticket to Seoul: I'm going in two weeks for a semester to study. Have you ever been there? It would be fun to go hiking and camping in one of their national parks if we are already on the same continent!"

I was stunned. I couldn't think of a more perfect proposition than hiking and camping in Korean mountains with Boogie – and this was her idea! There was the grim reality that I had no money at the moment, and an equally abject absence of prospects on the horizon. At this moment I had absolutely no idea how it would happen, but I had to find a way. This was precisely the purpose of leading a flexible solo lifestyle: to be ready for incredible opportunities like these.

After a spellbound and productive twelve days in Delhi, I hopped on a flight to Kochi, in the far south of India. I met kind and classy Aswin, Mother.Domains' longtime server admin, and stayed in his family's village near Angamali South. Graciously, Aswin lent me his bed while he slept on the living room couch. Kochi was productive in its own right. Aswin keenly showcased much of his state, Kerala, including jungle-like national parks, gigantic frothy waterfalls and a ferry, before we casually strolled around Fort Kochi. During the week I met Aswin's lovely staff at the GetMyAdmin office, and coached them in realistic English conversations and typical Western client communication.

I remained extraordinarily distracted, through scattered, twitterpated messages with Boogie, and the puzzle of how to make Korea happen, before time expired. I felt an odd assurance that something positive would arise, but I had no idea of the source. I put out feelers on social media, through my personal and professional networks, and considered, unprecedentedly, asking for financial help.

Out of the blue appeared Snake Catcher. Jason, a longtime expert Australian snake catcher, was referred by a dear old colleague from Red Bennies, Alex Schoeffel. Jason required a website overhaul, with a modern and mobile-friendly design that ranked well on search engines. I knew that the Snake Catcher website deposit would afford my flight to Korea, and its balance would help me stay afloat in Korea, for a while.

As I nervously waited for the deal to be sealed, my mind drifted in and out of accepting whatever happened. So many times in my life I'd looked forward to something, for it to come undone. There became an unbelievably ecstatic moment when the Snake Catcher deposit arrived. Past weeks of flight research confirmed the best possible airfares: from Chennai to Bangkok then Seoul, all for a few hundred bucks. I didn't book a return flight; I planned for a couple of weeks in Korea, check the vibe and adapt from there.

Night Bus to Pondicherry

Pondicherry is India's gateway city to the autonomous, experimental civilisation of Auroville. Situated on the east coast, three hours south of Chennai in the conservative state of Tamil Nadu, Pondicherry was a former French colonial enclave, now with a population in the millions. Alike other Indian cities, Pondicherry was large, noisy and crowded.

Despite packing the night before at Bangalore's Social Rehab, I removed certain items from my suitcase, repacked and reluctantly left behind several possessions. A momentary relapse of shopping restraint added two new kurtas (long Indian shirts), two kurta "pyjama" pants and a pair of jeans, that was originally my sole purpose for shopping. The weight from two bulging backpacks was uncomfortable, and approached 30kg. I was bogged down by an awkward tent, bulky sleeping bag, heavy old laptop, and thicker clothes that were unsuitable for India.

I spent the travel day in Bangalore roaming between cafes, enjoying coffee and snacks, while pounding out a few hours of work. While my bus' pickup from Shanti Nagar in central

Bangalore wasn't until 11:15pm, I had numerous loose ends to complete, including planning the new Snakecatcher website.

Back at the hostel, another fierce storm hit, cutting power. *Good thing I packed.* Occasional SMS from the bus company shared links that tracked the bus' progress: it might be half an hour late.

"Could be a buggy app!" exclaimed a choir of co-habitants of Social Rehab. "Don't trust the app!"

Urged to book a cab, one was twenty minutes away before it cancelled. Eventually, another ride share became available; again twenty minutes away. *10:15pm: tight.* My backup plan was to try to catch a taxi or rickshaw in the pouring rain. Amidst drench and lightning, the ride share pulled up by 10:40pm, and we raced to Shanti Nagar through steady streams of traffic.

At Shanti Nagar bus terminal lay four bays; each was a lengthy concrete line that bulged with buses. A random street person approached me and offered something I didn't understand. I recited: "Pondicherry. Pondicherry." The shadowy, sketchy bus station stoked my alertness, but this guy was fine. He directed: "Straight. Straight. Left." I motioned left, but, no: "*Straight, straight, left,*" he specified.

I headed in the general direction. Lane 1 was for local buses, Lanes 2 and 4 were filled with "sleeper" long-distance buses, and Lane 3 was for the Tamil Nadu bus company: more raw and battle weary. Lane 2 appeared correct, but something felt unsettling. The SMS came in: The bus was definitely on time. *Buggy app!* It was now after 11pm and the bus was nowhere to be seen, with the likeliness everything would happen hectically, and soon. Somehow I missed a phone call, but I couldn't ring the number back.

At Lane 2 was a young Indian woman wearing spectacles and Western brands. She went out of her way to assist me, ringing bus ticket hotlines – none responded – and asked around the station. Escorting me from the bus stand, the woman suggested I wait around the corner, to the (straight, straight) left, near other people and suitcases. She was certain this was the spot, as she was on her own way to Pondicherry, on a later bus.

At that moment, a Sam Tourist Bus pulled up; its headlights shone through the foggy night, then the bus sped away.

"Run after it!" the woman urged. "Quickly, go!"

After momentarily stopping to thank her, I bolted through the thunderstorm, after a bus that soon disappeared beyond other distant buses, then vanished altogether. Dejected yet hopeful, I retreated to the original spot, where another Sam Tourist Bus waited. The bus flashed its lights while I ran towards it, preparing to heave my body in the way if necessary. It was casually loading other passengers' bags, and the conductor was pleasantly surprised when I arrived: "Sea? Great!" I loaded my larger backpack in storage, and boarded.

Sleeper buses in India are an unusual but practical phenomena. There are generally two rows of steel bunk beds on dual levels. One side holds double beds for two people; the other sports a row of narrow single beds. Coloured curtains can be drawn for privacy, but there's nowhere to put bags. At first I generally found sleeper buses cramped, long and hellish, but over the years I've come to enjoy them. I was happy to catch this bus at all, and to have my own solo sleeper bunk, this time...

Flashback – Night Bus to Hyderabad

On my first visit to India in 2015, I was heading from Bangalore to Hyderabad Airport, on the way to a large but little-known city called Jabalpur, to meet my longtime developers, SRGIT. Having researched buses I desired no part of a "sleeper" bus. I specifically booked an ordinary bus with reclining seats, just like familiar Western ones. Unsurprisingly, on the afternoon of the journey I received a message: "Your bus has been upgraded to a sleeper bus!"

First, finding the bus was hectic. The meeting point was simply a parking lot, seemingly in the middle of nowhere. Occasional buses arrived, amid many people loitering around; some had suitcases. There were neither signs nor any indication that buses stopped here – only seasoned passengers.

Eventually my bus rattled in, only slightly behind schedule. Delighted upon boarding, I located a vacant solo sleeper bed and made comfortable space. Within minutes, another man came aboard, took a concerned look and chatted with the conductor. My actual bunk was in the opposite row, half of a double bed. On it lay an old skinny man, essentially in his underwear; he smiled at me, and enthusiastically patted the empty spot beside him.

"Come," the old man purred.

This became an ominous precursor to several hours of the bus lurching, bouncing and braking. I tried to protect my space and dignity while the old man slept. At one point he seemingly spooned me in his slumber. I acknowledged that death was a real possibility; we were surrounded by steel bars in what was tantamount to a cage, with no seat-belts and plenty of bones.

As dawn arrived, we approached Hyderabad. The old man saved the day. He informed me that Hyderabad Airport was far from city; it was best to disembark here, and take a bus or taxi. Insistently, he jumped off the bed and bounded to the conductor; the bus rapidly pulled over to the side of the highway. This saved hours of unnecessary and stressful transit.

I attempted to catch a taxi, before a small group of young men convinced me to ride the local bus: "Much cheaper." They helped me board, and I paid a small amount of rupees to the conductor. Another passenger had no legs; instead he walked on his arms. It was remarkable how he disembarked and strolled down the dusty street, on two hands like it was nobody's business.

Back! From Pondicherry to Auroville

Enjoying a single bunk and curtained privacy, I waited until the scheduled solitary bathroom break before wriggling into passable comfort to rest. It was difficult, with a small but lumpy backpack between my feet, and my six-foot body not quite fitting in the compact berth. Sideways or sitting were the only options. The bus frequently lurched from side to side, accelerating, braking swiftly and bouncing, for hours. Any accident would spell the end of everything. It added a certain danger and excitement to the occasion, alike flying: There's nothing we can really do about it.

After I managed to doze temporarily, brightness faded in. Trees succumbed to concrete neighbourhoods; the early bustle of Pondicherry morning hummed, and the bus groaned to a stop. People hastily disembarked, and the madness ensued.

"Pondicherry! Pondicherry!" exclaimed the bus' conductor.

Wearily, I clambered out of the bunk and collected my belongings. The typical slew of taxi and moto drivers attempted to capture my attention, but I was groggy and catching my bearings. I negotiated a trip with a bathroom and coffee break for Rs350. The coffee stop at a roadside shop was pleasant: Hot, milky, caffeine.

"Where are you from?" the cafe owner asked the most common question of all.

"New Zealand," I replied, accepting this would become my default answer, rather than rattle off five or six plausible nations. Spotting my unruly long hair, the owner offered me a little pink elastic to tie it back.

The driver, pink elastic and I set off in the rickshaw, along the tropical motorway. I was safely dispatched to my foresty Auroville guesthouse, Transformation. I met Samata – a German Aurovillian who'd resided there for decades – and checked into my uniquely circular room, while a studious German Sheppard prowled. After showering in an enchanting bathroom, featuring a spa tub that was converted into a submarine city for fish, I lay in my quarters' admiring its 70's-era architecture, then slept.

...

After my first week in Auroville I wasn't sure I liked the city. On the surface, Auroville was lifeless and touristy: a lonely place for a universal voyager seeking authentic connections. I remained distracted, longing time to pass, as I was juvenilely invigorated about Korean adventures ahead. I bonded with Transformation's golden-brown Tofu, who accompanied me for bike rides, long walks and scooter missions. Quality of food impressed me across Auroville's restaurants, while coffee and makeshift workspaces were acceptable, until I discovered the wonders of Marc's Cafe.

The first Aurovillian establishment to pique my creative interest was Svaram: a laboratory of experimental musical instruments. Its founder, Aurelio, demonstrated his unusual creations, like Stone Drum. Unravelling a twisted rope within a tree-suspended container, boomed thunderous waves that reverberated off large stone blocks cast in the earth below. There were giant xylophones made of pipes and wood, flutes, bells, strings and plentiful imaginative percussion.

My people connection came from another Transformation guest: Celeste, a kind French mother of two young children. Celeste introduced me to various local attractions. The underground cinema screened films in a comfortable theatre that was burrowed under City Hall. On another evening, Celeste led the way to a small hidden diner that served piping hot, freshly-made dosas under the stars.

With my confidence bolstered for the second week, I sought to experience as much as possible. I visited Auroville Radio, learning the history and realities of running the city's volunteer radio project and helped them address some website issues. I was treated to an inspiring lunch with brilliant Min, a master of advanced and conscious technologies, and returned to Svaram for a complimentary sound massage. The only downer was a gardener, who spoiled an otherwise-awesome day riding on his motorbike, by subtly molesting me on "Lover's Beach". Still, by fortnight's end, Auroville made considerable-enough impression on me to encourage a return.

No Prisoners in Regret Lane

En route to Korea was the matter of a short stopover in Thailand. In Bangkok I reunited with longtime Canadian friend and hip-hop MC Vandal, who was to co-host the international Spartan Race in Pattaya. In the capital we visited a spice-flooded food market for delightful kway teow noodles. The diner's television screened live Thai kickboxing, that pitted local Thais against foreigners. The host was a handsome, tanned and strong man; he mostly commentated in English, and introduced the fighters in a dramatic, almost wrestling style of pantomime.

In the morning, Vandal and I taxied south to Pattaya and the ultra-luxurious Siam Country Club. Spartan was frenetic, with long tables of festival administration and arriving athletes. The coordinator welcomed a break from her stress and treated us to a quiet, well-prepared lunch at the fancy restaurant upstairs. We sat on a shady patio with sweeping views of tropical trees, under hot blue sky and comfortably warm breeze.

Later, Vandal met his race co-host: coincidentally the very same TV celebrity from last night's Muay Thai battle! Surreally I listened, while they discussed plans for tomorrow's race. I wondered how one night he was broadcasting to millions, and now he sat smiling beside me. After their meeting, the celebrity's ultra-swish minivan whisked us to our drab hotel, that didn't seem to have a name, but was clearly inspired by the pinnacle of communist blandness. Service was lacking, headlined by a lazy and reluctant reception clerk, but the hotel room was comfortable, as was the giant swimming pool.

Vandal woke around 4am to host the race; I slept in and enjoyed complimentary breakfast, before churning out hours of work from the hotel room. A tropical storm thwarted my pool aspirations. Vandal returned and rested. We desired something closer to Pattaya Beach, for a Saturday night party that was organised by a hip-hop colleague of Vandal, and far from this North Korean-style hotel in the middle of nowhere. Exiting this particular property was a mission upon itself. The same lazy reception clerk, sitting behind a steaming plate of curry and potatoes, refused to help arrange transportation. He insisted that taxis did not come this far; odd in that it was a large hotel and money was offered. The clerk firmly suggested hitchhiking, and with no Ubers or Grabs available, our pleas fell on deaf, unwieldy ears.

Vandal and I headed to the small isolated road to catch a ride. Almost immediately, a pickup truck from Spartan Race rumbled into the hotel; they offered to shuttle us to a busier intersection, after they dropped off their passengers. Within minutes, another car pulled over. A lady rolled down the window, while a street vendor peddling a bicycle-powered food cart stopped to assist. Knowing the approximate ride share price between destinations – 250-300 baht – our initial offer of 250 baht was graciously accepted, and we gratefully hopped into the car. Upon reaching a busy village, we re-bundled into her brother's more taxi-like vehicle.

We arrived at the hotel in noisy and seedy Pattaya around sunset. Our hotel looked decent enough, despite no twin beds available – only king-sized. Vandal and I exchanged bemused glances; we'd try it for a night. A critical miscalculation was that the party organised for Saturday night was far away: it was an hour north, halfway to Bangkok.

Pattaya was a buzzy place, exhibiting the full stereotype of Thailand's seedy sex tourism. Venturing out resulted in being halted by most massage parlours and street peddlers. After dinner of scrumptious Thai food, we decided the party wasn't feasible: it was too far, time consuming and expensive for round trip. We didn't even know if it would be a good party. Instead we wandered around the oceanfront. We witnessed a televised chilli sauce festival at a shopping mall, with cheap beer, live music, food stalls, and mesmerising local babes touting chilli.

With a few beers in tow, we discovered the adjacent laneway, one we dubbed "Regret Lane" – because it so easily could have been. Each venue appeared to be zoned, where scantily-clad young Thai women and occasional transexuals prevented our ability to pass. Sometimes they twisted our nipples, and one transexual even grabbed Vandal's testicles. However, they remained strictly in their zones, and never crossed the invisible line whenever we managed to escape.

Following a televised Manchester United match at a low-key bar, Vandal and I stopped for delicious chicken kebabs, and agreed on "one more drink" before bed. He recommended a "chill" place up the road. At Shooters mingled two dozen young Thai dreamboats; several danced on stage with clothes. Vandal and I were approached by two particular stunners, and we conversed in broken English. The typical, "Where are you from?" although even my simplified answer was predictably baffling.

"My" girl, Elin, was petite, skinny and sweet, with delightful eyes and face – well, everything. She enjoyed cuddling. I asked deeper questions about her dreams in life; she recited shy and discrete answers, before periodically departing to the back of the club. One dancer on stage radiated mind-blowing charisma. She was gorgeous: long black hair, full curves, brimming with confidence, and earned admiration from all of the other dancers and perverts. She looked like fun, and in my inebriated stupor I wondered: *Was this the sort of girl I would pay for?*

Elin returned and hugged me; she told me she was exhausted, from whatever happened late last night until deep into the morning. She wanted to see me again; I suggested Pattaya Beer Garden on Sunday evening, to "continue the conversation". She seemed keen, so we agreed on a time: 9pm Sunday.

Vandal and I returned to our hotel and king bed, watching a bizarre old B movie that felt familiar. I contemplated my first exposure to Thai sex tourism, since I was thirteen-year-old boy visiting Phuket with family; back then I'd been concerned about frequently receiving attention from drag queens. In Pattaya there were pretty girls everywhere, and seemingly "cheap".

Yet, I couldn't stop thinking about Boogie. We were building a magical, rare bond, that was far more important than short-term drunken masochism. My inner demon: "*But nothing has happened with Boogie! You haven't even kissed her! You're not in a relationship! Nothing might happen at all!*"

On Sunday, Vandal and I walked along dirty, fish-smelling beaches, then through concrete plazas, pausing for occasional beers or coffees. When Vandal departed for a respectable massage, I headed to Pattaya Beer Garden. Beside the sketchy entrance to the restaurant, stood two bars filled with dancing poles and half-naked women. A smaller alleyway led to the restaurant, and a main bar at the rear. I didn't see Elin. She may have well been there, but I didn't recognise her among fifty other women in front, and I had no inclination to mill around for something I wasn't convinced was a good idea.

The portly waitress at Pattaya Beer Garden instantly took a fancy to me; she giggled with peers, and was noticeably proud each time we conversed. Presenting me a choice of drink coasters, she asked my intentions for the evening. One side read, "Lookin'"; the other: "Chillin'". I picked the latter, with its cute penguins. She thought it was sweet, then the manager attempted to set us up. Vandal joined later, after his fascinating but wholesome evening. We successfully departed Pattaya as good boys, without regret: only the picture.

Vandal flew home to K.L. on Monday, and I headed to Bodega, a party hostel close to Bangkok's weekly Bitcoin meetups. I wasn't a fan of party hostels but Bodega was pretty cool. It reminded me of similar boutique accommodation in Medellin, Colombia where my crew was a quartet of divine Lauras. At Bodega I made several connections; one was a touring UK DJ, who coincidentally also owned a Waves crypto wallet. At the evening's Bitcoin session, I met charming American nomad Lesley, who'd soon become a star in the global blockchain space.

After the Bitcoin meetup remained four men; two had extensive local experience. They brought us newbies into the heart of Thailand's action: notorious laneway Soi Cowboy, and straight to popular Crazy House. Our well-dressed quartet was escorted to the club's absolute front and centre, beside a stage filled with buxom beauties wearing little more than lingerie. While dancers prowled the stage, girl after girl approached us. One busty babe persistently sat on my lap, chatting, attempting seduction and receiving my shy declines. The dozen models on stage catered to the breadth of male fantasies: perky breasts, smoothly shaved bodies, giggling and confident, seemingly enjoying their lifestyle – and maybe they do. Upstairs near the toilet featured couples making out, and surely there were brothel rooms somewhere. Similar to strip clubs, the smell reeked of plastic, fake tan spray and pubic sweat.

After a final, eventful drink around the corner with another wave of random malcontents, I retreated to Bodega. I was euphoric about my late-morning flight to Korea, and not quite ready to sleep. I chatted at the bar for several hours with the friendly Thai-American receptionist and occasional guests. At one point, the receptionist asked if I smoked weed, and she covertly handed me supplies to roll for later.

"Be careful," the receptionist warned. "Highly dangerous if caught in Bangkok."

A few hours before sunrise, with her shift at its quietest, the receptionist led us down the alley, towards a bigger but generally desolate road. We found a snug spot between two cars; one protected us from street view. She was a cool young lady, full of stimulating conversation, and weed opened our minds into deeper discussions.

In the midst of one such conversation she stopped, paused and turned to me.

"Hmm... I thought I heard something. It's probably nothing. Let me check." She stood, spun away, stepped towards the road, then instantly raced back in fear. "The police! Hide it!"

I pitched roughly one-third of a joint, under the car in front of us. Immediately, two unsmiling, all-knowing police officers approached us. One was shorter and older, while the other was a beast of a man. We were in deep trouble. After their quick visual scan of the area, we followed their orders and slowly stood. I turned around, stepped back and placed my shoe on top of the joint's remains. The younger, larger officer with a video camera atop his head paced along the alley of the property, searching. The senior constable rapidly conversed in Thai with the receptionist. She was animated, almost pleading, but convincing. His deputy returned, and the officers chatted while I kept her relaxed with random, unrelated questions.

After the receptionist made the senior officer laugh, clinically and sternly he turned to me, starting with several simple questions in English. I continued breathing deeply and remained calm. Answering where I was from, my growing up in nearby Singapore was a benefit. Finally came the critical question:

"Have you smoked the marijuana?" the officer inquired. Exhaling a deep breath, I looked down at the ground, sighed, and nodded.

"When small," I replied, lowering my hands to the height of a boy.

The officer chuckled. "No! You smoking, now?"

I shook my head, for I honestly was not smoking, not right at this moment. With a satisfied glimmer in his eye, the officer rounded up his deputy, and they departed. The receptionist and I exchanged glances that blended fright and relief. We gingerly returned to the bar for a celebratory shot.

"You said something to him. Why did he laugh?" I asked. The receptionist's eyes brightened, almost apologetically.

"I told him it was your first time with a prostitute at Soi Cowboy!"

We treated ourselves to a cocktail from the bar, and shared the story with anybody else awake at the hostel. By now it was around 4am, and several others returned from their personal Soi Cowboy escapades. I learned of a performer who shot darts from her vagina, consistently and accurately bursting balloons from considerable distances.

Being caught with even a small amount of marijuana in Thailand would have, minimally, resulted in a night or days in prison, while etching a permanent scar on my record. There would be no flight to Seoul, possibly no Korean adventures at all, and the chance of serious trouble: short-term and long.

It was another lucky instance where the universe urged caution, while saving me in the nick of time. Consequently, this set the stage for a remarkable era approaching, the most magical of all. It's like the universe willed it to happen; at this transformational and almost bleak point in my life, I needed it.

45

Living the dream on Jeju Island, Hyeopjae Beach, September 2017

Chapter 4
The Dream on Jeju Island

On a sunny morning, the modern, high-speed train crossed a vast bridge from the airport at Incheon. Anonymous skyscrapers that loomed to the south comprised the outer megacity of Seoul, capital of South Korea. My head whirred with culture shock: a foreign language, grim-faced elderly Koreans sat opposite trendy youngsters absorbed in their phones. I felt mild jetlag from the Bangkok flight, relief from the near-miss with Thai police, and blissed disbelief.

Despite my preparing advance navigation as best possible, the hotel's incorrectly-listed address ensured several distressed hours walking around alien streets. I rapidly learned that English was rarely and barely understood. After hours of frantic coordination from a random cafe, I finally reached understated Hotel9: luxuriously modern at a budget price. Following a hot shower and nap on a plush queen bed, dependable Seoul transit delivered me to one of the city's legendary heartbeats.

Boogie and I met at Gangnam Exit 1. The divine Hungarian brunette appeared up the escalator, smiling with excited warm brown eyes. Harmoniously we bounced around vibrant and chirpy Gangnam, gathered Soju alcoholic drinks from corner shops, and chilled at a rum and cigar bar. After catching a glimpse at Itaewon – the international cultural hub of Seoul – with a brief interlude at a tacky commercial nightclub, we hailed a taxi to the hotel. I booked a room with two beds to reduce pressure: Boogie chose the queen bed, with me.

The weekend was about "hiking and camping in national parks". Boogie's idea was the spark behind our Korea plans, although she could have suggested "knitting and taxidermy", and I'd have found a way. Following another riveting evening together, on a sunny Friday afternoon we met at a central metro, each donning large backpacks; mine brimmed with the little green tent and sleeping bag. Plan A was to camp in the city's majestic northern national park: Bukhansan. Heeding spotty Internet advice about possibly camping in Bukhansan, we targeted an eastern entrance. After a brief stop through the local marketplace we commenced a slow ascent into Bukhansan. Lack of English throughout Korea was starkly evident, as the park rangers, after discussing among themselves, remained baffled at our hand illustrations of tents.

"No camping in Bukhansan!" was the verdict, with their arms crossed in the customary Korean, "No!"

I patiently summoned an online article, but English-to-Korean translation apps were inaccurate, if not misleading.

"No camping in Bukhansan!" the rangers repeated, friendly and tolerant enough.

We departed, but rebellious instincts stoked my need to impress. Shuttling one metro stop north, we entered a quieter gate. In a wooden lodge office situated halfway up a small foresty hill, the clerk greeted us. She better understood our intention to camp, but frowned and similarly crossed her arms.

"No camping in Bukhansan," she repeated sympathetically.

The deflation in our eyes prompted a flurry of the clerk calling around other parks, and she nominated several legitimate camping options across Seoul. They appeared to be bland touristy sites in the midst of commercial amusement parks; none well-rated, all overpriced.

We entered the park to at least take a look at Bukhansan, acknowledging the clerk's solemn concern about safely exiting the park before darkness. We laboured up the first hill, through tree-lined and flowery pathways. Not even fifty metres later, huffing and puffing, we paused to rest on rocks; our utter lack of fitness was evident. It was time for Soju, accompanied by skinny, fruity cigarettes and sips of almighty pálinka – a deadly Hungarian spirit – while swatting away fierce and persistent Korean mosquitoes. After catching our breaths we slowly headed upwards along the curvy forest path. A huge Buddhist statue and modest temple towered further, and we idled to the summit, gasping for oxygen. Thick green trees and colourful leaves clustered in the falling orange sun, while distant concrete high-rises shimmered in a valley, silhouetted by mountains in remaining flickers of daylight. The spot made for an ideal Soju and pálinka break, with the realisation that this was as much of Bukhansan as we'd discover. Solemnly we lit candles in a wooden box outside the Buddhist temple, and made wishes for those who'd departed.

The pixellation of sunset colours increased our urgency for Plan B. We descended through the park, past the wooden lodge office and towards the metro. Connecting to wifi presented a small list of available rooms in the nearby satellite city of Uijeongbu. One of two barely affordable options was American 1960's-style Heart Motel. The motel was tucked within the youthful vibrancy of Uijeongbu, an area bristling with abundantly busy bars, diners and shops.

A combination of exhaustion, potency of pálinka and queasiness of cigarettes blended the evening into blur. I recall a bar and televised baseball, busting a few moves on an empty dancefloor, and somehow stumbling to Heart Motel. Apparently I passed out instantly. Boogie explored the neighbourhood, before hours of delighted bubble baths in our spa. Meanwhile, I dreamed intensely, surreally, of cities and machines.

Chiaksan National Park

Groggy dehydration was overcome by a fresh morning's optimism, and we mustered determination for our mission. Researching from a nearby mega-mall's wifi, our options narrowed to a handful of camping-friendly national parks reasonably close to Seoul. We selected Chiaksan National Park in north-central Korea. Our economical interstate train rode to the city of Wonju, through green countryside, farmland and rolling hills. Waiting mid-afternoon at Wonju's main bus stop, an older man in baseball clothing practiced his English, cordially chatting classic rock and asking common questions.

"Ah," he frowned, after learning our ages, while I grimaced. "You are like her father."

We boarded a local bus to Chiaksan that weaved around valleys of lower mountains. After disembarking, we trudged uphill to the entrance. At a large park office filled with computers and photocopying machines, one of several rangers, stocky with glasses, assisted us with an increasingly familiar refrain:

"No camping inside Chiaksan National Park!"

After animated deliberations, the rangers indicated an official campsite in the vicinity. We lugged our backpacks down a main road, that sliced through mountains alongside a gushing river, and entered a small valley that housed Guryong Campground. Having exhausted my slender budget from Friday's unexpected hotel, paid camping was not ideal. We considered sneaking into the park but, with the sun starting to fall and recent Bukhansan lessons, instead we booked a slot at the campground – for the first night, anyway. We rented a patch on soft sand with a picnic table and plenty of space for supplies. Twenty groups of campers sprawled over larger sandy plots. There was an abundance of large kitchens, stand-up tent rooms, lounges, outdoor cinematic projectors, large screens, high-end audio, kids playing, cooking, eating and chatter.

As night fell, we sought food of our own. The fresh, crisp air complemented a panorama of mountains and trees, as the sky's darkness carved a hushed haze over the hilltops. Boogie, who was already in the country for two weeks, shared dreams and hopes for her Korean tenure ahead: "I want to eat at one of those restaurants where we sit on the floor!"

Only two dimly-lit restaurants were open in this remote little Chiaksan village. The first appeared empty. The second, featured floor seating.

"Dreams coming true already!" I exclaimed.

Our first traditional Korean dinner involved sitting cross-legged on a mildly uncomfortable hardwood floor, cushioned with thin pillows. Décor was sparse: a few paintings, traditional statues, and bunting in Korean white, blue and red. Unable to decipher the Korean alphabet, we randomly pointed at several cheaper menu items. This earned us a pair of hot steaming soups filled with noodles and vegetables, complemented by side dishes, including kimchi – customarily all-you-can-eat. The other diners – three older women – sat at the adjacent table, guzzling heaping plates of beef and pork from large bubbling clay pots. They laughed a lot, even while nearly fighting each other over demanding to pay the bill.

After our satisfying dinner, we returned to the tent and prepared for our exploration. Hands held under a pitch-black sky, we bounded up a hill, past deserted ranger posts, and into the eerie stillness of Chiaksan National Park. We stopped across an old stone and wooden bridge to watch the river trickle underneath, and stream through a cacophony of rocks. Further up and through trees we hiked, discovering a diminutive, pleasantly-sculpted Buddhist temple under renovation. Beyond was a massive, well-lit temple complex, that was blinding when contrasted by the night sky and trees. Avoiding lights and surely CCTV, we skirted into the shadows and curled along an unlit trail, across a small bridge, beyond boulders and upwards into a forest, that was black and silent. CRACK! A sharp noise halted us. We stood completely still among dull bark and fireflies. BANG! Like an invisible deer shooting through trees. I shrieked; Boogie giggled. We returned to camp with useful reconnaissance for tomorrow's hike. *Surely nobody would see us in here...*

Descending through forest and boulders, we crossed a small bridge, past the bright complex and smaller temple, then over the wooden bridge guarded by stone dragons. Traces of moonlight illuminated a serene backdrop of river, rocks and trees. The waterfall splashed across stones, spraying fresh mist in the air. I gazed into Boogie's electric brown eyes, and we kissed, scattering sparks of atoms that burst upon the creek below. Holding hands down the mountain to our campsite, snuggling inside the tent, inside, it all happened.

...

We inspiringly emerged into crisp daylight under bright blue sky and mountaintops. The campsite was abuzz with the clinking of dishes and chatter of campers, while most packed to reach home by weekend's end. After a slow and casual breakfast of oats and milk in my mammoth Argentinian silver mug, complemented by cups of sweetened instant coffee, we packed our belongings. We aspired to find somewhere inside Chiaksan to camp.

Now daylight on a busy Sunday, security was abound, while numerous hikers ventured through the park gates. Our hike commenced by retracing last night's steps: across the dragon bridge, past temples, into woods and through vast hectares of trees. A sizeable waterfall was the first major stop along Chiaksan Park's trail. Many elderly Korean hikers paused for picnics or snacks; some dared to dip their feet in the creek's freezing water. After touching the waterfall, we found tranquility beside the creek. Boogie created a quasi-traditional tribute, with layers of smooth rocks and stones.

Refreshed, it was time to climb the mountain. Fortunately, there was a security post. After miming to the park ranger, we were permitted to store our heavier backpack in their office. Ascending, endlessly scouting potential camping spots, each viewpoint brought further more stunning views of rolling hills and thick trees, with astonishing palettes of greens, like leafy pyramids beneath the sky. Higher, steeper paths required climbing over boulders.

At a certain point, exhaustion slowed our progress, around 1100 metres high. We'd set off too late to realistically conquest the difficult summit before sundown, and ensure a safe, timely return. Moments after we found a spot to rest, a ranger and his apprentice scaled from above, and apprehended us.

"Must turn around now," the elder ordered, politely but firmly. It was the office ranger from yesterday. "You entered park with two bags. Where is other bag?" he asked.

"At station down the hill," I replied, pointing downward.

He disbelievingly radioed into the unknown for affirmation. We made our way downhill, with the rangers behind us. The younger cadet gathered litter; I occasionally assisted, bewildering the senior ranger, who believed I was up to mischief. Losing patience with our slow pace, the elder ranger bounded down while the junior monitored our progress. Eventually back at the checkpoint, we collected the heavier backpack; the elder ranger was relieved. There would likely be no camping in Chiaksan tonight.

The campground was virtually empty. Large steel construction equipment stood ready for Monday's renovations. With the sun falling, we sat outside the office debating our next steps. The campsite was too expensive to pay full price again. To pass time, we took turns using the hot shower facilities, while the other waited, batting away hungry mosquitoes. Lovely Chiaksan attendants permitted our use of the office's microwave and kettle, and assisted with first aid of Boogie's recently-sliced finger from a kitchen accident at university. The attendant shift change came during Boogie's shower, and a kind older man beckoned me over. Using unrecognisable words with basic sign language, he motioned pitching the tent in a vacant spot around the corner. No charge. Freshly-steamed Boogie was delighted upon hearing the news.

Sleeping on the Streets of Seoul

The new day began with low-flying military fighter jets roaring through the sky, during escalating tension between America and North Korea. A bus to Wonju, then a sleepy train rolling through Korean countryside, returned us to the capital. I'd booked a room at Dream Inn for Tuesday and Wednesday, but couldn't spend cash Monday, and considered camping in the city. Boogie's university dorm was strictly gender segregated, and nightly curfew ensured that she wasn't sleeping there tonight. Dream Inn allowed us to store our heavy bags in the office overnight and chill on their cozy rooftop – perhaps an emergency crash pad.

At nightfall, we ventured into nearby parks and searched for plausible camping. The dark parks in this particular area, south of the Han River and close to Boogie's university, were neither big nor secluded enough to avoid potential observation by passing security officers or dutiful neighbours.

Boogie dropped her belongings at her dorm before curfew. I marvelled at the sprawling buildings of century-old Chung-Ang University: home to 20,000 students, including many foreign exchange. She proudly toured me through deserted neigh-bourhoods, while indicating typical cheap food places, markets and bakeries.

We continued north along city streets; the Soju buzz blurred the lights of buildings and skyscrapers. After midnight, exhausted from a weekend of fresh air and mountain hiking, we found seclusion behind a large statue and cement courtyard garden. Sleeping on the streets wasn't anything unordinary for those of us who've been homeless, but it was new for Boogie. Spooning on the ground, covered by our jackets, we dozed for ninety minutes, while our subconsciouses remained alert.

...

Snapped out of dreams, we dusted ourselves off and gingerly returned to the road. Our dazed return felt miles longer, particularly across the long bridge to her university. With curfew lifted at 6am, Boogie entered for rest before class, leaving me disappointedly on my own. I resigned to the unenviable mission of traveling cross-city to fetch my backpack, that was stashed at Hotel9. This public transit voyage consumed hours, including a rare McDonalds breakfast, and a long, slow bus to Dream Inn for check-in, shower and sleep.

Boogie visited after school both evenings; we scavenged free tasters from supermarkets and infiltrated hilly neighbourhoods. At Dream Inn we chilled with the cool owner of the guesthouse and his friend, while listening to classic rock and Korean hits. The older men were obliterated by one shot of pálinka, before they humorously mumbled a slurred, premature end to proceedings. After two deeply comfortable and electric nights, Boogie and I departed Dream Inn, into living dreams come true.

Jeju Island

We departed Seoul as sunset fell. Lights of fishing boats and island buildings flickered underneath, and we landed on a pleasantly tropical evening at Jeju International. We held no plans or reservations for six days on Jeju: only two backpacks, the tent, sleeping bag and an unrelenting sense of adventure. Our research uncovered plentiful camping-friendly spots across the island; one was a short distance from the airport.

We strode joyously towards the northern coast. The water's edge was loaded with small boulders; the eastern view curved around hotels, high-rises and a harbour, while the west was darker and more remote. Seohaean-Ro featured a park, sporting facilities and picnic grounds, where Korean families ate from bowls and drank Soju on blankets facing portable kitchens. We found a spot perfectly nestled in a secluded wedge between bushes and trees. We discretely erected the lime-green tent, stowed our bags, and ventured into the night.

Heading east along the coastline, we passed coffeeshops, restaurants and a plethora of truly convenient stores. These shops were particularly handy to acquire inexpensive Soju, including a fruity one with a pink marijuana-like logo: potent with 15% alcohol. Convenience stores were almost literally everywhere. They offered cheap food, such as tasty burgers and packet noodles, microwaves, boiled water and reasonably comfortable dining space.

Returning from late-night coffee, tipsy and curious, we entered a narrow multi-story building that housed several music bars and karaoke places with strange numbers – e.g. "7080". These signs described decades of musical styles, like 1970s and 1980s. The second floor greeted us with an enlarged Christmas tree, a broad bar, a sizeable stage in the centre, and a litany of musical instruments. With eyes alight, Boogie – a seasoned musician – a located a booth, nearby a handful of other people. Beer prices were expensive, but entry required ordering at least two.

The night's magic began. Various musicians scrambled to ready the stage, then expeditiously launched into rehearsed, passionate performances of Korean pop songs and 80s rock hits. An unexpected further half dozen beer bottles reached our table, accompanied by a massive fresh fruit platter: a gracious gift from one of the musicians, possibly the owner.

After several emotional Korean love songs performed by other guests, Boogie took the stage with an amplified acoustic guitar, and played a rousing rendition of Metallica's Nothing Else Matters. Then, with my shoulder-length blonde hair reminding some of Kurt Cobain, I was embarrassingly pulled on stage. Under the spotlight, Boogie sang while I played guitar to The Beatles' Let It Be, following helpful scrolling tablature, while aided by generously over-drenched layers of echo and reverb.

Departing the stage to ravenous applause, we returned to our booth. We chatted with friendly musicians, gulped our beers and ate delicious fruit. Many beers and Soju amplified a foggy, sleepy haze, not to mention our lengthy travel day from Seoul. Before sleep, first we headed to the sea, beside stones, hand in hand. Our connection was electric. The Moon, slightly past full, shone like a silver pearl through clouds in greyscale sky. The waves crashed and roared. We dipped our feet in the water. Under the Moon, while waves lapped our ankles with a warming wind, we made powerful love upon the rocks.

Gwakji Beach

Sunlight and morning traffic stirred us from sleep. Opening the flap revealed warm tropical air and blue Jeju sky. We lugged our backpacks to the nearby airport and boarded a modern 102 Express bus, that raced counterclockwise along clean, smooth highway, between sun-drenched trees and rock-lined coast.

At the top of Gwakji soared a carved stone statue of Dol Hareubang: the God of fertility, and protector against demons that travelled between realities. A lower waterfront walkway led towards Gwakji's main beach. In the distance, along a point that jutted into sea, I saw a large stage and screen perched on a hill. Soundcheck suggested a club or a big party brewing.

Upon approaching Gwakji Beach, I relievedly sighted three tents pitched on a grassy field that overlooked golden sands and sea. Gwakji comprised a superb area, featuring a pristine beach near a small cluster of shops and eateries. There were plentiful rock statues, like Dragon Head Rock, that organically formed in the shape of a dragon's head from long-ago volcanic eruptions.

Shortly around sundown, distant bass music boomed across the bay, and soundcheck had graduated to live hip-hop and raucous cheers. The music increasingly became louder, and enveloped a flurry of activity that emanated from a modernly minimalistic cube building. There were hundreds of balloons and plentiful guests: men in full suits, glamorous ladies and well-dressed young children. We climbed the grassy, rocky hill around the outside: clearly not the main entrance. It felt like we were crashing a fancy wedding or birthday party.

The courtyard hosted a large stage with sizeable speakers and substantial lighting effects. A duet performed to a hundred devoted Korean fans, who sang along and snapped selfies. Further inspection uncovered several tables loaded with buckets of bottles of Soju. Promotional staff informed us that tonight was the prestigious launch party of Jeju Soju! We were offered complimentary bottles of two variations – one strong at around 20%; the other "lighter" at 12%. While guzzling evermore Soju, we watched the remainder of the performance from the building's rooftop. More acts took the stage with a national level of artistry, evident from maniacal cheering as each took the mic.

Afterward, Boogie and I sat alone on the shadowy rooftop, and absorbed the moment with extreme gratitude. Famished, we explored the area for food, although by now everything beyond an elaborate octopus restaurant was shuttered. Heading down the deserted main road, we located a traditional Korean restaurant where fresh food was cooked on hot grills in the middle of tables. The sweet waitress was patient throughout challenging conversation and helped guide our order. She further encouraged our Soju habit by fetching a couple of glasses for the takeaway bottle.

"Wow! New Jeju one," the waitress exclaimed, peering at the unfamiliar "Jeju" logo on the bottle.

...

Upon emerging from the tent to sweet blue ocean and a golden beach, I was humbled. We didn't have to do anything or be anywhere. Boogie and I frolicked in warm water, swimming with jumping fish and tentative Koreans, many of whom wore full clothing. Some even waded into the water in their shoes.

In the early afternoon, we hopped a bus south along the coast. We'd vaguely heard that Hallim was cool, but accidentally stopped in the drab adjacent fisherman's city, instead of its more famous beaches. Continuing counterclockwise around the coast, past an astonishing belt of bright yellow sand and sky blue water, we reached a lively area near a series of sprawling resorts. Randomly, we entered the lush gardens of a posh hotel, and made ourselves comfortable on a bench facing the ocean.

"Do you know how to juggle?" Boogie asked.

I nodded, and proceeded to demonstrate. Starting with a single orange, I taught her to juggle with one hand.

"Become familiar with the feeling," I advised. "Soft hands. Sharpen your hand-eye coordination."

Progressing to two oranges involved the transfer of oranges between the catching hand to the tossing hand; Boogie aced this level again. Adding a third orange was predictably challenging. Boogie became frustrated; oranges fell to the ground and burst. We took a customary cigarette and Soju break.

"Your subconscious mind is working at it. Keep practicing when you're ready."

Boogie determinedly bounced up, and demonstrated marked improvement. "I did it!" she sang, as she consistently juggled for increasingly sustained seconds.

With nightfall and mosquitoes inevitable, we strode to the main road and stopped for cheap chicken and beer, while Korean baseball played on TV. Several older Korean men faithfully clad in baseball outfits glanced over with warm approval.

Random Acts of Kindness

After two glorious nights on Gwakji Beach, we were ready for further Jeju exploration. Boogie earmarked a pair of waterfalls near Seogwipo: the island's southernmost and second largest city. On the way we stopped at Jeju's World Cup stadium, from Korea's impressive 2002 tournament they co-hosted with Japan. Nearby was a large outdoor exhibition, populated with tents and steady streams of arriving Koreans. We entered the market, but lugging heavy backpacks was frustrating. I sad tiredly with the bags while Boogie wandered around the stalls. An older man from an adjacent tent observed our arrival, approached me and politely beckoned.

"Come try," he repeated in English. I reckoned he had something to sell, or perhaps we could leave our bags in his tent.

Instead, he led me to a double-length table filled with platters of freshly cooked chicken and rice. He nobly offered a bowl and a pair of chopsticks, encouraging me to eat. I feasted on scrumptious tender chicken with rice and broth, dabbing in sea salt for extra flavour. Boogie was astonished and impressed that I found new friends and lunch. The lovely people at the table attempted conversing in broken English. One man was heading to Boogie's native Hungary in December. He briefed us about the history of kites in Korea, and how certain kites represented different actions and movements at various points in war. Others came and departed, including the woman who prepared the meal, and a performing musician. Boogie and I wandered around, enjoying samples of teas and honey. Touched by this latest Korean generosity, I sadly realised that many good energies come and go, share short experiences, and we'd never meet again.

At Seogwipo City, our primary challenge was to find camping for the night. After trekking for seemingly hours, we settled on a spot by a river, near a waterfall tourist attraction. It was hidden by trees and a large street sign, but was perilously beside a swamp in the epicentre of mosquitoes.

"Good enough for now," I muttered, relieved to offload our heavy belongings.

After briefly watching thousands of meandering Chinese tourists transferring from a nearby marina, a lengthy stroll led to another waterfall, that also required admission fees. Instead, we ambled along the touristic oceanside trail, that was intentionally obscured by a fence, trees and rocks. Sitting, reflecting, grumpy from persistent mosquitoes and our uninspiring swampy campsite, particularly after three terrific nights near beautiful beaches, I knew we could do better.

Back at tourist parking, I studied an enlarged map of Jeju and scoured the immediate vicinity. I noticed a man observing us.

"Do you guys need any help?"

A blonde American sported disarming familiarity. Sharing our camping aspirations, I described our subpar default locale. He immediately listed enticing alternatives. Citronella – The American – had lived on Jeju for a decade, taught English as a university professor and recently married a Jeju-native Korean. Passionately into hiking, camping and surfing, over the years he'd discovered plentiful offbeat spots of the magical island.

His wife soon joined, and the four of us drove in their car around the coastline. First we exhibited our present campsite, then motored up a hill to gorgeous parkland beside ocean, with two rock pools at its base. There were numerous suitable places for tents. Boogie was delighted. Citronella mentioned other possibilities, including for subsequent nights, but he held imminent plans. Instead we were dropped in the city with suggestions for dinner spots; we were to meet later.

Boogie and I dined at a modern, youthful at-table grill restaurant. Afterward, we found nearby Pink Cafe, that featured a plump cat lazily laying about. Citronella arrived alone, and we sat around another cafe's outdoor tables. Boogie and I drank Soju while Citronella presented several small mushrooms. The eclectic evening began, with Citronella driving around the nearby coast. He pointed out potential campsites and hiking paths, while expressing his affinity for mushrooms.

"I know a few places," he explained. "We could go mushroom picking tomorrow." It was to be our final evening on Jeju, but his idea sounded like interesting and unusual plans.

Citronella drove us to an extraordinarily raw and isolated locale, at the mouth of a river that flowed from mountaintops. We edged through bush, along a narrow rocky trail parallel to bigger rocks, that barely separated land from sea. Through a clearing, passing huge spiders and thick webs, a modest wooden gazebo stood adjacent to a beach of boulders. Blackness was abundant, beyond faraway fishing boats and a sea of stars.

"Nobody will find you here," Citronella assured us.

The Wild Mushroom Night on Mount Sanbangsan

Morning sunlight reflected off a deep blue horizon. Our barren locale included rocky cliffs covered in vines, and boulders that led to a cove with caves. This was to be our final day on Jeju, with the next morning's scheduled flight. Boogie showered on the beach before she explored the tropical riverfront, while I worked from Hawaii-style Palm Cove Brunch & Chips. Later in the afternoon, we circumnavigated Seogwipo City, eventually downing beer and snacks at a rare New Zealand eatery.

The call arrived, and we again met Citronella at Pink Cafe. At dusk we drove through rolling hills. Citronella noted several plausible picking spots, before settling on one of his favourites. He led us through a shadowy trail of trees, fallen logs and rocks. Despite examining every nook and cranny, we uncovered nothing. Down into a valley, entering a broader pasture sat putrid remnants of cows, and acres of farmland. Time was becoming frustratingly late. Mushrooms are like mosquitoes, in that they might be everywhere, but it takes discovering the first to find many more. In a groundbreaking moment, Citronella spotted a small mushroom, and minutes later Boogie and I found more. Then, we collectively uncovered the mother load: two dozen fresh mushrooms scattered around the field.

Triumphantly, we returned to the car and sped along the empty country highway. Sitting outside a convenience store with moderate privacy, Citronella further examined the dirt-crusted mushrooms, and selected a few each.

"Can you handle this?" he asked me, displaying the largest cap.

Having frequently enjoyed mushrooms, I felt comfortable with any reasonable amount, but this was a new experience for Boogie, whose first taste was the nibble last night. We saved the big one for later, although Citronella added another sizeable mushroom to the pile in my hand, and another small cap for Boogie. In a ceremony akin to fungal "cheers", we toasted and downed our mushrooms with soft drinks or juice. Our fates were sealed.

We cruised along the coast towards Mount Sanbangsan: a spherical mountain formed from volcanic eruptions nearly a million years ago. Long a popular tourist destination, at this hour Sanbangsan was silent and murky. With the potent mushrooms activating, Citronella guided us up steps and past a giant Buddhist statue, that protected the temple and mountain. Colours and patterns intensified; despite panting for breath, we were mesmerised by ancient trees and greens, that contrasted the silver-greys of starlit stone paths. Intense wind whipped around the coast, shaking leaves in a crescendo, with a ferocious roar from crashing waves beyond.

Higher and higher, through elevation and psychedelics, the trail led through a veritable corridor to the top. Up one fleeting flight of stairs, we took a deep breath, and our jaws dropped. We entered a reverberant cave with a small temple carved within. A stone statue of Buddha meditated from the pinnacle of a slender staircase. A miniature waterfall rippled into a large basin. At that intense moment, it felt like the most stunning sight of my life.

Citronella removed his shoes, ascended the steps and engaged in a series of bows and rituals, before sipping from a goblet he dipped in the waterfall. I sat solemnly near the entrance, agape at the beauty of the temple. Enclosed by the cave, the mighty wind entered and ricocheted around; it was like sitting inside an enormous seashell. The cave's volcanic ceiling illuminated from dozens of flickering candles, that reflected off the silvers of statues and stone. With Citronella's encouragement, I ventured up towards Buddha, stopping, bowing and emanating gratitude, but I respectfully didn't dare drink the water.

After prolonged thoughtful silence, we departed the temple cave, faced the awesome roaring ocean and began our fragile descent. A landing halfway down afforded views of the coast, and a small hill at the end of a cliff. Almost everything was elegantly perfect – nature, trees and sea – other than an awkward commercial development.

"Chinese restaurant," Citronella sighed. This was yet another capitalist affront of the most sacred, majestic slices of nature.

Citronella detailed Sanbangsan's place in Korean folklore, and expressed his concerns about the state of the world. This unravelled to deeper discussions about the meaning of anything. Boogie was extraordinarily hushed; she listened, while occasionally standing against the railing and gazing out to grandness. Although I found Citronella articulate and interesting, Boogie was restless.

"Make him stop talking," Boogie whispered, with her head on my shoulder. Close to midnight and exhausted, she desired sleep before an early rise for our flight. Perhaps I should have taken this critical opportunity to politely request departure, but it felt like a rare, fleeting moment, shared with a captivating new soul in a spellbinding locale.

"It's okay," I whispered back. "It's interesting, and we're lucky to be here. Let's stay a little longer." Boogie nodded trustingly. Perhaps sensing our need for space, Citronella excused himself momentarily, likely to visit the bathroom.

Under the Moon, the rumble of waves harmonised with the thunder of wind, and clouds rolled through blackened sky. Outside the holy cave guarded by Buddha, with the girl of my dreams in my arms, it felt like the most perfect moment, ever. Profoundly brilliant, in a sweeping, windy instant, calm cascaded around volcanic rock. For the first time, I told Boogie: "I love you." We kissed, held each other, and admired the sea.

A while later, Citronella returned, and we migrated to the wooden deck floor. He asked about what I wanted from life.

"Right now, I'm thinking of selling my company and leading a simple life. Maybe live in a van near the water, and immerse myself in art and music. Do good things for the world."

He paused. "You travel and have these businesses. What were your majors?"

I looked back blankly, before understanding. "I never attended university. Finished high school. Learned on the streets. Self taught at everything."

Citronella appeared surprised and disappointed. He turned to Boogie, and asked about her university and career ambitions. Astonishing herself, she replied with an unconvincing medley of social norms: *having* to return to Seoul and school, and *having* to do certain things. I pondered, paused and spoke eloquently.

"Why is it that we *have* to do anything? Society dictates what we're supposed to do, and how we should live, but for what? Everything is manufactured and artificial, and we exist solely to be taxed and controlled." Both appeared captivated enough, and I faced Boogie, speaking more philosophically than realistically.

"Why do you have to go back at all? You could quit school. I could sell my company. We could live on the beach by the rocks, or in a van. A simple life: travelling around and playing music."

Boogie smiled warmly, closed her eyes and fell into imagination. Leaving her to rest in the shadows of the steps, Citronella and I returned to the bench. He shared his fortunate experiences that led him to Jeju, about marrying a Korean, and how he became a national hero in Korea, after saving a young boy's life.

The mushroom comedown began: sleepily but intense. At one point, Boogie stood from her shadowy corner, and peed under the stairs. She embarrassedly returned to my side, before falling asleep again. Not long after, out of a short but deep slumber, she woke crying and sobbing.

"Water, I need water," Boogie groaned, and the madness of the night was underway.

Citronella, a gentleman, raced down hundreds of steps, while I consoled her. "We'll leave soon, okay?"

The lights seemed to become brighter, as if somebody was warning us to depart. Minutes later, Citronella jogged up the stairs carrying several bottles of water. Boogie's eyes lit up.

"You *are* a hero. So nice," she beamed, as she drank.

"I think it's time to return to our tent," I insisted, and after some thought Citronella agreed. Slowly we stood and prepared to leave.

"Ah, one more thing." Citronella paused to indicate a plaque beside the staircase. "I saved this for last."

The plaque, inscribed in English and Korean, read:
"Altar to Pray for Honor
This is an auspicious place where a great general
or a man of great wealth would emerge.
A prayer at this altar prior to a big event or examination,
is believed to bring the wish to come true."
I truly felt at a crossroads. Right now, with whatever psychedelic or amorous sensitivity, offered only one wish: a happy and humble lifetime together with Boogie. While intensely contemplating, I heeded to caution within: that something so important must be carefully considered. *We've only been together ten days.* With that hesitation, neither wishing for eternal love nor peace for all beings, I nodded in appreciation and stepped away from the plaque. *I'll wish next time I come here, when I know for sure...*

Suddenly everything changed. Boogie's enlarged eyes, with giant brown circles, pierced vacantly beyond mine, frighteningly as if possessed. She kissed me hard, biting my lip. She chanted in Hungarian; even the clammy touch of her hands was unfamiliar. Undeniably freaky, like my karma for hesitation, I plummeted into a gloomy, irrational, psychedelic blackhole. It felt like Boogie suddenly changed her mind about everything. My extensive portfolio of crushed dreams and jealousy crashed upon me. Boogie acted vastly more attracted to Citronella for his valiant water act. One slow step at a time, Boogie rattled off Hungarian spells and Citronella dodged behind shadows, while we clumsily meandered down the mountain.

The pace was too slow and I needed the bathroom, sprinting down flights of stairs towards the public restroom; I left them alone near the large temple. The whole time I cursed in disbelief. Upon returning I noticed Boogie's pants were slightly down, revealing underwear.

"Water," she repeated. "I need water." Weeks earlier in Tamil Nadu, both the gardener who sexually assaulted me and the overly-chatty airport taxi driver referred to "sperm" as "water".

I'd seen and heard enough. The three of us staggered awkwardly towards the entrance. Boogie acted guilty and constantly mumbled in Hungarian with possessed eyes, while Citronella sheepishly skulked around the parking lot.

In the exhaustingly long car ride to a seemingly unknown destination, Boogie and I sat in the backseat. I was furious, while Boogie, sometimes stormy and distant, occasionally clumsily scrambled onto my lap, while I pushed her away. She frowned.

"Water, can I have some water?"

Boogie was inhaling litres of water. Without enough available water to quench her thirst, she began gulping potent Soju and orange juice.

"I don't feel well... I'm so cold... Water, please can I have some water?" She consistently touched herself in the genitals, further fuelling my misgivings. The loop continued, over and over. "Water, can I have some water?.. I don't feel well... I'm so cold."

At some point I suggested visiting a hospital. This added a new layer to the loop: "Can you take me to the hospital?"

Citronella continuously glanced in the rear view mirror, concerned and confused. He insisted on supplying her Xanax: a drug to force silence and sleep. My distrust was exacerbated by the extraordinary time we were seemingly driving in circles. At one toilet break, I was certain they'd find a private spot alone.

I shook my head: "I need to find the tent, pack my bag, and head to the airport."

I'd take a bus, and they could fornicate however which way: I'd had enough. I visualised prospective itineraries around South East Asia, ahead of retreating to Australia. I was crushed that a mushroom trip accelerated the end of this wonderful dream.

After seemingly hours of driving and repetitive loops, Boogie fell into Xanax-induced sleep, waking periodically to resume her chanting. The sun sprinkled light as we approached our hidden campsite. To reach the airport, we needed to hurriedly pack and catch the bus, but Boogie was in no state to walk or carry bags, let alone manoeuvre through airport security and fly.

While towelling a wet car seat I resisted Citronella's insistence on forcing her full of more Xanax, before dragging her into the bush – *then what?* We hoisted a battling Boogie from the car onto the pavement; she violently resisted like she never knew us. With day breaking and his wife waiting, Citronella advised we skip our flight, and insisted we update him when we woke.

After he drove off, I held a floppy Boogie, asking if she remembered me. She was content to sleep among swarms of delighted mosquitoes, that indulged in her blood-scraped knees while she sprawled awkwardly on rocks. Despite her initial reluctance, returned glimmers of normality in her eyes, even a mild smile, and she consented to move. She grabbed onto me, and we delicately hobbled through the trail to our secluded gazebo. Bundled under blankets, Boogie slept, but my head was buzzing. I'd return Boogie safely to Seoul, and continue my life elsewhere, alone.

...

We woke underneath the wooden gazebo in our remote little spot, near boulders and crashing waves. We missed our flight. Boogie barely remembered anything, while the entire proceedings remained stingingly vivid to me. Bits and pieces returned to her consciousness, although she had no recollection of the loop. She'd earlier watched me "depart her", that I looked at her differently, and that I was no longer with her. The earlier crying had come from happiness, with visions of our future, aged, having spent our lives together: a joyous place. Boogie also dreamt of family and friends, but deep-rooted sadness emanated from the absolute temporary state of being. That we all live and die. That nothing is forever, even our loved ones. She wondered about the point of anything, and it propelled her into an internal spiral.

I was touched at her visions of eternal togetherness. The experience bonded us exponentially closer: a magical feeling. We missed the flight, but it earned us a bonus stay on Jeju Island, with school holidays imminent. Everything was booked up for peak season: the few remaining airfares approached $1000, and hotels were scarce. *Somehow we'd find a way.*

Rain on Hyeopjae Beach

Boogie and I spent the night at a guesthouse in Seogwipo for a proper bed and shower. We braved incessant rain to investigate a bustling and scent-filled market, sampling plentiful free tasters and scrumptious food. Even skipping through torrential downpour was fun. We took breaks from the outdoors to practice deeper, multiple levels of intimacy, that elevated into sustained euphoria.

In the morning, I worked from the guesthouse while we washed and dried our grimy clothes. We navigated the maze of a large Korean hospital, for removal of stitches in Boogie's thumb and certain emergency medication. We returned along the coast towards Hallim, where we'd spotted its miraculously golden beaches and camping-abundant forestry. We arrived shortly after nightfall, with cloudy weather that was warm but windy. Beside substantial parking stood lush woods, traces of recent tents and glorious ocean aroma. In a little pocket of bushes, steps from the shore, lay a remarkable spot shrouded by trees. It featured wooden decking atop plastic crates, and ensured our stretched tent was elevated off sandy, grassy ground.

We delightedly skipped along the heavenly beach to assess our fresh environment. The main road held restaurants, shops and cafes with dozens of people strolling around. There weren't many available options for food, although one was particularly alluring: Container Yard. It was a miniature atrium constructed from shipping containers. It reminded me of Christchurch, New Zealand, where plentiful shipping containers were erected in the city's post-earthquake rebuild.

Upon ascending the metal stairs of Container Yard, we were greeted by an aromatic grill and a bespectacled chef. The menu was handwritten on wooden slats that hung from the roof. The articulate owner-chef answered questions in English and translated the menu. I shared my Christchurch impressions; he'd lived in New Zealand for ten years! Despite prices exceeding our budget, we sat at a corner table near the grill. The meal commenced with a couple of beers and a cylindrical roll of sliced tofu in soya sauce. The main dish arrived – a sizzling plate of fresh sea eel in decadent barbecue sauce, atop a bed of mint-like lettuce. It might have been the finest taste of our entire trip.

After dinner, the chef, Rain, joined our table. He invited us out, after he finished cleaning, while we mingled with guests and polished off our remaining Soju. With his duties complete, Rain guided us to a pleasant garden-style outdoor restaurant that was populated by buzzing locals. Rain was a known movie director, and a one-time celebrity in New Zealand. He shared his phone number, and insisted that we contact him should we need help. The rest of the night was a blur: I blacked out from excessive Soju, that was agitated by the unnerving head rush of cigarettes. I should have interpreted it as another warning sign.

...

I woke to the crashing of waves, next to the girl of my dreams. Our humble home was hidden under tropical trees, beside a golden beach and sparkling teal sea. It was the happiest time of my life. Working from any cafe mandated staring into blue layers of rippling water, while downing oversized coffees or pumpkin lattes in a sultry breeze. Writing was particularly inspiring. Meals were simple: usually budget burgers or noodles heated at convenience stores, and occasional pizza. I cut down Soju and cigarettes - a little, anyway. We couldn't afford much, but we didn't need much: we had all.

On the Sunday, several days into paradise, torrential storms gathered after steady, accumulating trickles. We spent the day inside a lovely cafe, that was perched beside a beach on a sliver of coast. The vantage afforded unfettered views of ocean and mountains, that were poignantly dramatic as water poured from the heavens. Thick sheets of rain prevented us returning to our tent, whose convenient elevation ensured our belongings remained safe and dry.

We called Rain: he urged we spend the night at his home in Hallim, the nearby industrial fishing city. Rain's hundred-year-old traditional Korean house was a humble and comfortable abode, with curved wooden floors, several cosy rooms, a kitchen, large bathroom and yard. His fourteen-year-old dog greeted us with her habitual yapping. Also visiting was Rain's niece and her boyfriend: a Christian couple spending time on Jeju. Rain admitted that he the outcast in his family. Our quintet visited a nearby restaurant for platters of noodles and bottles of Soju, before we returned to Rain's home for drinks and music. Rain insisted that we utilise his guest room, while he slept on the floor.

"As master of this house, you must obey my request!"

We slept well, and woke to freshly-brewed coffee. Boogie and I browsed the nearby supermarket, fetched food to prepare, played guitar and sang songs inside. Rain left us at home while he attended to his restaurant. He requested that we gather our tent, and stay at his place for our truly final evening on Jeju.

Later over tea, Rain commented on my seemingly inconceivable circumstances, with a much younger, beautiful spirit.

"Sometimes we live fantasies, that shouldn't be real," Rain cautioned me, compassionately. "Just remember to enjoy it while it lasts."

Karaoke Ferry to Tongyeong

Due to grossly overpriced flights, we preferred the more economical and adventurous ferry. This led to the only available destination: the city of Yeosu. After hours of waiting, mostly spent feasting on noodles and complimentary side dishes at the terminal's busy restaurant, we boarded a ship packed with holidayers heading to the mainland. The ferry sailed ahead of sunset, as we faced vanishing, magical Jeju. Its enormous mountains dissolved into grey clouds and mist, like a dream.

Boogie and I penetrated every cranny of the ship, while downing multiple "SoMacs" (Soju plus beer). Eventually, we discovered three adjacent, usually-locked doors that muffled the detuned wails and shrieks of karaoke. They were popular and seemingly always occupied, but at one point Boogie stormed into a room, revealing a man and his two young boys singing Korean pop songs on microphones. The father keenly welcomed us to join. Shortly after, his wife and the kids' grandmother entered, to their astonishment and everybody's amusement. For hours, we enjoyed Korean ferry karaoke; the father fed W10,000 notes into the machine, half hours at a time. Sporadically, Boogie and I were handed the microphone, and we laboured through various renditions of popular English songs, with thick reverb masking our mangled vocals. Everybody in the room delightedly clapped and rattled tambourines, rocking with the boat.

Summoning a notebook and pen, the mother, with simple translations from her young son, insisted we visit their hometown of Tongyeong, a few hours from Yeosu. They couldn't understand our affinity for camping, and offered to reserve us a guesthouse. As the ferry neared its dock, we exchanged contacts and heartfelt goodbyes. Boogie and I looked at each other and laughed.

In Yeosu at a tad past 10pm, we were magnetised towards psychedelic lights, that graced the walls of the sprawling Yeosu Aquatic Centre. We entered an empty amusement park, that housed abandoned rides, shuttered attractions and a huge circular ferris wheel, that stood perpendicular to a spacious outdoor amphitheatre. Nobody was around. With no security guards, and few CCTV cameras to spot us slinking through a relatively open fence, we found an appealingly flat patch of grass shrouded by shrubbery, for a welcomed night's campsite.

...

We woke in a deserted amusement park surrounded by bushes, rides and carnival attractions, near where dolphins danced, a huge aquarium and sea. After several hours at a cute cafe in Yeosu, we caught a bus to Tongyeong. Boogie dozed through thickening traffic; my attentive views offered tropical cinema, valleys and ponds.

The father and younger son greeted us warmly at Tongyeong bus terminal. Despite our bus' hour delay, the family had waited in the car without a trace of frustration. In a packed yet comfortable Hyundai 4x4, we set forth to find food. This was complicated by the prime of peak season, where every diner and hotel was fully booked, with visitors from Korea, Japan and China. Understandably: Tongyeong was a coastal city fantasia. Numerous waterways, gardens and mountains were mesmer-isingly blanketed by prolific parks and forests. With most of the family's preferred places full, we entered a traditional restaurant, that featured multiple grills and elaborate dishes prepared at tables. Conversation continued minimally and delicately, but it worked, and the family proudly shared a glimpse at their hometown.

After dinner, we visited the popular harbour around the former ship of legendary General Lee. Despite complete guesthouse unavailability, the undeterred mother discovered a cute room in Popcorn Hostel, that featured a bunkbed and pink dressing table. Back at the harbour, after treating us to ice cream and aromatic coffee, the mother presented us a bag of assorted dishes to assemble for the next day's breakfast: soups, rice and sweets. The father spread out a printed map with handwritten notes; he circled a nearby camping area, and penned his number should we need assistance. Impressed and grateful beyond words, we could only smile. □ □ □ □ □

In the morning we explored a nearby arts village, where Boogie tangled in giant spaghetti, before venturing to find camping. The father urged that we check "near Marina Resort". We trekked for ages, weaving through the bustle of Tongyeong, alongside rivers, and over a majestic bridge to a more plush foresty side. Buildings were adorned in colourfully painted walls; a church peered from the edges, mirroring a calming Buddhist temple.

After one stretch of uphill sidewalk, glancing at a miraculous approaching sign, I requested that Boogie close her eyes. When the time was right, she opened them to reveal:

KING ICE CREAM SALE

Boogie's brown eyes burst from her head. This large shop sold countless discount ice cream of all conceivable varieties, and with wild joy we pillaged plenty of it. Afterwards we discovered a cheap fried chicken shop, then a budget pizza parlour.

"This is the best street of all," Boogie solemnly declared.

We continued across a curving hill to Marina Resort. Several campervans and tents were spread around a grassy parking lot, that was otherwise bland and concrete. I knew we could do better and, as in Seogwipo before we encountered Citronella, I followed the urge to venture further.

"Let's walk to the top of that hill and take a look. We can always come back," I suggested. Defeating our weariness, we laboured up the hill beside Stanford Resort.

At its peak we gasped: a deep blue bay, green tropical islands with mysterious mountains, and national parks that loomed behind mist on the horizon. We noticed a sandy beach and several tents near the shore. Descending to the wave-lapped shore, we sourced space on soft sand, safely from the sea: our latest heavenly home.

Relievedly stashing our backpacks rebirthed our energy, for spirited miles of strolling back along the main road for food. With our appetites satisfied, browsing the area for nightlife suggested nothing happening, beyond multiple karaoke signs – and karaoke had led us to Tongyeong. The first two establishments were fully booked, but at the third, with its reception vacant, we skirted into an open room. Boogie and I performed before imaginary crowds, with my low *Ommm* sounds complementing her melancholy trip hop vocals, as reverb shook the fantasy stadium. We performed for ten minutes before door opened, revealing baffled faces and a gracious apology. Minutes later, a lady returned. She politely explained the rental costs for this room. The deal was W65,000 for an hour and three beers. We shook our heads.

"W50,000." We demonstrated "No money" with our fingers.

"W30,000!" Now, this was a good deal! But as thrifty travellers, this was a full day's budget for everything. We politely departed, and returned to the beach for heavenly sleep.

Hangover in Paradise

If Hyeopjae Beach lived the dream, Tongyeong was rebirth in paradise. We woke upon soft golden sands facing cool teal ocean, pristine islands and national parks. Unfortunately this was my most fragile hangover of the trip, that neared debilitating nausea. I'd not drank enough water and had definitely overindulged in alcohol. Boogie explored while I tried sleeping it off, and after several restful hours beside the ocean, I mustered sufficient strength to saunter out.

On our second and remorsefully final night, the Tongyeong mother treated us to dinner with her sons. She couldn't believe that anybody would willingly camp in a tent, particularly so close to the water. We politely declined her offer of another guesthouse, expressing cheerful admiration for our spot. After luscious dinner at a floor-seating Chinese restaurant with giant bowls of noodles, we were graciously dropped at the beach. This family demonstrated the essence of goodness in humanity.

Boogie and I further investigated the amenities around Stanford Resort. The adjacent building was a small luxury shopping arcade, with a bowling alley and other games in the basement. We played pool and air hockey, while cautiously downing smuggled Soju, before Boogie's bowling debut. We rode the resort's elevator to the rooftop; there were neither people nor cameras. Alone on the edge of the roof, facing parks and ocean, we crowned the moment, fast and pulsating.

...

In the morning, we packed the tent and embarked around a rocky cove, to the base of a hill. We boldly entered the luxury resort, and rode its elevator to the rooftop, that housed a now-open fancy spa and infinity pool. Pretending we belonged, we arranged ourselves comfortably on loungers near two hot tubs. For hours we delighted in complementary access to the resort's rooftop swimming pool, cooled in sky-blue water, and simmered in hot spas that faced ocean and green island mountains.

Navigating onwards to the coastal metropolis of Busan, following sleepy tropical life in nature, slammed the shocking contrast of a big, busy city. The vast sprawl of Busan and dwindling time required careful consideration of possible beaches. Knowing that discrete beachside camping would be acceptable, we selected a beach a little further north for the first of our final two nights before Seoul.

Songjeong Beach greeted us with a mile of sandy beach, that was popular with young adults and families. Countless candle-powered lanterns sailed into the night sky, and tents were scattered around the beach. We pitched at the far northern point, shaded by a curved corner of a tall rocky wall. We ambled along the beach and ate dinner at a cosy local diner.

The next afternoon we hopped on a bus, riding southward through the heart of gigantic Busan and its shiny metallic skyscrapers. Our final night's locale was manmade Songdo Beach: smaller and touristy, near a waterfall and buildings packed with restaurants and shops, but conveniently close to the central train and bus stations. We pitched the tent on a discrete, sandy corner, wedged between a rock staircase and wall. We snapped a tent pole, and patched it with tape.

A small restaurant broadcast a Korean Baseball League playoff game, and we took the opportunity for baseball, food and beer. The owner passionately supported his gutsy Busan side. The game extended to extra innings, and complementary plates of food accompanied extra beers, before Busan crushed to defeat.

"It's a whole new game tomorrow," I consoled. The owner looked down forlornly and nodded.

The next morning, after one final heartfelt glance at the sea, we trudged uphill towards Busan's central station. Outside the station lingered anti-North Korean protests, by clear supporters of American military power. Finding an available locker in the station was challenging; more so was solving its operation. We determined our best route to Seoul was an inexpensive national bus departing early the next morning.

With the day and night to spare, we headed to colourful and creative Gamcheon Cultural Village. After climbing steep hills we looked down on pastel palettes of modest buildings, and were constantly surrounded by fantasy character sculptures. Exiting downhill through twisting alleyways led past artisan bakeries, rainbow cafes, graffiti-adorned restaurants and galleries with brightly-painted staircases.

With the sun falling, we strolled behind streets parallel to Busan Station. We weaved aimlessly through a bizarre series of blocks: China Town, Russian Town and American-style. This was an ironic glimpse at harmonious superpowers fully kitted in stereotype. Beyond restaurants there were plentiful brothels – mostly Russian and American – with scantily-clad Koreans, foreigners, and older Russian women urging our patronage. Hours and miles of curious walking prompted my impromptu nap in the shadowy corner of a shuttered shop, while Boogie eagerly kept watch.

Back at Busan Station, several hours later we boarded the bus to Seoul. Boogie crashed into sleep while I relaxed and fell into dreams. *Did that really happen? What next?* Inspiration often surfaces long after the conclusion of magnificent occasions; one can neither force answers nor manipulate dreams.

Chapter 5

Fairy Tale Land

After our magical time on Jeju Island, there was no worldly reason to be anywhere but together, and that meant preparing for life in Seoul. We'd start with a month and take it from there. I held doubts, including that constant distractions might render me wholly unproductive, the prohibitive cost of living in Korea's capital, and wondering if it was better to leave on a high, say goodbye, and move on. Realistically, I had nowhere else to be. I was madly in love and, however improbable our chances, it felt worth making the most of a rare opportunity.

During my opening week in Seoul, I stayed at a Serbian-run hostel in Itaewon. I fiddled away on my computer from their restaurant, while the fog from Jeju cleared. At first everything seemed grey and unfamiliar, and days were long, cold and uncertain. Relievedly, I rapidly fell into a comfortable, productive routine. On weekdays, particularly Tuesdays through Thursdays while Boogie attended university, I bunkered into work from guesthouse lounges or cafes. Momentum accelerated for DigitalNomad.Blog, through extensive features about nomadic life in Korea, and I readied its website for launch. The litany of budget guesthouses and hostels ensured I experienced plentiful different districts of Seoul, although I most preferred to work between Hongdae – a vibrant university area – and Itaewon, the international, alternative-style hub.

Our weekends usually began on Thursday evenings, when we'd probe new parts of Seoul. There were some meals during school days, often at her highly-affordable university cafeteria. Every weekend was exhilarating and fulfilling. Contrary to losing steam from excessive time together, every moment remained invigorating, with the mid-week space inherently refreshing.

Moments of sadness were etched within the euphoria of this mystical era. Our first weekend upon returning from Busan was spent at the extremely low budget and poor quality Mini-

Residence, in south Seoul. Beyond unfriendly management, our windowless room was the size of a closet, with a single bed, a tiny desk, and awkward cupboards that were almost too big to open. Shafts at the top of each wall enabled infinite Korean kamikaze mosquitoes to swarm into the room for scrupulous feasting. The abject but affordable guesthouse prompted us to spend much time outside exploring the area. One evening we visited a music bar, at which Boogie performed with the owner. On another night we travelled miles to and from Gangnam.

Long into a nap at the dim MiniResidence mosquito abattoir, I awoke from pulsing notifications on my phone. It was from Bec, my ex-girlfriend of three wonderful years in Melbourne.

"Hey babe, just letting you know that Dawson passed away today from a skydiving accident..."

Startled, I jolted from bed and searched for any possible news. Peter "Awesome" Dawson was a friend of mine and the ex-boyfriend of Jess, Bec's younger sister, who I chaperoned around South America in 2014. Dawson was a professional skydive instructor, and was my partner for my first skydive, at Mission Beach, Queensland in 2011.

Groggy from the nap, with my mind in overdrive, I uncovered reports on the crash. It was top news on the international BBC news website. Three skydivers collided mid-air above Mission Beach, near the same spot of my maiden jump. Parachutes entangled without opening and all three divers slammed into the ground or trees. I took some solace in that Dawson died in the midst of his passion, in a spectacular area he loved.

A few weeks earlier we'd chatted about cryptocurrency's revolutionary aspects, and he was becoming increasingly switched on about the unpleasant truths of the world. Dawson's death put many things in perspective, including unnecessary petty feuds with friends and colleagues. There was not enough time in life for division amongst ourselves. RIP Peter Dawson.

Weeks later, while falling asleep in my bunkbed at Dustin's Guesthouse, I received a similarly sudden message from my Canadian aunt: "Sorry to have to write with sad news. Nanny passed away last night."

Nanny was my maternal grandmother and my last surviving grandparent, aged 93. She was the best cook I'd encountered, passing down her tasty recipes to my similarly talented mother. Once she dyed her hair purple to mimic my teenage sister's style, but her inherent grey and silver hair morphed into an embarrassing punk-like pink. Nanny was so mad! I held a cheerful memory from my grandparents' living room in the 90's, when she and my incredible grandfather spontaneously danced together. As children we were fearful of her, but she was paradoxically caring and loving much of the time.

When I returned to Canada in 2012 for the first time in seven years, our relationship improved. She finally saw me as an adult, instead of a mischievous, troubled adolescent. She'd chilled out considerably, albeit was skinnier and meeker, and any angry intimidating presence had long departed. The last time I saw her, was in 2016 when I visited her Toronto retirement home. I was impressed how cool she was compared to the other elderly residents. When we said goodbye, Nanny made the sign of the cross while praying to bless me, and that was my final glance. RIP Nanny Bernard.

...

Sandwiched between sad messages was a first voyage to the sizeable city of Incheon. The visit followed a tough week and mixed messages; I wondered what I was doing in Korea. To cheer me up, Boogie treated us to a special room at fun, California Dreamin'-inspired The Mamas and the Papas Guesthouse in Hongdae.

The next hungover morning of a cheery day, we boarded the metro for Incheon. I landed an excellent deal at Bunker Guesthouse for a modern, comfortable room. After wandering around neighbourhoods, parks and budget ice cream shops, we arrived at a lively area with numerous clubs and bars. We located a hidden Irish pub, O'Murphy's, for Boogie's first proper pint of Guinness. Back outside while eating street food, a young bespectacled Korean man approached Boogie at the counter.

"Your boyfriend is very handsome," he purred.

So began a bizarre night with our self-proclaimed guide, Ricky, who was excessively intoxicated, yet tried to hide it as best he could. After a nightclub refused Ricky's entry because of his hotel slippers and socks, he toured us around, while frequently patting us like furry animals. Ricky was "from New

York", spoke traces of broken Spanish, and returned to Korea three years ago. After I won a bet about which building housed a baseball game simulator, simply because I read a sign properly, Ricky treated us to chicken and beer. He didn't provide straight answers to simple questions like, "Where are you staying tonight?" Boogie and I demurred that he might not have anywhere to sleep, or perhaps he preferred to follow us around. Tiring, we said goodbye, and *maybe see you tomorrow.*

Nearing home, our virtually-deserted street was littered with miniature flyers offering sex services. Two men in full suits stumbled drunkenly along the street-lit pavement. Before crossing the road, I spotted a W50,000 note: nearly two days budget! We'd constantly discovered money and cigarettes on the ground throughout Korea: perhaps a result of Soju-intensified mindlessness.

In the morning we began our latest fairy tale, and one of our loveliest days. Chinatown was a central area for many hotspots of Incheon – including adjacent Fairy Tale Land. Chinatown featured several enchanting traditional structures and a quirky mesh of Chinese and Korean cultures. Fairy Tale Land brimmed with abundantly colourful walls, pastel murals and sculptures of cartoons, with photogenic sculptures, and a wide selection of dangerously delicious desserts. Fascinated sugar-fuelled children scattered everywhere.

The nearby cultural festival sprung to life, with a bustling laneway of food, coffee, chocolate and toys. There was an empty main stage with many hundreds of chairs lined along a narrow street, spanning several blocks up a hill. We strolled through a traditional market, where Boogie found the hambatan Korean pancakes she'd craved since Jeju.

Upon exiting the market we blended orange juice within a large bottle of the strongest Soju and passed a strange activity: people seemingly throwing chopsticks into a vase. Hearing live music, we turned down the next alley that revealed a small stage. It was a singalong karaoke-type event with a host, live musicians and a small audience. We clapped along to Korean pop music and rock covers played by dual guitarists. Several women in traditional dress, each holding percussive ins-truments, ushered us to a table.

The host on the microphone looked at us, greeted us warmly and made a joke; everybody laughed. An older rocker lady wearing sunglasses reached for my hand, and lured me onto the dancefloor. A man pulled Boogie up. Dozens of intrigued spectators snapped photographs, laughed and clapped as we shyly danced. At the song's end the crowd applauded, and we were presented a gift certificate for W5000. Our encore consisted of dancing along with the female percussive troupe. For the finale, one lady handed me a drum, draped the strap over my shoulder, and I banged the bass drum alongside the band. It was equally terrifying and therapeutically soothing. During the next song we stealthily departed, and returned to the thick of the festival. We learned that not only was this the Cultural Festival, but signs sunnily displayed "The Love Festival".

The day and night was perfectly romantic, but in a drunken garble I ruined it. At a nearby wine shop we found a bargain bottle of vino for W5000. After paying at the counter I spotted an eerily-familiar bottle of Remy Martin. I maintained an incomprehensible psychosis, that started at Afrikaburn in 2016, when I'd lusted for a certain Russian. A group costumed as Bolsheviks invited me into their circle, and a tall man donning a white Bolshevik outfit passed me a peculiar but luxurious bottle of alcohol. Since then I'd not been able to solve the identity of the liquor or the Russian lookalike, but seeing the bottle jolted my memories. I needed to see and feel the bottle. However, the shopkeeper was unwilling to cooperate.

"No. This one very expensive," he said curtly. I simply wanted to hold the bottle in my hands and feel its weight. "No. Sorry!"

Insulted and outraged, with a flurry of rude fingers and profanity, I stormed out of the shop, while a stunned Boogie tried to calm me. She didn't understand the backstory, but it didn't excuse my immature outburst. Considerately, she eyed fireworks while I sat on a bench blowing off steam; it took me half an hour to chill. My initial misguided anger at the shop-keeper turned into self-defeating disappointment.

Still, the rest of the night, if not a little subdued, was entertaining. We ate at a sushi train – Boogie's first – and enjoyed heaping platters of delectably hand-crafted fish and rice. At now-open Tantra Bar, classic blues and rock played from vinyl, and we covertly added our remaining Soju to otherwise expensive beers, creating a Korean concoction called "SoMac".

Two businessmen sat beside us at the bar and chatted. One shared a wish: "I would like to dance with your girlfriend."

I had no problem with that, but it was up to her. Boogie laughed and they danced elegantly on the diminutive dancefloor. The man bought an expensive bottle of Ballantine's scotch and poured us a drink. His friend was the CEO of a Japanese-based company; both of them handed us luxurious business cards. I learned that the first man and his girlfriend had argued earlier that evening; he held a noticeable air of despair.

"I really like your girlfriend," he sighed.

"Me too," I replied.

At some point, with forlorn faces, the men left. Boogie and I bottled the large amount of remaining scotch, and hopped on a late bus to the hotel. Still let down in myself, I resolved to make a more concerted effort to control binge drinking and my erratic alcoholic temperament.

A Warm Welcome to Traditional Korean Values

The first tangible assurance that my Korean fantasy would end, arrived upon booking flights to Bangkok. My unyielding visa expiry meant I had to depart Korea before December 13. Boogie was to return home to Hungary a few days later. Weeks of tracking flights led to an irresistible offer from Jin Air for less than €100, for an evening departure on Monday December 11. A few days comedown in Thailand, then figure out where next. Chiang Mai? Vietnam? Copenhagen? In the coming weeks I decided I wouldn't be returning to Australia.

On one particular mid-week evening, with the fresh frostiness of autumn foretelling a biting winter to come, I aimlessly wandered around Hongdae. At a corner I was approached by a young man and his bespectacled female friend; they peculiarly asked for directions to the massively popular Line Friends shop. After a polite introduction by the young man, Daek, the conversation detailed a breakdown in Korean values that had watered down spiritual concepts of Buddhism into today's bland consumerism. Daek was concerned about a lack of knowledge or respect from younger generations about their heritage. I cautiously accepted their invitation to accompany them to a special ceremony to learn more. It was an instance of, *Why not?*

A few metro stops away, we entered a mid-rise building off a main road, climbed steps and opened a door. Walls of shelves held musty shoes and I donned a traditional robe. A lady greeted us, and instructed the formalities of the procedure ahead. I entered a small hall-like room and faced a table filled with candles. I bowed in respect, replicating the footwork of others in the room: a few steps left and right, with some bowing.

With the ceremony complete, I was ushered to a tiny table where Daek and my guide sat. I was presented different fruits to eat in a particular order; each had a specific meaning. There was a scroll inked with my name and basic details. At the end I was requested to make a big wish. I was gravely reminded that this ceremony happens only once in a person's life, like a rite of passage. My wish, seeking to make amends for my failed opportunity on Jeju's Mount Sanbangsan, was straightforward: "I wish that Boogie and I could be happy forever."

Slightly puzzled, they frowned and encouraged me to rethink. "But she is so young!"

I shrugged, resolute in my desire. At the time I was unaware that my wish's semantics were open to interpretation, that didn't necessitate togetherness. With a shrug of their own, they accepted my wish, and solemnly burned the paper.

"You must not tell anybody of this ceremony for at least one hundred days, and not share the wish with anybody."

In the weeks to come, I was invited to a potluck dinner at their residence, and a picnic on an afternoon at Haneul Park, near Seoul's World Cup stadium. This glorious day featured a walk atop a hill through tall yellow sunflower fields, and views of the majestic panorama of the Seoul metropolis and Han River. During lunch one man shared several baseball gloves and balls; several of us delightedly threw baseballs in sun-chilled breeze.

Fascinated by my sudden social life, Boogie enquired what I'd been up to, and was intrigued at my mysterious answer:

"Sorry! I can't tell you for one hundred days!"

Penthouse and a Luxury Hotel

The latest weekend of randomness greeted us with the first of several wonderful gifts. Our original room booked for Thursday night, again at excellent Mamas and Papas Guesthouse, was occupied, and we were reassigned. I didn't expect much, but was thrilled to receive keys to the building's seventh floor penthouse. It was a family and games room, with two double bed futons, another single bed, a dart board, a full karaoke set up with multiple screens and a big soundsystem. Boogie was ecstatic at the surprise, and hopped over the beds like a frog. At night, all of the skyscrapers' lights illuminated 360 degrees. We wandered around Hongdae and enjoyed Korean BBQ, before christening the penthouse, making the most of every space.

A relaxed morning arrived, then in top spirits we ventured to Incheon. Following the hour's journey, we discovered our booking was cancelled due to another occupancy. Our inconvenience was rewarded with a free upgrade to a nearby, ritzy three-star hotel. Boogie was undeniably delighted – the girl from a poor Hungarian family had never previously stayed in a fancy hotel. She was particularly enthused about the prospect of free buffet breakfast.

The Charis Hotel in Incheon looked and felt more than three stars. Our deluxe double room on the eleventh floor featured a supremely comfortable queen bed, that faced a huge TV, with a spa bath and automatic toilet. The first night we piloted around the neighbourhood to accumulate snacks and wine. The early-morning buffet was served out of a large ballroom, with multiple long tables covered in white tablecloths and plates of fruit, breads, eggs, noodles, soups, salads and local delicacies. After a nap, we wandered around the area, visiting every open supermarket to devour their freshly-cooked free samples, and saved our appetites for the next morning's buffet.

...

Back near Hongik, with savings from our complementary luxury weekend, we stayed at Kim's Family Guesthouse, tucked away from the centre of Hongdae. In the evening we headed to source nightlife. We tried and failed to find an underground hip-hop club called Secret Society. The entrance was supposedly hidden behind a Coke machine, but the entire block around the alleged address bore no such landmark. Door staff confirmed that the old venue had closed: It was now Sink Hole. Inside featured hip-hop beats, reasonably priced drinks, and a fairly empty space that soon filled with patrons. A young American blonde, allegedly half Korean, invited us to share her bottle of Hennessy. She was overrun with attention by a drunken local, who was soon warned off by a clean cut European. The European asked where I was from, resulting in the usual complicated spiel. In return I was to guess his nationality.

"Hungarian," I predicted. His eyes opened widely, impressed.

"Close..." he replied.

I paused, and took a wild stab in the dark. "Lithuanian." He gasped – he was! Further astounded by my own Lithuanian heritage, he rewarded me with the first of several unfortunate shots of tequila.

The crowd thickened, music became ever louder and everybody thumped along. Recent attempts to slow down my drinking rapidly unravelled, and I lost control. In my sink-holing haziness it felt like people were unreasonably pushing me, so I pushed back, bracing my elbows like I would in a heavy metal mosh pit. The area around us cleared. Grumpy and disoriented, desiring to depart, I chucked our evil packet of cigarettes across the dancefloor; Boogie dutifully repatriated them. Boogie and I exited, and we soon passed out at Kim's.

Waking in a fog, Boogie was ill, while checkout was imminent. My hangover was a creeper, becoming increasingly unbearable. After hours of squirming uncomfortably on the couches downstairs, we induced vomiting, then relocated to the next locale: Dustin Guesthouse. Feeling wretched, I escorted Boogie to the train station before crashing in my bunk. There are only so many warnings we receive before the universe intervenes.

Reaching the North Korean Border

If our adventures weren't already exhilarating enough, we made an attempt to approach the volatile North Korean border, as closely as possible. The fresh autumn weekend began with a stay at the Itaewon Land Spa. It was a gloomy concrete building atop a steep hill, that housed segregated male and female hot baths, and several floors of simple, windowless rooms. After Boogie returned, steamy and relaxed from splashing around in the spa, we gathered our bags and rode a coach to the east coast city of Sokcho. Not having camped or hiked since Jeju, with winter approaching this appeared our final opportunity. Torrential, frigid downpour drenched us at the Sokcho inter-city bus terminal, in the darkness of Friday evening. The adjacent cafe shut its doors for closing at precisely the same time. The grumpy old security guard informed us that the bus station was closed, and we were back on the cold damp street.

We crossed the street to Red Light House, greeted by its faux artisan-looking owners. "W70,000" was the price for the cheapest available room: around three times our budget. Finding strong-enough wifi outside the shuttered bus terminal, we uncovered reasonable rates for a nearby guesthouse. While dodging raindrops along the way, another guesthouse glimmered in the streetlight: it was simply called "House". The owners, a couple, chatted on their phones while cautiously gazing at us, sopping wet with backpacks. A sign on the desk noted opening hours of "7am to 11:30pm" - it was exactly 11:30.

After understanding our situation, the man politely shook his head and informed us that they were fully booked. I asked about the guesthouse nearby – *Was it a nice place?* He nodded and motioned towards its direction, in the distant, rainy blackness. We wished him well, returned to the downpour and laughed – this was still fun! The owner ran after us: "Come back!"

We were offered a room for a very reasonable rate, "if you don't mind sharing single bed." House was a highly-reputable guesthouse filled with abundantly good energy. Messages of kind wishes and currency denominations adorned the walls. I gifted the owner one of my rare Malawian Kwacha notes. Our cheerfully-decorated, well-apportioned single room was extremely comfortable, with heated floors, a shower and a cute television. In the morning we enjoyed complimentary breakfast near other Korean and Western guests. The room was available again that night, at a slightly higher price, but we would first try our luck with Couchsurfing. Camping was ruled out entirely.

We hiked through impressive Seoraksan National Park: one of

the wonders of South Korea. Seoraksan was particularly splendid in bursting shades of autumn. Orange, red and yellow textures shimmered on trees under soaring mountains; some were coated with ice atop their peaks. The route passed a gigantic Buddha statue and small temples, before tree-lined and leaf-adorned paths led higher into hills. We paused for rest at the edges of steep cliffs, and on large boulders that looked into the panoramic vastness of beyond.

On the leisurely descent we moseyed down wooden bridges, through leaf-leaving trees, and into the central valley. A bus dispatched us to Sokcho's central market. Boogie's Couchsurfing matched us with a Canadian teacher and author, Mark Dake. Mark's flat was humble and cosy, with three bedrooms, a small balcony, kitchen and living room. A mountain climber from Slovakia named Robert arrived shortly thereafter, striking a friendly bond with his Hungarian neighbour. Our quartet discussed Korea, its education system, politics and mountains, while Mark's book, "South Korea: The Enigmatic Peninsula", included useful insights into reaching the North Korean border. Mark invited us back if we were unsuccessful on our random border mission.

In the morning, Boogie and I rode a bus to Goseong, alongside the northeastern coast. From there, a taxi to the Unification Observation point would theoretically take us as close to the DMZ as permitted. The bus ride showcased stunning but desolate coastline protected by barbed wire, probably to deter potential migrants from the North. The bus driver rightfully assumed that we didn't know where we were heading. He signalled us to the front and insisted we pay more to reach the end; misunderstanding we declined. Instead, we were dropped us off in the middle of Goseong. Afterward, we learned that was the final bus to the Unification tower. Instead, we explored this eerie little town. Its main street held the same Korean collection of smaller cafes and restaurants, yet there was no buzz or vibe, almost grim, with a market that was virtually deserted. We chilled in the sun reading books for a while. With no chance of reaching the observatory or witnessing the border, we stopped at a petite restaurant for heaping plates of grilled chicken and rice, before another welcomed night at Mark's place.

Our revised plan was to head to the North Korean lookout point near Haean. Known as the "punch bowl", Haean was a volatile town in a volcanic crater near the border, where many lives had been lost during numerous wars. Chinese squadrons had been perched atop the mountains, and there was a narrow pass that led countless soldiers through the hills into certain death. Recently, North Korean tunnels were discovered. This was a serious place in the middle of tense conflict – not helped that U.S. President Donald Trump was in Korea this evening, hours after the Pentagon's warning that the USA would deploy ground troops in any hypothetical battle scenario.

A bus to Inje led to further confusion from the next ticket attendant about our intentions, and there was a lack of suitable buses available. I was grumpy and rude with Boogie, that led to us walking in cold silence for an hour. We trekked through brilliant autumn trees alongside a river, before a couple of buses shuttled us to Wontong Bus Terminal. We learned that there was only one bus to Haean, at 6:30pm. This was unpractical, because we'd be stuck in Haean for the night, in the bowl of death with a minuscule budget. We couldn't find guesthouses listed on any app, and we had no clear means of returning.

Instead we roamed around the grim area, located a supermarket for snacks, and rested on a field to enjoy the remaining flickers of the falling sun. Something seemingly changed in Boogie's tone, like the first clues that she was considering other pathways in life, alone. The solemn reminder of war, and being in a historically painful region for Koreans, didn't ease our moods. Other battles were brewing.

The Worst Night

The longer I remained in Seoul, the more I gravitated towards Hongdae, particularly Dustin's Guesthouse in the heart of the buzzy neighbourhood. Dustin's featured a cozy, social, home-like living room, a good-enough kitchen with a work-friendly table, and comfortable bunkbeds. There were plentiful interesting guests, and I struck up a rapport with the cool manager. One guest was a storied Texas traveller: a discharged US soldier who survived being shot in the head – luckily, he'd worn a helmet. Another guest was a young pink-haired American, who enjoyed Seoul for his popularity with Korean women. Others came and departed, often shy Asians, including bandaged Korean women who sought refuge while healing from plastic surgery – this was rampant in South Korea

The landmark Dongdaemun UFO was a massive spaceship-shaped building that comprised the Dongdaemun Cultural Center. Boogie and I became lost in futuristic shopping, spun around on 70s-style space pod chairs, listened to a skilled pianist and scoured the local market for tasty samples. At our comfortable budget hotel room, we fetched a guitar from the lounge, played tunes, learned simple songs and sang together. The window glass was eerie and magical, with moving lights outside from cars or the flickers of streetlights conjuring ghostly shapes and ethereal colours.

My week was largely spent bolstering content for Digital Nomad. I worked late nights polishing various articles, while tweaking the site's content and appearance. Around midnight from a cafe across from the Dongdaemun UFO, I officially launched DigitalNomad.Blog. It was my first legitimate work accomplishment during my tenure in Korea.

...

The next day, Boogie and I returned to the Dongdaemun spaceship, and settled in at the bright and futuristic CREA cafe. Within hours, the first Digital Nomad ad campaign was underway and gained thousands of readers. We had no luck with Couchsurfing, and I was on the verge of clicking Pay to book a decent hotel. At that very moment, we heard from Robert, the Slovakian guest from Mark Dake's apartment in Sokcho. Robert was in town for the night and was considering a jimjibang spa. We floated the idea of sharing a room; one named Pipe Place in Myeongnyun was reasonably priced.

Myeongnyun was an unexpectedly lively neighbourhood, with a younger vibe similar to Hongdae and cheap restaurants aplenty. We loaded up on snacks and drinks for the night, including a fateful litre of potent Soju. Robert arrived with celebratory beers, that we downed while sitting on each of the three single beds in our small square room.

Enough walking outside in sub-zero freeze prompted a brief

interlude in a tavern. This led to an hour of further Soju, beer, cigarettes and food, before we discovered steps to a rooftop and scaled the very top of the building. Robert and Boogie watched while I showed off, by hoisting myself up a narrow ladder to the top of a satellite tower.

Up to this point we'd shared at least a litre of Soju, and several beers apiece. The head rush of cigarettes had fogged my senses and thinned out my consciousness. Upon stumbling to our cosy basement room, I blacked out and crashed.

...

Emerging out of darkness, I awoke drunk and desperately needing to pee. Bracing my heavy head, I stood slowly and staggered to the washroom. Looking to the right, I was startled and aghast: Boogie and Robert shared a messy, single bed, and he was spooning her. The entire place was a disaster: covered in bottles and wrappers, and sticky with beer.

"What the...?" I groaned.

Frowning, confused and not amused, I shook my head, grumbled and continued to the lavatory. The ghosts of my jealousy taunted me. Despite the cold, I considered packing my bags and disappearing into the subzero night. I stood under the awkward humming of overhead florescent lights, while judgement ping-ponged around in my mind. Eventually, my furiously jealous sensitivities bubbled like lava, and erupted.

I yelled out: "What the fuck!?"

Groaning like a hibernating bear, Robert appeared dazed, almost apologetic. Boogie remained motionless, seemingly sleeping and oblivious. I lifted a green Soju bottle, and flung it against the far wall, shattering it into pieces.

"What the fuck is going on?!"

Robert wasn't answering this fairly straightforward question. I pitched a mug across the room; it exploded through the glass window of a sliding door, that cracked, then disintegrated entirely. In the stunned aura of a very tense and silent room, adrenaline skyrocketed. Robert briskly packed his things.

In a calmer moment, I asked: "How do you think this looks?" Robert nodded in solemn understanding. To articulate my disapproval, I whipped a shot glass, 100km/h across the shambles of the room, before Roger's patience expired. He muttered in Slovakian, grabbed his bags, headed off and slammed the door. It was around 5am this freezing morning.

Boogie wasn't moving or responding whatsoever. I poured a cup of cold water over her. She turned over and groaned, apparently with no idea of anything. Infuriated, I hurtled her broken old iPod across the room, regrettably reducing it to ruins. Still drunk and confused, furious yet paradoxically remorseful, I calmed myself down. Breathing heavily, I lay in the opposite single bed, and coaxed myself to sleep.

...

After a few hours of painfully unsettling rest, my alarm blared. I woke to the pain of reality, with a throbbing headache and the biting sting of regret. There was an hour to pack before checkout, less the matter of scrubbing up my widespread destruction. The room was covered in a carpet of shattered glass, broken pieces of mugs and heaps of potato chips. A pool of Boogie's vomit, covered in toilet paper, lay beside her bed. Boogie wasn't moving much at all. After grunting and rolling over, she tiptoed across fractured glass to the bathroom. On her return, she observed the abject state of the room.

"What happened?!"

I cleaned up the floor while she lay hurting and immobilised. I swept and removed every speck of glass, including pulling remaining shards out of the door frame. I was worried, remorseful mostly about the iPod, and rehearsed a humble, pained apology to the owner.

As fortune had it, this particular room didn't require formal checking out: we needed only to leave the keys on a bed. Miraculously, I made the place spotless, and unless staff remembered a glass door partition, there remained no lingering clues. We slowly skulked out the room, and towards the metro. Thanks to a graciously-early check-in at the next guesthouse, Boogie was able to rest, and much of Sunday was spent in bed. That night we watched the epic film, Fight Club. The moral of abandoning everything material and imposed upon us by society lent a certain enviable freedom.

After a surprisingly good sleep, we explored nearby Hanok Village. We peered at the six-hundredth anniversary of Seoul's Thousand Year time capsule, that was to be reopened in four hundred years. Everything between Boogie and I seemed peaceful and fun, like we would survive this, although we were clearly repressing everything.

Cat Cafes, Time and Space

Over the course of a harrowing week, Boogie's replies on messaging became shorter and sparser. Wednesday was the first day since way back pre-planning Korean adventures, that I didn't hear from her altogether. I learned my actions that terrible night had deeply affected her. She'd "cried for days". She sought space; we weren't to meet until Sunday. Our messages became more heated. She refused to accept any responsibility for her actions, citing "alcohol", and that "nothing happened", during passionate discussions about maintaining trust. And that, "it shouldn't matter anyway".

Text-only contact has a means of rapidly deteriorating, rife with misinterpretation. Often it can cause irreparable damage. The relationship looked and felt finished. After further mixed messages, Boogie was insistent that I'd "have to change" to remain with her, before communication cut off entirely. Feeling paralysed in Seoul, I considered flying to Jeju.

There were some positive highlights from the week: I heard from my mother for the first time in a year. She reminded me that she loved me, and that she'd been depressed. I happily saw my first snowfall in a dozen years, when a small blizzard dumped buckets of snow upon Seoul. I spent much time alone, shivering in a shack on Dustin's rooftop playing guitar. I composed a wistful song called Boogie and The Sea, featuring an adventurous bass-line and a mournful countermelody.

I sent a heartfelt letter to my Mother.Domains business partners about my doldrums. That I needed to take time away from the Internet, and possibly exit the business. I mentioned my personal troubles, and hinted having contemplated ending it all. I'd habitually repressed my litany of frustrations of broken family life, failed friendships and expiring relationships. Of my utter disdain for corrupted society and the failures of this world, that I wore like a burden on my shoulders. Dear friend Alan suggested that I investigate Vipassana meditation: something I might have ignored in the past. At first I was skeptical, even nervous, about the prospect of ten days away from my habits, or that it might brainwash me. Still, I desperately needed help, and ten tranquil days was not the worst solution.

Sunday's peace session with Boogie came at Godabang Cat Cafe, in Myeongdong, not far from the Dongdaemun UFO. Despite its name, only one of the lazy cats rustled from their winter slumber. The creative confines comfortably stoked warm, broad conversations, while we sipped on steaming tea, and painted little square panels of imaginary cats. Boogie revealed that my violent outburst triggered unpleasant memories of her nightmare three-year relationship, with an ex-boyfriend who regularly beat her. I didn't have any excuses, but I was able to acknowledge repeat triggers: such as binge drinking, jealousy I was unable to stifle, ongoing money stress, deep loneliness and an ocean of insecurities.

Boogie was relieved at my Vipassana research: a positive sign that I was seeking to self-mend. I remained her "big love", and she authentically wanted our relationship to endure. It was clear that this could never happen again, and I was pretty certain it wouldn't. I learned after I passed out at Pipe House, she and Robert fetched more Soju from the supermarket, and returned to our room with a random guest – I slept through a party!

Relieved at peace, we donated our colourful art tiles to the cafe and walked through the cold towards my guesthouse. Side by side, step by step, we were together again, as strong as ever.

The End of the Dream

Time accelerated, as it does, and our remaining weekends briskly dwindled down. We watched traditional Korean drum performances, frolicked around Seoul's streets, and I made two minor presentations at Seoul's Bitcoin Centre. With Boogie's exams beckoning, I spent much time working beside her at the university's library. We'd guzzle cheap cafeteria meals before plunging into work. During one break, I phoned my old mate Jono from Melbourne. He was living in Cologne, Germany, and there was a cool synergy about our mutual tech projects. Jono urged me to visit when I arrived in Europe.

We remained busy and active until our final weekend. For our last days, I splurged on Patio 59 in the calmer north of Hongdae. The studio apartment had a small kitchen, a compact balcony, and a washing machine. Our time was joyous, although we were both devastated about the looming end. We celebrated our own little Christmas with popcorn, cards and gifts. One afternoon we headed to the 555-metre Lotte Tower, and its massive underground shopping mall. We sipped plentiful free Nespresso coffee samples, and gouged on complimentary food tasters from the gigantic Lotte supermarket. The mammoth, decorated outdoor tree, in the frost of winter, made it feel like my first proper Christmas in years. In the evenings we explored new parts of Hongdae, excitedly treating ourselves to Korean BBQ and discount chicken. Packing had an air of fate about it; Boogie kept my white Kurta from Borderland to help save me space.

On our final afternoon together we guzzled tasty Korean BBQ. Boogie's face smiled in delight at the flavours, acknowledging every taste. Disbelieving tears filled our eyes. We made the short walk to Hongik Station. We descended its tiled steps into the underground, and waded through packed crowds to find a more discrete spot, near turnstiles leading to the airport train. With my bags on the floor against a wall, we embraced, long and hard, plummeting into grief.

"I love you," I assured her, staring into her soggy brown eyes.

"I love you too," Boogie replied, something she'd never said. She consistently insisted that actions and energies spoke louder than words: for love, for self-improvement and for promises.

We were to reunite in a few months, likely in Copenhagen. After a final tight caress, we headed in wholly separate ways. I turned back to see her crying and waving, before I put my head down, sunglasses on, and headed on my way. Over the excruciating train to the airport, on the flight to Bangkok, across many gruelling months ahead, I never cried so much in my life.

Chapter 6

Night Train to Chiang Mai

Rhythmically rickety tracks preceded a mighty train that loomed out of dull darkness, as early specks of scattered sunbeams danced towards new day. Horizons rose out of numbing greyness, as the steel beast lurched around sharp corners. Inside the train, whizzed the tense metallic buzzing of overhead fans. A long night preceded a longer journey; the middle of a sixteen-hour ride. It was a couple of days since I'd awoken in a different bed at the same Bangkok hostel I'd departed months earlier. *Was it a dream?* Streams of memories flooded constantly and mercilessly, to be excruciatingly revisited at random will.

After the detour of Seoul, I was reluctantly on my own again. My first notion self-assured that I was merely killing time, until finding the means to reach Copenhagen. I didn't know how, but I had to make it happen, just like I made Korea happen. A more worrisome revelation foretold that something deeper lurked beneath the surface, one less resilient than our recent tear-soaked "goodbye, for now". The grimmest of clouds were only presently gathering, in a slow and clumsy dance of an unprecedentedly pulverising storm.

The train creaked and rattled through the mountains. Daybreak cast light through the trees, and colours slowly warmed greyness into more vibrant palettes. I regularly shifted positions to temporarily relieve backache, while unsettlingly unsleeping. My mind was a mess in all directions: heaving backward to the painfully fresh, and forward to the wretch of uncertainty. Many more tiresome hours on the train remained. Across multiple dimensions, time moved slower than ever, farther from an era that would never return.

Korea was a blur: a rapidly distancing recollection. Every single day had been exciting and adventurous: an intense microcosm of a lifetime together, compressed into months. The sickness in my stomach and gripping pain in my heart offered little reassurance that time would help it pass. On the contrary: there felt plentiful jagged layers. Recent events exposed my many shortcomings, and that my mistakes – perhaps even that one terrible night – had taken a fatal toll, the brunt of which was about to be realised. In this justified the tears, my anguish, self-doubt, and a blind resolve to endure.

After a couple of unsatisfying nights at the alcohol-obsessed hostel in overcrowded Bangkok, I headed to Chiang Mai. Chiang Mai was broadly regarded as the "Digital Nomad Capital of Asia", if not the world. Nomadic types across the planet frequently congregated in north Thailand's tropical mountain weather, before setting out to explore other wonders of South East Asia. This was my first visit to Chiang Mai. I intended to stay until the end of December, before a long journey to Kampot, Cambodia. Right now, I didn't care much for where I was heading: I was comprehensively absorbed in dismally replaying the past. This was a feeling I would soon learn more about: first through bottoming out, and later in unforgiving lessons of relinquishing attachment, whether I was ready or not.

The night train to Chiang Mai inanimately offered no answers; instead, it reliably and laboriously rollicked along the tracks. Greyness of dusk occasionally subsided for golden beams that reflected off lush trees, while sliced orange peels in the sky announced the imminently rising sun. The unabashed beauty offered temporary respite to my agitated mind and periodical self-loathing. The sunrise was one of the most sensational I ever witnessed, as the blue of sky, greens of trees and innocence of dawn welcomed the train into the day. The bells of the station chimed, and the stationmaster's voice through a tinny loudspeaker greeted our arrival. I bundled up my belongings, and embarked on a determined half-hour walk to the riverside.

My hostel for the weekend was ultra-modern Marktel&Coffee, perhaps the plushest hostel I ever visited. Situated southeast of central Chiang Mai, it was disappointingly far from the northwest's nomadic enclave, but the riverside afforded tranquility, pleasant walks and relaxed views. Shortly after checking in, I climbed the steps to my dorm, entered the spacious, clean interior, and located a lower bunk that featured a thick, comfortable mattress.

After a shower and rest, I caught the eye of a young brunette male who sat a few beds away. Harlequin was an uplifting 24-year-old Belgian who was on his first major travels. Harlequin was tired of the monotony and demands of normal Western life, and sought something purer. He anticipated spending time throughout South East Asia, before likely heading west.

"I'm thinking of embarking upon a spiritual journey through India," Harlequin shared, with his words causing an impactful ripple. He lifted my spirits with enlightened conversation.

We made a mission of finding weed; something allegedly in abundance, but wasn't the easiest task in strictly anti-drug Thailand. After no luck at a nearby reggae bar, we found a paranoid driver for an unnecessarily complicated, and expensive taxi ride, before being ripped off for a small amount of green. We were dropped off at the only bar open in town, that was tantamount to a Karaoke Brothel. A living room with televisions and catalogues of music books was entered by scantily-clad Thai prostitutes, who requested we pay for everybody's drinks, before we'd all sing along. It made for an awkward solitary beer while we stood outside dodgy reception; other prostitutes were warned away: "They only want a beer, haw."

In evenings, Harlequin and I dined at busy food markets or scoped riverside bars. During daylight hours, I tried working from several cafes as well as the classy hostel lounge itself; sometimes inspiredly on music, late into the night. Messages with Boogie sounded like everything was okay, and life began to warm as my shock wore away.

Christmas in Pai

After the riverside weekend I headed east, slightly out of Chiang Mai, for ten nights at Moonlit Pavilion. I'd landed a sensational deal for a private lakeside villa. Moonlit Pavilion featured an entire standalone four-storey structure, with a waterside-level kitchen, rock shower and toilet on the ground level, an elevated lounge area that peered into a small adjacent lake, and a modest wooden bedroom at the summit. Surrounded and secluded by trees, there were few neighbours around, and only one humble restaurant nearby. Less than $16 per night.

On the opening evening I relaxed in the outdoor lounge, caressed by a pleasant, balmy breeze. Regaining my inspiration, I ruminated about 2018: The Chinese Lunar Calendar's Year of the Dog. I jotted notes about my longtime film project, The Dogs Live On. Ironically, in the distance I heard screams of dogs, and a symphony of frantic barking. Dogs only shrieked this way when there was serious trouble. I listened further: a dog was being beaten hard, and repetitively. After one particularly horrifying sound, akin to a loud snap, the dog momentarily fell silent, before incensed other dogs howled in rage. Feeling distraught but uneasy, I considered marching through murky swampland to the house. I was unsure of my surroundings, or whether this violent man could cause serious trouble, such as being a police leader, judge or diplomat. Alternatively, I sought to learn the man's identity, and how to contact emergency services the next time an animal was beaten.

My conversation the next evening with Moonlit Pavilion's owner, Freddie Jumping Frog, was far more entertaining. Our chat was aided by Freddie's potent homemade eighty-proof whisky: more so coupled with awful, strong, cheap cigarettes. Upon hearing the dog story, Freddie expressed concern at his unknown neighbour's brutality, and promised to investigate. Freddie shared his vision for the property: it was originally intended as a sanctuary for gay couples to mingle. He certainly found me fascinating and attractive: I received regular compliments and occasional pats on the arm. While I amusedly smiled at his playful nature, I made no secret that I was straight, in love with another, and heartbroken. Confidently, Freddie didn't mind; he narrated a story of a similar such conquest.

A couple of hours of drinks later, unable to politely excuse myself to focus on the writing purpose of my stay, Freddie took me to a nearby roadside bar. The minimal and sparse shack held two stools, the shopkeeper, and a sizeable but empty industrial tent. The cigarettes, potent whisky and bottomless beers caused severe lightheadedness, while depressants in alcohol stoked my brooding. There was one person I desired, and it wasn't Freddie's pickup lines coming from the bar stool beside me. I was bothered by his frequent pats on my arm, and being insistently asked to kiss him while we were photographed.

My mood was firmly soiled through resentment of being taken advantage of, and I tumbled into a drunken stupor. I spotted a nearby pair of scissors, and briefly contemplated stabbing him and every witness, discretely burying their bodies in the jungle. A safer resolution pushed myself to leave and trudge home. After some reluctance, Freddie accompanied me.

I politely declined a further drink at his house and returned to my chalet. I let off steam during a call with Boogie, who was in otherwise upbeat Christmas spirits at her family home in Hungary. Added to the next evening's wounded, pained-dog rant about my disdain for family and hating Christmas, I was not putting forth best impressions during this delicate long-distance period. My little slice of low-key paradise had been tarnished, by the sexual advances of an unyielding gay man and the torture of neighbourhood dogs.

...

I needed a break from Moonlit Pavilion, so I rode a three-hour minibus up the mountain to Pai on Christmas Eve, for a few days to clear my head. For as long as I could remember, family Christmases were hit or miss – either passing astonishingly without incident, or typically featuring horrible and unnecessary drama. Christmas was a time I hoped passed swiftly, and my last few were intentionally spent alone.

My Christmas 2017 came in the hippie hilly town of Pai, in far northern Thailand. I was not completely alone, upon reuniting with Harlequin at Pai's Famous Circus hostel. Famous Circus was a huge and popular hostel, slightly out of the centre of Pai: full of Western guests, fire dancers and amateur acrobats. There was a small pool, a billiards table, a bar, restaurant and a pleasant view from its perch on the hill. Clientele included dozens of party-centric guests; none particularly impressed me. I was assigned a dilapidated bamboo bunkbed, where nights in the mountains were damp and freezing; I wish I'd brought my sleeping bag. I barely slept through discomfort, with a racing mind, bad dreams, and memories of sleeping rough in the cold decades earlier.

Harlequin joined me later on the first day, and we explored the town, ate street food and sampled wine. In the centre was a pedestrian street market, lined with stalls and trinkets for tourists, bong shops, cafes, bookstores and massage parlours. Pai had a calm but buzzy vibe, and we were gloriously surrounded by mountains, trees and soaring birds.

My Christmas evening was spent at secluded Sunset Bar. I waited hours to acquire green from a roundabout lady man, after making friends with a Cape Town Burner, a blanket-covered Romanian, an explorative German and other random patrons. I gathered extra weed to aid my writing and sleep-lessness back in Chiang Mai.

Upon returning to Moonlit Pavilion, I did my best to avoid Freddie and declined alcohol in his presence. Despite its beauty and tranquility, the place lost its lustre for me, becoming more of a slow-down refresher, in lieu of the productivity I'd aspired. Positively, no further dogs were beaten on my watch.

Emergency Funding, Revisited

A lengthy 28-hour travel day commenced: a taxi to the Chiang Mai bus terminal, an overnight bus to Bangkok, a taxi between terminus, and then the long onward journey to Cambodia. At the Thai-Cambodian border, Cambodian police manned a table on the street outside their office. Police sitting outside lured unwitting tourists to pay a higher fee for passport stamping than was legal or advertised. I didn't have surplus money and I could genuinely refuse, but other tourists ignorantly complied. The police threatened me for warning other people on my bus.

The border crossing was typically dodgy and slow, furthermore from waiting to hoard the slowest tourists back onto the double-decker bus. Old Cambodian ladies wearing elaborate hats, jewellery and colourful clothing, sold small merchandise on streets, while discretely serving as lucrative money exchanges: "The most powerful people in the area."

Cambodia sure looked like a different world: it was far less developed than Thailand. There were dusty streets, once-majestic old buildings and simpler, more earthy transportation, such as bicycles and oxen pulling wooden carts. Many hours later, by nightfall we arrived in Siem Reap. Traffic blockades prevented the bus from stopping closer to town. I politely refused offers of taxis and street food; instead I walked alongside the river into the glow of bustling Siem Reap. It was December 30th, and the city seemed excited about New Year's. I checked into the modern and well-situated OneStop Hostel, before strolling through the night market for food and beer.

New Year's Eve was unspectacular. I worked from a cafe, enjoyed an inexpensive massage at a reputable parlour, and ventured to a nearby multilevel bar for the midnight countdown. The packed premises was filled with hundreds of drunken and stoned guests; most were foreigners. After the crowds departed, I finished a pitcher of lukewarm beer with a pair of random British girls, and returned to my comfortable bunk, ready to hit the new year running. I removed my shirt and jeans, placed them on the floor beside my bunk, and slept.

...

On New Years Day, January 1st, 2018, ready to explore Siem Reap, I executed my habitual pat-down pattern of "Keys, Wallet, Phone". After one of the three steps astonishingly did not complete its check, I noticed that my wallet was missing. It was nowhere in the predictable places, and nowhere in obscure or hidden places: My wallet vanished. This is how my 2018 began: the first challenge of an endlessly testing year. The wallet's contents included my driver's license, USD$50 in cash, my primary bank card, and the rare vegan-leather wallet itself. I'd travelled with backup bank cards, although they presently held insufficient funds for minimum Cambodian ATM withdrawals. I'd have to wait a few days for transfers due to bank holidays.

The kind manager at OneStop Hostel reflected on my missing wallet and offered a fair solution: I could borrow cash – say $50 – and leave my passport as collateral. In the end this wasn't required. An intuitive young guest offered local cash for whatever foreign cash I was willing to trade – in the end, roughly $15 each of Australian and New Zealand currency. In Siem Reap this was enough for a couple of days, including an Angkor Wat pass and a rental bike. The stolen wallet would not prevent me from accomplishing my ambitions.

A few days after my departure, the hostel rang to inform me that items of mine washed up in their drainage. The wallet and cash were gone, and my cancelled bank card was useless, but my driver's license and medical card were intact. I believe the dodgy local guest in the opposite bunk spotted the wallet bulging out of the jeans I'd absentmindedly flung on the floor, and I slept through easy pickpocketing. This was a reminder to be more careful in hostels, as well as protecting online logins to banking sites and apps.

Sunrise to Sunset at Angkor Wat

I cycled north in darkness on Siem Reap's usually bustling and periodically broken roads. It was early enough before traffic woke, ahead of the opening slivers of sunlight. Yesterday's practice run to acquire an entry pass offered a fair approximation of the time and distance required. While I was groggy, my lack of sleep was superseded by the adrenaline rush of peddling along Cambodian highways towards one of the most historic ancient monuments on Earth.

As the preliminary sky blues deepened after the black of night, I peddled around a lake to locate an isolated vantage point. Ten minutes earlier I might have entered the old temple complex itself, but I was mindful that hundreds of tourists would already be there, and today I preferred solitude. A few hundred metres from the main entrance, with castle-like walls towering into sky, I paused by the lake, and sat upon a fallen log.

The pre-sky sun began its dance, with its movements mirrored upon the rippling lake. A cascade of peach and pink rose out of layers of steel grey. The foliage of trees surrounded the lake, and the unspoiled clearness of the water mystically afforded unblemished reflection. The water mimicked sky, the sky absorbed and recycled light, and clouds rolled atop temples. As yellows intensified, the opening unrepentant beams of sun morphed into the shape of an eye, heat brushed my skin, and light filled the horizon. The third day of the year was underway.

The freedom of a bike ensured that I was neither slave to excruciating tourist group dynamics nor pre-determined time limits, and I could explore as desired. While riding past the famous complex's entrance, I spotted predictable hoards of tourists and cycled further. Eventually, I discovered smaller temples that basked in satisfactory seclusion. The vivid blue sky, fluffy white clouds, ancient green trees and golden stones combined for exceptional spectacles and photographs. I strolled around chambers and marvelled at carvings of faces on high stone walls and statues. Paths led through cramped corridors up large rock-slab staircases and into old communal courtyards. Some of the temples were magnificently huge structures, that rose authoritatively into the air amidst their picturesquely tranquil surroundings. I imagined life a millennia ago when Angkor Wat – the Capital City of Temples – flourished.

The day's heat intensified, and constant hydration was essential. I guzzled water, while periodically stopping under trees for respite from the blazing sun. I biked across desolate, off-beaten paths, entering the rundown gates of the Temple of Death: a possible hidden, overgrown cemetery. After pausing at another serene lake, I headed to the famous cluster of central temples. Crossing a rickety floating bridge, I entered Angkor Wat's vast remains. To avoid crowds, I took a more circular route and wandered around the periphery, that afforded close perspectives of rising stone walls and hand-built Angkor towers. I explored once-luxurious hallways – many still held statues – and large windows that opened out to the water and jungle.

By sunset I'd visited the majority of temples. I returned across the manmade causeway, cycled around and found a narrow dirt path directly beside the lake. Parts of the path required carrying the bike across boulders and a creek. I found a small wooden dock, and sat on rocks facing the falling sun. The jungle of Wat was across the lake, and the daily dance of colours gradually filled up then departed from the sky. The sun dropped like a golden ball that plummeted atop a dark green, silhouetted horizon, while shadows of leaves scraped ripples across the pond. Corridors and entrances faced precisely down the path of setting sun, while steady breeze followed. It was perfect, natural, nightly theatre, in simpler times.

With only a handful of sunbeams remaining, I safely cycled through maniacal rush hour Cambodian traffic. The spirit of Angkor Wat filled me with great optimism. The experience reminded that the rising and passing of days, of civilisations and relationships, were as true as the sun and night. Like the sprawling temples of Angkor, even the most majestic loves and creations were temporary, and had their day.

Sometimes The Decision is Made For Us

Wearing myself out from prolonged cycling around Angkor Wat, afforded the exceptional benefit of my sleeping supremely well on the night bus to Phnom Penh. Following breakfast and a couple hours work from a nearby hostel cafe, the day bus to Kampot in the south of Cambodia unwound more slowly.

In the evening, I arrived at High Tide, beside the serene Kampot River, with two bulging backpacks on the back of an overly-enthusiastic motorbike taxi. I reunited with Skinny Rogers, an old mate from Australia and fellow digital nomad. Skinny'd long recommended I visit Kampot: the "green capital" of Cambodia. High Tide presented the most pleasant weather I'd possibly ever experienced: riverside in the shade with a warm wind, while sheltered from the sun. Skinny toured me around, introducing me to people and places. High Tide was very cool: good food and beats, refreshing drinks, and green-friendly.

On an ominous, otherwise innocent sunny afternoon at High Tide, the Gods conjured a screen in the sky, with clouds illustrating actors. Shapes in the sky unfolded. At first, a crow flew towards what looked like a lamb. The meek lamb and its thin neck transformed into a question mark. The sharp beak of the crow descended upon the lamb's neck, then pierced the question entirely. *What was the question?* My brittle confidence attempted petty interpretations, such as cutting the "question of doubt". A scary, all-knowing instinct warned that this symbolised rupturing any lingering ties I had with The Past. I was the weak lamb, there was a stronger energy consuming me, and the crow sliced any doubt to rest.

Something changed, I knew it. Conversations with Boogie had diminished almost entirely. She barely had breathing time while non-stop with family and friends in Hungary. Much was the same upon her return to Copenhagen, where she shared a room and a bed with her gay Hungarian friend, who was asked to leave to accommodate me. In one unfortunately over-needy email, I questioned Boogie's lack of stability, her reliance on her literally poor and overworked parents to sustain a life that she should be earning for herself, and a regrettable spew of bitter and lonely jealousy. I should never have pressed "Send", but it happened, and probably manifested her final doubts. The ultimate question was answered decisively by the Gods; the lamb's neck was snapped by the crow.

With my heart further sinking, after High Tide I headed to a more remote estate, that was lined with mangrove trees. Man'Groove was several kilometres east from Kampot. It featured waterside bungalows, and a restaurant surrounded by nature, laying beside a ghastly two-lane concrete highway. Man'Groove was my home for a couple of weeks, to build work momentum and begin making plans for the huge year ahead. My quarters, despite the comforts of a double bed and convenient desk, were flawed by a solitary narrow window to sunlight. Its steel bars were akin to a prison, feeling as much in the emotional sense, that multiplied over excruciatingly suffocating days ahead.

There was a point I could no longer wait for answers. I defied my lifelong resistance to phone calls, and rang Boogie. Astonishingly, she answered immediately. We chatted jovially enough. I updated her on my prospective arrival dates in Copenhagen. I'd swallowed the nerve to borrow a small amount of Ethereum from a close friend to afford my flights to Europe. I needed airfares to drop after holiday peak, and suitably convenient dates from Boogie, to confirm my arrival. Boogie reassuringly sounded excited, and she requested my flight information once I knew it. She acknowledged the need to evict her stubborn Hungarian roommate. Everything seemed back on track; I giddily grabbed on with naïvety.

Afterwards, the first long, bleak message arrived. No matter how many dozens of times I read it, as optimistically as I mustered, it was barren of solace. Boogie spelled out, undeniably articulately, our vast differences in age and experience, that long-distance was "not working", and she would call me "soon". This definition of "soon" I wilfully interpreted as hours, but it did not come then, neither the next day, nor the next – her birthday, and continued to delay the painfully inevitable. I became a cigarette and weed-smoking wreck, while waiting for the most devastating of phone calls. To distract myself I cobbled together a short film, detailing the start of my 2017 trip and highlights of our Korean adventures. I

depicted waiting patiently to renew our bond. On the Sunday –
Boogie's 24th birthday – two days after her foreboding message, I
sent her the film. Many painful hours later she replied: today
would not be appropriate. She was in bed with her roommate,
and preferred to chat in private. Meanwhile I sat around
Man'Groove, pale and self-destroyed.

On the Monday, after each agonising minute, for hours,
eventually the call arrived, blunt and short. Boogie's voice
sounded nothing like the warm and faithful confidante I'd loved.
She repeated much of her message about distance and experience, she didn't want to discuss it, and wished me well. I
gracefully thanked her, and the phone went dead. I cried for
hours. Unable to sleep, instead I smoked myself into oblivion.
That sobbing, poignant goodbye at Hongik University Station
wasn't "bye, for now": It was The End.

...

While I wallowed in grief, Trevor, the Singaporean-Malay
owner of Man'Groove, shared his sorrowful story. He recounted
his own dream relationship with a beautiful young woman;
together they explored Cambodia by motorbike. Everything was
perfect. With grim recollection, without specifying details,
Trevor looked down in remorse: his girlfriend died.

"Sometimes the decision is made for us," Trevor solemnly
surmised, with his head bowed. "There are things out of our
control."

Trevor maintained an impressively optimistic outlook, with
the shock having worn away over many years. Although my
relationship had died – the final question cut by the beak of a
crow – Boogie was alive, and hopefully healthy and safe.

Similar to my previous major breakup, I responded with the
opposite of habitual self-destruction: I detoxed. Harlequin
shared over the gruelling days I was waiting for the goodbye
call: "I believe aspiring for health in every way will bring you
much closer to self-fulfilment, self-love and opportunities to get
to be where you want."

I commenced with a water detox diet: A few days of nothing
but fluids – mostly water, with occasional fresh fruit juice. I
cleaned out toxins, before progressing to solid food. After
chain-smoking for days I lost the taste for cigarettes, and I

hated them; it's easier to quit when unable to bear the thought or taste. I termed my particular Kampot detox: "Water and Weed". This was pretty much all I consumed for several days. Otherwise I was lost, completely uncertain and unconfident. My biggest questions included what I was doing and, without plans to Copenhagen, where life would bring me next.

Make Art Not War

Turkish-Canadian Evren Ozdemir is one of my oldest, dearest friends. I first bonded with him during Toronto's legendary Abell St warehouse era in the mid-2000's. Evren was an accomplished music producer and a rapper, with a litany of quality albums, a Superbowl ad to his credit, a second-placed Eurovision finish for Turkey, and his latest standout project, Strangers on a Plane. Long married with a gorgeous singer wife, they'd raised two angelic, conscious and creative children.

Upon my waking mortified from a sleepless and restless night, into the first morning of my newfound single status, out of the blue called Evren. His message brimmed with unbridled enthusiasm and positivity, that filled me with pride for my unique life journey and timeless experiences I'd encountered along the way.

"Sea! Do not head off your path for anybody else. Focus on what you love. Focus on your art. Really focus on it."

Evren shared two forthcoming tracks from Strangers on a Plane's autumn album release. The songs were mostly piano, bass and beats layered around Courtney's melodic and soulful voice; sad but hopeful, intimate and intelligent. Evren urged that I ring him anytime. We agreed that there was a different, purer level of vibe with deep phone conversations, beyond any amount of digital messaging. We had to hear the voices of our friends.

Bizarrely, following Evren's uplifting call, Boogie called me immediately, stoking heightened confusion.

"Sea!" Boogie wailed. "I'm so sorry. I'm young. I don't know what I'm doing."

"What are you doing? Why are you calling me?" I choked, absolutely baffled.

In between tears, she paused. "Let's talk in a few days, okay?"

This was highly detrimental for the flawed, misguided part of the mind, in the wake of breakups, where one believes in whatever slim chances of remaining together. *Was it really over? Should I try to make it work?* Boogie's earlier reasons for our split, citing gaps in age and experience, remained undeniably valid, as were the patterns of my anger and emotional insecurity. On the Thursday morning after our breakup, with still no reply from Boogie, I sent her a flurry of messages. She needed a break from communication altogether, and would eventually pen me an email.

"It hurts," she whispered. We cut off all social contact. Days of suffering turned into weeks, then months, and infinity.

...

Something bubbled within me, that took a year to fully comprehend. Evren's words of wisdom rang truth: "Focus on my art" is what I genuinely wished to pursue. When all this business scheming, domain nonsense and social media imposterism were finished, I sought a simpler, placid life. I dreamed of my own home, lost in nature. I envisioned a comfortable creative studio, with sweeping views of trees and sea. Fresh fruit and vegetables would be grown from our garden, while happy animals frolicked in abundance. Art and love. Maybe a "wife" and kids. Everything else would take care of itself.

The subconscious is an underrated power of the mental multiverse. Teach it something. Research and ruminate a little, then return to the regular routine. The subconscious ticks away. I believe, and this will make sense later, that the anguish of lost love, my frustrations with life, and a desire to change myself and the world, triggered what would appear later in premonitions, and consequent future undertakings. Right now I had no idea. I didn't care, my heart hurt and mind ached. I felt like shit.

On the bright side, it wasn't the worst time ever. I was surrounded by magnificent scenery in the most pleasant of climates, with endless green remedies to sedate me, and abundant nature to explore. Cambodia was inexpensive, and I presently didn't worry much about money.

Overnight at Bokor National Park

Each morning the sting of loss remained, a micro-fragment less each day, but it hurt. Communication with The Past totally evaporated. I soon departed Man'Groove, the unfortunate, mistimed location where all of this recent heavy stuff went down. My next destination was the lovely and secluded riverside setting of Meraki. I found a barber to chop off some of my unruly hair, resulting in an awkwardly fluffy Cambodian haircut. I rose around 7am most mornings. Once the sun appeared, as soon as I drifted into consciousness, the first unsettling memories of The Past seeped in. I couldn't fall back asleep.

This morning I should have been more enthralled about an overnight trip to Bokor National Park. Today marked the first of endlessly interesting days over the rest of the year ahead, that included non-stop travel for a while. The entrance to the park was approximately 8km west of Kampot and another 32km to Bokor's summit: the second highest point in Cambodia. Bokor is home to the largest herds of wild elephants in South East Asia. The site was once a French army hill station, and was notorious for the remains of a war-era casino and resort. The old casino was recently succeeded by a concrete monstrosity; both were haunted by ghosts of colonialism and capitalism.

On this particular day, my last of three weeks in Kampot, the weather was abysmal. A low-lying storm shrouded grey sky, and the heavens opened with tides of drenching rain. Yesterday's similarly inclement weather prevented me from making the trip, but today was my final chance to accomplish this landmark mission. For the first time since our Korean adventures, I was to head to a national park with the tent we'd lovingly pitched on islands, beaches and mountains.

Amidst unrelentingly pouring rain, I set off from Meraki, mentally willing clouds to part, even just enough to drive. Although my backpack was wrapped in a garbage bag, it didn't lend to personal dryness. I waited undercover in the centre of town, long enough for thick raindrops to slow to satisfactorily intermittent pattering. Lowering my expectations, a subjectively milder trickle of rain encouraged my setting off, to attempt reaching the top of the hill before nightfall.

I raced down the bumpy Cambodian highway on my powerful Honda scooter, before torrential rain resumed. With dwindling optimism, I pulled the scooter beside a street vendor under a pair of large umbrellas, and took temporary respite from the rain. The lady and her little boy smiled at me and welcomed me in. There was was neither petrol nor English, but I drank a hot tea while occasional customers stopped in puddles for takeaway fried snacks or drinks.

After a temporary reduction from torrential to downpour, I reconvened along the abject road. Nearby, adjacent to the park's entrance road, a gas station afforded a large roof, that was ideal for squeezing out flickering specks of dryness from my clothes. I observed the entrance road, noting an occasional stream of cars and 4x4s departing the park, and few vehicles entering. In this rainy contemplation, under shelter with no indications of clearing skies, I was wet, cold, tired and dejected. There was no shame in returning to Meraki or spending a night at High Tide, to spare the embarrassment of failing myself.

The rain worsened and, counting my losses, I navigated the scooter onto the highway, resignedly heading back towards Kampot. I planned to smoke weed and chill out – although I could do that any time. Bokor was likely a now-or-never proposition. Not long after, perhaps from a temporary pause in the rain, or hearing a deeper voice within, I stopped the bike, waited for a lull in traffic and turned around. I'd come this far, and the mountain was close. *Ride to the top, see what's up there*, I urged myself, at a minimum.

Rejuvenated, I blazed through raindrops, past the street vendor and beyond the gas station, despite a nagging premonition to add more petrol. Two litres of petrol probably wouldn't be enough to climb the mountain and return. On the entrance road to Bokor there was no security check or national park admission fee, so I continued unencumbered.

Slivers of sunlight scraped through the clouds over the majestic mountain. The initial avenue led to a ragged, winding mountain road. Looping, tight corners approached every turn, and much of the road was rocky, with smooth yet slippery segments. The scenery was impressive: green jungle surrounded everything in sight, occasional waterfalls, there weren't many other people around, and the distant sea made everything feel worthwhile. Steeper I climbed, dodging raindrops, while clearer patches of sky were encouraging.

Near the summit were various rustic buildings, a small temple and a security outpost. Needing gas, I headed towards the ghastly "new" casino, with its sprawlingly empty, soulless concrete parking lots. The casino concierge waved me towards another part of the hill, where I acquired overpriced petrol.

Patters of raindrops returned, and the greying sky appeared evermore ominous. High up a mountain, approaching the end of day in endless moisture was a recipe for looming freeze, and I was soaking, dried ever slightly by onrushing cool fresh air. Sensing a need to take shelter, I stopped beside an abandoned building, parked the scooter and meandered inside. I changed into dryer clothes, shook out my wet items as best possible, and hung them from doors. I withdrew a pre-roll of one of Kampot's finest green samples and smoked it in the deserted, eerie concrete block, while rain pattered outside. I was proud I made it to the top of Bokor.

Calm and reinvigorated, matched with a respite from the rain, I felt I'd accomplished all that was necessary. It would now be acceptable to return to Meraki or stop by High Tide, dry off and excuse unfavourable conditions as poor timing. *I can come back next time*, I assured myself, if there ever was a next time.

Back on the scooter, I rumbled down the mountain road. The poignant view from the top, criss-crossing downwards, enthrallingly overlooked the watery horizon of the Gulf of Thailand. Darkness rapidly approached, while sporadic rain dropped. At perhaps four-fifths of the descent, a deep urge lent a final opportunity to fulfil my camping aspirations. I scanned the road for plausible entrances, perhaps somewhere to stop the bike and take a fleeting glance of this marvellous scenery. Minutes later an opening appeared on the left, beside an empty parking area. An adjacent gap allowed my scooter to penetrate through, and I drove into a field, that led up a small hill through a grassy clearing. I motored over rolling fields 200m further, halting near a row of bushes lining a cliff, with a supreme vantage of the bay ahead. Completely out of sight, I stopped the bike. *What a perfect spot!*

Delighted, as raindrops returned with a vengeance, I removed the tent, flattened the dry sheet, assembled the poles, hoisted the tent in the air, and hammered pegs into the moist ground with a large rock. In time for downpour, I sheltered in the cosy tent, as water pattered away on its green cover. After eating fruit and crisps I lit a celebratory joint, sitting upright as much as I was able. With the rain seemingly unending, I lay down, stretched out, and fell asleep.

...

Deep, mystical dreams later, I woke in the tent on an otherwise uninhabited hill, in the shadows of Bokor Mountain. Rain had ceased, and the sky conceded to lunar luminescence, with a silhouette of mountain peaks, a multiverse of stars and the rumbling of nearby ocean. I stood underneath the galaxies, impressed by the Moon and coast, raised my arms in the air, and peed into nothingness. Surprisingly, despite seemingly clear skies above, it was still raining: drops trickled atop my arms and face. With my heightened spirits, a little rain didn't bother me.

Then I heard a disarmingly high-pitched sound, that hinted it wasn't raining: The raindrops were mosquitos. *Shit!* The open tent was predictably filled with wild, hungry Bokor mosquitoes. I calmly entered the tent, zipped it behind me, and heard a torturous buzz of mosquitoes, inside and out. A flashlight helped me locate several mosquitoes that were aimlessly flying around. Typically, I strived utmost not to kill any creature, often saving struggling insects wherever possible, but this was an emergency. It would be impossible to sleep, or emerge unscathed from a closed tent that contained countless giant, scavenging mountain mosquitoes, or free them all without introducing persistent new visitors.

The first mosquitoes were easy enough to locate, seek and destroy. Slowly and predictably, they flew towards the light. I squashed them with toilet paper. After each kill I sat motionless, waiting for the inevitable next attack. After seconds of silence, a deathly hum emerged, and the latest kamikaze invaded. *Squish.* I wasn't proud. Four mosquitoes. Five. The final few of a dozen hid in shadows near my feet. Even one mosquito would ensure a sleeplessly stressful and itchy night. Eventually, the last particularly crafty mosquitoes were modestly exterminated.

With a combination of exhaustion and relief, I fell asleep into another realm of dreams.

...

I woke on the mountain moments after dawn, as early sunrise scattered sunbeams across the bay. My recent sad pangs of loneliness were replaced by serene accomplishment, and the vast splendour of nature. I determinedly packed, and ascended the mountain with a full morning to explore the peak of Bokor. With no set plans I joyously became lost, and drove along a multitude of paved and rocky roads. I didn't discover much of anything in particular beyond excellent future camping and silent party spots. With neither the time nor inclination to explore the old casino, I refilled petrol and commenced a serene hour-long descent down Bokor. Feeling warmth and accomplishment, I rode the scooter along the highway to Meraki, ahead of a bus to Phnom Penh. In the capital I checked in at a friendly hostel, ate at Happy Herb Pizza, and caught my morning flight to Kuala Lumpur. My adventurous spirit had been rekindled. Optimism radiated, and I was ready for everything.

Camping overnight at Bokor National Park, Kampot, Cambodia, Jan. 2018

Chapter 7

India, Revisited

Upon arriving in Kuala Lumpur I reunited with Vandal, to complete another surreal but welcomed bookend. Last time we met came in Thailand, days before I delved into the whirlwind of Korea. While I'd been elated before, I was now a barren, hollow shell. The daily sting of heartbreak lingered; each morning was a dagger in the gut, that foretold lengthy, tough, distracted days ahead. From traveling constantly, each morning arose marginally easier, despite preliminary biting thoughts of the same fading-away mirage, of the dreamy face I'd loved and lost. A low-key weekend with Vandal gratefully consumed several days. We chilled at his air-conditioned high-rise apartment, or gorged on tasty Malaysian cuisine. One evening Vandal emceed at a packed gig at Paradigm Club, while I lounged on the backstage couch and downed complementary beverages.

From K.L. I rode an inexpensive coach to Malaysia's southernmost city, Johor Bahru, that I hadn't seen since I was a teenager. I was curious about Johor's transformation, as its convenient location across the causeway to Singapore made for consideration as a potential South East Asian work hub. With not many choices for hostels, I selected nostalgia-themed Memory Guesthouse. It was built out of a local house, featured simple dorms with single beds separated by curtains, and was a half hour walk to the centre of Johor. The minimal, humble hostel off a noisy highway in a barren neighbourhood of a conservative city void of vibe, made for a long and dreary four days of emotional malaise. I spent the mornings working from downtown cafes, before strolling around the diminutive city's limited amenities. Container cafes and restaurants around the waterfront were fairly desolate, although a nearby street market buzzed in the evenings. Foolhardily, I penned a positive Valentine's card for Boogie, hoping to surprise her, and dispatched it to Copenhagen from a downtown post office.

My Johor visit was based around meeting cloud hosting startup RunCloud at their office. After meeting the upbeat and talented Malaysian developers, I coordinated Mother.Domains' Aswin to head their technical department, while initiating a global partnership between RunCloud and Cologne-based Wao.io, who my old mate Jono was representing.

Across the causeway, I returned to my childhood stomping grounds of Singapore. The island-nation had grown up significantly, nearly doubling in population since I was a kid. While Singapore was too expensive for budget travellers to stay long, one could usually find deals on basic hostel rooms and cheap food at local hawker stalls. One afternoon I power-walked through the city to the futuristic Marina Sands hotel complex. I spent time immersed in space-age botanical gardens and marvelled at the hotel's enormous atrium. Memories of my childhood streamed in from passing the Victoria Theatre and Singapore Cricket Club. At legendary Mustafa shopping centre, I scored a cheap pair of black jeans, and a replacement wallet for the one that was stolen. I reconnected with old friends, including "Reggae Queen of Asia", Masia One. She invited me to a specially-prepared dinner and show at a local apartment, that was hosted by a top chef, with expert musical performances to appreciative, intellectual guests. Later, I celebrated my first-ever Singaporean "green" milestone! In the two months since departing Seoul, this was the first day I truly felt happiness.

The next day I nearly missed my flight to India. Beyond late-running social plans in downtown Singapore, there was the matter of a ninety-minute deadline for international check-ins. The thorough check-in lady asked for my flight itinerary out of India. I truthfully informed her that my forthcoming two month work trip would determine whether I flew from Bangalore or Hyderabad – cities close to my prospective Vipassana courses. She consulted a manager, but returned with unfortunate news: I had to prove my pathway out of India. I'd heard of many travellers buying cheap intercontinental bus tickets simply for the purpose of proof, and then not using them.

I had thirty minutes to solve this, not the least was the matter of: Where would this flight money come from? Mere scraps remained in my personal bank account; perhaps I could afford a random bus ticket to Bangladesh. There wasn't much deliberation how to solve this: Mother.Domains would have to cover it. It was my only option, in lieu of defaulting flights, being stuck in expensive Singapore, working miracles to raise cash and pay for India flights again, plus booking the departure leg anyway. The Wao meetings in Cologne suggested I could justify it as a legitimate business expense. Months of researching airfares between India and Europe came in handy. Frankfurt was close to Cologne, and offered better prices to fly there. With twenty-five minutes remaining, I located an info kiosk, who provided wifi access after leisurely scanning my passport. With my bags plopped down upon a row of metal seats, I hurriedly searched multiple combinations: Delhi to Frankfurt, Bangalore to Frankfurt, Hyderabad to Frankfurt.

With time dwindling to fifteen minutes, I narrowed down to two options. There was a KLM-Jet Airways flight from Bangalore to Frankfurt via Amsterdam, with a four-hour layover. The alternative was Air France from Bangalore to Frankfurt via Paris, with a shorter layover and cost an extra $15. Just in case, I filled out both booking forms simultaneously: the first successful booking would become my flight.

Despite initial troubles with my bank card, with five minutes left the Air France booking was processed. On March 28 I'd be heading to Germany! This underwhelming moment was short-lived. I rushed back to the check-in counter with no other passengers in sight. With mere minutes to spare, I successfully checked in and raced towards immigration, before a leisurely wait for the flight. Sure, I was disappointed to use the company account again, but what else could I do? Relievedly, there was no further need to stress about money or spend time researching flights: Europe would happen, eventually. Now I could focus on a return to India, and each day as it came.

Winning is Not Everything

The jet arrived in Delhi close to midnight. An hour's bewildered taxi drive led to the southern satellite city of Gurgaon, and we eventually located the lodging booked for the Team Domainers cricket team. Navn greeted me warmly. At 1am, most of the other players were resting for the morning's match. My quarters were a room and queen bed shared with the bespectacled young domain wizard, Govind, who was fast asleep.

Hours later, alarms sounded, and the entire floor of the building jumped to life. Players showered and changed into their cricket whites, while I was presented a pair of white pants and a sky blue jersey, with "SEA" inscribed on the back. The young men, mostly in their twenties, were excited about the tournament match day. Several whom I'd previously met greeted me affectionately.

The amber hue of the sun began to intensify, casting a glaze over the frosty fog that rose from the streets. In breath-steaming single-digit temperatures, jacket-clad workers trudged to work while the sun rose and cows strolled along pathways. Hoodies were mandatory, and warming up was essential; a half-dozen of us enthusiastically practiced with tennis balls inside the apartment.

Several white Suzuki taxis filled with players rode through sunrise. We arrived at Gurgaon Cricket Ground: an impressive open air stadium. The huge circular pitch featured centre bleachers above a pair of concrete dugouts, a rooftop gallery, a sizeable double-level restaurant and several practice nets on the opposite side. Cows loitered around the field while the sun asserted its mesmerising early ritual. Glimmering luxury apartments soared into the sky a short distance away, and towered over the field.

Team Domainers dominated our opening match, although I was clearly distracted. While my sleep-deprived mind drifted to sadness of The Past, I heard the crack of a bat, looked up and saw the ball hurtling towards me. I couldn't catch it; the modified tennis-cricket ball bounced out of my hands, and scattered away. In the end this didn't affect the result – our batters dominated the match and we won handily. That night we celebrated one of our captain's birthdays. We bundled seven men in a little car and six in another, to dine at an excellent restaurant around the corner. In India the birthday person pays for everybody's meals: another welcomed surprise!

The next morning's match was not as positive. Our bowlers were crushed by big, quality batsmen, who frequently bashed balls through gaps for a menacing tally. Our usually-fearsome batters fell apart early, flailing at poor balls for easy outs, and we were losing by miles when my first turn at bat came around.

"Now batting... baseball player... Sea Ansley!" blared the stadium announcer. The crowd and opposition gasped in delight. *Who was this foreigner?* Teammates cheered me on, hopeful that several home run swings could put us back in the match. The gleeful bowler discretely chatted tactics with another senior player.

I locked in, ready. The tall, gangly bowler raced towards me. I watched his hand, the bowler fired his first ball towards the wicket. I braced for a mighty swing... and swung over the ball. The ball zipped under my bat and hit the stump: I was out. This was the final demoralisation for Team Domainers, and minutes later our last batter made the final out. The team sulked like the world came to an end. Later, spirits were somewhat elevated at the latest player's birthday that evening, when we visited a shopping mall for food.

Our prospects came down to Wednesday: with a big win we'd qualify for the semi-finals. Team Marketers were a player short and mustered a low target, that our mighty batters had little trouble surpassing. Mercifully, I didn't bat, but I did drop another ball after I lost it in the sun. We still won by miles. I was embarrassed about my unusually poor fielding performance. I'd expected GameX to be a fun tournament, like last year's match, but it was far more serious. I wish I'd practiced for the weeks leading up to it. That evening the Man of the Match treated everybody to dinner on the rooftop of our apartment, while Hindi dance beats blared out of my portable speaker.

The Thursday of the tournament was our off day. We had to wait on other results to learn if Domainers qualified. I spent much of the day working from a fancy art cafe in an oversized shopping mall, joined by Aswin, who was visiting from Kerala for the BlogX conference. In the evening I prepared for BlogX from the Pepper Pot Cafe.

When I returned to the team's apartment, something was clearly amiss, that I could feel and interpret despite not hearing anything. Several players at the apartment acted strangely; there were a few hints as though I knew the situation, and one of the players looked despondent. By virtue of other results, we qualified, and the draw was conveniently arranged for Team Domainers to avoid other favoured teams in the semi-finals. In an apologetic hush I was informed that I was not selected for the match: We had some "new" players – four, in fact. While I was aware that my mediocre performance at GameX was grounds for substitution, I was more disappointed for the others who didn't make the cut, including the last game's Man of the Match, and two younger players, one of whom sobbed.

I wondered what lesson this taught impressionable young men, who joined a team, worked and played hard, only to be replaced on the final day by outsiders. It was readily apparent that this tournament wasn't about fun or trying our best: it was all about winning.

Still, the games had to be played, and sports frequently furnish surprises. At the stadium I cordially presented my blue cricket shirt to a huge, bearded man, perhaps the largest player in the tournament. "SEA" now adorned his shoulders. The other new players were noticeably physically taller and larger than anybody else, with a calm assuredness as they assessed the day's requirements.

The semi-final brimmed with controversy. Representatives of other teams questioned why four new men, clearly powerful cricket players, suddenly became Team Domainers, while wearing shirts bearing the names of those of us who were sitting in shadows. The conflicted tournament organiser, himself a prominent domainer, curtly replied: "This is how it is."

At the halfway mark, with Team Domainers well in control of the match, opposing management formally protested the legality of the moves. They refused to let their players take the field until their questions were answered. Our new players were apparently not registered. In the heat of the moment and searing temperatures, there was a lot of yelling, in a comical farce. Match officials converged to animatedly converse while there was further shouting and accusations. In one huff the match was declared forfeited: we "won".

I wondered if this was the best use of my time, with a big presentation at BlogX tomorrow and a growing list of life-pertinent tasks to sort. In the midst of watching endlessly fruitless yelling, I'd had enough, and departed the stadium. For nearly two hours I gloriously strode through the dusty streets of Gurgaon, and headed in the general vicinity of our apartment. Upon my arrival, the benched, disgruntled Man of the Match waited outside with his suitcase. He'd packed and departed, similarly disappointed in the team's chosen means to win.

Despite the protests the teams finished the semi-final, and Team Domainers prevailed. In the grand final, with its new team dynamics, Team Domainers won the prestigious GameX tournament. Social media posted photos of raucous celebrations: of hoisting the trophy and hitting the town after. I politely declined invitations to celebratory drinks, citing tomorrow morning's BlogX presentation.

One of the trophy-pimping statuses from a Domainer, the young one who'd sobbed after being cut from the team, declared: "Winning is everything". I'd noticed the "winning over everything" theme of this young IT professional in his other posts regarding business and life.

These artificial pursuits never bring enduring happiness – there is always the quest for more – and, hence, dissatisfaction. It's like cheating on a final exam to receive the paper, but missing out on the valuable process of education itself.

From my extensive coaching experience, and eight championships I recall winning as a player and/or manager, I learned that the journey is ultimately the most important aspect. Our championship teams and our bottom-feeders worked hard, winning or losing together with the talent we had. Sure, there is a genuine pride that winners feel. But, days after victory, life felt exactly the same. Then it all starts again: Try again next year.

Winning is not everything; sport, like life, is about teamwork, sacrifice, the journey, and accepting the actuality.

…

The BlogX conference was a smashing success. My panel discussed the next phase of Internet growth in India, touching on current and future trends in the blogging scene, and wider Internet as a whole. Over the day, the packed auditorium at the Radisson Blu Plaza excitedly engaged in various presentations and interactive workshops. I was particularly thrilled to sit beside a stunning young blonde Russian named Inna, who was representing a video blogging platform. However unlikely my chances with her – and she had a boyfriend anyway – being attracted to somebody else was an essential step of healing, and reminded me that there were plenty of other fish in the sea.

The closing awards presentation anointed the freshly-crowned GameX cricket champions, Team Domainers. Donning my blue team shirt I was called up to stage with my teammates, standing front and centre while we were presented with medals and a giant cheque worth 1 Lakh (Rs100,000). As we hoisted the trophy we were cheered by the BlogX auditorium. In an adjacent hall, our team posed for numerous selfies with the impressive GameX trophy. The captains of the team pulled me aside and thanked me for my contributions. They assured me that I "played well" and that I was part of the winning effort. Notably, they understood my disappointment for the means.

"We only did it because the other team did it first," the captains explained, while appreciatively shaking my hand. I surely understood the impulses of passionate young men and the sporting drive to win. I bore no ill will – after all, they helped me become a national cricket champion in India!

A most pleasant surprise was an invitation to a Sunday picnic, with several of India's top foodie bloggers at famous Lodhi Park. These food critics, many with individual reaches surpassing hundreds of thousands of followers, shared homemade cooking with their longtime friends and colleagues. The quality food included curries, spiced rice, finger foods and endless desserts. We played games, and through my crafty efforts during a variation of musical chairs, I won a lovely scented candle.

I particularly connected with one attendee: Dipali Bhasin, a highly-inspiring writer. Dipali was a traveller, the daughter of a general and wife of an army officer. We talked deeply about life and love, with my anguish about the breakup readily apparent.

"Find peace. Life moves on." Dipali consoled me. Later she elaborated in a photo post: "Travelling is not just about garnering new experiences: It evokes one to appreciate life, and to give the confidence to explore the planet to know you'll be loved everywhere."

Back at the hostel, I chatted with a serene Israeli who'd recently emerged from his first ten-day Vipassana course. He'd travelled through India for seven months and was to return to Israel the next morning. Through Vipassana much clarity came to him. He recently disposed his mobile phone to live more fully in the now. Through his level-headed post-Vipassana afterglow, I more objectively reflected upon my lost relationship. I felt temporarily void of sadness, jealousy or clinging. With these revelations I was proud and grateful for the wonderful times I shared with Boogie. I wished her nothing but the best in life, love and happiness.

The Road Less Travelled

Mystical, tropical Goa rests on the southwestern edge of India, basking in the warm Arabian Sea, over 500km south of Bombay, and nestled above the fabled Malabar Coast. Following millennia of rich, ancient history, for centuries Goa was a Portuguese colony. This was evident through its Indo-Portuguese architecture, and vibrantly colourful pastels of homes and beach huts. In 1962, following relentless decades of warring skirmishes and non-violent resistance against its Portuguese occupiers, Goa was annexed by recently-independent India. Soon, Goa became a peaceful haven for hippies from across the world. Goa was granted full Indian statehood in 1987. Goa is renowned for its plethora of stunning beaches. It is particularly famous in underground music circles as the birthplace of the global psychedelic trance (psy-trance) subculture revolution, lending Goa's status as one of the most chilled out and progressive regions on the planet.

...

On a classy Vistara flight from Delhi to Goa I began reading the bestselling psychological book, "The Road Less Travelled" by M. Scott Peck. The book was gifted to me by a compassionate Taiwanese Christian at Seoul's Dustin Guesthouse, in the wake of my violent hotel room outburst. He noticed that I was struggling. It took some ego-conflicted courage and skepticism for me to dive into this book. The author's underdog reputation and objective viewpoints helped me accept his premises about Love. This entails love of the self, and what Peck interpreted as genuinely "true love" of others.

"Love of the self" has flowed in waves for me. The self-respect I maintained was largely from repeatedly finding atypical ways to survive. *Look at the adventures you've brought upon yourself! Remember the incredible people you've encountered! Consider what you've learned!* Whatever I might hate about myself, such as my anger or self-destructive habits, to love oneself, one must be unequivocally honest with, and forgive, ourselves.

True love of others? I found this concept harder to fathom. Truly loving another was to put their happiness and growth ahead of our personal vendettas or ego. This meant, whatever our partner was inspired to do, we should be supportive, even if it involved spending quality or intimate time with other people. Peck hypothesised that most ideal marriages would be "open". Even though we may be mutually granted the freedom to experience whatever we pleased, this did not necessitate *doing* anything. I'd further argue that trust afforded by this freedom can bring couples closer together. Still, I found this tricky to accept. Imagining my love with anybody else was difficult, even nauseating. My subconscious pondered this philosophically brain-twisting puzzle: I must continue working on self-improving every day, while affording freedom to those I loved in the future. Similarly, nothing and nobody should detract from *my* freedom.

...

Flying from Delhi to Goa's Vasco de Gama, preceded two weeks of writing and relaxing. Hopefully there'd be a party or two, and maybe I'd spark a new flame. Arambol sounded attractive, as the bohemian and artistic heartbeat of Goa. On my way from Goa's airport to a hostel in the north, I opted for the adventure and cash-savings of public buses. Taxi prices were exorbitant. They were monopolised by Goan taxi cartels – north versus south – and the state was void of modern ride share apps. Finding the colourful bus at the airport was simple; it safely and swiftly whisked passengers to Goa's capital, Panaji.

While I sat on a second bus, I received a message from Bower, my oldest Australian friend and a director of Mother.Domains. He was in Goa on his first visit to India, and was to perform didgeridoo at an Anjuna bar in an hour. I scribbled down details and, opting for a peacemaking opportunity, disembarked the bus and hired a costly taxi to Anjuna Beach. Upon my arrival a stern and tense-looking Bower neither said hello nor displayed any sliver of affection. I met his glamorous, dark-complexioned Caribbean girlfriend; the three of us sat in cold silence until their tardy musician friend arrived. I wondered why I spent money and time to come out of my way. Bower seemingly brooded about my abstract, survival-oriented approach to finance and business, while I harboured misgivings of his recent racist and out-of-touch millionaire worldview. Still, I was willing to forgive.

Hours later, after making plans to meet Bower next week for work discussions, I had little choice but to book another cab, that altogether obliterated my weekly travel budget. At around 10pm I checked in at off-street and offbeat Roadhouse Hostel, near the heart of Arambol. For my first five nights I booked an inexpensive private room, with a double bed, fan and bathroom, for Rs600 per night. I loitered in the well-positioned outdoor communal lounge, that was fluffed with pillows on mats around tables, around a tree in the centre. Guests included a local tattoo artist, writers and photographers, and several interesting, serene women. Conversations were easy yet stimulating, while hashish and weed emerged in welcomed abundance.

From the early outset, the lively cast of Roadhouse characters formed the core of a fortnight's crew: Jenny, a London writer with whom I clicked immediately, Adele, a long term American traveller, Alex, a young Swedish traveller, Constantine, a goth-clad conservative but curious Austrian, Pavitra, a local creative and social entrepreneur, K-Angel, a Bombayan stoner, and more. Each were on their unique paths, yet we all shared being out of the way in Arambol.

Much of our crew's time together loitered around Roadhouse, rolling some variety of weed, smoking cheap cigarettes or dabbling in occasional beers. Our group embarked on missions that included breakfasts, quests for superb coffee, sunset drum circles outside of Love Temple and late-night snacks. As days progressed we uncovered music nights and parties, assembling small convoys of scooters and motorbikes for each journey. One of our Roadhouse crew's customary morning routines included guzzling dosas and coffee from ultra-chill cafe This Is It, that was perched on the northern edge of Arambol Beach. Their comfortable seating areas, sea views and satisfactory wifi afforded relaxed, reasonably productive work. Through Jenny I met an intriguing, enlightened spirit: a Brit named Gauge. He was well along his path of healing and growth, one that was uncannily similar to mine in our recent loss of young flames.

Lost in the magic of travel, time ticked on its own paradigm. Seven nights at Roadhouse felt like weeks. Everything appeared welcomingly out of sequence; mystique and aura were abundant, and the stage was set for interventions of magic and fate.

Goa on Acid

On a warm and windy Friday evening, a diverse crew of six personalities set forth on our Goa psy-trance party night spectacular. I was suped up on countertop pharmaceuticals, to rapidly combat my increasingly uneasy queasy of "Delhi Belly", while we waited, and waited. For the occasion I donned my best black kurta shirt: its elegance was intentionally and ironically contrasted by glossy and grassy white GameX cricket pants.

While Hash – an Indian-SF photographer – arranged evening transportation and supplies, Constantine, the completely straight, black-clothed Austrian, made banter on the pavement. Constantine was broadly intelligent yet somewhat socially awkward. He mashed an unsettling combination of innocent but horrifically sensitive questions, that ranged from my recent single status through tenser parts of my family history. Meanwhile I battled growing nausea. Hash was supposedly heading around the corner yet took hours, while nightfall and fatigue asked their opening questions of dedication.

This greatly-anticipated party night was to be a respite from the turmoil and realities in our everyday lives. Acid – LSD – often reveals our place in the universe: our connection to the planet, time and space. My favourite LSD benefit usually came on the final nights of festivals, or when lost in nature. Through these experiences came necessary solitary reflection, that observed aspects in life where I must improve. There often came reassurance that the universe, when we emit good energy, will look after us.

First, we had to make it to the party. This felt rather unlikely from waiting endlessly on a shadowy corner outside Mandala Tattoo. Occasionally, Hash sent updates like: "Just a little bit longer!" I wondered why there were all these delays to find a taxi, but eventually Hash pulled up in a small car he'd rented especially for this occasion.

Marking the end of the season was a "big" psy-trance party, at a venue on Vagator Beach, and other trippy events if we were later inclined. My primary roles in the little car were to coordinate arrangements with others - Swedish Alex and two others had departed much earlier on motorbikes – provide navigational assistance, and to roll thick hash joints.

Sporting no ocean highway, instead roads in Goa traversed through hilly land, with subtle but specific interchanges that led to individual beaches several kilometres further. This added time, with wrong turns costly as we'd learn frequently. Another challenge was occasional police checks, who fined careless tourists for anything from motorbike drivers lacking helmets, to invalid license plates. At one blockade that nobody saw coming, suddenly we approached a police stop. I swept my veritable lap desk of rolling supplies into what I thought was a bag, but was mostly my lap, and, like cricket balls I'd dropped at GameX, the floor. My cricket pants were having adventures of their own.

By our eventual arrival in the filling-up parking lot at Shiva Place, the first giant hash joint was ready. With a ceremonial bump of tabs, Hash and I downed our acid, while Constantine thoughtfully observed. We promised to look after each other; Constantine realised he might be looking after us.

By the time we'd descended hundreds of steps to the beach, the mid-sized venue peculiarly switched off its speakers, while hundreds of people milled about. There appeared to be sound problems. We were happy to arrive, and the night was young.

"Sorry for kidnapping you, Constantine!" we joked. He seemed to smile, perhaps contemplating escape if necessary.

We sat on rocks outside the venue's seaside courtyard, perpendicular to stalls selling hot food, drinks and merchandise. Alex and her motorbike companions soon arrived. The music resumed thumping; dozens of patrons danced, and the vibe intensified. We sparked the joint: The party had begun!

Within minutes the music switched off amidst commotion. The police! A half dozen officers swept through the back of the club. We tossed the joint, hid the remains and tried to relax. Weed paranoia set in and partygoers scattered, including Alex and her crew. I stayed on the rock, calm but alert. The police didn't second glance at us. They had other intentions, clumsily dragging a protesting promoter to the police station, and possibly jail. There was no party here but it was too late to turn back. The substantial joint kicked in the beginnings of the acid, and we buckled in for the long haul.

...

For her first-ever acid experience, commemorating her milestone fortieth birthday, the effects hit as the rainbow of sunset fell on secluded Ashvem Beach. We sat together on soft sand in the shadows of a fishing boat, gazing at the rolling, frothing ocean. Reclining on sarongs, staring into sparkling heavens, celestial bodies orbited across the breathless brush strokes of the Milky Way. Other than a security outpost shack near a house on the point, we were alone. The guards' increased fidgeting sparked a concerned channel of my mind: the alert one that suggests exiting. Danger was not readily imminent, but I noticed the tide was rising, not only towards us, but enveloping the narrow point that served as our safe passage to shore. She was in deep reflection with her eyes closed, and I didn't wish to disturb. Instead I closed my eyes. The roar of the sea sizzled along sand and trailed up to the heavens.

A few minutes later, I noticed the tide rising higher. Scrambling from guards in the security shack and occasional flashing of lights, appeared to be an unspoken warning.

"We need to get out of here." I nudged her, and she rose to witness a rampaging tide that was closing in on us.

With waves enveloping us, we were becoming stranded. The way we came was now thick with ferocious monochrome waves that crashed against the shore. The "safe" route was to narrowly walk north towards Arambol, then a long loop to Mandrem, but that exhaustive and uninspiring effort would likely conclude this evening's voyage. From where we were perched, access to any shore – north or south – was extinguishing as the tide encircled us, ready to devour. A tad frantically, I held her hand, pulled her onto her feet, we collected our belongings and gingerly scampered towards the former gorge, that was now a raging river. There appeared no way through. Waves soared higher and taller, almost on top of us, while a fragment of silver Moon solemnly observed from the sky.

Surrounded by agitated ocean, on a scrap of dry land and mountains of roaring waves lurching towards us, with a deep breath and uneasy reassurance I waded ahead. My feet then thighs entered the churning water that was quickly shoulder high. I surged through the sea, while she followed. Plunging in, with buoyant waves cascading towards us, I knew at worst we could swim the remaining metres to shore. Somehow our necks remained dry, we held our bags over our heads, and we plowed through the water barricade.

Suddenly, shore met our feet and we barraged into safety, with a relieved sense of accomplishment. The waves were crashing in the same place and were no longer chasing us. We turned to each other and laughed. The humid air rapidly fanned us dry, while the Moon beamed. Damp and deliriously, we hopped and skipped south along sand and rocks, under cinematic heavens in seven dimensions. Perhaps our mistake was heading into a decent party hours too soon, when we could have further explored the coastline, but the music became a magnet. It was a puzzle to locate the maze of the venue's entrance, and upon entering, the party was only beginning. Sitting in adequate comfort, near the dancefloor at a long wooden table, the beats were enjoyable, but the inebriated coma zapped our inclination to move. Lighting the chocolatey blunt, I inhaled, deeply and thoughtfully, and passed it to her.

...

While sharing a joint, we drove slowly, back through main roads, then towards known hotspots. It was Friday night in Goa: surely there were other parties? Yet everything was dim and closed, almost like a curfew. Alex and her crew had departed on their motorbikes shortly after the police shutdown. For Hash, Constantine and I, there was no turning off. Hallucinations intensified, as if we were floating in a bubble, atop dusty night-grey streets in jungle. Occasionally we stopped to roll and smoke hash, blowing smoke out of open windows that cast ghostly fog through light beams. Adding to the surrealism was the architectural contrast of Portuguese, British and now Russian pockets of Goa.

After seemingly an hour of driving, but probably twenty minutes, we passed increasing numbers of party-looking pedestrians, while louder noises approached us. Braking cautiously down a hill, revealed parked cars everywhere and hectic dozens of people milling around a corner. Scooters, cars and motorbikes whizzed about, then stopped slowly in the centre. At the bottom of the hill, in the very middle of the vibrant corner, Hash parked the car, pushed back his seat and relaxed. Constantine and I followed, making ourselves comfortable, while the raver iteration of Paharganj madness bustled outside our windows.

Within minutes, anguished pedestrians politely requested us to relocate: Our car was blocking the already troublesome road. With astute concentration, Hash intensely reversed, narrowly avoiding people, bikes and cars, and expertly manoeuvred uphill to park. Overcoming temporary social fright, we emerged from the car and strolled down the hill. It had a bizarre energy: fast and intense, overly exaggerated, and with assertive vigour. We were in the Russian epicentre: the heart of decades of generations of Russians in Goa.

Ambling around the bizarre bazaar, a busy dessert shop fulfilled orders for alcohol. Large motorbikes growled, donning muscular, tattooed riders, male and female, with sketchy corner conversations everywhere. Everybody appeared willing but unable to party. Our odd threesome walked with forged purpose, yet tripping and confused. Constantine stood out in his all-black clothes, with his clean, straight brown hair in a ponytail; he was likely the only sober person in town.

Street word confirmed that police had shut down everything: there were no parties tonight. *Anywhere.* Unenthusiastically, for the sake of soliciting adventure, we hobbled up a bending hill into darkness. Snarling dogs barked warnings, as did a Russian pedestrian, who asserted that we should proceed no further. I imagined this was the road to mansions of grand Russian king-pins, queens and gangsters. Politely acknowledging the advice, our motley trio trudged back down into the frenzied epicentre.

"Try to act casual!" as we stood awkwardly. Mistakenly, I sat on a pile of broken glass.

Hash and Constantine were horrified: "Are you okay??"

"I'm fine!" I replied, embarrassedly brushing off glass. "I have a knack of doing, and saying, absolutely stupid things."

Constantine was noticeably disinterested through concise, silent body language, like yawning. There was a long, hard moment I pitied him. He was looking after us, but we should be looking after him. He was tired, holding us back, and our responsibility was to return him home safely. With a confident "*Eureka!*", perhaps while clicking my fingers, I spun to my feet declaring revelation.

"Constantine, we will put you out of your misery! We will take you home," I promised, to his relieved delight. Turning to Hash: "We can dump him at home, see what the others are up to, and find something happening near the beach." Hash nodded in approval.

We strutted with purpose to our parked car, that was seemingly hiding. Eventually, we glided out and away from the buzz, returning to state roads. The greyness overcame everything, and low-lying mist shrouded deep green trees. Lost temporarily in thought ensured furthermore aimless driving, taking turns to new places that didn't lead anywhere, reversing and back. Exhausted, back in the late-night ghost town of Arambol, the prospects of parties expired. Nobody was awake.

...

She accepted the joint, pressed it to her lips, and inhaled. On beach recliners outside deserted Shiva Place, we heard beats in the distance, while we were cajoled by a warm night's breeze. We peered out to the calm but diligent sea, and gazed at stars that rushed beyond shards of silver clouds. We didn't talk much; each of us were deep in inner frequencies, observing the distant universe and beyond.

After some time, the beats intensified from the adjacent hill. We dusted off and ascended a hundred stony steps to the road, magnetised towards the general vicinity of the sound. The loudest music disappointingly emanated from an overly posh and commercial nightclub, but the other beats blared from higher up a hill through shadows. This quelled an uneasy feeling, as the rocky road led into blackness. A spooky motorcycle approached us, and its shady driver creepily asked, "Are you looking for something?" With my mind swamped with hallucinogens and discrete warnings I could not reply; instead I held her hand, and we continued down the road.

Further lost through the mysterious night streets of north Goa, our scooter zipped around the coast, curling across gravelly pathways into murky neighbourhoods. One turn lurched steeply downhill; immediately we knew we'd come the wrong way. She hopped off the scooter as we were greeted by a gang of street dogs. Their leader, Skeletor, was a battle-weary and bony Pitbull. Skeletor's sharp teeth were exposed with a menacingly warm smile, and saliva dripped from his mouth. Skeletor took a fancy to me, jumping his paws on me, drooling over my arm with his teeth, while his curious dog army surrounded us. After politely but firmly pushing Skeletor away, I readied the scooter, the goddess hopped on the back, and we gingerly accelerated uphill, while the canine militia trotted behind us.

On our return, we were halted at a police check. I approached the officer with my driver's license. I respectfully presented it with my right hand and a courteous nod. I was mildly worried, as I knew my license expired a few months back. The officer peered back at me, before jotting my details in his logbook. He nodded at me, then returned my license. Weeks later I discovered that my license's photo had entirely faded away, yet there was no trouble with dog gangs or the police this night.

Baba and the Banyan Tree

Around noon, after hours of restless laying in bed, I woke alone, groggy and coming down from acid. Time for productivity: less dreaming, more doing. In the dead of the day, with the sun at its peak, I required cash. This wasn't an easy mission, as Arambol had few ATMs, and the closest was an hour's return mission through searing heat. I power-walked to beat any other pedestrian who might be similarly heading there. Alas, the ATM line at Arambol junction was lengthy, spread in two directions, with people in the queue baking under high-noon sun. I chatted with a pretty brunette in front of me; we mutually willed sufficient cash to remain for our withdrawals. This was not the problem, as neither of our dual sets of cards worked in the machine. While one of my accounts didn't have sufficient funds, this didn't explain my backup Qantas cash card, or either of hers. There was another ATM situated up the road, less than a hundred metres away, but far enough to thwart lazy stoners. My Qantas card worked, supplying me with sufficient cash for the weekend. Anna the Russian's cards remained lifeless; a new error instructed calling her bank.

The notion of exchanging foreign currency for rupees was a welcomed revelation for Anna, that turned into our miniature mission for the afternoon. After a quick stop past Roadhouse, for hours we chilled and chatted on the No Name co-working rooftop. The sun lost its sting, joined by a cool, flowing breeze, while we built a friendly rapport. Anna's excellent English had accumulated from tenures in Hong Kong and London. She was presently in Goa on holiday, taking a break from work, while considering new job offers in Delhi or Mumbai. She wondered if these big cities might be too noisy and extreme.

The next afternoon, Anna's message arrived: Did I want to accompany her to the jungle. *Of course!* We headed alongside the cliffs towards Sweet Lake. Visually spectacular, certainly not sweet tasting, this was a small lake cloaked by rustling palms, with the ocean on one side, and a lush hill on the other. Through the jungle we searched for Baba. One stop discovered tea served under a banyan tree by two wise old men. After, in the trees, a tall man looked like a Baba, scantily-clad in mud, a light robe and long hair; he approached us. Then an infuriated man ran towards him, harshly beating Baba with a stick.

"Baba! Fuck off and leave!" screamed the man at the Baba, while glaring menacingly at us. "I'm tired of fake Babas coming here and ripping people off!" He lashed the fake baba, who did not resist or request help. I considered intervening; my inner voice cautioned: NO.

Further through the jungle, we found a particularly large banyan tree with pillars of its branches dropping from the sky. In its shadows housed a court of participants: one was clearly the Baba: a withered but spritely old man adorning robes. A circle of people rolled smokes, played guitar, drank whisky and passed the bottle around. There was a snake charming act, with Baba's assurance that the snake was fine: he could be freed and "replaced anytime". We smoked unusual herbs and, summoned to sit beside Baba, I played guitar for one song.

Anna and I returned to Arambol for drinks. Steadily intoxicated, Anna became readily affectionate, holding my hand along the way. We paused for beverages at a bar that was perched atop rocks and ocean.

"Now or later?" she asked bluntly, tipsy and aroused. *It was on.*

Staying cool, never hurrying, I affirmed: whatever she preferred. Instead we chilled on the beach, and swam in warm ocean off the northern corner of Arambol Beach. We held each other somewhat passionately in the water, although she was a little heavy, and slippery from coconut oil, and I struggled to lift her. Compounding the tame first bottle of wine, the large strong Kingfisher beer took its toll. Head rushes from cigarettes were further unhelpful.

Still, we headed to Anna's hotel. She held my hand and kissed my cheeks. We shared another cigarette on her balcony, with enough time to wonder about authentic connections. Suddenly deciding she was too drunk and needed rest, our time together abruptly, mercifully ended. Sleepy from the acid weekend, and missing the lost love in my heart, I would not have been fully present. I was not ready.

Twin Flames and Strawberries

After Roadhouse, I upgraded to popular Love Temple, a thirty-minute walk down Arambol Beach. Love Temple hosted parallel rows of overpriced, underwhelming beach huts, and a huge wooden dorm, that I had to myself. Love Temple's centrepiece was a large and comfortable restaurant with plentiful shanti spaces to lounge and chill. Its vantage point on the cusp of the sea made for mesmerising sunset views.

Those clean-looking strawberries I'd bought last night from the local fruit stand held mysterious secrets, that my stomach could not tolerate. Unfathomably, I declined Adele's suggestion of washing them: a massive mistake that harmed both of us.

With great discomfort, I spent the ensuing days trying to sleep off an incredibly hot, consuming fever. Endlessly dehydrated, irrespective of my water intake, I shat my pants, but, palatably, no vomiting. Adele similarly suffered at Roadhouse. It was a stark reminder to wash fruit and vegetables in clean filtered water... and to heed our friends' sensible advice!

Shits and giggles aside, Friday's Mother.Domains meeting with Bower transpired better than I'd feared. Although it was little frosty at times, evolving the business discussion helped thaw our cold relations, and seemingly steered everything in an optimistic direction. While reluctantly offering to help with the drudge of accounting, it sounded like Bower was committed for the next - and possibly final – two years of the Mother.Domains journey. I did remain a tad unsettled from Bower's clenched body language.

Under the grip of debilitating diarrhoea, I spent the day working from This Is It. I chatted more intimately with Gauge, who impressed upon me the unusual concept of Twin Flames. Gauge was nearly a year removed from splitting with a younger beauty and his spirited soulmate. His story shared parallels to my own heartbreak, that followed intense, abbreviated affairs.

Twin Flames were more powerful and intense connections than soulmates. Over our lifetimes we may encounter multiple soulmates – of friends, lovers and even family – always pre-destined to depart us. Twin Flames were more of a reflection of ourselves. Often we'd share telepathic or psychic connections, with uninhibited passion and intimacy. This is why losing these particular energies hurts so much. The typical phases of Twin Flames start with internal yearning: as in imagined experiences, or attributes we desire to encounter. When we're ready, we receive a glimpse of them: perhaps in dreams, or a hippie trap sunset at Borderland. Upon being granted the opportunity to cross paths, falling in love comes briskly and easily, and the fairy tale begins. Inner turmoil ensues, often from ego, that causes breakdowns. One runs, one chases; cat and mouse, sometimes for years. After surrender and dissolution, outstanding issues eventually resolve, until Oneness and back together, strongly, forever. Or, so Gauge dreamed. His zen interpretation left open the possibility of my eventually reuniting with Boogie.

Flickers that I had any remaining chances with Boogie renewed purpose in my daily affairs. Following my lonely and toilet-oriented stay at Love Temple, while considering alternative parts of Goa for my final four nights, it made sense for me to remain in Arambol. My emotional regression returned upon waking up several times in the middle of the night, feeling sharp pain, and wondering if Boogie was similarly hurting. Uncontrollable diarrhoea was further unhelpful. I was disappointed with recent male acquaintances urging me to harbour (false) hope.

"She's young, be patient", advised Citronella, despite my depicting the impossibilities. I didn't feel it appropriate to wait around years for a young woman to eventually figure things out – or not. I had to continue along my path. Inevitably we'd become strong and stand again. When the time was right, new energies would emerge. It's when we desperately *wanted* love, that it fails to materialise.

My final few days in Arambol capped a prophetic, magical fortnight, and fluttered like leaves in warm breeze. I checked in at the comforts of La Cayden: a multi-storey budget hotel adjacent to No Name and opposite Roadhouse. The room offered a comfortable double bed, a small balcony over a laneway, and a private bathroom with hot water. Flights of stairs led to a chill rooftop restaurant that played sweet electronic music to an eclectic crowd. On my final evening in Arambol, ahead of a painfully early rise to reach the airport, I chilled on Le Cayden's rooftop with Jenny, Gauge and the Roadhouse crew. It was a perfect two weeks: everything I needed, and more.

Chapter 8
Auroville Fifty

At 10:30am on Wednesday, February 28, 1968, a special ceremony announced the inauguration of Auroville: The City of Dawn. Amidst the global despair of Cold War tension mounting between Russia and America, Auroville offered a varying glimpse at another prospective human civilisation: a city where people of all nationalities, beliefs and cultures could live in peace and harmony. The inaugural ceremony transpired under the sun, in an amphitheatre that seated five thousand people, on an otherwise barren patch of red dusty desert. Soil samples from 124 countries were delivered to Auroville, carried in marble urns by youths representing each nation. Each urn was laid down to rest in the centre of the amphitheatre. Prime Minister of India, Indira Gandhi, brimmed with enthusiasm and pride about this cultural and environmental accomplishment.

The Charter of Auroville was read by The Mother from her quarters in Pondicherry. The speech was broadcast to Auroville's amphitheatre, and nationally on Radio India to millions of avid listeners. Translated and presented in sixteen languages, the Charter read:

Auroville belongs to nobody in particular. Auroville belongs to humanity as a whole. But to live in Auroville one must be the willing servitor of the Divine's Consciousness.

Auroville will be the place of an unending education, of constant progress, and a youth that never ages.

Auroville wants to be the bridge between the past and the future. Taking advantage of all discoveries from without and from within, Auroville will boldly spring towards future realisations.

Auroville will be a site of material and spiritual researches for a living embodiment of an actual human unity.

There have been numerous attempts over history, as early as ancient Egyptian times, to create utopias based on cosmic and spiritual values, but none reached fruition. Having envisioned such a city for fifty years, The Mother understood Auroville would take time - "A hundred or a thousand years" - but that such civilisations were imperative for humanity to flourish.

We can ask ourselves: Is present society the best humans can accomplish? Are we living with freedom, in harmony and without fear? Auroville's growth may not be as rapid as envisioned, and there lingers characteristic human flaws and contradictions, but Auroville remains steadfast about honouring its founding principles.

...

At 4am, the first of five contingency alarms stirred me from sleep. Donning a long red-maroon kurta and comfortable black leggings, I gathered a ready-packed bag and wandered through dusk. Thousands of people streamed along, by foot, on bus, car or motorbike. Ominously, there were far more security and gatekeepers than I'd anticipated. I followed a large pack of people through the first narrow entrance to the Matrimandir, and tried my best to blend in.

"Passes please! Show us your passes!"

Security was left and right, with snakes of humans, four people wide. I remained in the middle, simulating frantically searching my backpack. My head was lowered and innocuous, while moving with the flow.

"Passes please!" a security guard demanded from the crowd.

Fumbling in my bag with my eyes diverted, pretending to be distracted, I tiptoed past the busy guard amidst a current of human energy, and safely slipped through the gate. *First checkpoint clear.* Then, security was everywhere, spanning all entrances to the main amphitheatre. Specific colours and letters on passes served as legends to specific seats and areas.

Overwhelmed by complications and fearing capture, I skirted into the darkness and away from the masses. Watching and observing, contemplating crowd flow, guard characteristics and apparent procedures, I was entirely under-confident. I considered climbing a nearby tree and hanging there. I wouldn't have been able to see much, and daybreak could be awkward.

After a few minutes I noticed a widening gap, between distant, onrushing guests, that led to plentiful vacant chairs on the amphitheatre's back edge. A large group approached an

136

overeager guard; then a pause. With deep breaths and a burst of adrenaline, I bolted. While the guard was distracted by the group, I briskly made my way to an empty seat. Immediately, another guard approached me.

"Sir," the guard began. "Do you have a VIP pass?" Defeated, I shook my head. "Then you need to head over there."

She pointed towards a general seating area on the right. Awed by any glimmer of hope, I courteously thanked her, and tiptoed through a section reserved for photographers and audio equipment. Moments before I exited, another earnest guard halted me.

"Are you here for the radio?" she asked. I was puzzled: Maybe I met her at Auroville Radio last year? *Take the opportunity.* I nodded. "Over there!" she pointed at the adjacent general seating area. I ducked through the media section and scrambled to find space on the concrete. I was in! I kept my head down, and didn't take it for granted.

Within half an hour, the bulging amphitheatre witnessed the solemn opening festivities of Auroville's fiftieth anniversary. The ceremony was serene and uplifting, mostly in silence. A nest of fabled banyan tree branches was lit on fire, before a lengthy water ceremony unified water samples from over two hundred places on the planet. One person of each ceremonial duo held a placard noting the water's origin, while the other carried water in a golden urn; it became a marathon procession. I considered "Hiroshima Peace Center" a fitting analogy for the war and peace that humanity needed to remember.

A live choir complemented orchestral instruments that shimmied sounds across Matrimandir's symmetrical amphitheatre, while the illuminated golden orb shone. Occasional reciting of text was presented in French, English, Tamil and Hindi. The procession was slow, contemplative and sedative – ideal to meditate and reflect. Others audibly described it, "boring". During flickering trickles of sadness, my mind wandered to The Past: I missed her, and knew she'd love this. In the midst of Aurovillians honouring The Mother, I thought of my own mother, and sought to help her, *somehow*.

At the ceremony's understated conclusion, many people departed. Others remained and mingled, encircling the stage that was blanketed by water urns and cinders of burning banyan leaves. The fragrant scent of fresh flowers, closer to the middle of the central area, delightedly melded with the fury of burning wood. Aurovillians greeted friends, sharing stories and uplifting energy. I wanted to honourably dispose of the Love Leaf near the legendary banyan tree, but it was roped off. Later, I attended another noble ceremony in a white, future-retro veranda. A hundred guests hummed "om", that manifested a communal, interactive choir. All of this contributed to the enlightening start of an eclectic and eventful day.

The Mysteries of Missing Mopeds

African Pavilion became home for my second visit to Auroville. My nomadic green tent was shaded between trees at the far edge of the Pavilion's forest campsite. The Pavilion was a modest premises. Its centrepiece was a main, angular wooden structure for group sessions and meditation, beside a circular semi-outdoor kitchen that faced an elevated compost toilet. Two open air showers, surrounded by concrete walls, stood adjacent to a shed that brimmed with assorted hand drums and gardening equipment. A little beyond lay two sets of narrow tables that formed hexagons around thick trees. Walking further emerged a forest, where pathways led to various clusters of tents; many were filled with hippies and backpackers.

Internal tension was abound. A rebellious French crew, an outspoken American and stoner Indians rudely resisted the strictly-enforced "No Smoking / No Drinking" rules, that particularly prohibited marijuana. Located beside the Governor's House, the Pavilion's two East African leaders understandably admonished illegal smoking and drinking on the property. However, the Pavilion's rules, although consistent with Auroville's code and strict Tamil Nadu law, were not accepted by the camp's rebels.

Following my check-in after a spontaneously shared taxi from Chennai Airport, I unwittingly broke a rule I didn't know, and was one of several ordered to leave. Within minutes of my arrival at African Pavilion, a young friendly Indian man approached me. *Did I want to smoke a joint?* I actually didn't, but

I was up for mingling. Several of us headed to a nearby bonfire pit that was snuggled in an earthy basin surrounded by trees. A younger man withdrew a pipe, added a generous pinch of weed, sparked the pipe and inhaled. He passed the pipe counterclockwise around a circle comprised of Indians and French. Seconds before the pipe was handed to me, anxious members of the group became worried.

"Hide it!"

"We've been caught!"

I casually placed the pipe underneath the bench. A fuming, diminutive, shaved-headed African stormed towards us. Apparently the group had been prior warned on multiple occasions. The first African agitatedly conversed with a dreadlocked African, before we were firmly requested to pack and vacate the premises. Even me. Having not smoked anything, I'd hence not breached any rule, and believed I'd be OK. This was more stressful for the others, who unsuccessfully pleaded their cases. In time I met Talib, the initially-fuming man and one of the heads of African Pavilion. In a calmer moment I shared with him that I'd arrived minutes earlier, and hadn't been informed of any rules. Talib relaxed with beaming eyes. He deduced that I was no nonsense and no threat: I was warmly welcomed to stay. I was presented with printed pages outlining the Pavilion's reasonable rules and expectations.

With the miniature city full of revellers and tourists, I was unable to rent a scooter. Instead, I enlisted a rickety old bicycle from the nearby Tourist Centre. A bike afforded leisurely commuting around Auroville's well-paved roads through red desert and rainforest. I learned the moped of a German guest from African Pavilion had been stolen the previous night. Two men from the rental "agency" confronted her outside the Pavilion, laboriously discussing the matter for hours. I'd spent most of the past hour patiently absorbing the stress of Amit, the bong-smoking miscreant who was yet to vacate. Amit frustrated me, and made matters more difficult for himself while often not listening. I emphasised self-reliance: not sitting around feeling sorry for himself. Why not make backup plans, just in case?

Meanwhile, the German girl Inke was fretting, while she argued incessantly with the two men. Other people tried to intervene, but it looked to be heading nowhere. I took a break from Amit's overblown worries, with my lifetime of anger brimming underneath. Marching directly to the bikes, I stared intently into the eyes of one man, and gained immediate respect. I introduced myself, shook hands with both men and assured rapid, satisfactory resolution. Within a minute, the owner of the bike was on the phone, and we were invited to her house "for a discussion".

Inke shared a bike with a male German friend, and we followed the two rental men around the twists and turns of Auroville Main Road. We whizzed through enough shadowy streets, that I temporarily questioned our safety. Our motorcade rolled up to a Victorian house. A portly drunken lady in a tight miniskirt scrutinised us from her balcony, before inviting us upstairs. The apartment reeked of weed, while bowls brimming with green lay across tables. The place was messy with dishes, papers and clothing everywhere. On the balcony the lady held a fat joint, for herself.

"What happened?" she asked, before the story was recounted. "Seems to me," she continued. "You owe me Rs5000 for the bike."

I presented myself as professional, pretending proficiency, and used long words. I withdrew a notebook and logged notes. The owner attempted to prove the bike's registration by plopping down the first random paper from a pile. This was not the same bike: it was a different colour and the plates were wrong! She pulled out another invalid sheet: at least the colour matched! I requested any and all details, yet there was no number plate on the lost bike. No proof of rental agreement. No payment, deposit or collateral. My calmness and procedural pragmatism spooked the owner into false bravado, and she challenged us to involve police or lawyers.

"I come from a military family!" she roared.

I reassured her that calling the police would be the last resort, and that calm and cooperative resolution was paramount. She insisted on Rs5000 for the moped, or a similar bike in return. We had until Friday to find the original; I'm not sure, "or else?"

Courteously, armed with information and a mild suspicion about this inordinately dodgy situation, we departed. The two rental men followed, initially demanding Inke's passport; I firmly refused. At the road's entrance, the men seemed to be relieved to be out of their master's vicinity, and they pleasantly wished us good evening.

Time for reconnaissance. We headed to an established rental dealership down the road. *Cost of such bikes? Had this man's bikes ever been stolen?* Friendly and professional, the dealer sympathised with Inke. With neither a written agreement nor any proof of the bike's existence whatsoever, there was not much the owner could do. He agreed that Rs5000 was the general replacement cost of such bikes, but that the lady's insurance should cover the loss. His advice was that Inke should calmly leave as planned on Friday. There was no need to worry about or contact the woman again.

In the end, we never found the bike, but Inke, fearing retribution, paid Rs4000. We wondered if the owner arranged her bikes to be "stolen", to scare and scam tourists out of money. A few days later, another bike went missing, sparking panic at African Pavilion. This time, an older Latino stoner forgot he left it somewhere else.

...

These bike incidents weren't isolated occurrences. Each day back at Auroville after my ten-day Vipassana course was full of surprise and adventure, but the craziest of all was the Thursday. In the morning I led an upbeat group circle at the fractured African Pavilion. My message reiterated tolerance and unity: to respect principles, the rules and each other despite our differences. In the evening I caught up with two French girls from Vipassana. We visited Vish, an Indian-South African chef who was staying at Transformation, and enjoyed red wine, organic brie, camembert and herb-seasoned crackers around the swimming pool. Every Thursday evening African Pavilion hosted weekly drum circles, and after drying off at Transformation's pool, our crew embarked in intermittent waves. With others on the road under blackening skies, I kept track of the French girls' bike by its headlights reflecting in my mirror. After a turn I could no longer see them, anticipating that they'd meet us at the drum circle.

At the Pavilion, with its bonfire raging, fifty people mingled. The French girls arrived on foot twenty minutes later – their bike had broken down. After recent experiences of missing mopeds, I didn't like the idea of leaving a bike anywhere, so Laurie rode on the back of my scooter as we returned to retrieve it. Between the grey sky and green of trees, Laurie was unsure of the bike's precise location. Her gut feeling led us to a spot, where presently stood a large motorbike, but no moped. Looping around the Solar Kitchen's roundabout, Laurie became increasingly adamant of that spot where the motorbike had idled minutes earlier. We disembarked, finding a path to a school and trails through to jungle, but no bike.

The recency of the moped's disappearance and the matter of the mysterious motorbike, prompted immediate action. Informing security officers at the Main Road entrance, we provided descriptions of the moped with its license plate number, and details of the suspicious motorbike. While security across Auroville would remain vigilant, the officer gently suggested we visit the rental property in the morning to check if, by chance, somebody found it and returned it there.

Returning towards African Pavilion, seconds after passing Dinesh Restaurant, my scooter slowed, stuttered and stopped. Fortunately Dinesh sold gas. Unfortunately, neither Laurie nor I held rupees at the time, and the payment machine couldn't connect online. Laurie's cash was with Lily, and I required an ATM, with none around for miles.

Back at the bike, standing in warm, stormy winds, under brain-shaped clouds that obscured a quarter sliver of Moon, we laughed. Laurie was super cool: unstressed and even excited by this curious escapade. Bike theft in Auroville appeared rampant. She was aware that the worst-case scenario meant paying Rs5000: less than €60. Dinesh remembered me from several visits and was willing for us to return with payment.

"Up for adventure?" I asked Laurie.

Her eyes gleamed. "Yes!"

Returning to African Pavilion accomplished the necessity of updating the worried others. Laurie collected money, while I gathered a flashlight, refilled my water bottle and rummaged up another bank card. I was mesmerised by the puzzle, piecing together clues like the motorbike, and debating the similarities to Inke's situation. I considered driving to the house of the miniskirted pot-smoking bike owner to scour her vehicles. Amit welcomingly treated me to a complementary steaming plate of African-style maize and beans, while I pondered.

With Laurie on the back of my scooter, we jetted along the road to retrace our steps. First: Dinesh. We tried my bank card again; after an extended connection delay, payment was approved. With a tank full of petrol, we drove to the main road and headed towards the rental shop. Their deserted dusty parking lot bore no traces of abandoned mopeds. Laurie and I shared a confident feeling that everything would be okay, perhaps from our afterglow of Vipassana. *Accept things as they are.* My imagination envisaged whisking Laurie into the rainforest and making passionate love, but I said nothing.

Eventually, we returned to Pavilion, in time for the fire circle's customary closing ceremony. A hundred hands linked in a human chain around a considerable bonfire. Gathering our crew, and resigning to resolve the bike situation in the morning, our motorcade returned to Transformation. To avoid disturbing other guests at Transformation, our group of Vish, the French girls, Spaniard Burners, and debilitated Tofu the dog, huddled in shadows at the adjacent kindergarten. Tofu consistently tried to sleep off his trauma following a serious collision with a cow. Music played at a low hum; wine was poured and cheese was devoured. Whispered chatting and much laughing underscored a glow of fresh but tight camaraderie: the special type that occasionally and magically arises on travels.

Rave in Auroville

On the Saturday before my Vipassana course, a large group from African Pavilion set forth to find a secret rave. The soundsystem was allegedly hidden amidst fields on Auroville's periphery. This was a wholly viral party, where younger and alternative types had heard *something* about it, yet nobody knew any details. The buzz lent hype and anticipation.

At African Pavilion, the mood remained hostile, and splintered from days of tense morning circles. Those who desired the freedom to smoke battled against others who didn't want to inhale it. By the weekend, differences were put aside. After a pizza buffet, baked from wood-fire clay ovens at Youth Centre, our group swelled to dozens of revellers. Spawning a motorcade of mopeds, bicycles and pedestrians, we meandered slowly through narrow bush, towards vague clues for the location. We followed booming beats from speakers that thumped from across the horizon, although we made plentiful wrong turns, with occasional spills.

Eventually we found the location and dozens of eager patrons streamed through the entrance. Dosas and "special" bhang lassis – green and strong - were served from two stalls. The stage and DJ setup were mirrored by psychedelic artwork, that glowed under black lights in a field adjacent to a farm. Hundreds of people gathered and mingled on the premises. The sandy dancefloor bumped to hyperactive psy-trance: a rare rave in Auroville, or even India.

Two bhang lassis later, I was buzzing considerably. That's all I needed. With Vipassana days away, I politely refused numerous offers of beer and joints. I no longer cared about alcohol, and didn't smoke anything. I fell into a typically introspective shell, with much to ponder: the past, present and near future, that included ten intimidating days of silence. Away from the dancefloor, a bonfire warmed forty guests who sat smoking and drinking. I chatted with the French and chilled with Africans, most of whom resided outside of the Pavilion. In one surreal moment, out of blacklight shadows, Talib from African Pavilion bounded through; his eyes were wild and vividly luminescent, almost yellow. The party raged on late into the night.

After a few hours, I lost steam. Neither fully confident about driving after bhang lassis, nor desiring an early departure, I invoked the faithful little voice in my head: *Stay until the end, see what happens. No doubt, interesting things will happen.*

Tiredly compromising, I located a thick old tree, secluded from populated areas. Climbing its weathered brown bark, I lay flat, closed my eyes and attempted to nap. I thought intensely while branches held me for hours. I'd been stung badly after a recent email from Boogie, despite the initial joyous surprise of hearing from her at all. Contact had been non-existent of late. Boogie was happy in Hungary with her family, and mentioned hanging with somebody who was "becoming more than a friend". I guessed it was the young musician who'd courted her and wooed her family for years.

I was fed up with my mental imprisonment and inane sentimentality. I had several opportunities to release the maple "love leaf", that Boogie secretly hid in my phone case during our Korean stay. She'd etched the leaf with "Boogie <3 Sea". I'd long clung to its expired symbolism of our magical times. Under the huge beaming Moon, I removed the leaf from its case. *Let her go.* With one final recollection, I flicked the leaf in the air, and didn't look back. The leaf danced through the wind and dropped into a carpet of other leaves through blackness. I felt an unexpected wave of relief.

...

Hours later, I woke in my tent in stunning pain: an entirely new and unusual sensation. The whole day was brutal. I could barely control my emotions, and trudged around trying to maintain tranquility. An upbeat Tamil festival near the Pavilion with live bands and four-legged egg races consumed useful hours. Much of my time was spent with caring, elder Louanna and Merlin, who were greatly sympathetic.

The next morning was similarly tough. On Monday while working from Marc's Cafe, I dispatched Boogie a reply. I wished her well in new professional and romantic endeavours. I assured her that she could always reach out to me, any time, and perhaps one day we might blossom a friendship. Pressing "Send" conjured furthermore relief. I felt in control. *I've let her go. I've accepted she's with others. I am at peace with it.* That night I dreamed my deepest dreams since Korea: full, exciting and fun.

New Windows

Separate instances of new acquaintances and adventures arrived after letting the love leaf fly away. By now I'd finished reading the "Road Less Travelled", and was particularly intrigued by its closing chapter on Grace. This detailed the psychic, mystic powers of the universe, and the vibrant signs and clues we're regularly presented, that help guide us along our way. There was a power in premonition, and to harness it we need only better tune in with it.

After my afternoon work session concluded at Marc's Cafe, I opted for an abbreviated return to African Pavilion. My plan was to find a restaurant from where to continue writing, but an inner voice suggested heading back to camp. Two African-Americans ladies, first time visitors to Auroville, arrived at African Pavilion around the same time as me. To their grateful relief, I carried their heavy bags to a tent. They appreciated my assistance, and invited me to accompany them for dinner.

On three bikes, we ventured around the corner of the main road. The first restaurant was closed. Then the second and third. I looked up another: Closed. The only open restaurant looked "fancy" from the outside, and was probably overpriced. However, La Signa turned out to be an exquisite place, with some of the most scrumptious and affordable food in the area. In La Signa's lush back garden, the two ladies and I became further acquainted. They were a pair of American teachers living in Pune who had randomly discovered Auroville.

A curious couple from the adjacent table politely interjected, then invited us to join them. Both Aurovillian-Canadians were actors and practicing clowns, having recently returned to Auroville after eleven months away. They taught us several quirks about Aurovillian society, as well the couple's amusing anecdote about first meeting each other. Dinner was sublime: some of the tastiest paneer I've eaten, with a perfect level of spice. The couple seemed readily curious about my creative projects and welcomed me to reach out after Vipassana.

On the day before my course, there was further spirited drama at the Pavilion. One of the few African participants at the camp, a helpful and peaceful but conflicted fellow, had inadvertently tarnished the camp's name, by informing recent visitors that marijuana could be found at the Pavilion. As he'd ignored prior warnings, he was relocated elsewhere in Auroville, for "better understanding" of the city's values. The vicious group circle became outraged at a "lack of compassion" for simply outing him, despite the chances he'd been granted.

After the fuss subsided, I spent an hour refilling twenty-litre water tanks. In the afternoon, I learned to craft a simple but supremely efficient plant watering system. This groundbreaking method conserved water by transporting small amounts of moisture, directly from recycled bottles to roots of plants and trees, via small ropes or string. Instead of vaguely watering plants, the bottles could be more conveniently refilled. This is how deserts, like in Auroville and Kenya, can be converted into thriving rainforests.

I was mildly concerned about the dwindling time remaining before Vipassana, and departed the Pavilion early to dive into work. I had a hunch to visit Bread & Chocolate, a modern and popular but overpriced cafe. I ordered food and set up my workstation on the only available table. Wifi problems resulted in a rare, "Please contact administrator" error. I mildly freaked out about bank transfer cutoff deadlines, and reacted tensely with those around who tried to help. My suggested restart of the cafe's modem solved the issue.

A pretty and confident brunette sat beside me and typed away on her laptop. Tina was Croatian-born and had previously lived in New Zealand. Her mother had married an Aurovillian. Tina ran a conscious organic cafe and yoga centre on the Croatian coast. We chatted about broad subjects, that included the socially-disruptive benefits of blockchain. I was invited to visit her Croatian cafe and conduct a workshop on conscious technology. After hours of electric chatter we refocused on our personal work tasks. Tina insisted I visit her family's house in Auroville, after my Vipassana.

I looked back on these days, where I listened to hunches that influenced decisions of where to go, and when. In both instances I met riveting and engaging new souls, while presented with future opportunities. Was there any correlation with letting go of The Past? Of Grace? I vowed to more acutely tune into premonition, a resolution that would transform and even save my life in years to come.

I thought back to Borderland, when a calm but insistent inner voice spoke to me at sunrise: "*Smoke your final joint. Take one more lap around the quarry.*" The rest was history: Here I am. Premonition can lead us into magic and adventure; at a minimum we could dare ourselves to see. We could always head home afterwards, but at least we tried.

Chapter 9

Hundred Day Vipassana

Shortly before 4am, a cacophony of analog alarm clocks beeped. Startled men jumped out of beds; some staggered straight to the communal showers, while others coaxed precious extra moments of sleep. Three slow, deep, reverberating chimes of a large gong bellowed, before complementary harmonic flurries of smaller and shorter bells. Pitch black, the Sun was asleep, as had been approximately sixty men and women who were segregated across two compounds. Fans whirred overhead, clicking and clattering, and provided cool respite from Indian humidity.

It was the opening morning of my first ten day silent Vipassana course, hosted at Dhamma Arunachala. The centre lay on the edges of the holy city of Tiruvannamalai, situated approximately midway between Pondicherry and Bangalore. Tiruvannamalai, home to centrepiece Shiva temple and several ashrams, was built around the "red mountain" of Arunachala: an ancient, holy hill. Every full moon, up to 100,000s of followers trekked around its 14km path, with many hiking its summit. The modest meditation premises was thirty minutes out of town, close to the literal middle of nowhere, and afforded amplified seclusion and tranquility.

Vipassana is 'the art of seeing things as they really are': the teachings of the living Buddha, that have been passed down for 5000 years. Vipassana's method of self-observation of inner sensations helps individuals acknowledge the truth of the moment. The process helps ease participations of pain, misery, craving and aversion, while bringing enlightenment along our paths to inner peace.

Vipassana begins with the awareness of breath: the truth of breath. How breath enters; how it exhales. Whatever the sensation may be: It is the reality of this moment. There is no inventing sensations. What if the mind wanders? No problem. Practice diverting a stormy mind back to the simplicity of breath. Accept each sensation as temporary, alike the absolute impermanence of all in the universe: the good, the bad, pain, elation and everything in existence. This is true for atoms, stars, humans and relationships.

Discovered several millennia ago by the Buddha, teachings have passed down across generations. Humble savants meticulously and scrupulously preserved the original technique into the modern era, most notably under the selfless tutelage of S.N. Goenka. Courses are free: teachers are not paid, and there are no charges for food or rooms. Instead, the facilities are financed by donations from past students, and are served by volunteers across approximately 1500 centres worldwide. Vipassana is non-sectarian and non-missionary: everybody, of all beliefs and creeds, is welcome. It is a technique that can help everyone, from inmates and wardens in the murkiest Indian prisons, to global leaders and angst-filled youths, who are rightfully confused and dismayed at modern realities.

I sure hoped it could help me. Throughout my past, I occasionally exploded, either through self-destruction, or violence of words and breaking inanimate objects. Sure, I was skeptical. It was like any foreign belief system: that it might brainwash me. Moreover, it was daunting to consider ten days of silence and solitude, away from the addiction of Internet life, digital relationships and distracting habits.

I'd arrived the previous evening after a rickety bus from Pondicherry to Tiruvannamalai. Unsure of the menu at Vipassana, I savoured a last supper of sinful food: notably exquisite hummus and warm pita bread with eggs, coffee, a majestic lassi and brownie, at the very chill Shanti Cafe. Afterward, an overpriced rickshaw dropped me outside a nondescript gate, that led into the meditation centre. While checking in with stone-faced Japanese assistants, few people spoke at all. With time to spare, I walked around the compound. The dry red clay of the earth led through stone-lined pathways; trees, bushes and shrubbery stood in abundance. Areas for men and women were separated; each had rows of dorm rooms, shower complexes and different entrances to the various meditation facilities. There were various shady trees, large rocks and benches for sitting. The impressively angular wooden building in the centre was the mysterious pagoda - or private meditation arena – with a hundred cells.

After a small meal in the dining hall, we gathered in the smaller hall for an introduction to Vipassana's key concepts. These repeated the rules, or Precepts: agreeing not to kill any living being, taking only what is given, not engaging in sexual deviousness, avoiding false speech (such as lying or breaking noble silence), and prohibiting intoxicants of any variety. The silence was to begin this evening.

After a short break, people filed back into the hall. Although I had no idea what to expect, it felt like authentic Vipassana. The teacher sat stoically, like a lizard king or snake, crossed-legged in his chair. The electric hum of the overhead lighting and fan buzzed at a tense frequency; much the only sound. Students sat on pre-assigned mats. Over speakers, a pre-recorded throaty voice sang a short song, in an ancient language called Sanskrit. This first session was simply breathing: Anapana, coached along by the audio recording. The hour sitting passed rapidly, then it was time for bed, ahead of the gruelling first morning.

...

Dazed students trickled into the meditation hall at dusk for the opening session. Two hours of Anapana was practiced under the audio guidance of Goenka, with most of us in sleepy haze. Two men sitting in front of me fell back into slumber, but were soon awaken by a polite, attentive Japanese assistant. An audio recording, first in English, then Tamil, instructed students to breath normally. We were to focus on the awareness of breath at the very edge of the nostrils, to diligently concentrate on the acute sensations of that narrow area, and practice diverting attention from any other thoughts back to breath.

After two long, uncomfortable hours, a gong graciously sounded. Breakfast was tasty: sweet coconut rice and hot lemongrass tea. Walks around the dusty red compound allowed me to fall deeper into solemn, contemplative solitude. Across three further sessions I practiced calming the mind; mine was cyclonic. If the mind runs away: don't stress, return to breath.

There was no dinner, but a small snack, as we learned disappointingly. This was reiterated during Goenka's engaging and occasionally humorous nightly video discourses. The recordings explained the day's particular lessons, and deeper philosophies behind Vipassana's subtle yet wide-reaching powers, such as teachings of the actual Buddha. Discourses granted a first opportunity to glance at other meditators. The vast majority of students were men, generally Indian, while most of the women were European. Did everybody else have lifelong demons or recent regrets for which to atone?

Day Two – More Breathing

The long opening day led to deep slumber and vibrant dreams. I recall sitting in the living room of a modern home. It was clean, white and cream-coloured everywhere, with all the latest gadgets. I was with a friend, who was a babysitter at the house. There were board games and video games to play. As a side plot, there was a middle-aged bearded man and his trusty brown dog. This motorcycle guy was voyaging through a mountainous country, running errands. I was unsure of his mission.

As dreams flickered away, a scattering of analog beeps was followed by three mesmerising gongs, then a flurry of bell chimes. Day Two was the most arduous of them all. The glow of the first day's novelty subsided to the brutal reality of sitting achingly for eleven hours. I found my imagination more difficult to control. Avidly concentrating on air tickling the edge of my nostrils could block out everything else.

This prolonged day agitated my hardest, most debilitating thoughts to the surface. My mind exasperatingly followed down violent paths, before returning to the serene awareness of breath. Time felt ever slower; I desperately willed the gong of relief to mercifully release us from this backbreaking focus. Sometimes it felt like the assistants completely forgot about ringing the bell. Some sessions ran longer than their designated times: perhaps a test of ridding expectations.

Another blunt lesson came through unfulfilled expectations. The first day's sweet coconut breakfast was so delightful, that I craved it, and expected it to be served again. However, the next day's menu was different, and my disappointment prompted helplessness and hunger. *Everything was a lesson.*

Day Three – Sharpen the Mind

Dream: I found a small, baby black snake. I kept it in a small box, pierced with breathing holes. When I opened the lid, the snake squirmed and wriggled, perhaps seeking freedom. After some time, I released the snake back into nature, and nudged it onto a grassy patch. Was this a reminder of letting go of attachment? Was I the snake?

This third full day of Anapana resulted in further more casualties, with several more men and women vacating the compound. One was a Ukrainian male I'd met at African Pavilion, and his Ukrainian partner. I was disappointed that people quit so soon. Eleven further hours of meditation reached the point that I had so much time to breathe and think, there was little left to ruminate. I wondered if all ten days would be this boring – and whether I could handle that. A sliver of hope appeared in the third evening's video discourse, when Goenka uttered the magic words: "Tomorrow you will learn Vipassana."

Day Four – Vipassana

The morning started with the customary two-hour session, that passed astonishingly quickly: perhaps from the blissful state between dreams and awake. Breakfast included that dreamy sweet coconut rice. The first session introduced Vipassana's fundamentals. For days we'd mastered Anapana, observing delicate sensations under the nostrils, by now with almost superhuman sensitivity. Building upon this sharp and calm mind, Vipassana senses each and every body part. Scans start at the top of the head, down to the tips of the toes. Piece by piece, part by part, we are in tune with each and every sensation within us. Every tiny rupture of pulse, heat or cold, itchy or scratchy, sharp or throbbing, subtle or intense, can be felt anywhere. One was neither to despise or avoid painful sensations, like debilitating aches. Nor were we to cling on to pleasant feelings, like a cool breeze relieving a scorchingly humid afternoon.

No longer allowed to shift posture felt like a worthy challenge, and encouraged me to work harder. I knew at this point that, unlike further more meditators quitting this day, including my roommate, I would persevere through to the end.

Day Five – Flawed Technique

4am gongs led into two hours of basic Vipassana. My mathematical mind calculated that breathing into every body part, for around fifteen counts each, resulted in a full body scan of approximately half an hour. This meant two full scans roughly consumed an entire hour's session. Focusing on body parts and breathing into them had the auxiliary advantage of soothing aches, while the counting in my head more rapidly passed time. I believed I had conquered. However, the audible, guiding narrative provided scattered clues of my incorrect approach. We were not sup-posed to recite, or mentally chant, or conjure imagery of deities, or anything similar.

At lunchtime, I questioned the teacher. Sitting cross-legged on a mat facing him, I explained my mathematical interpret-ation. The teacher paused, then calmly and patiently corrected me: There was to be no systematic counting, and certainly no breathing into body parts. The objective of Vipassana was simply to be aware of sensations: to observe without judgement.

"Don't wish painful sensations to leave, or try to heal them," the teacher explained. "Look closely at them. What do they feel like? Spend time observing each feeling, move on, then continue scanning the body."

I solemnly thanked him and departed for my quarters, demoralised. Despite my frustrations, I returned after the inter-mission, resolute to adjust and improve. At first it was more difficult, particularly now that I could not soothe pain through breath. Rigorous effort and steely determination brought me to the cusp of my first major breakthrough.

Day Six – Pulsing Orb of Energy

I greatly enjoyed the solitary, silent strolls around Dhamma Arunachala. While most of the sittings were focused on breathing and sensations, further reflection arrived during these walks: eyes to the ground, lost in oneself. By now, not much else mattered to me. I felt minimal heartbreak, no animosity towards anybody, and no stress about money, work or life decisions.

A highlight was the first opportunity to meditate in the central pagoda. Wooden beams converged into a pentagon-like shape, twenty metres in the air. Inside held a hundred solitary meditation chambers, with a lockable door and tiny window for each student. During my initial private session in the dark and silent pagoda, I resolved to discover less painful sitting positions. I removed my kurta, and sat on a thin mat and pillow in the humid, breezeless chamber. To this point, all sessions had resulted in numb legs and backache. I sat, switched leg positions, experimented with kneeling down, and even attempted the brutal and seemingly impossible Full Lotus, where each foot tucked under the opposite thigh. I narrowed down to two simpler positions, eventually concluding through hour-long tests of each, that cross-legged, left leg over right, was most comfortable.

After one of the intermissions I returned to the pagoda. I locked the door behind me and sat on a cushion in my undies, while heat seeped through the window. I closed my eyes, began Anapana, then scanned my body from the head down. In the perfect storm of a favourable position, and private space in which to experiment, despite the disarming presence of a nearby mosquito I would not kill, I mentally cycled. Free flow accelerated scans through body parts. Down and up; up and down. I felt scattered pins of pain in my back, and scars of an injured right pitching elbow: all were now tolerable. The flow throughout my body accelerated without pausing. I scanned multiple body parts simultaneously, rapidly naming body parts and feeling them: *Forearm.. Hands.. Fingers.. Neck.. Chest..* Faster and faster, breathing and pulsating, I couldn't name body parts expeditiously enough to keep pace with the flowing sensations. Words disappeared from my mind.

A delightful trickle of breeze tickled my right shoulder blade. Impressed, relieved, I revelled in it: too long. The pleasantries faded. The pulsating flow reconvened, in and out, up and down, feeling everything at once. Slowly gyrating, I subtly oscillated counterclockwise. The swirling energy was akin to my body as the centre of a galaxy that orbited around me, with each speck of sensation a planet or comet circling stars.

Another pleasant breeze tickled a similar spot; this time I accepted it unaroused, and continued scanning. Whatever consequence opened up an unprecedented pure flow throughout my body, my mind succumbed into blissful whiteness, and an epiphany floated to my consciousness. In the midst of this pulsating inner-galactic orb, I flashed back to a random, innocuous moment: the first time in my life, as a young teenager in my bedroom in Singapore, I masturbated. Following the curious pleasure of my first supposed orgasm, confused and curious, I had to tell somebody. Yet there were no male figures around or close friends in my life. I visited my mother, who was across the hall in her bedroom. Disappointedly, her reaction was aghast, almost horrified at the notion. She took a deep breath.

"Don't tell anybody," she admonished. I didn't. I kept it a secret, while definitely experimenting further on myself. It was never the same feeling, and was difficult to make recur.

What I realised then and there, in my isolated meditation cubicle, was its obscure but mighty relevance. For this was the exact indignant reaction my mother suffered as a young child under different circumstances. In the wake of an awful, violating incident, my mother raced inside to tell my grandmother – a devout Roman Catholic, and long a stern, intimidating woman. Similarly aghast, my grandmother instructed my crying, vulnerable mother: "Don't you dare tell anyone. Don't you spoil the family name, or bring shame to this house."

My sobbing mother silently agreed, leading to unforeseen consequences that rippled throughout the rest of her life. This moment put into perspective for me, my mother's long-fractured relationships with friends and family members, and especially her long-held animosity towards my grandmother. Undoubtedly, she repressed this incident, leading to a lifetime of hurt, trust issues and guilt.

I flashed back to my pubescent instance, finally understanding the almost instinctual reaction of my mother: "*Don't tell anybody.*" I realised how it repressed my own throbbing adolescent sexual curiosity. Shortly after, it resulted in what I considered, to that point, was the most sinful act of my life, in a series of juvenile perverse incidents, and an uncontrollably rising libido. Yet I had nobody trustworthy to confide in. The aftermath commenced years of psychiatrical tests and counselling, while lifelong frustrations and opposite-sex awkwardness brewed from my widespread repression.

At the peak of my delinquent and destructive energy, my exasperated mother bought me a one-way flight from Singapore to France, where my father maintained a humble cottage. Had I made the flight I'd soon have learned he wasn't around for months. First I'd have to locate his place, in a vague area of northwestern France, without knowing an address, in an era before online maps. Without a key or cash I'd need to survive for two months as a teenager. Likely I'd be cared for by nearby nuns. I'd have mastered French out of necessity, and Paris might have become home as I matured. The night before my trip, I played Metallica's Nothing Else Matters on my classical guitar, and my sobbing mother changed her mind. Instead, she resolved to find me better mental health care.

With the pulsating orb at its peak, I ceased meditating and wept. Like that first orgasm, the orb was never replicated, much as I tried. I was deeply sorry for my hapless mother, for my estranged sister, and for breakdowns across relationships of my family. My starkest observation: *it was nobody's fault*. My grandmother, bless her heart, undoubtedly survived unpleasant ordeals of her own, that influenced her cold and unfriendly mannerisms. My mother habitually blamed herself or others for everything, and prayed to God for forgiveness. My sister hated everyone: but no doubt she also suffered from the absence of respectable male influences. Furthermore, as a thirteen-year-old boy overpowered by natural human impulses, how could I maintain guilt and blame? Let it go: forgive the self, and others.

The rest of the day served no purpose than to shower, eat, practice breathing and sleep. The first major weight of my life had bubbled to the surface, and vanished.

Day Seven – Reflecting on Homelessness

Following deep sleep and dreams, I was eager to further my progress. I sought to resurrect that orb. I acknowledged that I was causing detriment to myself, by clinging on to retrieving even a sliver of those pulsating sensations, and sessions transpired with frustrating futility.

Back in the pagoda cell after a day of struggles, I simplified my approach, and returned to a respectable rhythm. While cycling through scanning I felt a glut of pain in a lower region of my back. I sharpened my attention to scrupulously investigate. Gazing here reaffirmed that pain consisted of temporary layers of vibrations, that were endlessly moving and pulsing. I cerebrally traced around the sore spot, almost tickling the circumference, and gently prodded its epicentre with brainwaves. I did not feel pain and didn't seek aversion from it: I was simply curiously observing.

Upon accepting the pain, sharp visions flashed into my mind. They crystallised the two years I spent homeless, living on the streets of Ontario, Canada, two decades earlier. My longest "home" during the era was a discrete rooftop, upon which I crafted temporary fortresses out of cardboard, old clothes and blankets. I frequently shivered on the rooftop in minus-twenty to minus-thirty degree winter temperatures. I long understood the circumstances that led to my homelessness, and appreciated the bravery I'd mustered to survive it. Yet this was the first instance I looked back with anything more than passing glimmers of recollection, and the first time I wholly respected myself for my efforts. One thing I had never done, for twenty years up until this calm moment in a meditation cell in the middle of India, was cry about it.

Other than this unusual year, crying was not something I did much. Sure, after breakups or deaths, I'd be more emotional, but these were never on the scale since my goodbye to Boogie in Seoul. The pagoda revelations offered fresh perspective about my homeless era. I should be proud - integral to "love of the self" - of surviving, particularly through a brutal Canadian winter.

What could I do to give back? I imagined a concert at a majestic theatre hall in Toronto, possibly the coming Christmas. After a comedic opening hosted by Omie, the professional clown character of my friend Dave McKay, a video screen presented the introduction. The short film cinematically depicted the realities of homelessness in Toronto: a huge and infinitely growing epidemic. An act depicting homelessness was performed on the stage, portraying the all-familiar snapshot of somebody sleeping on a street, while the hustle, bustle and righteousness of the trickle-down economy in major metropolitan cities passed by.

The concert featured acts including friends Evren and Courteney's "Strangers on a Plane", and a volunteer orchestra. At the evening's conclusion, Omie requested that all former and present homeless people who were scattered covertly around the audience to stand. This revealed many dozens of well-dressed, humbled people in attendance, including myself. On the screen there was a subtle mention that the night was produced by somebody who was homeless, "twenty years ago this Christmas". Standing ovations rained down for the performers and the homeless guests, and the charitable event raised thousands of dollars for local shelters and aid groups.

Day Eight – Sun Moon Sea

The more I devoted to practicing Vipassana, the less I remembered dreams. I didn't recall sleeping so well in my life, especially on a thin mattress. I mentally conjured concerts performed by full orchestras, and discerned symphonies in varieties of halls and outdoor stages.

Another breakthrough came during one of my restful periods. I envisioned the security wall in Gaza, built by the Israelis purportedly for their nation's safety, yet it simultaneously segregated and disabled Palestinian society. Its wall, the ultimate symbol of division, was a fact of life: a souvenir of actuality in human history. Ideally it served as a stark reminder, like Berlin's, of why there shouldn't be walls. But, whatever our opinions, the wall physically exists in the now.

I pictured a hypothetical peace orchestra uniting Israeli and Palestinian musicians, performing epic music while 3D video projections illuminated stories atop bricks. Scenes included daily life in both societies, as told by their people, including projections of harmonious futures. Brick by brick, the virtual wall fell down, affording a glimpse at prospective unity, without divisions or barriers. Nothing more: no politics, no blame, but an uplifting collaboration of cultures demonstrating a will for peaceful co-existence.

The peace orchestra was a concept I'd long-considered to live-perform soundtracks to my films, It would be steadfastly uninfluenced by the perversion of money, suspect marketing or intrusive technology. It must be acoustically viable to perform without power if necessary. During meditation breaks, I chipped away at solving certain essentials, such as what would be its name? The power of the Sun, and the attentive hope of the Moon, had nurtured the life of the Sea. Their cosmic influences helped manifest the name: The Sun, The Moon, The Sea.

Day Nine – Bhanga Nana

Dream: I was in a cafe, the same establishment as I'd dreamed a few days prior. I saw and smelled a fresh bakery, with its long clean counter, and an outdoor area with a wooden bench and table seating. I was famished, yet I inexplicably refused to pay Rs36 or Rs39 for samosas. Later I saw delicious chocolate cake offered for "good value" at Rs110. In the end, I decided everything was too expensive and ordered nothing. I woke up starving – my punishment for craving – or indecision?

If I craved anything, it was the menu of Shanti Cafe. I was deviously delighted at the recollection of homemade hummus, warm pita bread, eggs, lassi and chocolate coffee. While the food at Dhamma Arunachala was consistently tasty and always wholesome, portions were small. Every meal was welcomingly vegan, and much was organic curries, rice, sprouts, fruit salads and plentiful vegetables. Once day four began we were not to take second helpings, following the precept of taking only what is given. The less energy that the body expends on digesting food, the more the mind elevates with focus.

The Bhanga Nana technique, after the customary free flow of energy throughout the body, starts with a 3D scan of sensations within. Now the mind can smoothly cut through the brain, like a thick-bladed saw. This was a revelationary exercise, as the acute sharpness of my mind readily bore through solid body parts. I could feel the mush of the brain, the gums in the teeth, or pulsing through the heart. Any encountered lumps or clots typically opened up and relaxed, simply through concentrated observation. I could depict the insides of my arms, heart, intestines and testicles. I could tickle the length of my penis with my mind; this was actually unhelpful, because it ensured my awakened testes were unbearable to sit on! I was blown away by human mental powers, and wondered what else could be discovered – particularly with an intimate partner.

After scanning with free flow, unhindered by blockages, 3D mental focus began at the base of the spine, pushing upward through the centre of my spinal cord. I was surprised how many blockages were prevalent in my spine, and these frequently thwarted my progress. Practicing further in a subsequent session, after an hour of scanning and free flow, I tried again. On the verge of the end, I spent less time concerned by clots in the spine. I pushed higher up to each subsequent notch, eventually ascending to the tip of the spine, and intense energy surged into my brain. My entire body radiated with a warm, pure feeling: a throbbing light of bliss. A few minutes later, enveloped by glow, instead of clinging to the delightful sensations, I restarted from the basic up and down scanning of body parts.

Over the final days, I attained Bhanga Nana twice. My next effort was the best; despite uncomfortably numb legs, my body was otherwise free flowing. I carefully spent time inside my spine and stopped at each blockage for careful observation. There was no hurry or forcing anything, and my spine slowly loosened up. Higher and higher, clot by clot, up the spine, to the next ridge, out to the brain, and profound euphoria.

Similar to the inner-galactic orb in the pagoda, I could not force Bhanga Nana. Most meditation sessions barely resulted in free flow whatsoever, with at least one painful blockage preventing progress. Sometimes, full hours were required simply to calm a raging mind.

Day Ten – The Silence Ends

At the end of the tenth day, well-integrated into an enjoyably tranquil routine, noble silence ceased. I held no further revelations, only small flashes of bridges I could mend, and memories of distant people from long ago. There were no epiphanies about my father, work or recently-ended relationships, and there felt like no point forcing anything.

At least half of the meditators excitedly resumed their inane oral banter. Some couldn't wait to speak again; they cheated on their strolls around the compound a day or two earlier, pretending to hush as others passed by. Why were humans so insistent about chattering?

The tenth night's discourse led to a captivating film about brutal, notorious Delhi prisons. Under the inspired influence of Kiran Bedi – the progressive new female Inspector General of Delhi Prisons – Goenka organised a mass Vipassana course at Tihar Jail. Past trials in Indian prisons demonstrated the positive effects of Vipassana, not only on prisoners but also increasing compassion in guards. At Goenka's monumental ten day course at Tihar, over a thousand meditators – including guards, wardens and inmates – practiced, with impressive results. Internal crime rates and re-offences plummeted. Soon after, a dedicated Vipassana wing was opened at Tihar, and numerous jails around the world incorporated Vipassana into their programmes.

Day Eleven – Back to Reality

After a short morning session, our Vipassana course concluded. People holding curiosities about each another had their first opportunity to mingle. The men I spoke with compared our experiences. Only one other man attained Bhanga Nana. In fact, he also described a pulsating orb of energy, on the same day, at around the same time. His meditation cell was the one beside mine. Had our energies and electricities interconnected?

Of sixty meditators who began the course, around thirty reached the end. Almost everybody I spoke to briefly considered quitting at some point. Similar to gasping through the painful end of a two-hour meditation session, those who worked hard and finished earned the full glow of success. A few others shared the sentiment of wishing for another ten or twenty days.

After ten days without exercising vocal cords, chatting was difficult on the throat. I thanked the teacher – who preferred not to be thanked. He provided advice on maintaining practice, even for a constant traveller.

"On a flight, or bus, close your eyes and practice Anapana. This will help relieve jetlag. In the morning, after waking, at night, before bed: focus on the awareness of breath."

Timing enabled almost everybody to wait roadside together outside Dhamma Arunachala for a late bus. This crazy ride, with blaring music that shattered all prior tranquility, bounced around on broken, rocky roads, while our group squeezed tighter. Bags were compacted wherever they could fit, as evermore locals boarded. Several young Tamil men held onto bars and hung off the bus as it lumbered towards Tiruvannamalai. Everybody laughed the whole way.

Rallying up willing participants, I led an "afterparty" to Shanti Cafe for lunch. I ordered exactly the same meal I'd enjoyed before Vipassana. Naturally, it didn't taste as extraordinary as I remembered, but it was still utmost satisfying.

Mikey, a German, and Vashu, an Indian, accompanied me on the contemplative three-hour bus ride to Auroville. Mikey and I further satisfied our sweet tooths by stopping for fresh fruit juice, a coffee and sweets, although this was to soon cause illness and dreadful diarrhoea, that betrayed the ten days of our organic, vegan diet. I suffered for days from succumbing to the weakness of my cravings.

One Hundred Days of Practice

In the blissful wake of Vipassana, I maintained practice for an hour every morning and night, irrespective of my location, for around a hundred days. Some sessions were easier than others, particularly the week after the course. The more that I reintegrated into the noise and hum of society, the less sharp my mind, and this led to increased difficulty concentrating and scanning. Still, I tried, finding any placid place I could, sometimes under trees in parks, on the floors of hostel rooms, and often in my green tent.

Back in Auroville, I relocated my tent to a quieter part of African Pavilion. Numerous of the camp's negative energies had departed, but the Pavilion's cleanliness and discipline suffered. Elsewhere I made several new connections as part of a crew. The French girls, Laurie and Lily, became regular companions, and I randomly met two Spanish, Berlin-based Burners: Alejandro and Paula. We spent time at Auroville's lush Botanical Gardens, and made several visits to Marc's Coffee. With Vish, the South African chef, we all tried, and failed, to crash a party on my final night in Auroville.

I made my first foray inside of the golden, spherical Matrimandir: The Temple of the Mother. Following a short video presentation, shuttle buses whisked a large group from Visitor's Centre to the Matrimandir's entrance. A guide led us further into the central Peace Garden, where an old-time Aurovillian shared foundation philosophies and facts, before questions from our group of around forty. One answer reiterated that Auroville was not about religion.

"The failure of religions is… because they were divided. They wanted people to be religious to the exclusion of other religions, and every branch of knowledge has been a failure because it has been exclusive. What the new consciousness insists is: no more divisions. To be able to understand the spiritual extreme, the material extreme, and to find the meeting point, the point where that becomes a real force."

In solemn single file, our group moseyed along a bronze-clay path towards the golden ball's centre. Up close, twelve giant manmade petals encircled the Matrimandir; each reflected a principle, such as Gratitude. They were matched by a selection of complementary organic flowers and contained smaller meditation chambers, with ceiling-high glass that overlooked a central pond. In the basin at the bottom was the Lotus Pond: a convergence of waters. Sunbeams entered the Matrimandir at the solar peak, and reflected onto a specifically-crafted mirror and lens that projected single light rays onto a special crystal. Light travelled through and illuminated the entire structure, into the sacred water at its base.

One at a time we slowly entered the cavernous gold-lined geodesic dome. This space-age sphere of whiteness and light was the most majestic structure I'd ever entered. Long, slow spiral staircases ascended dozens of metres in the air and overlooked spherical spaciousness. It felt like a movie, or a human base on another planet. At the top, entering a vast open floor lit by sunbeams and crystal, a solitary ray of light pierced the centre from roof to floor. Individually on pillows, the large group sat around a wide circle. Taking in everything, awed and impressed, I meditated. I could feel everything in nearly complete silence, other than occasional coughs that ricocheted around the dome like cannons.

As travels blurred into the realities of everyday demands, maintaining practice was challenging. Slipping out of the twice-daily Vipassana routine became detrimental. It was easy to fall back into undesirable habit patterns. Upon returning to regular meditation, peacefulness was restored.

Many months after that horrible, destructive night in Korea, and several more since my heart was wrenched away from living dreams, I saw the purpose of bottoming out. Those ten silent Vipassana days were a living testament to my endless resolve of improving myself. Whatever the means, I needed this change.

A Rooftop in Bangalore

The night bus from Pondicherry growled and weaved through the heartlands of Tamil Nadu. After temporarily pausing for the journey's sole bathroom break, the bus hurtled along the desolate highway towards Bengaluru. Thanks to a welcomingly early check-in at Social Rehab Downtown, I napped a few hours in a curtain-lined upper bunk, before emerging into the day.

After my rest, I sat on Social Rehab's sizeable living room couch, adjacent to a balcony of sunshine and the bustle of Bangalore. I researched prospective shopping locations that might stock winter jackets suitable for chilly spring nights in Europe. I settled on Commercial Street, that was a short walk away. While I was preparing to ready myself for the shopping excursion, a pretty blonde woman with medium-length hair and visible tattoos descended Social Rehab's stairs. We locked eyes.

"Hello!" I greeted her.

"Are you German?" she inquired.

"No... But I'm flying to Germany in a few days."

"Do you speak German?" she asked.

I shook my head, in the "No" sense, not the Indian "Yes". Fortunately, Aura's English was immaculate. Aura's plans similarly included a shopping visit to Commercial Street. She shared a passion of finding great coffee, and was up for breakfast along the way. *Super!* Breakfast at famous Koshy Restaurant included their puzzlingly-named "Special Coffee", that was simply strong coffee. The bustling Commercial Street featured roads and alleyways that brimmed with shops, eager vendors and hoards of dawdling tourists. Our first stop was surprisingly successful: the well-known Eastern Store. Ironically Eastern Store was on the west side of Commercial Street, while Western Store was on the east. I skeptically tried numerous no-name winter jackets in all sorts of shapes and styles. The warmest and most comfortable of the jackets came in a subtle grey-blue. Initially I dismissed it, favouring black or tan.

"It really matches your eyes," Aura mused about the blue.

I tried on several alternatives, then reconsidered the grey-blue jacket. I did like it: It had heaps of pockets, including some hidden ones. The jacket was warm, fleece-lined and comfortable. Its price was a fraction of the cost of a comparable jacket in Europe or Australia. I put the jacket aside, not wanting to commit at the very first shopping stop. I sensed I'd be back, as did the shopkeeper.

Aura hunted for particular shoes, while I searched for boxer shorts or trunks. Our stops included cold coffee and chatting further in shade, while she smoked cigarettes. Aura was a nurse and had recently quit her mundane, long-hours job to begin her era of travel. India was her first overseas voyage; she'd arrived a month ago, with another two months to follow. Despite her low budget traveling, today was a rare burst of indulgence. We shared similar interests in music, festivals and trippy inebriates.

At a nearby shoe stall, a young man carrying several hand drums approached us. I liked the little drum of mango tree that he allegedly hand built, as well as his humble vibe. For the first time on this trip I was intrigued at such a purchase. With the neighbourhood ATMs neither functioning nor holding sufficient cash, Aura and I were down to Rs500 between us. I explained the scenario to the young drummer man: if Aura liked a pair of tribal shoes, I'd previously promised to loan her my final Rs500. Otherwise that cash would be available for the drum. Alas, the shoes Aura desired were not available. The young man – Bika – delighted in the news, and I bought the cute little drum at a discounted price.

After returning to Eastern Store to retrieve my new winter jacket, Aura and I continued voyaging through Bangalore. We paused for lunch at the posh White Room, treating ourselves to freshly-made salad and sandwiches, sipping green tea before indulging in cherry-topped Panna Cotta and ice coffees. We strolled down famous Church Street; most of its recent construction was now complete. Before we reached the end of the road, an older man carrying drums approached.

"I am not trying to sell you anything," the man began. "I am curious about your drum. How much did you pay for it?" He believed the Rs500 I paid to be a fair price. To showcase a bigger drum in his arms, he banged on its rock-hard surface. "THIS is mango wood," he exclaimed, and tapped out a much deeper and louder sound than the one I was holding. "Your drum: the skin is made of paper."

He peeled away part of Bika's drum. The sound and quality of the bigger drum were superior, although I preferred Bika's drum's aesthetics and back story. The tout pressed me to upgrade, noting its original asking price of Rs2500. I hesitated for various reasons – money, size and sentimentality – and was firm on allocating only Rs500 further towards the purchase. After minutes of "last offers" by the vendor, he agreed to my price and the swap was made. This earned me a larger, louder, stronger drum with lovely resonance and deeper bass, while still reasonably travel friendly. As we began to leave, the man appealed to us once more.

"Now," he pitched. "Would you like to upgrade your drum again? I have bigger ones!"

Aura and I giggled. We walked away while the man banged and tapped on alternative percussion. Fatigued, Aura and I discovered a secluded space to relax on the rooftop of Social Rehab: an ideal spot to watch the approaching sunset. The idea for beer or wine on the roof arose, and we revisited Bangalore's busy roads. Finding a bottle shop was simple; sourcing a shop selling cheese was futile. This didn't stop us from hiking aimlessly for further more hours through Bangalore. Map apps were extraordinarily ineffective. We couldn't find any grocery stores whatsoever, and sunset had expired by the time we returned to Social Rehab. This didn't dampen our spirits in the least. Following an hour of fruitless (or cheeseless?) exploration, we stopped for ice cream, and shared creamy mango and coconut scoops. Resigned to the fact there may never be cheese, we compromised by ordering the cheesiest pizza we could find at a popular roadside diner, while waiting for the meal in a vacated children's playground.

On Social Rehab's roof, we enjoyed our red Sula Zinfandel wine and satisfyingly cheesy pizza. Chatting deeper, we discovered we shared similarly fractured family pasts. Affection and intensity had culminated over the gloriously electric and spontaneous day. There was constant, casual touch whenever we crossed busy roads, or during particular points in conversation. In the wake of heartbreak I bore no mojo or pheromones, and maintained a cautious, consensual approach.

The breakthrough came while our legs dangled off the top of the roof. After some deep and sincere reminiscing, compounded by a half bottle of vino, we hugged. It evolved rapidly: stroking and caressing. There was no doubt of our mutual attraction. We relocated to the sleeping bags, and it began.

In the midst of her delightfully receiving particularly intimate attention, suddenly Aura stopped, and glanced towards the entrance. Through holes in a wooden wall, I noticed jeans walking our way. Seconds after we abruptly draped ourselves in sleeping bags and whatever clothing within arm's reach, a head popped around the corner of the roof. I timed an over-exaggerated gulp of wine from the bottle, to divert focus from us sitting around in our underpants.

"Hello!" a young man exclaimed sheepishly, before he turned back towards the door. This provided ample time to restore basic clothing.

We invited him to sit with us. The rooftop was his sanctuary for cigarettes and occasional beers, away from his dominating and opinionated mother. We talked for nearly an hour, despite him bashfully questioning if we truly wanted to socialise. Eventually, he politely excused himself.

With the roof to ourselves again, Aura and I exchanged amused glances and laughed. Another person accessed the area to remove their laundry from the washing line; they were far more stunned to see us. Becoming uncomfortable in our overly-accessible location, we ventured around the roof to a more secluded section.

Monumentally we continued, all the way. Prior interruptions helped build anticipation. I battled a litany of emotions: mostly the flickering flashing of The Past in every breath I took. I could see her when I closed my eyes. On a Bangalore rooftop, under the smiling, half-full Moon, the light of a few watchful stars pierced through pollution and city glare. I felt neither sadness nor regrets, and I didn't covet anything more: only gratitude, about how special this random day had been.

...

After an hour's sunrise Vipassana on the rooftop, I was ready for my final full day in India. I largely shared it with Aura, and spent several hours working from a Church Street cafe. We each bought a miniature sewing machine from an old man on the corner of a bustling street. For lunch we stuffed ourselves at an all-you-can-eat Chinese buffet, where waiters intentionally loaded us up with filling appetisers, to cut down on our time at the ritzy buffet. Mutually exhausted, we fell asleep in my bottom bunk bed, with the curtains drawn for privacy.

We celebrated our third and final morning together with a hearty breakfast at Church Street Social. We swapped "The Road Less Traveled" for "The Hidden Life of Trees": about the interconnectivity and intelligence of forests. Later, Aura and I gathered our backpacks, bid farewell to Social Rehab and headed to the road to await our respective taxis.

Aura slipped me a small sheet of paper. A message was etched with pleasantly rhythmic lines, punctuated by:

YOU WILL NEVER FEEL CLOSER TO LIVING THAN THIS

It was goodbye for now, and see you soon. Life, ever full of magic and surprise, was beautiful. I departed India with renewed vigour, brimming with purpose.

Chapter 10

Living Examples of Grace

The silver aeroplane landed on the runway of Paris' Charles de Gaulle Airport in torrential, chilly spring rain. The weather had no bearing on the cancelled connection to Frankfurt, and no further explanation was provided. I was handed a compensatory meal voucher worth €10, and was rebooked on another flight, departing five hours later. The delay forfeited my pre-paid train reservation from Frankfurt to Cologne. With hours to spare, I trudged through the cold, old concrete airport, and hopped on a shuttle connecting terminals. The small regional waiting hall was packed with dreary, listless travellers, including several toddlers who were puzzlingly fastened to leashes. I set up base on an empty table at the sole cafe; €10 barely covered coffee, a croissant and juice. The replacement Air France flight was also late: Delayed boarding, take off, disembarking, and baggage pickup. One might expect Europe to be vastly more efficient than the "developing world", but countless experiences demonstrated that the "developed world" was comparatively unhappy, unfriendly and more prone to systematic breakdowns.

Time was evaporating before the departure time for my newly-booked coach to Cologne. Rain bucketed down in chilly nine-degree weather; I raced through raindrops towards the small bus station. Fortunately, my bus had not yet arrived. I sought to refill my stainless steel water bottle at the adjacent bathroom. A bedraggled hobo dragged a filthy, muddy towel with his feet, and vehemently prevented anybody from entering. I dummied left and right, but he blocked my path each time.

"Are you okay?" I asked, compassionately staring at him in the centre of his weary, hostile eyes. Calmly, while frowning with a hint of rancour from my own troubled street days, I pointed to my water bottle and insisted on a refill. "It's been a long day." Begrudgingly, the hobo let me pass.

The bus departed twenty minutes late: perfect for my own

tardiness. A few hours later I arrived at Cologne Airport, before an express train whizzed to the city centre. At Cologne HBF I was greeted by my old Australian mate, Jono. This was the first time in a decade since we'd last met in Melbourne; he'd grown in all directions, and was a big boy. While he chatted with clients at Starbucks, I grabbed a quiet corner to write, with an ice green matcha and an overpriced vegan wrap.

Our first stop was to meet one of Jono's friends: Ronald, an American-Latino. We fervidly chatted over dinner and beers at a German restaurant. Ronald had lived in Germany for years, and was similarly a traveller and programmer. Afterward, Jono led me to his apartment, where I met his German fiancee: tall, slender, brunette Miri. I was toured around various cafes, bars and restaurants of their buzzy Friesenplatz neighbourhood.

The next sunny day, while Jono and Miri worked at Sevenval's downtown office, I strolled to the centre of Cologne. I was amused at Germans, who strictly obeyed mundane, double red man pedestrian signals, even with no traffic around. It was quite a contrast to the controlled chaos of Indian roads, where it was more of a deep breath and prayer, before plunging into traffic. I registered a German mobile number and bought a travel-friendly beard trimmer. At lunchtime, Cologne's Philharmonic Orchestra opened its doors to the public for a free rehearsal. I sat in the back row, marvelling at serene strings playing underneath rehearsing vocalists.

Brainstorm sessions at the apartment were tailored around Jono's beloved whiteboard. We discussed projects as diverse as foreign expansion and relocation services, Mother.Domains, a memory sharing and collaboration concept called Memtell, and blockchain. Something prolific was bubbling within Jono, but what he'd soon dedicate his life to was unclear at that moment.

Jono and Miri spent the weekend in Holland, enabling me to bask in the peaceful headspace of an apartment to myself for the first time in ages. Upon Jono's return, we again met with Ronald. Every cafe was fully packed, closing or both. Ronald literally ran into a busty brunette on a pretty, vintage bicycle. They were friends; she was opening the corner pub for the evening. We sat outside with tall frothy beers while Ronald shared several humorous, somewhat naughty stories. My turn to talk detailed the circumstances behind changing my name to SEA, the depths of my homelessness, and endlessly resolving to better myself and the planet around me.

Sympathy subsided when talk came to business. Ronald was rightfully cautious upon hearing the latest hype from "high-profile sales guys". We chatted for hours; occasionally it was contentious, yet slowly productive. As we departed, the Colombian waitress cheekily scribbled her number on paper and passed it to me.

The following evening's meeting with Ronald was wholly unproductive. He was in a grumpy mood. Ronald dictated that the only way he saw a path forward, was for Jono and I to become blockchain evangelists, under his command. As I'd just arrived in Europe and was only beginning to consider my options, I resisted. Ronald called me a "hipster", and that he knew "many people like me." Ronald's proposal sounded like a lot of dedication to the drudge of blockchain and its slimy undercurrent, for an end result that was unclear. I questioned how his elaborate scheme would benefit society, in any way.

Ronald huffed, and retorted: "What social projects have you accomplished?"

"You can buy my book and find out," I calmly replied.

"I'm not buying your book, man."

The three of us sat in awkward silence, while clock hands ticked, agonising and slow. Ronald was wound up with his arms crossed, while frowning intensely. Jono rocked back and forth, customarily pensive and musing. I looked around at the busy, loud bar. Some guests had been paying slight attention to us; most continued as they were. Fortunately we were drinking non-alcoholic beer.

Pfad Nach Berlin

The bus from Cologne to Berlin raced through rain and bolts of lightning, navigating past clusters of traffic. Near Berlin's deceptively-named Central Bus Station, I waited for an S-Train. "Time to next train" constantly flashed "3 minutes"; sometimes it flickered to "2", then back to "3". Then, in mirrored parallel, dual S-Trains, one on each platform, rumbled in simultaneously. It caused much confusion; humans scattered in all directions, like unmusical chairs. I picked the train on the left – the eventual "winner". After an M5 tram and a short walk along Sandino-strasse, I arrived at Sandino World Improvement Network, a little before 11pm.

Shami greeted me warmly, with a hearty handshake and a broad hug. We chatted about India, our hopes for the coming summer, and the questionable state of the world. A furnace warmed his brick semi-cellar quarters, while I wolfed down eggs, brōt and beer. I was led to my temporary room; we wished each other good night, and I slept deeply into the Berlin night.

...

I woke with the familiar, disorienting feeling of the unknown: *Where am I?* Yesterday I was on a plane from Bangalore. I emerged into spring Sun, and gathered boxes of groceries from a nearby discount supermarket. Shami and his assistant fulfilled pre-season construction duties. Shami offered me the freedom to feel at home, with a wing of the hostel and a kitchen to myself for a few weeks, until Sandino opened for the season. This afforded me comfortable time to acclimatise and figure out my plans. At this point I had no idea what would come next, but I was open-minded to a plethora of possibilities.

Traveling on my New Zealand passport entitled me to stay 90 days within the Schengen area, that comprised most of mainland Europe. This meant that, after accruing 90 days within Schengen, I could not return on my NZ passport until 180 days after arriving in Europe: the end of September. With Borderland looming in July and several mainland plans over the summer, I had to balance time out of Schengen as much as possible. The UK – my birthplace – was an enviable destination to spend several such weeks, while non-Schengen Balkan states and Russia were possibilities.

Applying for a new Canadian passport, from my experience neither the easiest nor cheapest task, would allow me to juggle the whole year between my citizenships. Critically, this wouldn't aid my ability to fulfil business ambitions, or legally take on jobs, if any. I'd still have to depart Schengen and re-enter. For digital nomads and freelancers, there was a handy but cumbersome Berlin Freelancers Visa, that required undertaking German

172

bureaucracy and subscribing to expensive health insurance.

The solution came from an unexpected source: My father. His email made a simple suggestion: Why not apply for my UK passport? I'd lost mine twenty years earlier. Logistically, this application was difficult, with my birth certificate and other necessary documents under care of my dear friend Ash in Melbourne. I set out small tasks to complete the whole assignment, although I still needed to visit England to temporarily pause the Schengen clock, just in case my passport application was unsuccessful.

A plausible travel window fell between Sandino's launch at the end of April and Bonobo's concert in Berlin end-May. Airfares from Berlin to London were cheap: €15. On the way back I considered stopping through Copenhagen, mainly to meet participants related to Sun Moon Sea in the Pyramid at Borderland. Admittedly, I hoped to cross paths with The Past, as my aching heart still pined for her.

...

I couldn't sleep much last night. There were lucid dreams I'd forgotten. I felt sharp twinges of helpless money stress. Europe was expensive, although Berlin was relatively tolerable, as I had a place to stay, for now. Ongoing chats with Shami suggested I could barter website assistance in exchange for space for my tent. After rent, it was food, travel and impulses that become expensive. The need to remain out of Schengen for around forty days amplified much to coordinate, on top of adequately maintaining multiple work projects at high levels. My van plan, that I debated daily, might provide the answer. With a van I'd have a mobile home, and could comfortably spend time out of Schengen, anywhere. As time progressed, I realised my attachment to the unrealistic complexity and expense of the van further stoked my money stress.

My evening chats with Shami were consistently stimulating. Shami was a peaceful, kindred spirit, similarly healing himself from earlier anguish. We'd frequently sit around his bar-top table and chat a litany of deep topics, often smoking giant blunts that were undesirably overpacked with head-spinning tobacco, over-amplifying the green effect. Shami was curious about meditation, and Vipassana specifically. We agreed on the present-day pertinence of a truly viable World Improvement Network – but what would that entail?

To attempt building a social life, I attended Tuesday evening's Burners Pub at Castle Berlin. This was hosted in a quaint old bar, where a half-dozen Burners sat around several small circular tables beside candlelight. I chatted with a Turkish girl named Fortuna, who amused me with tales of her solo attempts at silently practicing her interpretation of "Vipassana" – to the horror of her mother and confusion of the local pharmacist, who received handwritten notes.

The next morning's meditation whizzed by in my half-asleep state. After accomplishing work duties, I booked a 10am flight from Berlin to London for €24. Two weeks in the UK were to commence on May 3rd. No plans or return tickets at this point.

After several emotionally stormy days, my productivity and momentum heightened. I sourced a new lead: a PR firm that managed and promoted blockchain ICOs – Initial Coin Offerings. I secured $1000 in grants for the ambitious Sun Moon Sea project in Borderland's Pyramid, on the night of the full blood moon. I also received a lesser amount to host an "Introduction to Vipassana" workshop, covering the costs of organic vegan Indian food and lemongrass tea. My intent was to coach Anapana through Goenka's recordings, while providing tranquil meditation space for all.

...

April 13 is a special date in my life. On April 13, 1993, I attended the inspiring, groundbreaking Metallica concert in strict Singapore. I knew after that electrifying concert, that I desired a life based around music and and riveting live experiences, however long it might take to come to fruition. On this particular Friday April 13, 2018, I attended an experimental MALMO concert at Petersburg Art Space. The night was marked with torrential rain, lightning and strong winds, ensuring drenched walking through cobblestoned streets, as I searched to find the back-of-a-warehouse venue. Performers banged out beats and blips on modular synthesizers, analog drum machines, looping pedals, small MIDI keyboards and DJ gear.

On Saturday morning I met up with Fortuna. Our date commenced with a Palestinian-Israeli breakfast at a restaurant named Kanaan. We were graciously served platters of hummus, warm breads, olives and vegetables, although the establishment appeared to be closed to the public while it underwent renovations. Six diverse, clean-dressed actors sat at an adjacent table, filmed as they sampled the buffet, stuffing themselves and smiling at their good fortune.

Under the splendid Sun, Fortuna and I wandered around historic Mauer Park in Berlin. We scouted the many different vans and small buses parked in the area; Fortuna was similarly contemplating van life. We strolled alongside the scarred remnants of Berlin's divisive wall. Heading south to Kreuzberg, a vibrant Turkish neighbourhood, we scoped out the NDBK art space, where artist groups were competing for €50K in grants to commemorate the gallery's fiftieth anniversary. The groups showcased cutting-edge proposals; several embedded sharp political satire. Some were scribed by children. We sneakily enjoyed complementary finger food and bottled drinks.

At Kreuzberg Park we chilled on rock benches in the Sun, while hundreds of revellers drank bottles of club mate or beer. Many smoked marijuana, while a few portable sound systems blasted beats into the open sky. Fortuna's mission in Berlin was to find a place to live, a job, and a boyfriend – not necessarily in that order. Numerous Africans milled about selling weed, furthering the stereotype that Auroville's African Pavilion strove to avoid. While strolling through the park, at the last second I glanced up and jumped out of the way of a homicidal young child, who was on a tricycle, barreling towards my legs.

As night fell, Fortuna and I sat on the top deck of a hostel boat on Berlin's Spree River. We sipped teas, and draped ourselves in blankets for warmth from a chilly breeze, under blackening skies over city lights. I trustingly shared my deepest secrets from childhood, that since my Vipassana's revelations no longer seemed so horrible. Fortuna thought that, whatever my age, these incidents were "kinky". We exchanged erotic desires, that contributed to rising sexual tension. Inevitably, we kissed.

...

On a warm and optimistic Sunday, the day of the week I forcibly ween myself away from "normal" work, I helped Shami complete Sandino's first vegetable garden. I potted plants and laid down seeds, revelling in fresh air with my hands dirtied and dried by soil. The two resident chickens – Roxanne and Maxine – clucked around, curiously examining me and slowly mustering trust. Sandino and Berlin, cold and grey upon my arrival, were slowly, optimistically, blooming into colour and light.

On the weekend, Fortuna and I visited Babylon cinema for a midnight film that depicted a famous photographer's video portfolio. We sat inside the vintage art deco auditorium, mesmerised by fast-paced photographic effects and scenic stories. At its conclusion, walking her bike alongside me, Fortuna returned with me to Sandino as my first invited guest. I should have asked Shami, who was clearly agitated about it the next morning. We stayed awake deep into the night, until the chirping of the birds ahead of the morning Sun. I moved forward emotionally and physically in further more ways.

...

Early in the week, the first staff, Jack and Jill, returned to Sandino. Canadian Clara arrived days later. Mid-week, I flew to Cologne to progress discussions with Jono about prospective collaboration. Of all his intriguing ideas, Jono gravitated towards Memtell: the process of attaching audio recollections to photographic memories, and encouraging family collaboration to nurture them.

I returned to Sandino ahead of its ceremonious opening weekend. Saturday was a glorious day of sunshine, music, and table tennis. At nightfall, a fire in the courtyard raged at the core of a social circle. Patrons downed drinks and smokes while excitedly chattering. Fortuna arrived with a bottle of wine. Her behaviour was occasionally odd, such as interrupting group conversations to specifically ask me unrelated questions. Alejandro, the Spanish Burner I'd met in Auroville, arrived later. The party was laid back and low-key: a smooth start into a magical season ahead.

...

Fortuna snoozed beside me, while rain pitter-pattered against my newly-loaned tent, in the far corner of Sandino's garden. I woke with the uncanny premonition of danger on the brink. Suddenly, steel exploded; there was a horrible bang and crunch. Two cars collided at the nearby intersection, on the other side of Sandino's wooden fence. The two German drivers were polite and efficient, before driving back to their realities.

Waking to a car crash the first morning in new confines was ominous. As the morning progressed, I deeply debated about how and when to cut things off with Fortuna. I knew she wasn't the girl for me; remaining together was only impeding both of our progress. I thought about delaying the split, preferring to keep it as tame and civil as possible. Perhaps after my UK trip?

"Be free from your aversions," Goenka's voice boomed in my head. My mind simulated realistic scenarios: some plausible, others painful – Why hurt the other person? "Be truthful," my inner Goenka persisted.

I recalled about ten years earlier, when I visited my dear Sri Lankan-Australian friend Shanks, during his final days living in Perth. My heart was falling for a particular tall brunette model friend of his. After months of intense online conversations with her, I wanted to gauge if there was any vibe. In the end, there was none, although she became a close friend for many years. Shanks' father observed my intense, flustered rumination, while we shared glasses of his beloved scotch. He imparted an everlasting message of wisdom and decisiveness: "The sharpest knife cuts cleanest."

Fortuna and I sat on a blanket in Sandino's garden, while chickens clucked around us. I made a few subtle references to being consumed with another energy, repeating that I was unable to fully be present. Initially it flew over Fortuna's head, before the message sharply sunk in. Upon a brief but firm discussion, that detailed my suffering from a recent breakup, Fortuna understood. She wiped tears from her eyes and gracefully, solemnly departed. I felt a distinctive gut kick in the stomach, before ripples of relief.

Seeking solace, I chilled with Jack, Jill and Claire in the front corner of the bricked courtyard of Sandino. Confiding in them, I embellished upon my personal situation, namely my post-Korean anguish and consequent spiritual journey. Despite my enduring heartbreak, I felt love flowing through my heart. Love for all the universe. Appreciation for recent times and kind people. I definitely still loved Boogie. I realised a breakup didn't mean we suddenly had to stop loving them.

...

On Workers Day, May 1ˢᵗ, I headed into the city. Berlin was flush with outdoor music stages and thousands of revellers. Historically, Workers Day has descended into chaos, amidst occasional anti-establishment violence. Thick carpets of shattered glass from drink bottles littered the pavement, and police were out in force; several rode horses. Kreuzberg Park was thick with crowds, that bumped to various small stages of techno and other electronic beats. I didn't feel like partying; I preferred rest, ahead of my first summer in Europe.

A Long Overdue Return to the UK

For the first time as a solo traveller, I missed a flight. Everything was under control: I packed the night before, early rise, meditation, and calmly rode Berlin's S-Train to Schönefeld Airport. My mistake assumed that the UK, as part of Europe, was "Domestic Europe", although it was actually International. I needed to be there ninety minutes before departure. I was further stalled in the winding human abattoir of laborious airport security checks. Eventually, I reached the other side, that revealed no mention of my flight anywhere. After asking bewildered staff, I sprinted miles through narrow, congested corridors, reaching the supposed gate, that was long since shuttered. Plane be gone.

Plopping down back at the check-in hall, I searched for alternatives: everything from prohibitively expensive flights later in the day, to shuttling to London from Edinburgh or Birmingham. A seat on the same flight the next morning cost €100: four times the cost of my forfeited fare. *How much did I want this?* My inner voice: *Fun plans in London. Need to pause Schengen. Adventure. Do it!*

On the bright side, the test run was excellent practice for my identical journey the next morning. Beyond departing an hour earlier, I opted for a shorter, speedier security station, upstairs at Schönefeld. A further benefit was one less night overpaying for pricey London, or imposing upon friends. After the first few nights on a friend's couch, I had nowhere confirmed to stay. Living off around €120 a week meant I barely had budget for anything, even less now after buying replacement flights. I considered locking my bag in storage and sleeping on the streets of London. *For the story.* My former inner-homeless knew that surviving any one night was breezy: Stay up until dawn, find a cafe, then nap in a park or a library. I didn't feel like partying, but I would, if I had to.

The ebb and flow of a random one-way flight, with nothing locked in, on a shoestring budget, were romantic for a traveller, but, inconveniently, red flags for British national border security. Polite and professional, the tall middle-aged UK customs officer at Stansted Airport, nowhere near London, recited his list. "Ah, New Zealand passport," he mused.

"I am also applying for my new British passport."

"When is your return flight?" the officer asked.

I paused. "I don't know yet, Sir. I'm not sure if I'm flying back through Copenhagen next week, or direct to Berlin."

"Copenhagen? Why Copenhagen?" (Christiania alarm bells.)

"Well... my ex-girlfriend is there. I want to say goodbye."

"Who are you staying with here?" he inquired. I provided Wiki's name and mobile, but she didn't answer. "Can you provide a bank statement: Proof that you can afford to cover your expenses while you're here?" I couldn't and, with my actual bank balances totalling a few hundred bucks, I'd better not connect to wifi! The guard continued: "What do you do for work?"

"I run a domain company. I'm a digital nomad. I've been working on the road for a year now." He skeptically examined my business card, having seen a lot of counterfeits.

"Where do you call home?"

"I lived in Melbourne for twelve years, but I'm not going back."

"Are you returning to Berlin after England? For how long?"

"Yes, I'm heading back to Berlin afterward. I'm helping out at a friend's hostel: Sandino. Computer stuff and odd jobs. I'm staying there until I figure things out."

Further frowning, yet caring and sympathetic, the officer was posed with a professional dilemma. "Do you see my predicament?" he asked. "My job is to satisfy requirements, and everything you've answered raises questions. A lot of New Zealanders and Australians try to settle in the UK. I believe you, but I need proof you won't be staying beyond the time limit."

The matter of my British birth and pending passport application intrigued him enough for closer investigation. I was escorted to a segregated lounge area, that was walled by mid-height glass: short enough for scrutinisation and judgement by long slow queues of bored, groggy passengers. A younger, almost Maori-looking security guard was certain that all would be fine. I practiced Anapana: awareness of breath, calm the mind. At worst, if fate resolved for my entry to be denied, I'd return to Berlin. *Not so bad.*

The younger guard returned; he was less confident than earlier, and almost bewildered. Further sleuthing revealed details of my previous UK passport, that I lost twenty years ago, on the brink of homelessness. This essential passport information, once verified, confirmed that I was a legitimate British citizen. Relieved, the elder border officer returned.

"You should have told me about your past UK passport," he murmured patiently.

"I lost it a long time ago. I'm sorry."

After leading me to a quieter customs desk, he flipped a few buttons, and nearly forget to press something. He turned to me, adding in a serious, fatherly tone: "Good luck finding what you seek in life." His eyes made sure that mine acknowledged his words. I nodded respectfully, and thankfully.

Free to proceed, for the first time since the turn of century I stepped foot in my country of birth: England. I rode a modern coach towards Shoreditch, followed by an invigorating walk, through warm spring breeze to South Hackney. I reached the home of Wiki, New Zealander captain of our Underdogs Softball Club: 2009 Melbourne A-Grade Champions. Wiki had recently been living in London with her partner, Anna. I slept on a comfortable couch, at a home with stimulating and caring beings, for the opening nights of my English adventures.

Rave at an Underground Mushroom Farm

For the first time in five years, since a legendary party at my St. Kilda Beach apartment, pop star friend MZ Wood and I renewed acquaintances. I visited her spacious warehouse in Homerton, northeast London. Cooked breakfast was complemented by coffee and champagne, while we felt the foreboding, twitter-pated anticipation of revelry and naughtiness ahead.

Alongside MZ's housemate Bonkers, we taxied to the pre-party meeting spot, The Cause. Under remaining beams of the Sun in a covered laneway, we downed drinks and rolled smokes, while more guests arrived. Five luxury coaches rolled up, although not the double-decker buses that were promised in party marketing. There were loads of traveller drinks on board, and other naughty things were shared.

An hour into the journey, with two hundred revellers busting for a toilet break, the buses paused at a service centre. This was our last chance to grab supplies, concocting a queue for alcohol, mixers, smokes, conspiratorially expensive condoms, plastic water – for those not with reusable bottles – and snacks.

The buses drove further from modern civilisation, into rustic, hilly countryside. After exiting the main road, our slow elephant conga of coaches initially took the wrong turn. The smaller street was too narrow for the buses to turn around. I was busting to pee again, as were hundreds of others. I couldn't hold it; it was painful, and furthermore excruciating when we know that relief was many long minutes away. The buses very delicately backed up the long country road. I resigned that I would pee my pants.

The doors finally opened. Everybody barrelled out; dozens bolted and staggered to pee. There were rainbows of glorious, simultaneous golden splashes into sunshine and grass. *Pants Down, Panties Off; Smiles, Relief for Everyone.*

Upon mutually drip-drying, fellow P-crew member – a lovely blonde in a curvy red dress – paused for a Deep and Whimsical. We hypothesised repopulating post-apocalyptic civilisations.

"Want to get started tonight?" the curvy blonde enquired.

"...Um..." I blushed. "Sounds good!"

Nodding and grinning, we parted ways, while a stream of humans rumbled towards big beats that emanated from a barn. Indeed, it could be that kind of night: populating magical new civilisations, under worlds architected by mushrooms.

The horizon's panorama was cast upon a bright blue spring afternoon, beside a wooden barn in rolling English countryside. The orange Sun set over yellow fields and a grassy green hill. A prestigious Funktion-One soundsystem pulsed inside. A humble yet sizeable and popular bar was stationed outside. To revel in the rarity of warm English weather, most guests sat on the grass basking in sunshine, although it was still chilly in the shade.

As the evening unfolded, I danced away for hours, interspersed with rest breaks outside, that often encircled a fire. At one point MZ danced behind me, but we were on different planets, barely capable of speaking. In the end, there were no mushrooms – another unfilled promise from promotional spiel. It was still a pretty good party.

In flickering blackness, the fire warmed our bodies and souls, while collectively we all came down. Buses shuttled everybody back to The Cause, where most people departed, including MZ. Bonkers and I remained. We danced a little more; it soon became a handful of wasted guys dancing alone in darkness. On the cusp of daylight, returning to the warehouse with Bonkers, I attempted sleeping on a couch, while my serotonin levels began depleting. Lonely, I fired up Tinder for the first time in while.

...

After a few hours of sort-of sleep, on late Sunday morning I accompanied MZ to Hackney Marshes. There was a pair of open air parties that were adjacent to family football pitches. A queer party called Hot Box brought together all sorts – transgenders, pansexuals and more. I never even knew what a pansexual was, until this visit – basically, somebody who sleeps with any orientation. The other stage featured hardcore electronica, run by alleged squatters. Most people were off their chops: there was blatant and open drug use. On the football pitches, cursing sweaty ball-kicking men and anguished referees paid no notice, as disinterested wives sunbathed and kids ran around.

I stayed a while after MZ departed, before I embarked on the long, captivating walk home. I cruised past a major daytime music festival, that was loud and completely cordoned off by fences. Down tranquil canals and through lush parks, eventually I reached the botanical edges of Victoria Park, and then to Wiki's. Just as I was about to leave the empty apartment, Wiki's housemate Adolfo returned home. We chatted for hours while cooking spaghetti bolognese. Wiki, Anna, and Kelly – a meditator from San Francisco – arrived not long after, for a lovely evening.

Deep sleep and an early rise led into my first hour of meditation in days. With depleted serotonin, I deliberated about flying to Copenhagen to gain necessary closure with Boogie. London to Berlin direct was expensive, but Copenhagen prices were cheap. I didn't know if I was emotionally ready, but I wanted it done with. Either way, I booked a flight to Denmark.

An Italian in London

My flurry of lonely, almost desperate Tinder messages after the non-mushroom rave, resulted in a match. Subsequent friendly conversations led to organising Monday bank holiday plans. Meeting near the centre of London Fields, Milly and I grabbed a pair of exquisite wood-fired pizzas and bottles of juice. We sat on a park's thick, lush grass to become acquainted.

Milly was a 41-year-old petite Italian blonde, who'd lived in London for over a decade. She was in crisis: fresh out of a one-sided ten-year relationship, with a dominating man who had frequently cheated on her. Her father recently died. She was imprisoned by the drab corporate world and social taboo. My male hormonal inclinations evaporated, instead offering safe listening vibes for her. Milly confided that during her prior relationship of four years, she unwittingly discovered her partner was a radical Islamist – two years into the relationship! The final two years, she played the role of a submissive Islamic female. It sounded like Milly desperately needed her own self-freeing journey.

We wandered around London Fields at the peak of the Sun, visiting a petting zoo void of animals; perhaps they were also escaping the heat. Our first pub stop afforded a sliver of sunshine on a front patio, while we enjoyed a pint. Milly proposed another drink, suggesting a legitimate beer garden "closer to home". We sat comfortably in the back veranda of The White Hart. At one point Milly joked that she was a man, and sported manlike qualities.

"Do you have a strap-on?" was my best response. It surprised us both, as well as the eavesdropping table beside us. Milly blushed and shook her head. Yet, the question appeared to unlock a portal within her. After laboriously explaining why she *no longer* had a strap-on, she paused, and peered at me with a mischievous twinkle.

"Are you staying over tonight?" Milly asked. Impressed, I started to shrug in faux-cool acceptance, then her focus sharpened: "Would you like to have sex?"

I nearly fell off the bench. The two curious men at the adjacent table froze, similarly awed at Milly's frankness. Taking a long, calm breath to maturely process the request, I slowed down the Macarena lines of "Yes!!" that danced in my head.

"Sure..." I answered, as cool as I could muster.

The rest of the evening spun a comfortable, increasingly affectionate haze. We returned to Milly's modest third floor apartment in a row of dreary community flats. We downed leftover pizza, a bottle of wine and unpleasant cigarettes. Her living room featured a large, framed photograph, depicting the drab outside wall of a maximum security prison. Surely, staring at this every day could only agitate one's own emotional prison.

Milly's past included a short tenure as a part-time escort. She suffered from real estate ownership stresses, and nurtured deep, if not sometimes acrimonious, ties with her elderly Italian mother. Milly communicated humbly and matter-of-factly, without any apparent apathy, despite her recent sadness. At some point, conversation made way to mutual massages. Milly trampled over my back: an odd but pleasant sensation. A few times I woke up in the middle of deep dreams, alone in a comfortable queen bed. Milly couldn't sleep – noises from downstairs convinced her that the neighbours had entertained a succession of cheap prostitutes.

...

Like me, the morning came. After a chilli scrambled egg and coffee breakfast, we headed into our days. Milly bussed to her office job; I epically strolled around London, that included cafes and co-working visits. After satisfactorily completing work, I trekked an hour to London's glitzy Southbank. I eyed the bizarre Eye ferris wheel, while feeling apathy towards the tourist and commerce bustle of the prestigious riverside.

In the evening, I met Milly outside St. James Cathedral. My first double-decker bus of the visit shuttled us to a pizza parlour, for a dinner of tasty, thin-crust vegetarian pizzas, smothered with copious amounts of chilli. We picked up a bottle of Australian Malbec red wine, and returned to Milly's for the evening. She was more relaxed in some ways, but not sexually. She held lingering thoughts of her ex; naturally, I understood.

Singapore, Arambol and Auroville Reunions

At a coffee shop in the modern St. Pancras International Station, I met up with Wes, a classmate from our United World College days in Singapore. We hadn't seen each other in twenty-five years, since we were teenagers. Wes was married with children to a Malaysian wife, and recently concluded his job at a fitness company. He was seeking his next career opportunity, hoping to balance travel with family life.

On my way to the gigantic British Library, I stopped through a local museum, that was hosting an exhibition showcasing visual patterns of science in nature. Adorned atop vastly high modern walls were depictions of microscope enlargements of various cells, including the magnified eyes of fruit flies, and other random biological shapes. At the nearby library, many hundreds of people worked away from every available desk and corner. It was only on the top floor, at a small table, where I located a spare spot, albeit without a power outlet.

From the library I walked east, eventually resting under a secluded tree in London Fields. Anxious about my impending visit to Copenhagen, I indulged in an hour's Vipassana. I sipped tea at an independent cinema's bar with Nadia, one of the Australian sisters from our Discordia camp at Burning Man 2016. Nadia treated me to a complementary yoga class that she taught nearby. I had no place to stay for the night, and didn't want to bother Milly or other friends, so I booked a hostel near London's centre. This was the first time I'd seen, or slept on the top of, a triple bunk bed. The bunk was in a small, lightless and dusky room, that required midnight ascension up a long, tricky ladder: unviable for toilet missions.

In the morning I returned to the British Library, minutes before it opened; a huge queue wrapped around the block. Once inside, I located an available desk with an adjacent power socket. I worked productively most of the day. Notably, I sent a short and concise email to Boogie, to inform her of my impending arrival in Copenhagen.

I strode north, past London Fields, around Arsenal's Emirates Stadium, that was draped in a monstrous "Merci, Arsene" banner. I strode up to Finsbury Park, where Auroville's Louanna and Merlin awaited. We sipped fresh tea, occasionally relaxed in their hand-groomed garden, and enjoyed vegan treats. I was again astounded that Louanna was over seventy years old, and I had no idea of Merlin's age. The concept of age held dwindling importance to me. More crucial, was what we do with our time.

A fitting touch came a few days later, when many of these diverse energies converged, for a glorious evening picnic in Victoria Park. The serene spirits of British writer Jennifer, from our Arambol Roadhouse crew, Yasmine, another schoolmate at UWC in Singapore, and Auroville's Louanna, mingled over luxurious wine and ice cream. In the falling Sun we threw a tennis ball around. It was the most upbeat and promising my life had felt in a long while.

A Living Example of Grace

The power of Grace is clearly articulated towards the end of M. Scott Peck's book, The Road Less Traveled. Grace suggests the omnipresence of premonition, something that scientists are yet unable to explain, but clearly exists, as we are personally aware from our living observations. Clues and signs are revealed to us on a daily basis.

The weekend transpired at the sleepy seaside city of Brighton, in the south of England, for a rare live Thumpermonkey gig. I was thrilled to reunite with Thumpermonkey's singer, guitarist and songwriter Billy Tascademo, who I'd last seen when he visited one Toronto winter, fifteen years earlier. Billy met his eventual wife, Obijazz, on my old Universal Metropolis forums, and this was the first time I met her in person. Obijazz shared my birthday of June 23. Thumpermonkey's unique, intelligent, unpredictable math-rock metal, despite the sick absence of their lead guitarist, was unduly satisfying. Billy T barked over the microphone, balanced with soulful vocals, before raging walls of complex distorted rhythms churned under ricocheting percussion. At the show's end, as the DJ played to vacating space, we said our farewells. I walked forty minutes alongside the dormant Brighton coast, before a good night's sleep.

For breakfast, I sat down to coffee and toast in the dark musty basement at vibe-less Sobo House. This particular Sunday morning began with a surprising reply from Boogie. She confirmed that she was unable to meet during my Copenhagen visit. Coincidentally, hours before I was to arrive, she was flying home to Hungary as her mother's birthday surprise.

"The universe is playing a funny, random game on us. :) Probably for the better," Boogie mused.

The unusually lengthy email continued. Boogie seemingly recited every recent textbook she'd studied in her university psychology class. The email raised questions of attachment, patterns, psychological and philosophical ideas, rationality, emotion and so forth. I couldn't read it thoroughly; much of it felt robotic and contrived, although I was impressed she felt the need to share. In another way, I was tired of thinking about her. Yet, this email offered great relief. It took the edge off my Copenhagen trip, and meant I could enjoy it without stress. Our time to meet would come, when or if the universe decided. Hopefully we'd make our peace by Borderland.

Another useful email arrived, from the UK passport office; odd in its Sunday morning arrival. The message confirmed the existence of my previous UK passport. They requested that I submit a Lost/Stolen form, and handily provided my long-lost passport's number. Optimistically, this suggested a solid chance of my passport application's approval, perhaps expeditiously.

After this handy start to a reasonably hungover Sunday, I ambled to Alcampo Lounge in the heart of Brighton, to meet Billy T and Obijazz. After a decadent Hollandaise breakfast, we strolled to the heart of the ongoing Brighton Festival. We were lucky to locate a sun-shaded table at The Warren's busy beer garden, where we devoured several Grapefruit India Pale Ales. With both Brighton Festival and Brighton Fringe in full effect, we were frequently visited by comedians and performers touting their upcoming shows. A woman approached our table and presented a flyer for her forthcoming production, simply entitled "Grace". After listening to her spiel, I asked if the name was inspired by the magic of premonition: the mystical power of Grace. After thoughtfully deliberating, the actress murmured that it was not intended, courteously thanked me for the new interpretation, and departed. A flickering moment of familiarity prompted a further scan of the "Grace" flyer. The presenter was listed as Katie Reddin-Clancy.

"No way!" I yelped, startling beer-guzzling Billy and Obijazz.

Katie was an old colleague from the Red Bennies cabaret club era in Melbourne. Katie's social profile photograph matched that of the "Grace" flyer, and I bolted after her. I waited patiently while Katie delivered her spiel to another table.

"You bought me chocolates years ago!" I exclaimed. Katie stared back at me intently and inquisitively. "We are Facebook friends!" I presented the Facebook app on my phone. She remained puzzled but intrigued. Removing my Harry Potter-style glasses, I looked her in the eye. "Red Bennies!"

With huge wide eyes, Katie recognised me, and beamed. Six years ago Katie departed Melbourne for the UK. Before leaving she rewarded me with a "thank you" box of chocolates for helping her show.

"This is exactly what I meant by Grace and Premonition!" I proudly reiterated. After a routine catch-up, we continued back on our independent paths through the galaxy.

Shortly thereafter, Billy and Obijazz headed home to Croydon, and a few days later I joined them. In their creative den, I survived the wrath of a legendary house cat, plodded through a nature reserve with Billy T, that afforded distant hints of the tips of London skyscrapers, and enjoyed recollecting sounds and memories from our curious Universal Metropolis past.

Today transpired the first true sliver of magic on this trip, something that can never be forced, and usually emerges towards the end. When aware, Grace is regularly observable. Sometimes we stumble upon it.

Lost in Copenhagen

After waking early morning in Croydon, I bid farewell to sleepy Billy and Obijazz, and rode a long and expensive train to Stansted Airport. I rushed to check in, past hoards of dawdling awaiting passengers. The jet landed in the Danish capital on a balmy afternoon. I rode a modern train downtown, and stepped out in glorious warmth at Copenhagen's central station. I walked through joyous sunshine to my canal-side hostel, Bedwoods. Optimism was evident from the hundreds of devoted cyclists, and pedestrians who basked in the heat.

I organised my belongings around my bunkbed, that was built with strong, polished wood, and featured useful privacy curtains. I set out on a brisk stroll to the mystical autonomous civilisation of Christiania. Copenhagen was prohibitively expensive. *I'd have to love somebody to live here.* The hostel was €36 for one night. Two cans of beer, a package of rolling papers and a cheap lighter cost nearly €12. A gram and a half of "Super Sativa" ran another €12.

While sitting in the popular amphitheatre in the heart of Christiania, I rolled and smoked a mediocre, wind-disabled joint. The Sativa elevated my reflection. I felt plentiful colliding forces swirling around: This was Boogie's domain. It was, virtually, the closest we'd been since our farewell – even if in energy only.

Two men from Ghana sat beside me. They were impressed of my affinity for Malawi and lengthy stays in Cape Town. Denmark maintained waste recycling programmes that, like Berlin's, served as a popular income stream for migrants and the destitute. However, while specific cans and bottles were popular, a particular type of soda bottle was frequently ignored: Faxe. Why? Because the recycling station for these bottles was farther away. This prompted a social experiment engineered by one Ghanian man, who asked each collector why one bottle was good enough to take, while the other was not. Why not gather both to help dispose litter? The exercise broadcast metaphors of discrimination in its own way.

At some point, I rolled another joint. In a flicker of a flinch, during a self-defeating thought related to The Past, a fierce breeze blew. Futilely, I grasped to catch flying weed, while simultaneously dropping my phone; its screen smashed. This felt like appropriate karma for breaking Boogie's iPod in Seoul that angry, drunken November night. The material damage from breaking my phone had minimal effect on me, but spiritually I felt I deserved this.

With the wind causing havoc, I delegated a neighbouring group of youngsters to roll my remaining Super Sativa. They presented a phenomenally giant and potent joint laced with tobacco. Not long after smoking, my head rush kicked in to the max. I needed somewhere in nature to close my eyes and chill.

After bidding adieu to the Ghanian men, I walked around picturesque Christiania. Strolling around the lake, through trees, I found a park bench and attempted to meditate. Fatigued, l lay on the bench and briefly napped, of the unsleeping, head-spin-control variety. Eventually, I my gathered senses, chose a random direction, and became lost in Copenhagen. The eerie walk alone reiterated that The Past was entirely that.

...

Time cascaded pleasantly and slowly, with a full day in Copenhagen before a prospective overnight bus to Berlin. I was open-minded to postponing my return, if I was inspired, or if new opportunities presented themselves.

At 1pm I met Luna, an erotic sound artist, with whom I considered collaborating at Borderland's Pyramid. Luna toured me around Christiania. We lounged at a miniature, sandy beach, amid a scattering of topless sunbathers. I had the privilege of meeting Esprano, one of Christiania's earliest residents. His boat bobbed, as we reconnected with the tides in our bodies. We discussed a range of alternate societies, including the uniquely progressive movement behind Christiania. Esprano shared his big news: that very day he fulfilled a lifelong dream of acquiring a particular sailing vessel.

After parting ways with Luna, the Sun began its descent. I rushed through Christiania to my next appointment: an interview about Auroville with Boogie's classmate. *Who was this guy meeting me? Why did Boogie choose Auroville as a school project, and interview me for it?* Thankfully, the meeting was delayed, and I ambled further through the lushness of Christiania. Sitting cross-legged in adequate seclusion, I began Vipassana, surrounded by peaceful insects and other creatures. By meditation's end, inner resolutions composed themselves, while powerful gusts of wind whirled around me.

Outside Christianshavn Station, I met Boogie's classmate: a handsome, bespectacled Syrian named Mazen. He was a tad nervous, a dash excited and wholly respectful; a gentleman from beginning to end. There seemed an impressed curlosity wilhin him, and I wondered what he knew of me. With a pair of ginger beers, we sat on an umbrella-sheltered bench outside a cafe in Christiania. The first twenty minutes of our recorded interview discussed my impressions of Aurovillian society. There were elements I couldn't answer, such as individual Aurovillians' sentiments about certain topics, or the exact process for how decisions are made: seemingly slowly. We recorded two smaller segments about Auroville's innovations and certain hinderances to the city's growth. When asked about cultivating similar societies around the world, I shared an ongoing rumination: of re-vitalising abandoned mining towns in Australia and elsewhere. Yet, instead of dedicating a lifetime to each project, the objective was to research and draft how-to technical papers. These blueprints would help inhibit communities anywhere to set up autonomous, self-protected miniature states.

"Interview over!" Mazen exclaimed, as he packed away his gear. He was clearly captivated about my regular life and travels. After a pause: "Are you in love?" he asked bluntly.

I pondered the present truth. "Yes," I responded, solemnly. "I am in love with somebody, who does not feel the same."

He peered at me compassionately over his spectacles. Mazen, an artist, had lived in Copenhagen for over two years, following stints in Istanbul, Beirut and Damascus. His impressive cubist-impressionist painting style was alike Picasso. Mazen similarly considered Berlin as a potential base. He wanted to know where I thought of settling, if there was any particular spot. I did not then know the answer. "Auroville is one possibility." I might have mentioned Goa. I also raised the van idea.

He beamed at me: "Next time you're in Copenhagen, you have a place to stay, with me!" As we walked towards the train station, he continued his questioning. "What would it take for you to settle down?" Mazen asked rhetorically, not necessarily expecting an answer. "For me: a woman."

I understood what he meant. Prior to my recent return to a solo path, I'd have moved almost anywhere for the "right" person. Despite initially hesitating, I agreed.

"I see what you mean. Yes, if the right person was somewhere in particular, I would spend more time there. However, I would still travel as needed. Especially in winter."

Before we bid adieu, something still puzzled him, like a final unsolved mystery.

"One more thing." Mazen paused. "About your love. Did you meet her in Denmark?"

"Yes, I did."

Seemingly relieved at unfolding a riddle known only to him, Mazen's eyes gleamed again. Our final philosophical musing touched upon objectivity: How to accept pain as temporary. To embrace joy as momentary treasure and, when blessed to experience it, enjoy every moment. Mazen relaxed into his farewell. With care brimming in his eyes, he grinned.

"About your love. Be optimistic." Mazen shook my hand, firmly and graciously. Perhaps his curiosity was how Boogie and I knew each other. She must have said something. "*Be optimistic*"??

Enlightened from new mysteries, I returned to Christiania to fetch several small bags of Sativa. Next was a power walk towards Copenhagen central station, for my final meeting of the trip, with Jay, the organiser of Borderland's orchestra. The meeting was an hour away, but I hoped to find a cafe or restaurant for writing.

With little more than a vague idea of the station's direction, intentionally avoiding online maps, I walked through Copenhagen's deserted inner-city streets. Silhouettes of historic buildings reflected off shimmering, wind-swept canals. The roads weaved and bobbed, while construction blockades occasionally thwarted pedestrian progress. To reaffirm that I was on the right path, I asked a group for help; a local man helpfully confirmed that I was correctly heading in the general direction. There was any combination of streets I could take. I revelled in being lost, weaving around curving foreign roads, crossing diagonally when appropriate.

On one avenue, I stopped to check the clock and messages. Forty minutes remained before the meeting. I looked at the property beside me. *Oh my...*

MOJO BLUES BAR

This was Boogie's favourite place in all of Copenhagen. She

regularly played bass here on Thursdays; tonight was Thursday. Taking a deep breath, I entered. Mojo was a small vintage rock venue, that was popular for its open jam nights. Its well-stocked corner bar stood straight past the entrance. The stage could comfortably hold half a dozen musicians.

I sat with a fresh pint of chilled pale ale. Jay was to meet me here. A few tables to my left was a couple. The slender brunette wore glasses, with the same hair as Boogie, and my mild psychosis returned. I wondered if it was her: *Perhaps she lied and never went to Hungary*. I was at peace with that, and even if that was her new boyfriend. Yet, I knew the real Boogie would have a wholly different reaction to me sitting there.

When Jay arrived, we chatted about Borderland, the ambitious Pyramid as an experimental sound structure, and bolder concepts. Sometimes it was hard to hear each other above the music blasting from the stage. Towards the end of the first blues band, three pretty young women entered the bar. So they could sit, I pulled two seats from an adjacent "Reserved" table. The musician who'd left a guitar there seemed happy elsewhere, so I moved the guitar to the edge of our table, and pushed our spare seat towards the girls. The ladies were delighted at the courtesy; the brooding musician was not so appreciative. He scowled, while heavy-handedly relocating the guitar to another table. Grumbling, he glared at me for ages, doubtlessly sharing the story to chums, of the betrayal of his male privilege. I sure left my mark at Mojo.

After Jay cycled off through the night streets of Copenhagen, I navigated the fifteen minute walk to the bus terminal. Exhaustedly crammed in a seat, next to another tall and gangly man, I pondered everything: this busy trip, today's magic, Mazen's questions and his advice. How could I wander, absolutely lost through a foreign city, and stop outside the favourite landmark of the girl I missed and loved? The powers of Grace and premonition are often unwitting to the conscious mind. Today was the spell's final ingredient, built from each preceding day, punctuating a journey that only becomes magical upon its whole.

Roxanne, resident chicken at Sandino World Improvement Network, Berlin

Chapter 11

Chicken Meditation

Aural frequencies from Radio Paradise shimmied a diverse assortment of eclectic sounds and beats across a quaint, red brick courtyard. A pair of eager, shirtless young men whacked away at table tennis, and others milled, with any combination of breakfast, coffee and smokes, in the numerous comfortable nooks and crannies scattered around Berlin's Sandino World Improvement Network. Guests read books or caught up on writing; many were absorbed in digital life on their phones, while others simply basked in sunshine, amidst a pleasantly open and inclusive vibe. The communal open kitchen was abuzz with the clanging of pots, pans and plates, with guests' supplies stashed between two large fridges and numerous cupboards.

Three restored buildings of the former East German sausage factory joined with reception and the main lounge to create walls that encircled the classic European courtyard. A small iron gate opened to a spacious, grassy garden, that was adorned with tents of varying shapes and sizes. A large teepee towered in the centre of the garden. The nubile vegetable garden was complemented by spring sprouts on branches of big old trees, and freshly budding plants.

At certain intervals, arrived the careful clucking of Sandino's two resident chickens: mischievous Roxanne and shy Maxine. The friendly fowls were uncannily able to observe and recognise strangers from afar. Once confident, the chickens would cautiously emerge to greet their guests, slowly and thoughtfully, as full as love and trust possible from the favoured prey of plentiful carnivores on Earth.

"There is nothing more sincere than earning the trust of animals," mused Shami, during one of our many invigorating conversations.

Sandino was the gracious host of my first European spring, and became my home for most of the summer ahead. The hostel loaned me a bigger tent, that was tall enough for comfortable meditation, and sufficiently wide for visitor sleepovers. Erected in the shadiest, far corner of the garden, the tent was protected from the Sun by well-established trees and a high wooden wall. On most mornings I woke around 7am, and plunged into an hour's Vipassana meditation. The blend of organic nature in the garden, the calm placidity of chickens, the presence of readily-available herbal supplements, and laid back nature of Berlin, combined for a serene and satisfying atmosphere.

The barter, in exchange for my tent (saving me €70 a week in rent) was assisting Sandino with everything web: social media, improving the old website, building a new one, and general tech assistance. Every week I uploaded dozens of photos and stories from a given year in Sandino's history, accumulating a growing visual timeline that was popular with staff, guests and community followers. I hand-coded two mobile-responsive booking forms, in English and German, that resulted in sharp boosts in direct reservations, and saved Sandino cash by eliminating third-party booking fees. My solitary struggle was devising the new website: What platform to build it on? I was loathe to deploy WordPress or pay developers to set it up, but the alternative required a lot of my time programming. Whatever, we seemingly had time to figure it out.

I helped keep Sandino's kitchen, lounge, garden and courtyard tidy. I fulfilled errands for staff upon request, such as running to shops, and sought to help settle in guests, particularly the shyer ones, as comfortably as possible. Occasionally I facilitated internal activities, such as World Cup screenings and group hangouts. For most of my tenure I ran popular group meditations every morning. These were not part of the barter, but were tasks I was pleased to undertake, to help nurture a stellar Sandino atmosphere for everybody.

My intimate chats with Shami resumed daily. At 8am, Shami would sleepily, frantically pace around reception, initiating his duties for the day. I attended to emails and tasks over coffee and breakfast. As the Sun rose towards its peak, more of the holiday-minded guests casually filtered into the lounge; it became too distracting to work there. Many of the guests brimmed with curious questions, about my adventures and freelance nomadism. In the afternoons I generally vacated to a circular table in the back garden, that afforded privacy, peace and solitude, with occasional appearances from the clucking chickens. When his shifts finished, Shami joined me, conversing further about life, love, books and society.

One of Sandino's most distinct early guests was a large, whimsical young man named Flowa. He was a devout participant in the underground electronic music scene, affiliated with local Berlin clubs and bigger festivals, like Fusion. Flowa's creative passion was concocting powerful ginger shots, and blending ginger with other fruit and herbs for potent, energising juice. Flowa was a regular, naked guest at legendary underground sex club, Kit Kat Club, and was flamboyant in his colourful clothes and extroverted persona. However, he was completely straight: no drugs or alcohol. Flowa lived in the central teepee, metres away from my corner tent.

Meditation became a vital complement of Sandino's activities and lifestyle, that lent to heightened tranquility. I met one of the new guests, Percival – an American B-movie writer and director – who was a past Vipassana practitioner. Astonishingly in this summer's early days, Sandino hosted at least four Vipassana mediators simultaneously. Percival's uncertain business hustle sought to package pre-recorded guided meditation for profit, but for a few days he coached free sessions for Sandino's willing guests and eager staff. He and I bonded well, at least at the beginning; we chatted frequently and played long cooperative matches of table tennis.

After a few sessions, Percival lost interest in facilitating group meditation, seemingly in conflict with his inner-capitalist. The others encouraged me to continue and lead the morning sessions. Daily meditation held several inherent benefits. The hostel's vibe became increasingly more chill and upbeat. The two chickens absolutely adored the serenity. Whenever our circle of poultry-eating humans closed our eyes, the chickens understood their blessed safety, perhaps even sensing the magical electricity emitting around our concentrating group. On regular occasions the chickens clucked around us, with Roxanne often sitting near or on her chosen meditator of the day. Sweet Maxine observed from a little further away, while sometimes braving closer. Upon opening our eyes, we were regularly greeted by the chickens' contented basking in glorious sun.

Whether it was our core quartet – usually Shami, Clara, Jill and myself – or up to thirty guests who joined for the session on Shami's birthday, the chickens mingled, integrated and meditated. This is how we coined one of the summer's defining phrases: Chicken Meditation.

J-Man, Jono and Bonobo UFO

Guests at hostels are transient, coming and going like space travellers to faraway planets. We meet people, make acquaintances and share time. Then one, the other or everybody heads off on their separate, distinct paths through the cosmos. With particularly kindred energies where orbits are compatible, we may cross paths again, but the only certainty is movement and change. We are all constantly barrelling through the galaxy.

An epic weekend was brewing for Bonobo's live concert at Berlin's UFO Velodrome. Eminent Captain J-Man – fellow New Zealander and jet-setting international Burner – flew in from Sydney for an impromptu catch up.

Disappointing news arrived, upon word that my main contract was cancelled. The project was to develop a bland but sizeable and well-compensated mortgage comparison app. The client was messily separating from his wife, who was also a registered business partner. By missing out on thousands of Euro from the remainder of the project, it confirmed that my van would not materialise this summer. It also predicated further months of financial scramble ahead, and an urgency to uncover new leads.

Deep in one meditation session in my tent, during the final garden flickers of the Sun, I felt trickles of anguish towards my father. I was disappointed that he may not live long enough to truly learn the meaning of happiness. I acknowledged our time remaining on this planet together was limited.

Additional stress accumulated through the nearing proximity and expectational magnitude of the Sun Moon Sea concert, scheduled for Borderland's Pyramid. While I prepared for a simpler iteration of my ambitious dreams, there still remained much to coordinate. My tasks were distracted by ongoing heartache. I battled myriad imaginary simulations of crossing paths with Boogie, an awkward meeting that would undoubtedly materialise at Borderland.

Between all my dilemmas, I was overjoyed and relieved to catch up with genuine old friends. J-Man arrived on the Friday morning donning his customary sailor cap; he instantly loved Sandino and Berlin. Jono's arrival later that evening was a surprise, as he never confirmed his visit! Jono and J-Man met for the first time. Preliminary niceties warmed their first conversations, and on Saturday we began tackling each of our challenges. After sharing our personal projects, we agreed to pick one each for primary focus, and we'd help each other how we could. I selected Nomadic Cloud, that I misguidedly believed in at this time. Jono by now was passionately reviving Memtell. J-Man's choice of venture was Death Counter: a social calculator that tallied one's individual footprint of death and destruction, caused by our personal purchasing decisions and lifestyle habits.

On Saturday night, J-Man landed a ticket to the Bonobo concert, while Jono headed to meet friends elsewhere in Berlin. Our multinational concert crew included a pair of lovely German brothers, a tall Dutch named Thijs, Percival scored a last minute ticket, and a new pal from the Berlin Burners pub night – Rachel from Taiwan. Pre-drinks were complemented by a hearty BBQ, served by retired Michelin-star chef Carsten.

The tram and stroll to the appropriately-named UFO brought us into the thick of thousands of awaiting patrons, who filed slowly into the Velodrome. We entered to witness thousands more guests already inside, with the blurry stage far in the distance. Unperturbed, I led our crew along a narrow pathway between the gigantic left wall and large throngs of spectators. We walked alongside the wall to the very front security railings, that separated the crowd from backstage. Then a sharp right, following the stage's railings into sufficient space. We were one row from the front, a few steps left from dead front centre. Best spot in the house! Impressed members of our group took turns to load up on drinks and pass around cheeky smokes.

Bonobo's concert was characteristically professional. Simon Green, a.k.a. Bonobo, stood on a central riser, with a controller, keyboards, a mixer, sampler, effects, cymbal and a bass guitar.

The supremely proficient band was comprised of a drummer, keyboardist, guitarist and horn section, divided on opposite sides around Bonobo. White spotlights shone from behind the stage, underneath a mammoth visual projection screen. The humble band truly enjoyed their music, heads down with no ego or fuss. Perhaps there was a hint of the melodramatic, when wasteful tons of single-use glitter fell from the ceiling upon the band's dramatic finale.

After the concert, many thousands of enlightened concert-goers shuffled outdoors. During our group's uncertainty about where next for everybody, the voice in my head urged remaining longer. We descended a staircase and followed the sounds of cheers, reaching a joyful mass sing-a-long, with an excellent busker who played outside one of Velodrome's lower exits. I sat by the arena's outer wall and rolled a big joint for our crew, while others danced and sang along.

As I stood and sparked the joint, the buzz kicked in. From a distance I noticed two gorgeous, well-dressed women chatting with each other; the brunette stared at me. Then, with unbridled German confidence, the women headed our way, and cleverly integrated with our group. The brunette approached me in the midst of my speechless, post-spliff paranoia. Both girls were interesting and interested, Percival was up for accompanying and, after the rest of the group departed, our foursome headed into the electric Berlin night.

At this point I didn't know many suitable clubs, and the girls weren't from Berlin; instead they hailed from a smaller, more southernly town. My vague recollection from last year's Berlin trip led us to a man-made island off the Spree, and we entered an outdoor club called Ipse.

Jenni and I hit it off immediately. She was comely, smart and charismatic. Both of the girls' English was perfect, after years living in Australia. Eventually we moved inside into a darker part of the club, on a discrete level above the DJ booth. There was a sudden moment the girls decided to leave, that felt like they lost interest. Contrastingly, our goodbye outside under the stars featured Jenni pulling me towards her, then kissing me long and hard. Her friend appeared as astonished as I was.

...

Back at Sandino, an eventful week was brewing. Top chef Carsten cooked up impressive communal meals, almost nightly. He graciously relented to, if not humorously grumbling about, vegetarian requests from "pacifist hippies". Carsten prepared luscious salads with fresh dressings, juicy burgers with creamy and fragrant sauces, and sizzling, tender meat for the carnivores. Many of the vegetables and herbs were picked from Sandino's nubile garden.

A wave of good news greeted a balmy thirty-degree day: Jenni from Bonobo found me through the Plan Sea website. Camping plans near a remote lake sounded like a fun possibility. On the money side, an Air Help legal claim for my cancelled Paris to Frankfurt flight unexpectedly earned me hundreds of Euros in compensation. Jono, J-Man and I made substantial progress. We vowed to narrow our focus to a handful of concurrent projects, instead of our attention scattered across dozens of ideas.

Jono departed earlier in the week, while J-Man remained another few days. On his final afternoon, J-Man gulped a first bottle of white wine on an empty stomach, that rendered him wholly incoherent by midday. At night, having ingested several further bottles of wine, J-Man interrogated a surprisingly-accommodating Clara about the deepest secrets of her life. There were numerous, classic J-Man bouts of awkwardness, in the wake of his piercing but honest questions. Stunned onlookers sat in bewildered silence, while Clara, after pauses, willingly yet carefully dove into intimate rabbit holes.

The drunken Captain J-Man was highly reluctant to depart Berlin. Waking him required my throwing several pillows and glasses of water on him through an open window. He eventually stirred in time to sleepily grab his suitcase and catch his flight, with a wretched hangover. J-Man had an important Burning Man Australia meeting to attend in Sydney. He intentionally left his prized sailor hat at Sandino.

One of the guests was a twenty-year-old yoga instructor from America. She took immediate curiosity in me, participated in group meditation, and occasionally taught post-meditation yoga sessions. Easy to talk with and mature beyond her years, she frequently visited me in between pockets of my writing and Borderland planning. The vibe was comfortable enough, open-minded and playful. On the final evening of her stay, before she ducked out to the supermarket for food, she approached my seat on the cushioned metal swing near Sandino's entrance.

"Would you like to meditate tonight?" she asked innocently.

"Sure..."

She smiled, nodded and headed on her way. Although my inner-male pondered her intentions, I didn't overthink, and certainly didn't raise false hopes: She was young. Later, we chatted late into the night, while most guests lay in tents and beds. She repeated the request: Did I want to meditate? I had a feeling where this would lead, although I'd experienced a lifetime of misinterpreting female intentions. We headed to my tent, and attempted to meditate in silence. We sat on the mattress facing each other with our eyes closed, and began deeply breathing. After a few minutes, I detailed reflections of sensations. She turned around, with her back in front of me; I casually brushed her skin, and it was on. By early morning she headed onto her next universal voyage..

The tents in the garden were close enough that practically all sounds were audible to everybody else. Several fellow campers heard everything from my tent. Playful gossip eventually reached the impressed curiosity of Shami the following afternoon. I was shyly discovering my unprecedented attraction to a whole range of desirable women. The sole element dragging me down, was my blind, devout attachment to The Past, with our daunting reunion beckoning at Borderland. This was an encounter I naïvely imagined would be the final border between healing, and over it.

Rekindling of an Indian Flame

In a lifetime of special connections perhaps, the most inspirational person I've encountered along my travels was Dawn. Age 88, Dawn spawned wisdom that transcended millennia. He was fit, spry, healthful and upbeat. A regular, lifelong traveller, Dawn did good things in the world, including previously operating an Amazon rainforest NGO. He was born transgender, eventually became a boy, although he brimmed with motherly instincts. He loved ballet and had written books.

Presently he was studying ancient Chinese numerology. Dawn's secrets to everlasting vitality were: Water, Walking, Weed (no tobacco). His prodigy grandson was also visiting; together they'd voyaged the world. Dawn proved that age was a concept. There was no acting one's age, or as anyone else at all. Unless, of course, you're an actor.

Before one morning's group meditation, of which he'd not yet participated, Dawn depicted an illustration of the circle, noting that the group's optimal alignment would factor meditators' astrological signs. With the 11am Sun towering from the south, backing Cancer – my sign – he suggested my back should align with the south. Capricorn, the polar opposite, should sit across from me, facing the Sun. Dawn humorously theorised that people born below the equator would have the opposite star sign, as stars in the southern hemisphere appeared differently. No wonder Australians were so confused!

While becoming better acquainted with Dawn, I awaited news from Aura, of "A Rooftop in Bangalore". Aura was returning from India and heading to Berlin. She'd experienced an unwitting detention by Indian authorities for overstaying her ninety day visa by nine days. For her Indian visa, the ninety days began from the date of the visa's issue, not the date of her arrival. Under the responsible care of the Deutsche Botschaften, the process required around a week of painstaking bureaucracy before clearance for departure. In the meantime, she was minded in a plush Delhi flat with a cook and cleaner.

I weighed postponing my Schengen border run plans to the following weekend, versus not seeing Aura for months. Postponing my latest UK trip meant abandoning a mystery romantic rendezvous, in Glasgow with one of two Italians. I'd found a cheap flight to Scotland, then I hoped to discover Manchester for the first time, stay a day or two in London, then fly back. It was a quick mission with a solitary objective: depart Europe on my NZ passport, and return on my new British one. The Glasgow rendezvous was cancelled anyway, but I had the flight, and needed to make the trip.

Aura's inconvenience became my saviour. I found another cheap flight to London a week later. The original flight to Scotland would have arrived hours before the awful Glasgow

School of Art fire – not the happiest or safest vibe in the city. Another benefit, beyond skipping pointless, expensive travel, afforded more focus on my projects. I plugged away on wireframes and mockups of prospective new Sandino websites, and continued mingling with guests, particularly Dawn.

In the wake of the death of author and chef Anthony Bourdain, I opened an online discussion about the right for somebody to take their own life. *Why was suicide so prevalent and rising in artificial, man-made society? Why was there no media uproar about the suicide pandemic?* My advice to anybody depressed enough, is to radically change a few elements – location, relationship, job, friends, hobbies, etc – and embark upon a new quest. Even a few tweaks or alterations can make a large impact on our psyches, while being aware of whatever energies or elements drag us down. One must have something worthwhile to look forward to, and be driven by purpose.

"You only get this human life once, and it's short." Dawn looked me dead in the eye, as if he suspected my recent in-difference to continuing this mortal existence.

June 13, 2018, arrived: a multifaceted milestone. Aura was to arrive from India this evening. It was the first anniversary of my departing Melbourne. It was the birthday of the late father of my first girlfriend. His passing away in 1998 expedited the end of my acrimonious relationship, and instantly spurred my two years of homelessness. Additionally, this marked nine months since I landed in Seoul.

On the same day, word arrived that Borderland, due to petty zoning issues in its political jurisdiction, might be moved to a new venue. There was a chance the festival would be cancelled altogether. Without the Pyramid, my original Sun Moon Sea vision was impossible. The whole art of the idea was based around experimental sound design in this specific structure. I leaned towards selling my ticket and ridding the headache altogether, as The Past had become nothing but a distraction.

Three months since we parted ways in Bangalore, I greeted Aura at Berlin's Tegel Airport. Aura bounded through her gate with her eyes and face glowing. I carried her bulging Indian army backpack, and we headed towards public transportation, making the fifty-minute journey to Lichtenberg. Our first evening at Sandino was low-key and lovely. Shami was pleased to meet a German friend of mine. Timeless Dawn held an avid fascination of Aura's independent female journey through India. Aura and I prepared fresh salad, red wine and platters of cheese. We sat around the fire, sharing stories and tales, wondrously relaxing. It had the special energy of reuniting with a dear old friend, even though we hadn't known each other for long.

Jet-lagged, Aura fell asleep easily, while I suffered a chilling vision, either from Indica weed or premonition. My mind sharpened on one person: Citronella. The mystery of what happened on the mushroom night on Jeju Island flashed back. My revelations were unprecedentedly painful, sharp and puncturing. I wondered if he wanted Boogie to himself. Emotions revisited my pining for The Past, and a self-inflicted sting of futile, misguided jealousy, that should not matter.

...

The next afternoon, Aura and I embarked on another random walk, infinitely heading southwest towards the Sun. We discovered an excellent Vietnamese restaurant with creamy mango-coconut shakes. At a nearby park we sat outside in the shade. We more deeply shared our recent relationship encounters. I learned of her ex; they'd mutually agreed to move on. Aura learned the fundamentals of my own sadness, the gist of Korea, and my months of recovery since.

The next day, Friday, was one of those weird energy days for everybody; probably something in the stars. Cancelling the morning meditation amplified its impact, particularly with Shami stressing deeply about a legitimately grave hostel issue. Shami had a limited window within which to solve it: we dubbed it the "B Situation". I was alongside Shami the moment Jack delivered the bad news, and it unwittingly stoked the beginning of the end of good vibes at Sandino.

One of Sandino's more prominent guests was Dutch-African Rose. Rose was a big girl, pumped up with dangerous anti-psychotic medication, that had a knack of ballooning its recipients' bodies, as though they were obese. I'd mistakenly assumed Flowa was grossly overweight, but, like Rose, he was on anti-psychotics. Rose felt a need to interject her boisterous opinions into every passing conversation, relevant or not. Her behaviour became more erratic. Compassionately, but losing patience, I politely requested she consider the art of listening.

Granted, it was Rose's idea for Aura and I to attend the open air cinema screening of Wes Anderson's *Isle of Dogs*, at historic Freiluftkino in Kreuzberg. Uncannily similar to my own dog movie I'd intended to release in 2018, Isle of Dogs was a strange story about outcast, post-apocalyptic canine society in Japan.

After the film, further inebriated from another bottle of addictive chocolate wine, I became lost in thought, while feeling mentally and emotionally fatigued. Aura and I maintained some distance during the walk and on the train. Aura this interpreted as an insult, while I saw it as creating a modicum of space. With people constantly around at the hostel, I rarely had time to myself. This, with the exacerbation of unfriendly messages Aura received from her disjointed ex, led to the first rift in our harmony. In a huff, Aura felt inclined to prematurely depart for her home of Dresden the next morning.

On Saturday, after a refreshing sleep, we woke rested and abundantly optimistic. The morning group meditation, dedicated to the impermanence of pleasure and pain, was a boon to Sandino's collective spirits. Aura opted for a later bus, affording us to spend the day together. Following lunch, barefooted Aura and shoe-clad I walked north to Weissensee Park. We found a cozy spot under shady trees, beside a lake where ducks paddled and splashed around. With a bottle of wine and rolling tobacco, we opened up deeply, invariably becoming closer. I bared my heart, and revealed everything that troubled me. It exposed raw wounds, that inexplicably battered me as viciously as the day Boogie and I split. Aura learned she was the first after my ex, and how challenging that night on the Bangalore rooftop had been for me. Her ex was hurt that she was spending quality time with me.

Our time at the lake was upbeat and unifying. Aura and I strengthened the bonds of a unique, blossoming relationship. We remained solid on our individual paths, while destined to sporadically interconnect at various intervals. Aura was a sensational energy with whom to share a sliver of life. However, irrespective of what I felt for her, she was my rebound: a bridge between the past and future. Without a bridge there was no crossing, but the bridge can neither be the departure nor the destination. In many ways, it was true, open love, but it's difficult to accept, and possibly impossible, as one person always, inevitably, wants more.

24 Hours in London

The Schengen Assignment arrived during a welcome time to take a break. Cracks began to surface at Sandino, in an otherwise dream season to date. The initial negative energy was Percival. He resented the popularity of our group meditation, for my continuing to run it, and me in general, even though I only took the role when he quit on everybody. Percival clearly ignored me, and exhibited oddly anti-social behaviour, confiding only with Brighton, our usually-delightful resident gay, during their animated, secluded evening chats.

Percival's disdain for me was so intense, and timing as such, I wondered if he'd meddled with Danish council politicians to disrupt Borderland. Once he offered everybody at Sandino an apple; mine, passed to me via Shami, appeared to have something welted in it. "A poisoned apple?" Shami asked, only half jokingly. I chucked the suspect apple in the corner of the garden. Other times Percival won favour by cooking for everybody, but ensured that I had the last helping, if any.

The B Situation started to blow up. Several guests became aware of the underlying issue; some chatted loudly about it, while staff attempted to keep everything hushed. Meditation helped smooth the overall vibe, but in Shami's dedication to desperately solving the B problem, he skipped numerous sessions, exacerbating his struggles to cope. We all knew this was a hugely stressful period, with Sandino's reputation on the line. However, Shami's outbursts – that predated the B Situation – were always unpleasant, sometimes shocking, to receive. Like a family, we were patient, we forgave and we battled through. We knew Shami was stressed, but why be cruel?

Perhaps the craziest day of the entire summer was the Monday, days after Aura departed. On the morning following Jack's fun, late-night birthday at various Berlin clubs, we arose late and feebly to a highly peculiar energy around Sandino. Rose, who was amped up on her anti-psychotics, was about to explode. Her loud domination of conversations and attention-seeking, elevated to fever pitch, and she became universally ignored by other guests. This influenced her to try harder, becoming louder and angrier.

Sucking back several, big puffs of a tobacco-stuffed Indica hash joint a guest unwittingly left on a table, plunged Rose into irreversible paranoia. It triggered extreme mood swings, where she crashed and writhed around on the ground. Rose dropped and smashed glass and bottles, while helpless guests further ignored her, or unsuccessfully attempted aiding her, as she spiralled lower. This drama endured for many hours. Shami and staff handled it as well as possible, albeit embarrassingly explaining the situation to arriving guests. It caused prolonged uneasiness across the complex.

At a certain point, after hours of Rose's nonsense, Shami's patience expired, and he rightfully ordered Rose to pack up and leave. Eventually she did, wheeling a bicycle loaded with her bags to the front gate, before (seemingly) accidentally dropping more bottles. Then, with one final glance before leaving, seconds from the drama mercifully concluding, her bike toppled over, bags and bottles crashed on the courtyard, and Rose lashed around the floor.

A dozen police arrived with an ambulance, a mental health unit, and a team for cardiac arrests. Fighting the police, Rose – a large, strong girl – was handcuffed on the ground, kicking and screaming. Four officers strapped her to the ambulance's stretcher. She furiously blamed and threatened all of us. After Rose was carted away, despite a welcomed onset of peacefulness, Sandino was collectively exhausted from the tedious ordeals of the day.

...

My critical passport trip served as a timely respite. Following minimal sleep, I rode to Schönefeld Airport and hopped on a red-eye flight to London. There was no trouble, either exiting Schengen on my New Zealand passport, or during rapid processing at London Stansted on first use of my fresh UK credentials. I didn't see the previous border guard. A two-hour, traffic-stalled bus transfer to London's Liverpool Street Station dispatched me in the middle of the city. After breakfast in a historic old building, I headed for the Barbican Centre. The modern complex featured art galleries and music studios, with the sprawling Barbican Library at its core. I found a long, quiet bench table, and typed away for hours.

Listening to an inner-gospel choir full of premonitions, I made the critical decision to cancel my Borderland plans. The change of venue disrupted everything I desired to attain in the unique Pyramid space, and amplified what was already a major, unnecessary distraction. At peace about postponing my lofty ambitions of Sun Moon Sea, I transferred my Borderland ticket to a friend of Alan's, receiving much-needed cash in exchange.

I wearily packed up and headed for Shoreditch Park, that was a lengthy walk away. At the park, I found shade beneath a tree, rested my back against its thick trunk, adorned sunglasses and napped. An hour of Vipassana followed. With hours to spare, I found a bar from where to write my book, not coincidentally called The Book Club.

Milly arrived at around 6pm, looking markedly happier and healthier. She'd dated a few men: a Finn and a Scot. She was spending much time cycling as part of a group, in preparation for a 100km bike ride, and regularly attended hot box yoga. There was a devious twinkle in her eye, as we chatted playfully while downing sizeable glasses of Malbec.

"You've lost weight," she admonished.

"Everybody says that," I replied. "Yet, I weigh the same."

"We need to fatten you up."

I'd heard this plenty over the years. Still, Milly tried, ordering a round of microwaved finger food, and later she bought me two scoops of ice cream. Back at her place, we chatted openly. Neither of us minded that the other had been with anybody else. She repeated that she liked me. A few random ideas for mutual travel plans were casually interjected into conversation.

"Costa Rica!" Milly suggested, presenting me a keychain adorned in the Central American state's flag.

After the early morning's blaring of multiple alarm clocks, I cabbed to Liverpool Street Station ahead of an early train to Stansted Airport. I flew from London to Hamburg to meet Bella, an old friend from Afrikaburn. On the way to her St. Pauli place,

I loitered around Hamburg's majestic Elbphilharmonie, where I was to attend September's David August's concert. The structure's shimmering sea-blue glass reflected off the bobbing harbourfront. My few days with Bella were predominantly spent watching World Cup football matches, from her local tavern and the living room of her impressively-decorated apartment. Occasionally her friends visited, and Bella toured me around more creative parts of Hamburg. Maintaining numerous charity projects in Africa, Bella was a cool, kind, driven woman.

On the road to Berlin, I had much to think about. The London trip was a blur. My Schengen mission was accomplished: I could now legally live and work in Europe. I mused over the fateful decision to sell my Borderland ticket. It welcomingly shut a door to the past. I appreciated that the decision cleared ten days in summer, to do anything and be anywhere.

For ages I clung to the idea of attending Borderland, simply to make this book more exciting. There would be peace made, or further anguish, but definitely resolution. However, life is not about telling tales: it's about living them.

Chapter 12

Festivals and Hungarians

As the decades-long Cold War peaked and began to ease in the 1980s, vibrant new musical genres and subcultures blossomed across the planet. Hip-hop was an outlet to express the rage of repression of Black America, during a societal peak of unsafe metropolises, brutal ghettos, violent crime, unbridled inequality in Reagan's America, and widespread frustration with The System. Of all the cities in the USA, Detroit was in particular decline, with its automotive industry crash, mismanaged city finances and escalating poverty. Countless other American cities suffered through skyrocketing crime rates and street drug addictions, while AIDS, with its connotations of racism and fear, was the global health pandemic.

In contrast to the broken beats of hip-hop, came the house music and techno scenes, particularly in Chicago and Detroit. Lowkey parties found their way into abandoned factories and warehouses, while house pioneers rummaged up events at local churches and YMCAs. Performances rigged drum machines, groove boxes and strobing lights, layering and looping percussion, pads and textures, for long nights filled with hypnotic, soul-affirming soundscapes.

Over the Atlantic in England, the streets shared similar disenchantment with Thatcher-era politics and conservative white power, that ensured British life was difficult and dangerous. Youngsters infiltrated warehouses to immerse themselves in veritable galaxies, that helped escape the dismal realities of society. This movement spawned the rave scene, and countless "electronic" sub-genres that continue to thrive today.

Across the Channel, Europe was undergoing its own cultural transformations. While Paris and Amsterdam were early players in electronic music, the heart of techno emerged in Berlin: the formerly-divided German city. Berlin's social issues were far more complex and divisive than other cities, for Berlin was the epicentre between Western democracy's capitalist ideals and brutal Eastern communist regimes. The Russian-American superpowers were a Tinder-flick away from nuclear missiles plunging the world into Armageddon. At the same time, social revolutions rolled through Poland, notably the labour union movement in seaside Gdansk, that helped topple the Soviet empire. On November 9, 1989, the Berlin Wall fell, eventually leading to German reunification and the end of the USSR. The wall falling was a joyous and freeing occasion, uniting Berliners who were otherwise split by a physical totem of twentieth century ideology. Berliners headed to warehouses, docks and decommissioned factories to lose themselves in raves. The era inspired new art, and much social and technological progress.

This is relevant for several reasons. One, is that here in the 2020's we find ourselves in a new Cold War, including an alarming War on Truth. Through this, the next generations of art and subculture will flourish, despite whatever draconian restrictions or global gentrification are in place.

...

In large part to its history, Berlin is universally regarded as one of the ultimate arts and music centres on the planet. The city's long and storied history, through plentiful wars and social revolutions spanning centuries, contributed to the power, poise and rebellion in its creations. Berlin helped pioneer everything from architecture, 3D graffiti and techno. Galleries, arts warehouses, classical concert halls and cutting-edge exhibitions are grandly prevalent around the city throughout the year. Berlin's clubs feature prominently in lists of top underground destinations in the world.

Berlin's clubs maintain a reputation for unwieldy and ruthless door policies. At Berghain – Berlin's most famous club – partygoers can queue for hours, only to be rejected in an instant. It's not about fancy clothes or upmarket style; this is more likely to be rejected in subtle, low-key Berlin. Furthermore, there are no photographs permitted inside many venues, as privacy is paramount. The door policies, strict as they are, ensure a quality, more peaceful crowd.

Hence, there was no guarantee that any or all of our motley crew from Sandino, would be permitted access into club

Sisyphos this particular Saturday night. Accompanying me was Pedro - a young Spanish party monster, Jonathan the Scot and Thijs the Dutch. We rolled up around midnight to queue in a huge, winding line. The entrance was chaotic at times, with many hundreds of prospective guests filing into sheep-abattoir style walkways, parallel to the similarly lengthy but more expeditious guestlist queue.

Twelve male British tourists stood ahead of us. Our group was now five males. I didn't like our chances. After scanning a few rows back in the line, I summoned a group of petite females standing behind us, and positioned them before us. Within twenty minutes we approached the security check. Predictably, the large group of British tourists was rejected. The grateful girls in front of us were admitted. We split our group in half; Thijs was my partner. The door man barely blinked our way, as we appeared to fit Sisyphos' criteria. Thijs and I successfully cleared the challenge, as did our trio behind us. Security patted us down, and placed stickers over our phones' camera lens.

Sisyphos was like a miniature village. The venue featured several shops, a pizza restaurant, bars, storefronts, and a spa that offered massages. Slamming techno boomed from all directions. Many alternative-styled personas were dressed down, and there were numerous subtle ravers; everybody bounced around energetically. Not long after we entered, a short brunette approached me.

"Have we met?" she asked. I didn't recognise her. "Are you Sea?" she continued, piquing my curiosity.

She was Andi, the Israeli-Australian DJ I'd hung with last year in Berlin. Andi looked vastly different, having shaved the sides of her hair. Andi offered a guided tour of the vast venue. One doorway led to two separate techno rooms; one was further, deeper and darker. The "beach" was sand and grass that encircled a small pond. People were chilling everywhere, rolling all sorts of smokes.

Drinks were surprisingly affordable, yet I largely refrained from alcohol: A few beers and cocktails, but mostly water. Complementary water refill taps were located near the bathrooms. Under the influence, my head spun comfortably, including a typically intense, blurry period I don't recall, but likely included dancing to pounding techno, and multiple trips to the loo.

To take a break, I headed outside to the huge outdoor patio, beside the small lake and ironic beach. I noticed a woman dressed in black intently staring back at me. The tall brunette approached, and greeted me in minimal English. We located a spare bench near the lake. Cara was Deutsch, 28, and another psychotherapist. We didn't have much in common, with communication hindered by the language barrier and our substance-enhanced minds. Cara repeatedly proposed heading to the bathroom for a "pick me up", but I was comfortable cuddling on the bench, and insisted on rolling a joint: a mistake. The downer of a mistimed Indica joint spelled a rapid end. In my mind, I pushed her away, and she felt it. The vibe became uncomfortable; Cara sat up thoughtfully, and paused.

"I think I'll go home now. There was a dark moment there." Cara sauntered away, and I never saw her again.

The momentary downer was like a flicker of a daydream evaporating in mist. I took refuge in a techno bunker on a packed dancefloor. There was no sign of any other Sandino crew. I headed to a brighter and emptier room, that had a more soulful and upbeat vibe. A colourful dancer flowered around me, intentionally, repeatedly bumping into me.

"Oh... sorry!" she feebly apologised.

We shared the shy incapability of speaking to each other, or, for me, speaking much at all. A portly man named Maurice, a friend of her group, took a liking to me. Maurice was bespectacled with short brown hair and a mild olive complexion, and today was his birthday. Maurice led me to a private area, where he shared some of his exotic birthday treats. Not long after, Maurice inexplicably plunged into bizarre paranoia; he briefly blamed me for something he lost, before looking harder and finding it in his pocket. After profusely, embarrassedly apologising, Maurice exited to brood in a shadowy corner.

With early light beginning to fill the morning sky, I exhaustedly rested on the patio beside the dormant outdoor stage. The day party soon commenced, and the dancefloor filled with hundreds of people grooving away to a solid DJ. A blonde German male with a brown goatee approached me, offered greetings and complimented my aura. Shiva introduced me to his friends, all of whom were generous with drinks and smokes.

Back on the dancefloor, doing my thing, female energies swirled around me, distinctly attempting to capture my attention. Three model-grade stunners danced directly beside me, with one of the most gorgeous women I'd ever seen, looking intently into my eyes. *I'm too shy.* Babes realise this instantly, then they move along. Another tall brunette donning black sunglasses constantly peered at me, then slowly inched my way, while occasionally freezing with fear. Her friends offered her moral support. *Could anybody unfreeze me?*

"Sea!"

An Australian trio from Sandino arrived, helping practice my social skills and exercise my mouth muscles. We held a fantastic spot – front left of the stage – while the patio was packed with happy, bobbing revellers. Rave hours flew by, alike disappearing inside black holes and popping out another side.

By the end of the evening, whatever interactions were in progress led to underwhelming conclusions. The tall girl in sunglasses inched closer to me, with further encouragement from her friend. Close enough, unexpectedly and without uttering a word, she handed me her glass of wine. *The opportunity!* I was delighted that somebody made the effort, and a night of silence bubbled up into talking too much.

"Thank you!" I took a couple of sips, before blurting: "You look like a really interesting person. I like your minimal dance style."

We were mutually baffled by my astonishing flood of words, and she couldn't respond. Upon silently tiptoeing back to her friend, they earnestly discussed the interaction in length. The friend appeared frustrated with her. Sunglasses-Girl eyed me cautiously the rest of the morning. The dancer who'd earlier constantly bumped into me, made a final attempt, deliberately strode towards me, paused... then hid eye contact. *Look me in the eye! I will say hello...*

Alas, this night was not to be with anybody. Following a full night and day dancing to techno, 24 hours later, exhausted and sleep deprived, our ragged group returned to Sandino. A final fireside joint led to prolonged sleep and, whatever self-frustrations, I woke in a positive headspace with no real regrets.

Birthday at Sisyphos

My 41st birthday was celebrated in Berlin. It commenced with tranquil meditation, early on an overcast morning. Pleasant birthday surprises included tasty chocolate cake for breakfast, and a hefty bag of weed. Messages and greetings poured in from all over the world, although I felt a biting sting that The Past did not write. I'd hurt from seeing Boogie's recent profile picture: her angelic face was covered by a bigger love leaf.

In the early evening, our crew – including a sizeable Irish contingent – assembled for a new mission to Sisyphos. Braving torrential rain, we headed to the club early, wagering that an emptier time should improve our chances of entry. Indeed, we strode uninhibited alongside the winding metal barriers to the front door.

"Heute ist mein Geburtstag," I garbled to the amused doorman, where my Geburtstag (birthday) sounded like "Garbagetag" (garbage day). The doorman chuckled, politely corrected my phonetics, and waved us in.

Under rain pouring from grey skies, our wider group gathered in an ironically-sheltered treehouse structure, until everybody we were expecting arrived. With hands conveniently stamped for rapid re-entry, we set out to find food and a screen showing the pivotal Germany-Sweden World Cup tie. While watching the match from a cosy kebab shop, I received a wave of Citronella messages; none of which had anything to do with my birthday. Every time I heard from him was a downer; an inherent reminder of The Past, that I was trying to move on from. *Were he and Boogie collaborating?*

Back to Sisyphos, now buzzing with guests, we bypassed the bulging main line, with our hand stamps providing express entry. The group dispersed into darkness, and most ventured deep into techno bunkers. Hence commenced the game: "Where's Pedro?" The diminutive, handsome young Spaniard was usually front and centre in a techno pit, wearing sunglasses, and charging to beats for hours.

To honour my birthday, Sandino's Jill impressively cycled forty minutes through storms. She cheekily whisked through the shorter guestlist line, before admitting to the door person that she wasn't on any list. Jill was waved through for her bold attempt. Our group remained surprisingly intact for most of the night. The rain kept most people confined inside. Bountiful techno blasted in the middle room. Fragmenting from the others, I found a discrete dance spot near the rear of a techno hall, in front of a pillar. During one swarm of feminine energy, beside typical alpha-male interjections, my head flashed an unusual alert: "*Danger. Danger.*" I seemed to be drawing adverse attention. I departed for fresher air and a stroll.

I sat outside, perched above the treehouse, on a reasonably wet, wooden chair that adorned a deck. Early light scarred through grey rain clouds. I closed my eyes and pictured where I most wanted to be: Warm visions of my pillows, mattress and sleeping bag comforted me. I returned into the techno madness, searching for our group, knowing some of the others would also want to return home. Our remaining crew totalled five: Pedro, Jonathan the Scot, two Irish and me. We charged away on the techno floor, lost in suspended time that could last forever.

Further worn out, I retreated for more Sea Time under a sprinkle of rain. I found a secluded spot on a wooden plank, metres above ground level, with my inverted jacket insulating my buttocks and dignity. Although it wasn't the most graceful effort, I capably rolled a final joint of the morning. I had to find a lighter, and probably people with whom to share.

From the perch atop the treehouse, a sharply street-dressed man descended, and confidently approached me. He beckoned me to come, before repeating his welcoming gesture. I intriguingly obliged and joined his crew. Their group was aligned in a U-shape, with a tough, cut up, frowning man sitting in the middle of the worn couch, and an elegant lady on either side of him. Assuming I was somebody of importance, they guessed I was a champion surfer. I smiled and shook my head.

"My New Zealander uncles were champion surfers, though."

"Are you an artist?"

I paused thoughtfully and beamed. "Recently, I realised I am."

After some chatting, I followed one of their crew down to the Tea Room, where hot herbal teas were freshly prepared. I ordered, "*Eins Minze Tee, hier.*" The minty fragrance steamed pleasantly into my nostrils. I returned to the hill with a mug of steaming tea. The icy man on the couch between the two ladies, coldly looked through me as before. I fetched my water bottle, cordially thanked them for their hospitality – albeit in English – and bid adieu. He nodded with blank eyes; he was on a heavy trip of his own.

The craziness began. Worn out, simply heading to the techno alley to find my crew, I sought one last dance before heading home, alone if necessary. As I crossed Sisyphos' miniature village's intersection, I was halted by a loud, crowd-stopping yell, in a splatter of nasty, angry swearing. To my bewilderment, it was directed at me. Under a covered area protecting from falling rain, sat a scruffy, short-haired brunette man, with big, bloodshot eyes and a labouring scowl. He repeated his shouted denigration, stunning everybody in earshot. Wondering what all this was about, I boldly walked up to him. Face to face – him seated, me squatting and looming over the other side of a short wall – I calmly asked for clarity. He swore to himself in German, before commencing his finest chivalry.

"Do you speak any German?" he asked, staring and snarling.

"I'm slowly learning."

Scowlman raised his right hand, as if to shake mine. I peered at it: not the cleanest, with cuts and grubby smears, but I accepted the gesture and reached to shake it. Like a child or bully, he pulled back, made annoying, pig-bleating sounds, and swore further. He sneered at me with contempt, composed a straight face, then made a concession, once more offering his hand. Again, he pulled it back, with a noise alike a dying horse.

Tired and bemused, I glanced at his mildly unconcerned skinhead friend - a large, lumpy man – and our eyes locked. Immediately the skinhead softened his expression, almost sympathetically, and bounded over to me.

"My friend... he is in another world," the skinhead apologised. The otherworldly friend rolled his eyes, sputtering and swearing. Relieved that there was absolutely nothing of substance worth further discussion, I stood. With a short bow, I wished them both a wonderful day. The grubby miscreant again swore for my attention, that I ignored and waltzed away. After a few steps I stopped in the rain, and smiled.

Standing on the porch of the brighter Wintergarten DJ room, I

peered beyond rain towards the techno bunker entrance. I
sipped my remaining tea and calmed myself down. Staring out,
in contemplation of it all, a profound new energy began to
materialise. Acknowledging me from across the pathway, an
Australian staying at Sandino nodded goodbye to a pretty and
familiar-looking girl nearby him. The Australian approached me,
and wished me birthday happiness.

"Such a lovely day," he demurred. "No reason to head home or
sleep. Enjoy it!" He patted me on the back, and made his way
into the party. These were the sorts of clues from which magic
often appeared out of nowhere. *Was it a hint to stay?*

Suddenly, Boogie appeared from the doorway, and shuffled
closer to me. *No way.* Everything about her looked the same:
Height, hair, breasts, shape and style were a spitting image.
Upon closer examination, she bore a new-looking tattoo on her
left arm. This was a stunning doppelgänger of the girl from my
dreams. Flabbergasted, I could not ignore this divine woman,
who was further inching towards me. I had to say something.

I turned to her, mustering my best, while remaining cautious.

"You look very familiar. Have we met before?"

She looked me dead in the eye, and shook her head. "No... it's
impossible." Her accent had changed; it sounded more Eastern
European than Hungarian.

Circumventing the clear-cut or superficial, I posed a deeper
question, digging for clues: "What is your favourite language?"

She paused slightly, thinking. "Well, I'm Polish."

I laughed. "You didn't answer the question!"

A miracle: Her speaking floodgates opened. In my sleepy,
inebriated daze, I had no idea what she was saying. I was unable
to decipher simple words; my mind was blown and my head was
spinning. I was tense from the recent altercation, and recalled
Citronella's messages. *Was this an elaborate birthday surprise??*

In my blur of radical self-confusion, whether this was Boogie,
or not, I no longer cared. In the middle of this gorgeous clone's
rambling, I moseyed off towards techno. Hesitating, I felt a need
to share the truth. I returned, to her stunned, bewildered face. I
leaned in apologetically and assuredly.

"I'm sorry. You look exactly like my ex-girlfriend... We broke
up six months ago." I turned around and headed away.

"You are... *such*... an idiot!" she seethed. Maybe it *was* her!

Unperturbed, I stormed into the techno bunker. I relocated our Sandino crew and we visited the Tea House, where the party animals debated staying versus leaving. While guzzling hot tea, I boogied in the corner to the best beats of the night: a groovy and downtempo respite from techno. In the end, our group departed together and returned to Sandino by 10am. After updating a proud Shami and curious Clara, I crashed out hard.

What was all that about? Boogie had become a mild, unwanted psychosis, alike my constant fantasy of 2016, from Afrikaburn through Burning Man. Back then I believed, through distorted, inebriated illusions, that I saw a particular Russian everywhere, and that she was frequently trying to surprise me. I wanted no further reminders of the Past, or games.

Fusionella

Fusion is one of Europe's pre-eminent underground music festivals. It spans six days and hosts many big underground electronica acts. The site becomes a transient home to nearly 80,000 spectators, at an historic former military premises. Through not announcing the performers or lineup before the event, people buy tickets for the vibe, and everything else was a surprise. Inside there was no media, photographs or Nazis.

My free ticket came from being part of Flowa's Ginger Juice crew. A minibus shuttle from Berlin's creative arts Greenhouse was arranged by DJ friend Andi. The pleasant, leisurely drive headed a few hours north of Berlin towards a decommissioned Soviet air base, nestled behind a village near the city of Lärz. The other passengers were members of camps or marketplace stalls, such as food, or arts and crafts. As the gates hadn't officially opened, I didn't yet have a crew pass, but with Andi's urging I made an attempt to infiltrate the venue. Timing the moment perfectly, taking cover from a truck that temporarily blocked security's view, I snuck in with my bags and tent. We trekked a mile through the bustling festival setup, and I pitched camp in the farthest inhabited corner, near rows of portapotties.

My first mistake was endlessly waiting for Flowa. I spent hours reading Shantaram from the Crew Care area, near the festival's entrance. This was where volunteers and workers queued for wristbands and meal tickets. Flowa continually assured me over messaging: "I'll be there soon."

With daylight falling, I sought to muster sufficient phone reception to coordinate arrangements with Flowa. Once outside the gates – the only spot with viable mobile reception – I could not convince security to permit me reentry without a pass. Worse, Flowa casually informed me that I'd see him "tomorrow". I'd have to climb a security fence and sneak into Fusion properly, or be without my food, shelter and belongings, overnight in the cold. After several mind changes, Flowa arrived with his father for the drive to their nearby family home.

The solid sleep and early morning rise at Flowa's house preceded a hearty breakfast, with coffee, fruit, bread and cereal. We rode Flowa's tandem two-person bicycle through his village to Fusion. Thousands of festival-goers loitered; many waited in a long line, that eventually resulted in wristband passes.

Back at Flowa's quaint house, our joyous juice quartet consisted of Isabel, Flowa, his mother and myself. We chopped and squeezed fruit, while Flowa added his magic spices and crushed ingwer into gallons of fresh juice. Occasionally we were offered samples of his concoction, that resulted in a pleasing, organic head buzz.

With the first juice-making shift complete, I rode the tandem bike with Isabel on the back, and we slowly cycled around the festival site. Stages were plentiful and impressive, built into existing airport infrastructure, including hangars, bunkers and radio towers, while thousands of guests milled around. Eventually Isabel located her friends, and I was the lucky benefactor of accompanying three German babes – Isabel, Josie and Klara – through the festival's exciting and explorative opening night. We wandered through various stages, some of which were stunning pieces of futuristic architecture, pausing to dance momentarily; more a taste, and move on.

Fusion spawned an entire village of food stalls, catering to eclectic tastes from traditional German cuisine and European staples, through Asian and Latin American. Talks and workshops sprung up around the venue, with theatric performances in smaller atriums. There was a magic forest, illuminated by shades and layers of yellows, purples and greens. Stages and air base installations were brightly configured, often donning geometric shapes and patterns. As the night progressed and fatigue heightened, we made our way to the front of the indoor Kino, and fell asleep to whatever film was screening. By dawn we staggered back to our respective camps.

...

After a deep sleep I unzipped my tent, ready for the day. I was astonished to discover a half-dozen tents encircling mine. My new neighbours happened to be an international Burner party crew. Comprised of a German male, Austrian female, two Americans and two Australians, together they'd attended numerous global festivals. I shared part of the first full day of the festival with this group, and their painfully slow indecision.

Gratefully on my own a few hours later, I loitered around sunny Sonnendeck for hours, hoping to run into Jenni from Bonobo. We'd agreed on vague pre-festival instructions like: "Meet me at Sonnendeck on Thursday around sunset!" Despite hundreds of partiers around, there was no sign of her. Spotty mobile coverage was impossible to coordinate plans, with messages delayed by hours.

Aura, who'd landed a job at German bakery stall, Zeit Brot, was thrilled to see me. I collected her at 4am, upon the conclusion of her shift. Sharing a magic pill, with our arms linked we roamed around the festival. We chilled in various spots, including watching the creek in a tree-shaded area, and glided through the enchanted, illuminated forest. We danced temporarily at numerous stages, chatted incessantly, and eventually crashed out at our separate tents.

Communication breakdowns resulted in nobody around at 10am for the Ingwer juice meeting. With thousands of new campers, I couldn't find Flowa's teepee. Absolutely exhausted, I crashed for the afternoon, waking at 5pm. I missed a message from Isabel about a 2pm juice shift. Instead, the evening ensured further solo roaming. I settled in the northern party zone, randomly hung with generous K connoisseurs, and became giddily wonky for hours, before an "early" 1am crash.

The theme of this Fusion for me was apparent: it was a solo journey. I neither ran into Aura again, nor saw Jenni, Jono or other friends. The neighbouring Burner crew was hindered by a male Australian dolt, who was selfish and unfriendly to me. Comparably, the German, Austrian and Americans were more welcoming, almost apologetic for their friend's behaviour.

Fusion's Saturday was a super trippy night. The vibrant Moon beamed, adjacent to sprinkles of twinkling stars, as clouds breathed and swayed in the wind. Colourful lighting, lasers, futuristic artwork, fire pits, magical forests and art installations, were mesmerising and captivating. I ventured into inspirational spaces of sound and light, and danced near the front of stages. Tripping, I danced and fast-walked for miles, dodging hyped-up people who seemingly appeared from all directions. The more I partied, the less I wanted to speak English, or at all. Halfway through the night, impressed with everybody else's low-key aesthetics, I swapped my long maroon kurta for a dressed-down hoodie, jeans and t-shirt. This was much more relaxed! I tried visiting Aura twice, but she appeared to be on a heavy trip of her own, and she didn't recognise me standing nearby the bakery. I didn't want to stalk her, so I left.

Many hours later, I made "one final lap" around the venue. I passed a packed Acid Pauli sunrise performance at the Palapa stage, towards Penne Eichel, and dismissed dancing any further. I was wholly worn out, with the party comedown well underway.

...

Sunday's final juice-making session fulfilled the remaining obligations of Flowa's arrangement with Kater Blau. Fresh fruit was chopped and squeezed by the hands of three past Vipassana meditators. I chatted with the mystical, stunning Sonja: perhaps the most captivating woman I met the entire summer. Flowa prepared his proprietary recipe of herbs, spices and ginger. This batch held a late, sharp bite. With our shifts complete, I received a VIP backstage wristband. I relaxed on the stage behind the DJ booth, bobbing along while many joints were passed around. As the night wore on, I frequented more dancefloors, with hours on each, despite barely enough space to move.

Seeing the orange flickers of early sunlight, I felt I'd attained everything I desired. There was no need to party hard, or further force adventure. It was time to rest, and begin cleaning my system. Big changes in life were coming.

Festival Infiltration with a Hungarian

A few days after Fusion, I voyaged out with a new friend from Sandino. Hajni was a tall, svelte Hungarian who bore a striking resemblance to my past flame, and was an avid psychedelic trance fan. We discovered a festival of ten thousand people called "Freqs of Nature", a couple hours south of Berlin. Expensive and sold out, this was the final night of the festival – ever – but I was confident we could sneak in. Even if not, the attempt would be fun!

A Sunday afternoon tram and a couple of trains dispatched us to the town of Jüterbog. We shared a taxi with several other waiting festival goers, before exiting in the middle of remote countryside, a mile before the first security entrance. Veering off the main road, we strolled down a dusty country path. Hectares of cornfields with tall green and yellow stalks separated us from the main road and festival. Seeking to avoid detection, we entered the cornfields, a half-dozen rows in. On hands and knees we slithered through stalks, towards flashing lights and thumping sounds from the forest. Camouflaged by corn stalks, we occasionally paused and took breaks. I imagined making love to Hajni in the cornfields, like my old Hungarian flame would have adored, but I said nothing.

The sound of an abnormally loud, artificially-buzzing bee froze us: a drone. *Was it security?* Taking no chances, we lay face-first in soil, waiting for the drone to pass. This was soon followed by a small airplane flying in the sky: either scanning for infiltrators, or simply a joyride on a clear sunny day. We crawled on our hands and knees through cornfields for nearly two hours.

Eventually, we reached the edge of the forest that lined the festival site. A few passer-bys did not see us. I didn't fancy our chances of entering during daylight. As night fell, we boldly entered the adjacent forest. Immediately through the clearing, a man resting on a hammock stared back at us intently. He spotted us, but did nothing. Still, we bolted through tall weeds and grass, finding a trench burrowed in the ground. At least one flashlight scoured the nearby forest. We needed to stall until the sky was completely black: another ninety minutes away. Making ourselves comfortable, we took a short nap in the trench, and when we woke, darkness was virtually upon us.

After some time, roughly 11:30pm, I covertly popped my head up, and decided it was our prime opportunity. We ran for the forest, and skidded down varying levels of woody embankments. We stopped every so often in silence, gauging any possible reaction by prospective security. A high fence stood in front of us. A chillout stage was erected on the other side, with further more stages and structures beyond. Sporadic festival-goers lurked near the fence; random men occasionally peed. We headed right, that was more detached from the festival site. Adrenaline was at a maximum. With great fortune, we located a huge gap in the fence. We didn't even have to climb – we walked straight in! After a minute we were perfectly integrated. We wandered around, checked out the food court, visited the drum & bass stage and charged up. Hajni was ecstatic.

We swiftly discovered that this was merely one smaller part of the festival. To enter the main area, we had to pass a stricter security check. These guards stopped everybody, even regular staff, to verify wristbands; ours were self-created mock wristbands we'd hastily crafted out of red and white police tape found on a cornfield fence. Not perturbed in the slightest, we paced around the entire perimeter, back and forth a few times, looking for openings or opportunities. Our best prospect was navigating through a small hole under one of the fences, near a stage. I slid under the fence and Hajni passed me our bags. A short tiptoe through trees and shadows led to the main area. There were two psy-trance stages and one techno. I made a few friendly acquaintances, although Hajni and I were noticeably fresher than those who'd been partying non-stop all weekend.

Around 9am, Hajni and I were exhausted from hours of dancing, and it was time to leave. Would we sneak out the same way we came? Or humorously try our clearly-fake wristbands through security? I opted for the latter: the first mistake. This German security pair was particularly diligent about wristbands, seemingly brimming with pride about the meticulousness of their team's efficiency. At our chosen exit, a security lady with short blonde hair and her tall male assistant stopped us dramatically. They knew immediately that our police tape bracelets granted us no legitimate access. While radioing a Red

Alert, she held me firmly, wrapping one arm around me, almost like a lesbian sister. Hajni looked mortified. I openly shared with the guards that we didn't have tickets or wristbands.

Through the time waiting for more senior security to arrive, I engaged in increasingly amicable conversation with the female guard. I learned about the festival, harsh realities of Berlin life – not as wonderful as the tourist perspective – and her various leftist views on Germany's government. She appreciated my level of societal consciousness and awareness, and that I wasn't a Berlin party tourist.

Eventually, the head security guards arrived: big beefcakes of men. They seemed surprised that our placid energies might be causing trouble. After the security team chatted in German, the bigger man scrutinised me, hard and calculating.

"You need to remove all your things, and exit the festival," the head guard ordered, firmly but politely.

"We don't have anything here," I calmly replied. "We've only been here a few hours."

His relieved eyes opened wide. "Ah! Then you must vacate the festival, and leave through the front gate. I will arrange a car."

The big man departed. The other big guard asked how we entered: Perhaps we lost our wristbands? I confessed that we didn't have tickets to begin with; instead we'd simply "walked straight in", through an opening in a gate. Unfortunately, this wasn't the best answer. The lady scolded me, "You shouldn't have said that." Apparently the police had to be notified, and would be waiting for us at the front entrance. At this mention of "police" I did worry a little, but I knew everything would work out. There were far more serious problems in the world, and surely even at this festival. I was more concerned about Hajni; she stood tall, silent and thoughtful.

Quite a few minutes later, the head security guard returned. He beckoned us to approach his vehicle, while we were escorted by the other giant. The female security guard and I bowed respectfully towards each other. In the back of the car, I focused on breathing; Hajni looked relaxed enough. *Maybe she hadn't heard "police"?*

We arrived at the front gate security office, and slowly exited the car. The head guard: "Here you are. Have a nice day!"

And we were free! There were no problems, and certainly no police. A guarded escort to the entrance saved us a twenty minute walk, or – for nostalgia's sake – two further hours of crawling through cornfields.

While tying my shoelaces, I shared with a jubilant Hajni that I sensed somebody would soon offer us a ride to the train station. She wasn't so confident, almost disbelieving the possibility. Over our hours of conversations in the cornfields we'd discussed premonition and Grace.

Sure enough, almost immediately, a blue van pulled up.

"Need a lift?" asked the British driver.

We excitedly jumped in the van, and sat on crates of bottles that were heading to a recycling station. These fellows comprised a British psy-trance crew, who were wearily and dustily driving back to England. A couple of hours of trains and trams later, we returned to Sandino, a sliver after noon. While tired and famished, Hajni and I were invigorated by this enchanting, spontaneous adventure. It sure beat sitting around doing the same nothing, talking nonsense at hostels or wasting time on our phones.

This exhilarating latest infiltration enticed me to consider sneaking into Borderland's new venue, for the night of the full blood Moon. Festivals are exciting, like small, temporary cities that converge in frenetic energy, and there's an inherent romance about their myriad possibilities. Anything could happen. For a while, we can live out our dreams. At some point, like everything in the universe, the party is over. So, dance like our lives depended on it.

The cornfields along the slow way to Freqs of Nature festival, July 2018

Chapter 13

Night of the Full Blood Moon

Blood Moons occur during total lunar eclipses of Earth's Moon. From our planet, the Moon appears in luminescent shades of vibrant red and reddy brown. These are because the edges of sunlight bend around the surface of Earth and fall onto the Moon's surface. The Blood Moon of July 27, 2018, was the longest total lunar eclipse of the century. Furthermore, it was the night that planet Mars shined brightest in the night sky; Mars' closest proximity to Earth since 2003.

It seemed that all the converging energies from my spellbinding 2018 were to culminate at this year's Borderland. Although the festival was relocated and Sun Moon Sea was postponed, the full blood Moon was to appear on schedule, unperturbed. Would I sneak in and chance fate?

Following three eventful months since my arrival in Berlin, changes were imminent. That I remained this long at Sandino was a real surprise, but it felt like mystical new energies were beckoning me to explore, elsewhere. A few developments required specific travel to fulfil them. Opening an Estonian bank account to complete my eBusiness registration, mandated a physical visit to the country. I was keen on sculpting a first Baltic adventure, particularly from my grandparents' Polish and Lithuanian heritage. I had tickets to David August's concert at Hamburg's Elbphilharmonie at the end of September. Wilder prospective stops through Moscow and Budapest further stoked my imagination. My usual drawback was a complete lack of funds for anything beyond extreme budget travel.

In Berlin I'd become disenchanted, almost stir-crazy at Sandino. I felt in loops and ruts of being in the same place, following a similar routine in a deteriorating environment. Hostel life typically distracts, and are often counter-productive, frequently disrupting small pockets of momentum. Yet, hostels aren't supposed to be private or secluded workspaces, but socially-enabling gateways to cities for travellers. I had no authentic privacy, sharing facilities with around thirty other guests, many of whom demanded, or were worthy of, attention. Space at home alone – or Sea Time – was impossible. I was in a rut with work, detesting much to do with web hosting support or web development, particularly inane and uninspiring WordPress sites, that seemed to be all anybody wanted.

There was never a shortage of quality interactions at Sandino, whether with staff or visitors. I spent time with an Australian and British couple, who owned a houseboat on a London canal. I met a broad range of wonderful Bavarians, including an open-minded religious businessman on holiday, and a pair of adorable young Bavarian beauties. Temporary friends included a Spanish traveller and his Australian girlfriend; we'd often hang together in the garden, or enjoy excursions out of Sandino.

As with everything, in life and at hostels, people and experiences congregate, share a sliver of existence, then disperse along independent paths. Transience can be tiring: meeting new people, coexist a little, then somebody leaves forever – constantly. My whole life was like this.

To further agitate my frustrations, relations at Sandino slowly disintegrated. Increased stress from dreary internal issues at the hostel put everybody on edge. The daily overload of hash and tobacco provoked head rushes, that I often couldn't recover from. I observed how moods swung deeply and profoundly, in everybody. Cumulative Indica in the bloodstream stoked a rabbit hole of drowsiness, anxiety and paranoia. Shami was particularly struggling under the weight of the exploding B Situation. He sensed my lessening enthusiasm, and constantly criticised that I didn't work hard enough around Sandino. Although my weekly social media engagement, coordinating group activities and curating of photography albums were appreciated, we struggled to complete the new Sandino website. A lack of Shami's feedback stalled the project altogether. This breakdown was a handy source of blame whenever Shami lost his cool; more regularly as the B Situation reached its climax. I believed a month's break for the Baltic Trip, before prospectively returning to Sandino by the end of the season, would craft necessary space, and allow the situation to blow over.

On what became my final Friday at Sandino, making rare sustained progress on mockup designs for Sandino's website, several of us, including Shami, indulged in magic cookies. These were the tasty variety, that one doesn't feel anything for a long time, eat more cookies to top up, and eventually they hit, strong and long, with sensations and side effects that last for days. A few hours after eating the cookies, they kicked in hard. With waves of head rushes from fat Indica joints, I felt hideous. I hurriedly packed up my workstation and crashed out in the tent; I slept for eighteen hours.

...

All of Saturday was hazy, like an awkward dream. Staff and guests had long-planned a visit to nearby Mensch Meyer. Originally, Shami unprecedentedly suggested he'd accompany us, due to the club's local proximity. Shami was comfortable within his own castle, but rarely elsewhere; he felt "old" and "out of touch". During a short, terse conversation, he informed me that he was not attending, to my noticeable disappointment. Coldly referring that I was "on holiday" and was "incapable of understanding" his work, Shami proceeded to insult my latest website efforts. At that moment, I finally had enough.

I'm wilfully patient with most people and situations to an extraordinary point, even at my sacrifice (it's more peaceful to say nothing). By letting it accumulate and build up within me, eventually I'd explode. There's a limit to how much one-sided abuse anybody can take. Once I'm over something or somebody, it's done with: there was no going back, for a long while anyway. I pondered departing Sandino, deeply and gravely for days. My mind processed plausible next steps, and debated the more freeing and inspiring possibilities of the Baltic voyage.

Mensch Meyer was a typical Berlin underground club, and was conveniently twenty minutes from Sandino. Contrary to other Berlin establishments, Mensch Meyer's door policy was most accommodating, even friendly. Our dozen-strong crew lined up at its nondescript entrance, surrounded by high-rise apartment buildings. Hajni was my partner, and security, after asking a few simple questions, amicably waved us through. We entered the lobby into a small outdoor courtyard with a hundred mingling guests, that led into a concrete, old school-like building, with several rooms blasting techno, a washroom area and various bars. Dancefloors were packed and sweaty, structured in a way where doorways were overly congested, but rooms were too full to push through to the other side. I particularly enjoyed an alternative, colourful space, that was more Bohemian and funky. Much of our time was spent loitering outside. I wasn't in the best mood for partying, while others in our crew exhibited similar fatigue. Before sunrise, most of us returned to Sandino together.

After a couple of stimulating but thoughtful days, on Tuesday I broke the news to an agreeable Shami: I would soon depart Sandino. I intended to return – perhaps for the end-of-season party, the weekend after the David August concert. Shami agreed that a temporary break was for the best. With the air clear, I shifted my headspace back into solo adventurer, in the murky crossover between infinite traveller and homeless.

The rest of the surreal afternoon featured a trippy walk around Berlin with two guests: Bosnian-American Maria and Chinese Joanna, who enjoyed her first LSD experience. We began at famous East Side Gallery, where slowly-unfolding visuals warped around classic post-war graffiti. Colours throbbed and lent 3D forms of heroic and historic imagery. We breezed through the heart of Berlin along canals and parks, that were a wonderfully understated feature. Sometimes we paused for ice cream or beer, sat near community playgrounds, or marvelled at modern technology and architecture. We ambled to Potsdamer Platz and the edges of Tiergarten Park, resting on post-modernist sculptures, before passing Brandenburg Gate, then the pizzazz of the historical embassy district. Tens of thousands of trippy steps later, we slowly returned to reality.

The timeless 88-year-old Dawn returned to Sandino to conclude his European trip. On Wednesday, I spent much of the day chatting with him and his prodigy grandson. Dawn was one of the most inspiring people I'd ever met. He lent hope that, as long as we're mentally fit and treat our bodies well, our journeys can endure a very long time. I sure hoped I had another fifty years of self-growth and accumulating wisdom. I've known several active seventy-year-olds, who ran marathons, aced university courses out of interest and blossomed purposeful, creative livelihoods. I doubted I'd ever "retire" - there would always be something to do, learn or teach.

I prepared for a major voyage of an unknown duration. I acknowledged how many unnecessary items I maintained, and vowed to further minimise. Everything seemed bulky and heavy, particularly after not recently lugging around 30kg of round-the-world items. Packed and ready for uncertain adventures, my final night at Sandino was welcomingly low-key. I cooked dinner for the staff: luscious basil pesto gnocchi dotted with feta cheese. We shared several bottles of red wine. Shami remained silent and contemplative. After nightfall, a quartet of us played music and finished wine across the street at an empty sports park. Maria and I spent further hours chatting.

On my final morning at Sandino, I woke in my tent feeling the sting of realisation. Perhaps sensing my situational gravity, an older Dutch couple presented me a specially-prepared hash joint with great affection. They'd appreciated my making them and other guests feel welcome at Sandino. The potent Dutch hash set the tone for a calm yet surreal day. I led a final meditation, recording the session for the group to continue with daily practice, irrespective of the absence of a leader – they could replay the recording any time. The chickens clucked away contentedly in the background. To a dozen meditators, I focused on the theme of the transience of everything: of pain, of pleasure, of people in our lives, and of experiences. That it was normal and OK: Everything arises and passes away. Particularly at hostels.

I ate breakfast with a thoughtful Maria and a sombre Shami. I gathered my bags, and shared long hugs with those who'd been closest to me at Sandino: Jack, Jill, Clara, Jonathan the Scot, Hajni, Maria, and other guests. Even the chickens clucked goodbye! With Shami, in our final moments of an intense three months as friends, as brothers, and even as a reluctant father and son, we embraced.

"Sorry if you're mad at me," Shami uttered, solemnly.

My eyes brightened, and I smiled. "Not at all!"

"This is a break. We will see you again soon."

For over three months, Shami graciously welcomed me into his private, hand-crafted world of Sandino. He'd generously offered me a comfortable and loving home, and a Berlin base. I encountered unrelenting waves of remarkable souls and unforgettable experiences at Sandino. At some point, every relationship has an expiry date, and we often drag out tenures longer than necessary, usually out of sentimentality. But, perhaps this is the path of the universe: that it was exactly meant to be.

For that, I felt nothing but gratitude for everything: the good, the bad, the revelationary, our circle of tranquil souls, and the love and trust of curious chickens. There was an air of finality as I exited the iron gates of Sandino, and as I waved goodbye to its merry cast of characters, who'd been my family and my friends.

From Dresden to Děčín

Having departed the drizzle of Berlin's skies, the weather warmed as the bus rollicked along the highway and entered Dresden. On a sunny evening, Aura greeted me outside Dresden's Neustadt railway station. We made our way to her ground floor apartment near the Elbe River. After stocking up on several key supplies from the nearby Netto supermarket, Aura baked tasty polenta, while I rolled joints for the evening. We carried a nice bottle of Prosecco to the riverside, where we laid a blanket beside an old industrial crane. The Sun fell as the water trickled along the Elbe River. I confided about the breakdown at Sandino, and voiced my trepidations about the forthcoming Baltic Trip. Aura was deciding between life in Dresden or Leipzig, and she was to bake bread at more festivals in the summer months ahead.

After night fell, with adequately buzzing heads we roamed around Neustadt. There was not much happening at all: not one solitary lively or interesting bar. On the way back to Aura's house we heard techno beats in the distance. Following our ears, we uncovered a small club, with neither door charge nor security. There was a bar, and a large walled room at the rear, with a pair of DJs taking turns spinning to a dozen dancers. The smoking area was particularly friendly and welcoming, despite less English. After 4am, the music stopped, the club closed, and we returned to Aura's. A final bottle of Prosecco was transported to the rooftop patio, where we enjoyed an evolving sunrise of scattered yellows, oranges and pinks, embracing under a blanket.

...

I woke up in an unfamiliar room, while comforted by a warm and familiar caress. After a breakfast of Johannesberry porridge and coconut milk, we located another tranquil spot alongside the river. At the appropriate time, I gathered my hefty bags, and we strode to the train station, in the nick of time. My traveller life had returned in full abundance. There was an exciting, refreshing energy about this – at the beginning of trips, anyway!

The train to Prague rumbled along the tracks, and pierced hill-lined countryside that lay alongside the Elbe River. As the edges of the German border succumbed to the frontiers of the Czech Republic, the landscape's architecture and farmland transformed. Houses looked a little older, but they were more colourful, frequently in shades of pastels, while trees appeared thicker and greener, and mountains soared from beyond.

An hour later I arrived in Děčín. New Zealander artist Peter Czech and his young teenage son greeted me at the vintage courtyard outside Děčín's train station. Děčín was a blast back in time, with its historic architecture and humble low-rise buildings, that were spread around parks and the centrepiece of the river. Děčín was surrounded by mountains and dormant volcanoes that lent to Bohemia's mythical aura. Unfortunately, the former border city was plagued by concrete and commercial excess, with a major, noisy highway that ran atop the town, and hectares of garish, sprawling supermarkets, parking lots and fast food complexes. Much of the city appeared run down, with buildings in disrepair, and a ghetto vibe throughout. Contrastingly at night, particularly around sundown, it was one of the most comely and enchanting places I'd visited.

From Peter's charmingly dilapidated building, he prepared for his journey to Borderland. Peter was disappointed that I was no longer accompanying him. He understood my underlying reasons, although asked on several occasions if I might reconsider. I certainly debated the exhilarating possibility of sneaking in, incognito. Yet, I could imagine the inevitably awkward encounter with The Past. More starkly, I needed to generate income. Ten days at a festival didn't feel like the best use of my time or headspace.

My temporary residence was Peter's excellent top floor studio. The flat had a simple mattress on the ground and a large wooden desk in the corner, joined by a modest but satisfactory kitchen. Outside the window overlooked a block of smaller buildings, with views of the river, mountains and horizon. Several Czech guests resided in the building on lower floors, most of whom I never encountered, and there was no English anywhere I visited in Děčín.

After Peter pulled away in his packed stationwagon for Danish adventures, I was left on my lonesome. This was truly the first Sea Time I'd had in many months. I stood in the living room, and it all sunk in. During a moment of clarity I acknowledged that falling in love might be the most marvellous experience in the world. Boogie should enjoy that pleasure a few more times in her young life; as should I. And with that, I forgave Boogie for dumping me.

The colours of the falling Sun took on new liveliness. I relaxed deep in my heart; waves of joy filled me. I was grateful for the privilege of staying in my friend's studio, in this pretty Czech town. I had the power and freedom to choose where to be, and to do as desired – whatever the struggle. I'd use these next couple of weeks, in lieu of parties, distractions and comedowns, to take the next vital steps on my growth. Out of a sheer need to survive, I had to work hard and make things happen.

Magical Mountain Forest

A few days after Peter left, Aura and I reunited outside Děčín's station. We strolled around the antique city, trundling over an old stone bridge while pastel colours reflected beneath the vibrantly setting Sun. We searched for open bars with any vibe, but by 10pm little was open. Eventually, we stopped at a modest tavern in the town's main square. The unsmiling Chinese or Vietnamese owner assimilated well with the grumpy nature of other elderly Děčín residents.

"Ahoj!" We greeted him. "Do you speak English?"

"NO!" he replied, so sternly that it was amusing.

We flashed two fingers and asked for "pivo"; the barman nodded, before grumpily pouring our beers. It cost less than a Euro each for tasty pints of frothy Czech lager. Aura and I sat outside, sandwiched by two long tables seating local Děčín residents. There was minimal activity in the ghostly town square. The owner/bartender handed us a note with "2300" scrawled on it: closing time. We finished off our beers inside the bar, before venturing home through the artistically illuminated streets of Děčín.

Come daylight, Aura and I further explored Děčín. Crossing the river helped gauge the neighbourhood around the central railway station. We feasted on a picnic at a small park, that was filled with older tradesmen and delinquent youths; maybe not the best place to remain after dark. Sharing the trippy remains of particular festival goodies aided our exploration of magical Bohemian valleys and forests. We detoured at the uber-relaxed Čajovna tea house for juice-infused tea. Afterwards we ascended a trail to a castle on the nearby hill, affording a handsome viewpoint across the valley. The tourist-oriented castle was underwhelming, so we continued hiking up the small mountain, through a forest so still and silent that even the breeze was muted. Magical glows shone within the woods, as if the light uttered a godly message through the trees. We rested upon benches and sculptures, taking moments to meditate and reflect. The vibrating colours, scents of grass, flowers and leaves enhanced the mesmerising tranquility. Eventually, we ambled down the hill, back into the little old cobblestoned town of Děčín, alongside the river, around a shimmering lake, and returned to Peter's building.

The next afternoon, Aura departed. The sadness and starkness of my loneliness returned. Aura and I shared a unique relationship, that was undefined beyond its unspoken openness. It was love, in another way.

The Full Blood Moon

In a parallel universe, Thursday's full blood Moon witnessed Sun Moon Sea performing a rousing orchestral concert at Borderland. Simple, classy and solemn, cascading notes of strings, horns and woodwinds ricocheted around the Pyramid, inspiring those in attendance. Later, Boogie and I sat by the sea, conversing for the first time since our teary farewell in Seoul. We smoked joints while revisiting pleasant and unbelievable tales from Korea. It was the anniversary of the magical night we met at Borderland: the spark of everything that was to come. Alan, Peter and I hosted a popular camp, with Alan's huge soundsystem a welcomed tonic for guests seeking broken beats. Peter's "So Beautiful" live visuals blended erotic dance and effects-based projections. Everything culminated at the festival's conclusion – Boogie had clearly moved on, spending time with somebody closer to her age. I met enough enchanting feminine energies to soothe me about future prospects. Our wider crew sat around the festival's final campfire, in a solemn yet joyous contemplation of the week that was.

Alas, it was not to be. Instead I spent the full-moon weekend in Prague. Renting a cheap, comfortable bunkbed at central Hostel Marabou, I was a solid stroll away from most of the historic city. On the invitation of Berlin-based digital nomad Benno, I attended a small house party with Benno's crew of freelancers, who'd been working the summer from Czech's medieval capital. Their living room floor featured an inflatable canoe, that was surprisingly comfortable for up to three people, while sporting sufficient space to conveniently hold drinks. At one point we attempted to sight the full moon from the adjacent neighbourhood, but thick clouds and an imperfect latitude thwarted any realistic viewpoint. I remained at the apartment late into the night, for mostly unremarkable but fun-enough escapades. Eventually, I exited for a brisk dawn walk to my hostel, past drunken revellers and stumbling tourists, as the orange of sunrise filled the sky.

The following afternoon, I trammed to an open air techno party south of the city, in a sparse and industrial area. I followed the sounds of nearby beats, and entered a small concrete bowl that enclosed a DJ booth, speakers and a hundred guests. A long bar sold Czech beer, cocktails and water. While gazing at the early ripples of the dancefloor, I noticed somebody was trying to capture our attention. Klima, a kind Czech gentleman and techno enthusiast, politely approached us. He looked after us with much generosity. Our small group of Prague-based nomads and Klima indulged in many hours of dancing, drinking and chatting. We spent most of our time in the cement bunker of the dance area, or through bushes in a more serene spot.

When the final beats fizzed out, hoards of people returned to the city. Many attended the official afterparty, at a location I don't recall. The venue featured a pitch-black techno room, with a small but popular outdoor smoking area. Inside was too dim to see anybody, and too loud to hear conversations. Outside, I chatted with several Czech techno enthusiasts, while my crew slowly splintered home. Trying to dance alone in strobe-interrupted darkness revealed that I was supremely fatigued.

I was awake long enough to witness another glorious Prague sunrise, then stumbled back to Hostel Marabou. I crashed for a few hours, before the alarm clock blared, coaxing me to groggily and rapidly arise. Prague's pearly cobblestoned streets were filled with thousands of tourists, who snapped photos of intricate cathedrals, 19th century architecture and the nearby Vltava River.

After riding the scenic train to Děčín, I rested in Peter's studio apartment, before tackling tasks and plans. There was much to accomplish, while my finances were almost completely depleted: €12 remained in my bank account. Thrifty shopping manufactured several days of meals for €10. Money stress was temporarily outweighed by the awe of existence, and I felt confident, in that life had an uncanny knack of finding a way.

...

Ten days after he departed for Borderland, a bedraggled and exhausted Peter returned home. I helped him unload boxes and bags from his dusty stationwagon, carrying supplies up five flights of stairs. After a week of tranquil independence, Peter's return burst my mental solitude bubble. I returned to a cliff's edge of anxiety. I nervously anticipated Peter's depictions of encountering Boogie, no doubt brimming with tales of her frolicking naked, and orgying with Scandinavian savages.

"Was it all worth it?" Peter asked rhetorically, before hinting at wanting to express something, but holding back, for my "sanity". This made me feel increasingly uneasy, but the next day I learned he never met Boogie, and didn't see her at all. He asked: "Was she even there?" Honestly, I didn't know. I doubted she'd skip her beloved Borderland, even with its constant reminders of me. I wondered if she'd tried to find me. Or, maybe it still hurt, too.

Mornings became increasingly productive; I rose by 7am to meditate, before diving into work. Afternoons and evenings remained entrenched in contemplation and creativity, and I was certainly stressed about pulling off everything with unreliable income. Occasional long wanders through Děčín helped improve my psyche. One evening I hiked up the mountain, as a thunderstorm loomed. Before sunset I was perched on a boulder, that had required a careful hop from a cliff. I meditated on the boulder's edge, before lightning flashes prompted my rapid evacuation. Under falling rain and bolts of lightning, I had to leap from the boulder, with the stark risk of a thirty metre drop to the ground if I slipped. Filled with adrenaline, I took several breaths, jumped across, grabbed onto the cliff and hoisted myself back into safety, while the storm raged around.

Czech Mountain Rave

On the final weekend of my Děčín visit, I reunited with a longtime German party friend, Nicole. She was working in nearby Vienna for the summer. Klima invited us to a festival "on the top of a mountain", somewhere in the western Czech Republic. We hadn't crossed paths since our Melbourne years, likely somewhere on Chapel Street at one of Windsor's many stellar establishments. Nicole and I spent the night wandering around Prague's glimmering riverfront, where we popped into occasional bars, or drank cheap takeaway beers beside the water. Many hours later, we enjoyed a good night's sleep in separate rooms of old, cheap Chili Hostel in central Prague.

Nursing mild hangovers, Nicole and I ambled to Cacao Cafe for a stellar breakfast, before arriving at Florenc station. Ninety sleepy minutes after departing, the double-decker bus dropped us off at a muted Czech town called Lubenec. A dozen other passengers disembarked at the stop, where we met other festival-goers. Most shared a similar dilemma: How to reach the festival? Train? Hitchhike? Long walk for hours? We bonded with a young French man and his Czech girlfriend, and stocked up on cider and beer from the only open shop. The four of us set on our way, hiking along the main road for a journey that could prospectively take hours.

Five minutes later, as if dispatched from heaven, a kind angel stopped her stationwagon alongside us. She was heading to the same festival, with four available seats and enough room for our bags. Perfect! Within twenty jubilant minutes, we arrived at the buzzing gate of Povalec festival. Smiling but exhausted Klima greeted Nicole and I at the top of a hill, and led us to his crew's spot. I pitched my green tent next to his camp, before Nicole and I scouted the rave. The stage highest on the hill blasted house music, while a larger stage featured rhythmic techno. Other stages across the festival were geared towards live music: some experimental, others were folk. Family-friendly areas were abundant. Beyond a thick forest was a massive other part of the festival, near a stage that blasted death metal.

At our comfortable perch atop the hill, we charged up a little more, and mingled. Nicole became highly talkative; she criticised my lifestyle, relationships, job prospects and whatever else. It seemingly came out of caring, but I found it unwelcome. I'd come here to take a break from my engrained realities, not for more things to ruminate about, whatever the love or truth behind her words. Did I need a relationship to settle down? Perhaps, but not for the sake of it – it had to be the right match. Mercifully, Nicole became tired, and crashed out in my tent, as did Klima in his, as he'd been awake since yesterday.

A small group of Czechs graciously adopted me, led by Lenka, Krystyna and the latter's apparent boyfriend. Lenka sported an electric smile and comfortably familiar vibe. Our small group danced, and frequently explored the festival. As daylight beckoned, Lenka and I roamed off on our own. We found a large tree in a secret, overgrown garden, behind an old wall. I learned about her life dreams coming true, with a boyfriend and young family; they'd soon commence the slow, gradual building of an idyllic home in nature.

Lenka went to bed, and Nicole rose shortly after. I lay under the sky, enjoying the clouds, the air, the sounds and smells. Scattered festival beats sketched a dreamy Sunday morning soundtrack. After Klima groggily resurfaced, we bundled up his car for the ride back to our independent worlds.

Back in Děčín, my days became about preparing for the Baltic trip. This was an astonishingly ambitious undertaking, considering I had single-digit Euro in the bank, and minimal prospects on the horizon. Yet, the most critical step of this long journey was underway, one that would shape the rest of my life forever. Departing one day earlier, or later, would have altered everything.

Chapter 14

The Baltic Trip, Part I

The Baltic region comprises the northeast of continental Europe, specifically the nations of Lithuania, Latvia and Estonia. While Poland's coast touches the Baltic Sea, and the isolated Russian exclave of Kaliningrad is perched between Poland and Lithuania, neither are considered Baltic states. The Baltics are an historic and tranquil region, shrouded in forests and abundant in lakes and sea. They provide convenient ferry access to Scandinavia, and St. Petersburg was a short drive away from the Estonian border.

For centuries, the three Baltic republics were absorbed by the Russian Empire; eventually they gained independence after the first World War in 1918. While conflict, turmoil and strife were constants for a millennia – including the bloody reigns of the Northern Crusades or Teutonic Knights – increased atrocities were suffered during World War II, when the states were annexed by the Soviet Union, and later ruled by the Nazis.

The Baltic people were not known as warriors, but resisted in other ways. A decade of civil uprisings against the Soviet Union in the 1980s culminated in an August 1989 protest. Two million people formed a human chain called The Baltic Way, that stretched 600km from Vilnius to Tallinn. True independence was restored in the early 1990s after the collapse of the Soviet Union. Since joining the European Union in 2004, the Baltic countries began to thrive economically; particularly Estonia.

...

The original version of my Baltic Trip – that one might refer to as Plan A – projected roughly fifty days beyond departure. Draft plans forecast a weekend in Krakow, a few days in seaside Gdansk, a Warsaw afternoon, several days each in Vilnius and Riga, leading to Tallinn, to complete the setup of my nubile Estonian e-Business. I'd hop to St. Petersburg, before an undoubtedly crazy week between there and Moscow. A cheap flight to Budapest would precede a stop in Leipzig or Berlin, on the way to Hamburg. Friday, September 21 marked the date of the David August concert at the Elbphilharmonie. After that, anything could happen. Perhaps I'd find a place to slow down and settle, even for a little while. The journey provided a first opportunity to retrace my maternal grandparents' Lithuanian and Polish ancestry.

Plan A was a rough guide, drafted from sourcing the most affordable means of getting to and from anywhere, such as flights from Russia to central Europe. I was keen to experience Budapest – a reputed digital nomads haven – and I certainly was enamoured with certain Hungarians. Leipzig sounded like a cool German city, and Aura might be there. The trip became a logical conclusion for Plan Sea: Might I find love or connection at Hamburg's Elbphilharmonie? Would there be a happy ending at Sandino in Berlin?

My limitations included the constant of a minimal budget: roughly €120 per week. I packed my tent, as there were several hostels, notably in Vilnius and Budapest, that offered reduced rates for camping. I could further save money by limiting meals, and refraining from expenses like elaborate breakfasts, overpriced coffees and alcohol. This tilted the balance to booking hostels that included complimentary breakfast – then I'd only need to afford one proper meal per day.

Back at Děčín, in the wake of a few serene weeks in the Bohemian valley, I methodically prepared for an unknown voyage. I left behind a small blue backpack with several kilos of unnecessary items, such as snowboard pants, old notebooks and superfluous clothing. Following fond farewells to New Zealander Peter, I hefted my main backpack, now weighing a more reasonable 15kg, hoisted my smaller 8kg carry-on pack, and lumbered towards Děčín's train station.

On Day Zero, the train to Prague was ultimately destined for Budapest. Eerily reminiscent of departing Berlin, the afternoon was overcast, cloudy and grey, betraying the greenness of surrounding forests. The train ride was slow and stopped often. I stared out at Bohemian hills and the flowing Elbe River.

The final physical attachment I held to The Past was Boogie's ominously-faded passport photo, that we'd swapped the day after that terrible night in Seoul. I disposed it in the train's trash bin, with a couple of my passport photos I'd given her: one final adventure together. Following a flickering flutter of sadness, seeped a wave of relief, and opened space, like a portal, that new energy would soon fill.

Upon arriving in Prague, a storm hit, and I took shelter at photographer Jan's apartment. After the rain ceased, we wandered towards Prague's famous 130-year-old exhibition centre, to film a nerdy video interview for RunCloud. "I love RunCloud!" I gushed. We ventured further into the park, behind a hipster container bar that was cloaked by lush trees shimmering in the wind. At 9pm I met with Lenka, from the Czech mountain festival. We chatted over soft drinks at the rainbow-bright National Gallery of Art cafe, and she gifted me a box of chocolate. Lenka dropped me off at Florenc bus terminal. She departed to her family and home-building.

A Date in Krakow

My journey from Prague through Poland steadfastly navigated to the medieval-styled, progressive city of Krakow. This historic Stone Age-era city dated back to the seventh century and was revered for over a millennia. Krakow (pronounced "krac-koff") frequently attracted high-brow political visits from European dignitaries, and suffered fierce raids from savages alike. Like a fortress, Krakow's lengthy castle walls encircled an inner core, while the mighty Vistula River flowed alongside its perimeter. Krakow was Poland's capital until 1596, and is widely regarded as one of Europe's most attractive cities.

As I awoke from a nap at modern and clean Mundo Hostel, the weight of this trip sunk in. As I was definitely open-minded to encountering female energies, I reinstalled the Tinder dating app. I updated my page with whimsical depictions of spiritual journeys, and flicked through prospectively-compatible profiles. I was impressed at how many cool and progressive women were prevalent in Krakow, and many match notifications blazed in.

Taking a brave breath into foreign territory, I headed into the castle-like old centre of Krakow. In the midst of fulfilling writing tasks at the magical Magia Cafe Bar, I received an email reply from 88-year-old Dawn. Short and simplistic, Dawn's email hit a raw nerve in its truth:

"Enjoy your travel, and remember that the key to success in life is to build a reputation for good service to those who employ you."

I wondered if he was specifically referring to the breakdown at Sandino, or a general interpretation from his observations of my struggles. I looked back to numerous of my contracts that petered out, from breakdowns in communication or overzealous demands from clients. Dawn's words hurt, as truths told about ourselves often do, but they helped me improve. I also needed to be more selective of the clients and assignments I took on.

On my first fatigued but inspired evening in Krakow, I met up with a Singaporean nomad. Ray delighted in showing a fellow South East Asian around several vibrant Kaziermierz taverns, where we indulged in impressive Polish pivo. Comfortable Mundo Hostel afforded a productive Friday morning's work, after a satisfying, well-cooked breakfast. Sitting in calm breeze, I chatted with a pair of young Turkish men about work, travel and the planet. They were rushing through Europe on their annual week-long vacation. I couldn't fathom how anybody would agree to any job that only offered one week's holiday.

Despite a few interesting encounters, the trip already felt lonely. Still, Krakow was a surreal city, like living in a castle. It was easy to stoke the imagination of past times: medieval ceremonies, peasants, dignitaries, and preparing to defend battlements. While tomorrow featured a charity-oriented underground music festival, I held no plans for tonight. Deep down I desired female accompaniment. Reopening Tinder sparked stimulating conversations; there were several intriguing matches, but perhaps not tonight.

There was one particular match I hoped would reply. Her simple opening message asked: "What kind of writing do you do?" Her profile was simple and soulful, with a warm genuineness about her. There was a particular photograph that revealed the care in her eyes; it attracted me to her heart, before I'd encountered it. Still, it didn't matter if she never replied, and I bounced between friendly conversations with others, ready to confirm plans with whoever committed first.

In the late afternoon, around the time my work concluded, a surprising reply arrived from the match I desired: "Any plans for this evening?" Arrangements developed rapidly. Shortly after 8:30pm on a rainy Friday evening, Magia and I met in the foyer of Hard Rock Cafe, in the ironically modern part of Krakow's Old Quarter. First impressions make considerable impact, and Magia was a striking figure. She wore a singlet and short red shorts, with light brunette hair tied atop her head, and piercingly playful eyes. I donned my silver-grey Indian kurta shirt, and black jeans, with my hair neatly in a man-bun.

At the cozy second-level bar of the Hard Rock Cafe our initial conversation progressed, over pricey but well-prepared mojitos. Magia, a svelte 39-year-old psychotherapist, was similarly a writer, and curious about my travels. We chatted about writing, work, travel, life perspectives and a hint of family, that sounded like it'd been a struggle for both of us. Clearly mutually comfortable, Magia proposed visiting Kazimierz, the Jewish Quarter, for further beverages and conversations. She navigated us through winding, cobblestoned streets to an absinthe bar. The bartender's specially-prepared apparatus caramelised sugar cubes into our glasses, that sunk underneath the syrupy, bright green absinthe. Ice cubes were useful for distilling, although after one sip the strong alcohol swiftly made its impact.

On rustic old leather couches, Magia and I opened up more deeply. Her early childhood had been rough, frequented with physical abuse from both of her parents. I learned that domestic abuse in Poland, and other Slavic states, was rampant. Raised as a strict Catholic, Magia was a late bloomer, while her last name "Dziewic" translated in Polish to "Virgins". My first! A rebel underneath an otherwise good girl, Magia was engaged at 26, waiting for sex after marriage, before she suddenly ended the relationship. She'd been anorexic for fifteen years; skinny as a pole. In the midst of all this, she earned four university masters and three bachelor degrees, across a broad range of subjects.

I confided with her about my homeless era, twenty years earlier. Magia barely batted an eye, and it brought us closer. By now there was regular, mild physical interaction. Our knees touched, and there were occasional, playful caresses against each other's backs or arms. With a strong buzz in tow, we departed the bar, and Magia led us towards the majestic Vistula River. I put my arm around her; she reciprocated, and we walked in sync. We crossed a modern bridge, adorned with life-sized figurines of comic acrobats. Approaching a large old church and a hill on a silent street, Magia's eyes gleamed.

"I've never done this before at night, but let's walk through this park."

The overcast drizzle lessened the likelihood of miscreant energies pottering around outdoors in the shadowy park. I held her hands and gazed into her sparkling eyes. Comfortable and relaxed, it felt like the time – perhaps this was our only night together. We kissed; strong, enduring and juicy. Taking a deep breath, we entered the darkness. The path of the eerie park curved clockwise, with a mammoth brick wall that towered up a gorge on our left. After a while, we passed a ramshackle shelter. Circling around, we reached the other end of the church. Two drunk men appeared on the street below, and made their way into the blackness behind us, as we idled under streetlights.

"Want to chill at my house?" Magia uttered the magic words. I was impressed at her forwardness and my good fortune.

Before crossing a different bridge over the river, we smoked a little ganja from her broken, miniature pipe, while she was cautious about police. "Very strict here," she warned. Sitting on the corner of the road, ready to book a taxi, her eyes squinted, then she grinned. "Want to go to a gay bar?"

I frowned, and laughed. A sign that looked like "Colon Club" faced us from across the street. Asking myself what was the worst that could happen, I accepted the challenge. For the sake of roleplaying, I was gay and she was my lesbian friend. We strode to the entrance and entered easily. Several dozen gender-balanced LGBT Poles mingled between the various spaces of the small club. Cheesy, upbeat dance music blared under blinking LED lights. Some guests were clearly in drag; others left enough to wonder their orientation. Magia ordered drinks, while various passer-bys brushed against my body.

"That man is raping you with his eyes!" Magia exclaimed.

We sat on a couch in the dance room, watching the energetic, happy crowd. A handsome Amazonian beefcake with long blonde hair caught a glimpse of me from the corner of his eye.

He moved his gyrating Tarzan body across the room, jiggling beside me, but he was similarly too shy for eye contact. I pretended to not notice his distinct attention; I was not acting as a very convincing gay.

The next round of drinks was mine, and I attempted to order two mojitos in garbled Polish. The bar's lack of mint ensured an English conversation, and I opted for the bartender's recommended daiquiris. Magia, craving affection, decided our roleplaying was over; we kissed. She was definitely up for anything, but left it to my comfort level.

"Let's have one dance, and leave," I suggested. Magia's eyes smiled.

The DJ spun his best songs of the night to a heaving dance-floor. Pairs of women and men surrounded us, occasionally bumping against us. The tall blonde Thor peered disappointedly at us from a distance.

Twenty minutes of a taxi zipping through night led to Magia's apartment, in a modest three-floor building in Zielonki. It was slightly out of Krakow, near a huge national park. I was instantly impressed at her flat's inviting ambience, greeted by modern ceiling lighting, and wall-high red-black graffiti of a city scene. Magia owned and had designed the flat, and for over a decade accumulated an impressive interior of artwork, figurine dolls, and a hundred healthy, colourful plants. Two large and happy but cautious cats mooched on couches.

"Czupur is the man of the house. He doesn't like any guys who come here," Magia cautioned, as the big, black, fluffy Maine Coon sidled curiously around me. I cooly pretended to ignore him, knowing he'd eventually try to capture my attention. Ten minutes later, Czupur was my best friend for life.

Much of the serene time was spent between Magia's living room and the spacious balcony. Early flickers of daybreak ricocheted across the horizon, with a backdrop of trees above a creek. Throughout the night's events I was filled with gratitude for the experience, and the connection that bound us. Magia, while constantly radiating happiness, confided that she felt similar, regular thankfulness for life.

In our lifetimes we are destined to encounter particular souls and energies. It took a mobile dating app for the introduction, but it enabled Magia and I to share a remarkable sliver of life together, even for a weekend. This trip could hardly have started better.

A Spell in Lublin

Following Saturday evening apart, on Sunday Magia and I visited nearby Ojcowski National Park. We strode through the stillness of diminishing light in an ancient forest. Huge, rocky cliffs mirrored a couple of castles, one where a guard insisted that we not sit on its wall. On Monday evening, after swarms of embraces, Magia cheerfully waved goodbye from Krakow's Główna station. I rode an uncomfortable night train to the coastal city of Gdansk – formerly Danzig. In the humble carriage, a family of three faced me; the two young kids spread out around their mother, who graciously afforded me extra leg room. I sat beside a large athletic man; we all barely had sufficient dozing space.

Ten restless hours later, in the wake of sunrise, I arrived at Wzrescz station. I stretched my legs, and strolled through local streets to the address of fellow Burner, Dane. We'd camped together in 2014 at Burning Seed's The Orphanage – where Captain J-Man and Miss Hannah-gin were our adoptive parents. Dane was an Australian teacher who'd moved to Gdansk with his Polish girlfriend, Kasia, whom he met in Australia. A groggy morning opened the way for a couple of days of exploration. Dane and I travelled to Sopot Beach, downing quality craft beers, and peering out towards Scandinavia, that loomed in the distance. In the evening, Dane, Kasia and I moseyed around Gdansk's Old Town, pausing by a traditional Polish folk performance. Dane and Kasia's small strip of land within a communal garden ("działka") enabled a refreshing Wednesday evening, pulling weeds and planting seeds, before sunset wine and sausages. Later we visited the modern Container Yard, in the middle of Gdansk's old port area, then we sipped on drinks at a quaint local cafe closer to their home. Dane confided with me about intense relationships with Slavic women, and the challenges faced by English-speaking foreigners in Poland. I was beginning to understand both of these.

The next day, a bus from Gdansk dropped me at the northern edge of Warsaw, before a hectic M1 metro rush to the cross-city bus terminal. These were my first fleeting impressions of Warsaw; it appeared to be a fast-moving and busy city. A second, emptier bus glided southward to the historic city of Lublin – Magia's hometown and birthplace - where she awaited me under streetlights.

This was Magia's first visit to her grandmother's apartment since her death a few months earlier. After the big wooden door creaked open, it revealed an old but homely flat. It was reminiscent of my Polish-Lithuanian grandparents' house in Toronto, decorated in yellow wallpaper, flowered curtains and picture frames. There were plentiful religious artefacts, including one with the Pope from 1932, and worn-out photographs of beloved family members that adorned the walls.

Magia's grandmother was a remarkable woman, having survived the Second World War by luck and steely determination. She avoided capture by the Nazis, and escaped brutal encounters at the hands of bloodthirsty Ukrainians and fierce gypsies. Ultimately, she was detained by Russians and was transported to Siberia, where very many people perished – on the way, or there. She craftily asserted herself as a useful and indispensable driver for the Red Army, eventually marrying an officer, himself a Pole. This enabled an eventual low-key return to Lublin, where she lived in hiding for years, under the shame of collaborating with the Russians.

During the responsible and respectful first evening in Lublin, Magia curiously and craftily departed to the kitchen. She returned with specially-brewed tea, that may have contained witches potion. Magia later admitted to reciting a spell before serving the tea; the spell sure worked on me! In the morning, we ventured into the quaint centre of Lublin, that was surrounded by looming castles and intricate cathedrals. The evening featured a popular community festival, with traditional Polish dances and folk songs. We roamed around the old city and its peaceful riverside, indulged in quality yet inexpensive pivo, and tried without luck to find any music bar oozing vibe.

On Saturday morning we departed Lublin, and drove east towards the Ukrainian border, to a secluded campsite in the woods near a creek. This was Magia's first camping experience since her teenaged years, but she acclimated well to humble living. Our modest food and drink were heated by a gas burner. Later, we straddled a blanket in our candlelit corner of the campground, underneath stars that sparkled through the night sky, beside a gurgling creek.

Our lovely Sunday unfolded with heightened relaxation. We heated coffee on our gas burner and ate baked goods. We paused for lunch at the hilltop city of Sandomierz, a former royal enclave. Sandomierz historic Old Town was set within a giant, walled castle, rich in churches and cathedrals. Refreshed, we returned to Zielonki, greeted by thoughtful black Czupur and mischievous silver Xara.

Home is Where the Heart Is

My time with Magia in the little Polish village of Zielonki became increasingly comfortable. Her cats adored me; they spent much of their waking hours demanding pats or lounging on my lap. Czupur was particularly alluring: a sensitive, contemplating creature, endlessly observing and learning, sometimes noticeably frustrated that he couldn't speak. It's like he sat there for ages, trying to think of something to say, and all he could eventually muster was: "Meow".

Every corner of Magia's well-decorated apartment was filled with hand-crafted love. The spacious living room adjoined a roomy, modern open kitchen. The long balcony was lined with plants, flowers and herbs, such as mint and two varieties of basil. There was a pair of bathrooms: one for the cats, and the other was smooth and tiled, with a future-retro space-capsule shower, steps from a sizeable bathtub. The bedroom was massive, featuring dozens of healthy plants, and a soft, thick king-sized bed adorned with metal posts. A humble rocking chair with a blanket sat nearby the bed, but it wasn't for humans: it was Czupur's "throne". Overnight, Czupur guarded our dreams. Otherwise-rebellious Xara never dared approach Czupur's throne, and she rarely even entered the bedroom.

Contrastingly, the last room was a small, undecorated square, with a cluttered desk, ceiling-high mirrors, and a curtain-covered wardrobe, void of plants or soul. The room was mostly a pile of old magazines, and a heap of laundry on the floor.

"A mess!" Magia declared. "Much like my life and my mind at times – it all comes here. One day I plan to clean it all up."

Magia's casual, twice-weekly roster as a psychotherapist fulfilled her professional ambitions, affording abundant time for her writing and pastimes to flourish. It afforded us excellent space during those days. I'd wake early, and Magia would drop me off near the city, where I'd work from various Krakow cafes. We'd often meet for lunch – usually a pierogi place.

...

One evening while cuddling atop her spacious bed, I proudly shared my pleasant sentiments.

"You have such a comfortable home. Friendly, happy cats. A lovely apartment. Such a nice life you've set up."

She beamed at me with her magnificent sky-blue eyes, almost blushing. She paused thoughtfully, then answered decisively: "You are welcome to join us."

And with that, I questioned everything I ever wanted: Here, right now, I had it. A deeply intelligent and compassionate woman, who'd procured a comfortable existence in the wake of three decades of struggle. She'd left herself open to be filled with a complementary energy, but didn't necessarily *need* anybody else. I often witnessed pure love in her eyes, contrasted with occasional flickers of resignation, as if she acknowledged the reality that our time together was not forever. Sometimes she looked at me with disbelief that I appeared in her life.

Czech Mountaineering Film Festival

One Friday afternoon, Magia and I embarked towards the Czech border. Our primary, loose objective was to visit Teplice nad Metuji, an area famous for its massive rock landscapes, and an old town of stone. We sought to camp near the Polish city of Wroclaw, explore the city for a night, then continue to Czech. Overcast clouds transformed into a gigantic panorama of blacked-out sky, preceding hours of torrential rain. With our camping ambitions quashed, I researched private rooms at budget hostels, deciding on Friends Inn in the centre of

Wroclaw. The hostel was simple but pleasant, in a vibrant nook of the buzzy city. Despite the drizzle, we set out for the night and waltzed around the vintage central quarter. Our first stop was an Indian restaurant: Magia's first taste of India. She was impressed by the complex, complementary flavours from layers of spices, in dishes of paneer, rice, mango chutney and butter naan. She particularly appreciated the mango lassi. "I like Indian food!" she glowed, as I shared stories about my Indian travels.

"You should join me in India, one day," I proposed, to her delight.

With our stomachs full, amidst a pulsating chilli buzz, we strolled around, readily impressed by Wroclaw's vibe. Nobody appeared in a rush; there were minimal tourists, and even they were relaxed. Usually tourists clucked about aimlessly and hurriedly, like chickens running out of time.

...

The next morning, after meandering around Wroclaw, we returned to the highway and rode towards Teplice nad Metuji. We detoured via the historic Ksiaz castle and its surrounding gardens. We scouted a lavish, royal forest with hectares of thick, ancient trees. The castle's exorbitant entry fee prompted us to successfully slip in, through the hotel's temporarily unmanned side entrance. Rain drizzled down while we sat watching the periphery of the main castle structure, with crisp fresh air reinvigorating our lungs.

The drive further through Polish countryside brought us to smaller roads, through nearly-deserted former border towns. Passing a narrow, innocuous bridge marked by a discrete Czech Republic flag, we crossed the open border. Soon we were surrounded by trees and forests, of a national park that featured impressive cliffs made of boulders. As we approached the town, an overwhelming onslaught of humans came into view. Unbeknownst to us, on this particular weekend the town was hosting the 35th annual Mountaineering Film Festival. Mountain-climbing enthusiasts from across Czech and the planet descended upon Teplice nad Metuji, for a weekend of film, music, camping and every conceivable type of related retail.

The festival solved several challenges. The first was that we could camp for free in the middle of town, next to hundreds of likeminded campers. Proximity to the festival ensured that we had a quality local selection of food and drink, instead of heating up tins of beans. At the far end of the central park, we erected the little green tent on a grassy patch, in front of the car; a perfect spot, with nobody else too close to us. We wandered around the festival, passing stalls that sold the latest in mountaineering gear and accessories. There was a sole beer sponsor, who poured the least impressive Czech beer I've tasted. Everything was overpriced by Czech standards, but remained wholly reasonable. Despite being in the middle of it all, I'd not felt so out of place at a festival; Magia concurred.

We returned to our camp and prepared sandwiches. I'd lost my taste for alcohol, and didn't drink any. I crashed out early, after encouraging Magia to roam around the festival. I felt a need for rest and space. Occasionally I woke, hearing muffled, amplified music from the main stage. Magia returned to cuddle after stimulating hours of roaming.

...

On a fresh Sunday morning, we indulged in a chocolate croissant breakfast, instant coffee and a wake-and-bake. The crisp air hinted at autumn. After efficiently packing the tent, we bundled off to find truly big rocks. The main tourist gate of Teplice nad Metuji demanded lining up for expensive admission. I couldn't locate any particularly easy alternative entrance. Instead, we drove a little further up to Adersbach, where many more tourists lined up to overpay for parking and entrance. A short walk uncovered a narrow creek and rocks; we crossed with minimal wetness, and easily entered the national park without detection. Once inside, we marvelled at a miraculously green-blue lake, that was surrounded by enormous rocks and boulders. Forests glimmered as thousands of trees waved in the wind. With too many tourists for our liking, we followed a path with no signs; it led us to a hill through a forest, to a small cliff that overlooked a valley.

Magia sat on a rock and closed her eyes, facing a wall of mountain-sized boulders. I ascended higher, almost to the peak of the hill, crossed my legs and meditated. My grumpiness and restlessness had grown over the weekend. I considered whether it was hunger, or the onset of money stress – as I'd nearly run out of funds again – or fatigue, although the long sleep should have remedied that. I wondered if I'd already had enough of Magia. Here I'd come again, two weeks into seemingly a new relationship, and I was already tired of the other person. I'd not met anybody as perceptive as Magia, and she could sense something troubled me.

During my meditation on the hill of Adersbach, in a vast forest of tall trees and ancient boulders, I reflected on my emotions. I coveted space. Not in terms of a few hours apart, but it was a long time since I'd been alone by myself. I missed pacing around in private; experimenting, creating, joyfully productive in solitude. My sentiments were rarely the fault of another person. I looked back to my past relationships, and where I'd become frustrated. Nothing in my existence had lasted a lifetime – such as friends or homes. I was a self-raised free spirit, who particularly thrived alone, preferring nobody else around who could disrupt my headspace. Most relationships were demanding: lovers, family, housemates, colleagues and pets.

I'd been with Magia for ten comfortable but intense days. Other than my few days in Gdansk, Magia and I had been together every morning and night. I hadn't enjoyed even one soothing "Sea Time" evening. Days in the city working alone from cafes or workspaces, or lonesome strolls through city woods, weren't the same. This wasn't Magia's fault. It's not like I gained the freedom I desired when staying at hostels or friends' places. This was an inherent drawback of travelling: there was almost always somebody else around. The idea of a van remained appealing to me – I could drive into nature with my mobile home and studio, then return to society when I'd refreshed. Wherever my path led in life, I needed healthy periods of Sea Time.

To afford immediate space, I considered a mid-week trip to nearby, inexpensive Budapest, or staying at a nomadic retreat in Poland. But, my next attempt at the Baltic Trip was to begin shortly. I already knew I'd miss Magia. I didn't know how long I'd be gone, and what new encounters might engage either of us while I was away. This might be our small window together.

In the late afternoon, we ate traditional Polish food at a charming restaurant perched atop a mountain. The gospoda afforded scenic views of Polish countryside. Magia and I sat in renewed comfort and unspoken understanding, while exhausted from hiking and fresh air. Time apart would allow for authentic reflection on where Magia stood in my life. A powerful question remained: *Had I truly healed?*

Sinking at the Titanic Hotel

The first cracks in our relationship arose following the initial Krakow Nomads meetup at Truckarnia. A lovely Italian student named Fabio started a Krakow Digital Nomads group for his university paper, and randomly invited me, as an experienced nomad, to help bolster the group. Truckarnia bore the delicious scent of freshly cooked burgers, Polish food and Oriental cuisine, that emanated from multiple food trucks, adjacent to a bar. Over a chatty evening, we met writers, developers, tour guides and community organisers. Later, Magia acted clingy, pulling me to kiss her in front of everybody. I felt uncomfortable and resisted, preferring to maintain professional conduct. She was visibly incensed, and tension lingered overnight.

The next evening after a frosty day, we chatted openly on a Vistula riverboat. The piercing weapon of communication cleared the air. We celebrated with her first-ever Espresso Martini. Afterward, we chilled on the grass at a riverside picnic commemorating Collaborate Krakow's second anniversary. Some of the sentient souls meditated near the river, while snacks and progressive ideas were shared.

Over the weekend, Magia originally had plans to fly to Malta to meet a recent American marine fling. Out of respect for our budding relationship, she cancelled the trip, and let him go. I didn't influence the decision whatsoever. Magia was my first relationship where I implemented my worldly lessons of openness and freedom. She was free to do whatever she desired. Following Magia's conflicts with her ex-best friend and mother, our time together became more regular and intense. These factors multiplied against a lack of necessary creative space, and the rapidly-approaching, revised Baltic Trip. Compounding the stress, was that I now had to cram seven weeks of travels into a fortnight.

The enticing Up To Date music festival in the eastern Polish city of Bialystok planted seeds of new ideas. My original target destinations of St. Petersburg, Moscow and Budapest dissipated. Bialystok was close to Lithuanian capital Vilnius, and offered a useful springboard for necessary travels further northeast. The two-week window was certainly not conducive to relaxed, advance-planning traveling. Flights to and from Tallinn were predictably expensive, but nearby Riga matched up with plentiful budget possibilities. A €15 Ryanair flight from Riga to Berlin, days before the David August concert, was almost perfect. Booking this flight locked other plans in place. After Hamburg I'd decide where next.

With a week remaining before my departure, the matter of an open relationship unexpectedly but necessarily arose, when Magia enquired about our status. I took a few moments to compose myself.

"You are free to do whatever you desire. If you feel the urge to do something, by all means: go for it. Please don't sit around waiting for me; get on with your life. Then, whatever happens, enjoy it, and it nobody's mistake." I recommended she read The Road Less Traveled: *"True love is accepting and appreciating the growth of the other person, whatever that might entail."*

Magia took the reply in stride. I knew she wanted more, if not everything. Sometimes I thought she craved it too much: hence the clinging. It felt like a considerable spiritual journey lay ahead for Magia. I wouldn't make any major decisions until I was able to adequately reflect over my solo journey to come. More than anything, Magia was a definite energy and friend I wanted in my life, whatever our status.

...

"Am I too skinny for you?" Magia once asked me, with sad, wide eyes.

Undeniably, Magia – a former longtime anorectic – was thin. After a few days of lessened eating, it was particularly evident. In many of our intimate interactions, Magia was as gorgeous as anybody I'd met, and I'd never been so lost in somebody's eyes. But, she was not the sort of girl I typically went for, and didn't have my typical "look". She was certainly original and unique: this I greatly appreciated.

With our bags packed, we hugged the cats goodbye and hit the road. We stopped in Warsaw for a night, at a slick, modern apartment in an otherwise dodgy suburb. The next morning's drive was compounded by prolonged, tense silence. Various triggers from our unpleasant childhoods trickled through, such as long road trips with parents or partners, that stoked anguish and impatience. There were plentiful hours where we barely talked to each other; instead we listened to electronic music, lost in our thoughts.

Our nubile relationship was under strain by the time we checked in at Bialystok's Titanic Hotel. Camping wasn't desirable – the prospective campsite was far from the festival, and entirely secluded and sketchy. The unlit part of the remote property where we'd pitch our tent, featured neither other tents nor security in sight, while three dodgy men burned something from a makeshift fire. Rapid searching on Booking.com cultivated a small list of choices; most were too far from the festival's venues to reasonably walk, while others were very expensive. The only legitimate option was the aptly-named Titanic Hotel. On the way, barely speaking to one another, we rushed to fetch our media passes. Our tardiness unfortunately skipped Sarah Davachi's cello performance, and we weren't able to meet Jan, the media manager who'd arranged our access.

The Titanic Hotel was shaped like a boat from the exterior, while fitted with a tasteful vintage ship interior. Perhaps from absolutely rock bottom expectations, while our relationship was seemingly plummeting, we were greatly impressed with the Titanic; the service was sweet and lovely.

Standing on the carpet of our modest hotel room, Magia and I cleared the air. I expressed my various frustrations, including my stress about this Baltic trip, and the unknown of where I'd head after. Magia's frustrations emanated from absorbing my frequent grumpy energy, her admitted hypersensitivity, and triggers of unfortunate memories from past relationships. Out of nowhere I uttered magic words, that appeared to be a welcomed surprise, even shocking, for her to hear.

"I think I'm also stressed because I'm leaving you soon, and I'll miss you. I'm sad about that. It feels like Love. I hope to see you again after this trip – but who knows what will happen?"

Magia had expected quite the opposite, and my optimistic words eased the mood considerably. Peace was made. The remainder of the weekend was uplifting and exciting, complemented by the pleasant but slothful effects of overindulging in heavy, magic weed-laced cookies. Fatigued from a long day's drive, and the rollercoaster of a relationship crisis, with a long night ahead we opted for a necessary nap, instead of confirming our first interview. Without rest, there was no way we'd be able to endure the late night ahead.

After midnight, rested, showered and dressed, we arrived at the stadium hosting Up To Date Festival. We were among the eldest of a very young crowd, many of whom were unable to handle their alcohol. There were several stages scattered around converted parking lots outside the arena, with an impressive food selection. Several hours later, delayed messages from Jan arrived. I hastily prepared for my interview with French techno duo LUXOR, before their world premiere set. Jan fumed at me from the periphery, although I'd never covered a festival with such last-minute notice for interviews.

Magia and I remained at the festival through drum and bass pioneer Goldie's early morning set. Particularly impressive acts included fellow spiritual nomad Aisha Devi, and Lorn, of epic track Acid Rain. On Saturday the festival moved into a large old hall: more of a sit down and closed-eyes consumption of artistic music and soundscapes. No further interviews were scheduled; Jan deleted me from the press mailing list, and I never heard from him again.

In the morning we checked out of Titanic, and gouged on a late breakfast from a cafe near the bus station. Magia and I stood on the concrete tarmac beside the coach to Vilnius. We exchanged warm embraces, and stifled tears. I knew from her deep touch that we'd see each other again, and that newfound love filled our hearts.

Chapter 15

You Cannot Force Magic

With my unexpected Krakow detour aside, the Baltic Trip resumed. The journey still hinted at myriad possibilities, as though something special remained out there. To allow my heart and Grace to guide me, I had to remain open to everything. Disappointingly, I had minus-$120 in my bank account: a stressful state of financial affairs.

This hastier Baltic leg began in the quaint Lithuanian capital of Vilnius. I arrived in Vilnius after sunset on Sunday evening, following a six-hour bus journey from Bialystok. Vilnius was submerged within a small, royal enclave covered by forests, with a large castle situated on one of many pretty green hills.

Downtown Forest and Camping was alike a bigger and more mature Sandino. It featured a huge tree-lined outdoor garden, a funky wooden bar, and layers of chillout areas that were sculpted into a steep hill. One could rest in a hammock, or swing from a large, antiquated tree. An old building was converted into dorm rooms, and the front lawn offered space for parking, vans and tents. For this short trip I left my tent in Krakow – another reason to return. Downtown Forest's warm vibe and its inner-forest outdoor patio lent instant comfort.

On Monday morning, I roamed around Vilnius. Locals dressed smart-casual, reflecting an upbeat, fresh, progressive vibe. I attended to work tasks at Huracan Cafe, fuelled by a coffee-filled, otherwise-empty stomach. I munched lunch in sunshine on a cobblestoned pavement outside Cozy Cafe. Directly across the street, sat a bedraggled homeless man, who was humbly enjoying a cigar. Multiple passer-bys conversed with him; several selflessly offered him change, bananas, candy and cigarettes. He was grateful for all of it; he ate hurriedly, clearly starving. Respectfully, he collected his rubbish and crossed the street to dispose it in a bin. Then he returned to his backpack and small shoulder bag – undoubtedly containing his entire world, just like us globetrotters. A patrolling security officer firmly warned the beggar away. The streets of Vilnius appeared to keep clear of riff raff and the destitute. As homeless, we're told to leave; we move on, find another place for a while, and the cycle continues. Yet this never really solves deeper issues.

Back in the privileged comforts at Downtown Forest, a motley social group was forming. Our crew included a party-inclined vacationing New Zealander cop, another Kiwi named Bob, his British party friend Yamesh, a cool German named Cora, a Brit cycling through Europe and an Austrian hitchhiker. Joining later was Flora – a vivacious Lithuanian who lived in Copenhagen – uncannily, another spitting image of Boogie.

In the evening several guys ventured to a techno party at the top of Vilnius' old city. In an enclosed courtyard, a tiny outdoor stage faced a hundred avid dancers and revellers. The DJ played to an enthusiastic crowd, under flashing lights. I took occasional breaks from dancing to chill with our crew, while mingling with friendly and welcoming locals. Several were impressed of my Lithuanian heritage. One lethal blunt passed from a music promoter absolutely destroyed me. I felt unstoppable head spins from tobacco and drowsy THC, amplified by double-strength beer, on top of the many beers I'd consumed earlier. I doubt I drank enough water. A similar effect on habitually disgruntled Bob the Kiwi, led to his feeble attempts at imposing misguided social-political insight on stunned Lithuanians.

"Of everybody in the wars, nobody suffered more than Poland."

Bob drunkenly argued with bemused, frowning Lithuanians, whose families undoubtedly suffered from generations of poverty and killings, throughout the violent twentieth century and earlier. Later, after I read James Mitcham's epic historical novel, "Poland", I better understood Bob's point: Poland was greatly fortunate to have any country or population after a millennia of crushing crusades. Yet Bob's remarks in Vilnius were insensitive. Several locals sat beside him, patiently but passionately debating the topic.

Unable and unwilling to intervene, with my head-spinning on the cusp of dangerous, I had to leave and rest, rapidly. While staggering along cobblestones towards the vicinity of the long way to Downtown Forest, I spotted a small church that was cloaked by shadows. Encircling the church's perimeter, I crawled into a little concrete corner, and slightly but sufficiently blocked the chilly and wailing wind. I lay down, blanketed myself with my jacket, and passed out.

...

Probably a half-hour later I awoke in blackness, with an inner voice urging I depart. I groaned, stood, then stumbled down hills, eventually reaching the comfort of my bunkbed. In the morning I felt violently ill, and tried to repress everything. I loathed vomiting; instead I hoped to sleep it off. Usually it worked. My immobility prompted my solitary annual sick day. After a few hours napping, I felt slightly better, and moseyed delicately onto the communal patio. The goateed Austrian hitchhiker challenged me to a chess match and pulled out a hefty wooden board. Unfathomably, I accepted offers of vile cigarettes, and puffed on a joint that tossed me over the edge. I hurried back to my bed to sleep off the inevitable.

Starving for food, weakened by an empty stomach, in the late afternoon I headed for dinner in Užupis with the Kiwi cop. Užupis was an autonomous region and UNESCO heritage site within Vilnius, close to Downtown Forest. Užupis' authenticity was betrayed by consumerism and hipsterism, that spawned countless expensive restaurants and cafes. For instance: a Lamborghini parked outside one lavish diner. We found a reputable, affordable restaurant, where I struggled to digest soup and salad. With chemical reactions boiling within me, from the previous night's beers and blunts, but also dangerous residual effects of the space cookies I'd ingested in Bialystok, I rushed to the solitary toilet inside the restaurant. Fortunately it was unoccupied, and also that the restaurant was loud.

"I'm proud of you," the cop fathered, as I gingerly returned, and nibbled at my food.

The next day, feeling rejuvenated, my productivity and liveliness returned. I chatted with Flora, who I was definitely attracted to. She had the look I liked: brunette, svelte and cool. The Copenhagen connection was also peculiar. All these coincidences instigated mind games. Smoking a few joints in the evening during an upbeat vibe helped kindle a distinct feeling of all-encompassing magic - like Borderland, Burning Man or

Arambol. My strange psychosis of blurry identities returned. Temporarily, I wondered if Flora was really Boogie in disguise, and part of another elaborate surprise. *She cared enough to see me.* Even though I knew the reality, this part of my imagination had tricked me for years, and always while under the influence.

I was conflicted by my characteristic loyalty, to the love who was presently consuming my heart: Magia. Even though our relationship was left "open", I'd long-ago deleted Tinder, with no plans or intentions to hook up. I would not go out of my way. Yet, I wasn't ruling anything out. I hadn't embarked on this lengthy soul-affirming journey to compromise my freedom. At very least I was free to imagine without guilt, and it welcomingly took pressure off everything. Incredibly, this mindset eradicated any awful clinging impulses, such as worrying about what Magia might be up to, or with whom. Jealousy be gone.

As it was, minimal opportunities with other women presented themselves. I was certainly curious about Flora. There were only vague signs of potential mutual interest, with no time for us to scrape past superficial surface layers. There was one moment she and I lounged around Downtown Forest, when I adventurously suggested Flora postpone her return to the drudge of corporate lawyer work in Denmark. Maybe she'd be up for a weekend in Palanga? Surprised at the idea, Flora sighed, about *having* to head back. The Kiwi cop who was sitting beside us shook his head, "Why would you skip work? Don't do that."

A Weekend in Palanga

The next morning a group from Downtown Forest visited the Museum of Occupations and Freedom Fights, dedicated to the city's history of genocide. The former KGB headquarters wasn't a huge building, but sizeable enough to enact numerous atrocities of brutal twentieth century history. We visited prison cells, interrogation rooms, torture chambers and execution halls, with plentiful walls filled with memorabilia, photographs and visual presentations, that depicted the unrepentant atrocities of Soviet and Nazi occupations. The visit was surreal and unsettling, reminding how fortunate we were for today's world, whatever society's failings. Today's mass genocides were conducted in far more subvert means, while few countries are legitimately worried about invasion or violent occupation. Nowadays, most people need fear their own governments and corporations, instead of other nations.

After dusting off the sobering cobwebs of recent history, I gathered my bags, bid farewell to our Downtown Camping crew, and headed to Vilnius' train station. Accompanying me to the coast was the charming German brunette, Cora. Both of us were consumed by other loves; Cora was pursuing a traveling jazz musician, who'd visited her for one steamy night in Vilnius. This was entirely a "friends" affair. Cora and I waited for hours at a teashop near Vilnius' train station, where we met a Chilean nomad, who was on also his way to Tallinn for Estonian e-Business. Cora and I rode an evening's express train through Lithuania, sitting backwards and windowless through the countryside journey. We were lucky to have any seat at all – the evening's trains were otherwise fully booked.

Palanga rests on Lithuania's small apportion of the Baltic coast. It was renowned for its beaches, parks and, puzzlingly, nightlife. The town featured a frightening commercial dance megaclub. I found a super deal for a private flat, with a deck that faced a trace of sea, using Airbnb credit to further lower the price. In the middle of this hectic Baltic rush, I had a calm place from which to meditate and write: essential Sea Time.

A late shuttle from Klaipeda preceded a twenty-minute walk from Palanga's bus terminal. Eventually, we solved the mystery of locating the flat's door, and the hidden key to open it. Cora crashed on the comfy couch, while I enjoyed the bedroom's queen bed; the distant waves were audible. In the morning we strolled through the sleepy town to source coffee. Cora headed to the enticingly isolated peninsula of Nida, near the Curonian Spit. The peninsula sounded ideal for prospective van journeys.

The overcast Saturday in Palanga opened its skies, as rain fell across the Baltic coast. A small Baltic celebration parade, thick with traditionally-costumed participants, marched a block away, turning on my street towards the centre of Palanga. I sat in the apartment facing my laptop, and slowly completed my LUXOR article from Up To Date. I distractedly exerted much energy researching buses, hostels and happenings for Riga and Tallinn.

A year ago this weekend, I'd landed in Korea. Boogie and I'd hiked through Seoraksan's blackened forest, across a dragon-lined bridge atop a gurgling river. I lovingly reflected on the equally adventurous Magia, who'd appeared so (too?) soon on my journey. Magia was rapidly becoming my soulmate. I was already closer with her than I'd been with nearly anybody.

Most of my time in Palanga was restfully spent inside the apartment. To take breaks, I headed onto the streets, and wandered around local neighbourhoods and supermarkets. I roamed through a nearby forest, to the roar of the Baltic Sea. The coast was simple and grey-blue, with rocky sand, and a few piers that jutted into the chilly water. Palanga was pretty, with its manicured parks, well-maintained streets and rock-lined sea. Its soul felt sapped by its distinct tourist vibe, as though the town served little other purpose. I stood at the end of the pier, stared out towards invisible Scandinavia, then eyed the Lithuanian shore, as wild winds lapped around.

A trip-altering downer came in an email from Sandino's Shami. He apologised for taking a while to respond.

"I appreciate all the nice things you did for me and Sandino, especially the good vibes. But you also brought bad energy in my house, and you left them behind. Take care Sea, enjoy your adventures. Let's meet another time, but not that soon. Shami."

While I sensed the pain in Shami's sincerity, I was encouraged that he was open to eventually revisiting a friendship. I knew he'd be in touch again when he was ready – perhaps in months or years. Conveniently, being disinvited from Sandino's closing weekend, made the decision for me, and further opened up post-Hamburg plans. Space is useful in all sorts of relationships. True love and friendship come back.

The Blur of Fast Travel

Traveling from Klaipeda to Riga through flat, forest-lined countryside, revealed impressively huge, glimmering lakes, that hinted at abundant beauty in Latvia. Glorious nature eventually succumbed to the concrete realities of smaller cities and shop-lined towns. The scenic Latvian capital of Riga was surrounded by the Daugava River, with the city's compact medieval square and cobblestoned streets reminiscent of other historic European centres. I spent the night at Riga's acclaimed Tree House Hostel. It brimmed with sentient feminine energy, in a modernly-appointed interior that spanned a few floors of a humble inner-square building. Riga's old town was besieged by tourists, ensuring overpriced restaurants and cheesy "western" entertainment. Few establishments remained open after 10pm. An Indian-run, late-night döner-kebab place was a welcome and tasty find. I wandered around the old town's streets, peering at the cathedral-like House of the Blackheads in the centre.

In the morning, I was back on the road again. I departed northern Latvia through Estonia. In Tallinn I arrived the week after the season was unofficially over, with most nomads having vacated. For my sole Sunday in Tallinn, I spent the night at comfortably-shanti Music Guesthouse. There was only one other guest, and the sizeable music lounge, fitted with a stage and plentiful musical instruments, was empty. The Melbourne owner was intrigued about my book and musical projects, and warmly welcomed me to return and present them. Later in the evening, Bob and Yamesh from Downtown Forest visited me for dignified drinks. Yamesh was supposed to be on my same Riga-Berlin flight in a couple of days. The next morning, a drunken Yamesh ferried to Finland, became a public disturbance, and was detained overnight by Finnish police. He had to book expensive replacement flights to London.

I had only Monday in Tallinn to attend to my litany of Estonian tasks. I strode through Tallinn's modern streets and predictable city blocks, before entering the bright, spacious lobby of LHV Bank. After loading up on complementary faux-gourmet coffee from a well-stocked machine, I signed away to nonsense terms, for the matter of a simple, soon-unnecessary business bank account. I'd written a letter protesting LHV's callous and exorbitant monthly fees, even if there weren't any funds in my account. LHV Bank never replied, despite several attempts, and this accelerated my disinterest in Estonian e-Business. My next meeting was with friendly LeapIN, who astutely serviced e-Business startups with Estonian-language accounting and compliance. LeapIN's office was miles out of downtown Tallinn, in a remote, developing industrial area.

With my successful day complete, I returned to Tallinn's bus station. I guzzled plates of buffet-style cafeteria dinner, before a deluxe Lux Express coach to Riga. This was one of the best buses I ever travelled on, with comfortable seats that afforded plentiful leg room, a DIY coffee and tea machine, wifi, movies and not many other passengers. Cora awaited me in Riga; she was refreshed from her rapid dash into Lithuanian peninsula tranquility. We split different rooms at the cheap Central Hostel, a twenty-minute walk from Riga's old square. Cora pined for Jazzman, while my heart was magnetised to Magia.

Kit Kat Club

The budget flight from Riga landed in Germany's capital on a sunny afternoon. After dropping off my bags at Flowa's Friedrichshain apartment, we biked through bustling inner Berlin to Südstern station. There were social plans with Flowa's original Berlin party crew: renowned circus troupe Zirkus Mond. For their ringleader's birthday, the group creatively assembled several tables, benches and chairs outside the metro station, opposite a public piano where random performers expertly played for pedestrians. An extension cable precariously dangled from their fifth floor apartment's balcony, affording the illuminating glow of a vintage lamp. Dinner and drinks were served during a respectable affair, although only a few of us were not German speakers. Roaming police requested a conversation about the classy public takeover, before an apparently-coincidental busker humorously intervened, with his rousing Deutsch rendition of "Gangsters Paradise". The police laughed, and walked away.

While I munched on home-cooked food from the buzzy Berlin neighbourhood, Flowa popped a devious question.

"Sea! Come with me to Kit Kat Club!" Flowa's eyes filled with a devilish twinkle, before softening. With an air of responsibility: "For the ending of your book!"

How could I refuse a naughty dare on the eve of my book's originally-intended finale?

"Okay..." I slowly and cautiously agreed, before Flowa's eyes widened and gleamed.

The Kit Kat Club was a legendary Berlin institution: a notorious, world-renowned underground sex club. I didn't even fully know what that meant, but I imagined dark orgy rooms surging with leather-adorned gimps. I'd said "No" to these invitations most of my adult life, although I'd unwittingly attended similar clubs simply by chance. *What was I afraid of? Being coerced into awkward, uncomfortable situations?*

Joined by a busty blonde Canadian, the three of us ventured to Kit Kat on bicycles. Navigating past tricky Berlin bouncers was our first challenge. Next was stripping off my shirt: a disarming prerequisite for all males. Inside a couch-lined entrance lobby, under warm but dim lighting, I undressed in front of a large coat check, manned by three busy multilinguist clerks wearing panties. The lobby had the hustle and bustle of coming and going, with guests transforming between their street clothes and fetish gear.

I entered cautiously, and shuffled slowly past vacant couches in the lobby's black-painted corridor. I was wearing black boxers, short black socks and my faithful, well-worn running shoes. I headed towards banging industrial beats, that emanated from the supposed DJ room. Stepping through a doorway onto a packed dancefloor, I'd never felt so many simultaneous eyes intensely locked upon me. Unperturbed, I strode to the back of the dancefloor, where there were perhaps sixty people in a reasonable square. The vibe and guests' attire reminded me of late-90's gothic clubs. I became lost in dance, undistracted by the encircling energies trying to gain my attention, be it curious, leather-clad babes, or space-dominating alpha males.

A bathroom visit made for its own mission: I waited in a busy line at wet and steamy co-ed taps, before sourcing an available stall that was in surprisingly respectable condition. Some sections of the club were closed for this mid-week occasion. I entered a large lounge, located beyond a shuttered swimming pool and fountain. At certain couches, a couple of naked couples casually fornicated, while everybody else minded their own business. I took refuge in downing an overpriced gin and tonic at the bar, and stood sheepishly. My eyes were unsure what to observe. Other shy types mingled nearby. One was a hetero Spanish male in his twenties; he was mutually relieved at a simple, non-threatening conversation. Kit Kat seemed to be a nightclub that happened to have revellers in underpants, with occasional nudity and discrete sex; not dissimilar to elements of Burning Man. Admittedly, this was a "quiet" night - apparently weekends were far wilder.

My ultimate objection to being at Kit Kat, was that I had plans with an old friend from Melbourne, Spikey Tee. Spikey was DJing at another Berlin club, and I hadn't seen him in years. Flowa was completely naked at this point; his big belly cast shadows upon his dangling dong. He'd originally promised that I could enter Kit Kat Club, stamp my hand for re-entry, visit Spikey, and "come back" - or not. In the haste of our arrival, our collective items, including clothes, wallets and phones, were split between three chaotic lockers. Trying to repatriate all my items frustrated already-busy staff. It became such an ordeal, that remaining at Kit Kat seemed simpler.

"Sea! Not good. Don't cause trouble, PLEASE!" Flowa, sweating and flustered, apologised to everybody around. "You might not be allowed back here."

That didn't bother me in the least. I hadn't wanted to come here anyway, and I was presently unsure of any desire to return. Without my phone I couldn't update Spikey, but I resolved to stay a while longer, even though I was too shy for much at all.

After a drawn-out gin and tonic, and more time on the dancefloor, I again attempted departing. Recovering belongings from whatever first locker, resulted in a jacket, pants, and keys to Flowa's apartment, but no shirt or phone. I had no means of digital navigation or communication. Back on the streets, I followed hunches and instincts to weave along unfamiliar territory. I was lost in Berlin in dusk, while wearing a bizarre combination of clothing. It seemingly took a couple of hours, and the two male passer-by's I tried asking for help weren't the friendliest. Alas, instincts guided me well, and I reached the flat. I woke up a few hours after sunrise to open the door; Flowa was accompanied by a playful guest, who wore little at all.

In the end, Kit Kat Club wasn't so bad. We might never know something until we try for ourselves, and we usually survive - even enjoy it - in the end. I was proud I made the attempt, and I remained open-minded to one day returning. Sending apologies to Spikey Tee: "Sorry, man. On the way to your gig I was kidnapped at Kit Kat Club. Then, they wouldn't let me leave!"

David August at the Elbphilharmonie

The culmination of this prophetic European summer built up to the monumental David August concert, at Hamburg's harbourside Elbphilharmonie. The bus from Berlin delved through rain and unusual dust storms, before arriving at Hamburg's central bus terminal on a chilly and cloudy evening. The lively and mischievous former sailor brothel neighbourhood of St. Pauli was bustling, with multiple venues hosting events at the huge annual Reeperbahn Festival.

Money was extraordinarily tight. With no Bitcoin ATMs in Germany, I was at the mercy of minimal available funds – less than €70 for the weekend. I cancelled my hostel reservation in completely booked-up Hamburg; it was to cost over €40, for a bed I might not use. Instead, I stowed my backpack in a locker at Hamburg's central train station, allowing for freer wandering through meandering crowds, to Hamburg's shimmering waterfront. The Sun set, atop bobbing boats in a haze of purple sky, while brisk breeze suggested the onset of autumn. The wind roared through streets and trees, amidst a thick aroma of fragrant flowers and sea.

Hamburg's stunning Elbphilharmonie sliced through port-side air like smoothly-cut shards of glass. Strong, salty wind blew and breezed, while boats bobbed, clouds accumulated and thousands of chattering revellers scattered, like ants chasing falling sugar from the sky. I entered the Elbphilharmonie's futuristic entrance, and boarded a slow, slightly-slanted silver escalator, that ascended through off-white walls with circular faux mirror panels. At the top was a dim, square entrance, akin to riding into an abyss. Windy, sweeping views screened Hamburg's nighttime skyline, mostly of the harbour and its ships. After another escalator came further more stairs, that led in every direction through a cavernous, futuristic atrium. I sipped on a generous glass of in-house Rotwein on the thirteenth floor, while guests filled the steps and balconies of the foyer. At 10:45pm, I entered the hall's G section and headed to my seat. Delightfully, I was four rows back behind the stage, dead in the centre. The hall filled with patrons: mostly low-key and German. A gorgeous young woman sat to my right; a young, thin man in glasses to my left. I didn't say much, beyond polite hellos. There were numerous empty seats; Magia easily could have scored a ticket. She hadn't wanted to risk driving all the way from Krakow to Hamburg, to be refused admission. I thought the attempt would have been exciting and romantic.

The concert began: A solitary spotlight beamed in the centre of the stage. To rapturous applause, Hamburg-native David August entered the great hall, and headed to his complex workstation. The stage was sparse: A piano, guitar, harp, several keyboards and synthesizers, drum machines, a laptop and tall racks of effects. Ambient tones from David's recent, experimental album rippled through the hall. He played reverberating piano atop it, adding complementary layers and textures of sound. Occasional beats erupted; some stood and danced in the aisles; most, like myself, nodded along in our seats. A harp player accompanied around one-third of the way through the performance. For ten minutes, they crafted walls of ambience, with melodic flurries of the harp that weaved in and out of electronic tones. Sometimes heavy beats thundered through. Towards the end, a saxophone player wailed away.

The finale hinted at David August's melodious, crescendo best. He built up walls of emotive sounds, with much anticipation and feeling, before allowing the remnants of the concert to softly fade away for reflection. The lights came on. Thunderous applause ricocheted around the great hall; David August bowed, accompanied by his harpist and saxophonist. The eclectic concert at the Elbphilharmonie was over.

…

Meiko, an acquaintance I met at Afrikaburn a few years back, was the only other person I knew who attended the concert. His personal connections with the Elbphilharmonie gifted him a front row seat on the stage's other side, almost directly across from me. After the concert we shared beers at Mojo's jazz cafe, and chatted about Burns, travel, relationships and blockchain. Needing to pack for his next day's flight, Meiko departed. I was left to roam the festival streets of Hamburg on my lonesome. I was drained from the whirlwind, frantic Baltic Trip, and now I had to stay awake until morning.

What next? I sought out the best electronica I could find. A small club off the boisterous main drag, Baalsaal, required paid admission; its vibe didn't inspire much confidence. Another possibility was Uebel und Gefährlich, a vast warehouse thirty minutes away. A line of forty street-clad patrons queued outside, while slamming techno emanated from beyond the walls. A couple of young men were rejected firmly but politely at the door, rehashing memories of Berlin clubs' strict policies.

I sat on a concrete barrier in the biting windy cold, snugly in my grey-blue winter coat, observing the line. The crowd was young; several coughed from excessive smoking. I realised I didn't want to enter. I'd lost my appetite for partying, for dancing, for forcing myself to stay out long enough, or willing some sort of last gasp adventure to satisfy the far reaches of my soul. It was time to head "home". Patiently waiting for me was the overflowing love of a beautifully-spirited woman and her two fluffy cats, in a warm, comfortable environment that felt as much like home as I'd ever known. I sought peace, stillness, consistency and some stability, to focus on work, self and blossoming vibrant new relationships.

One cannot force magic. Magic happens when we least expect, when many variables intersect perfectly, or sometimes when timing for everything feels so wrong. Magic comes out of nowhere: it illuminates within, it encompasses everything, it is omnipresent. For me, magic was alive and abundant in the sincere touch and embrace of Magia. The power of Grace can be right in front of us, as much as we might resist it. Yet we should embrace it, roll with it, appreciate it and enjoy. Nothing lasts forever; cherish the special moments while we have them.

Waking in the Woods

Outside Hamburg's chilly bus terminal, I patiently and exhaustedly waited for a coach to Berlin. An earlier bus to Amsterdam crossed my mind that, under different, quantum circumstances, perhaps I'd randomly hop a bus there. At the cusp of sunrise, my bus departed Hamburg. To spend a three-hour layover in Berlin,

I located the acclaimed Cafe Lotti & August, situated on a quaint street away from main traffic. I attempted to order a cappuccino and croissant for breakfast, but the older baker didn't understand me. His two pretty young waitresses and a comely older patron assisted.

I was waved over to join a table occupied by the elderly lady. I learned about her community housing group, that represented six thousand participants. With Berlin's gentrification well underway, her group helped keep rental prices affordable. Many of their buildings were a hundred years old. Just as this fair lady departed, another old woman arrived: her friend. She was handed the awkward baton to humour me in broken English. As a relief to both of us, another friend entered. I graciously allowed them the table, and relocated to a larger table, near a power outlet. An eccentric older man regularly demanded evermore coffee, while busy waitresses crafted intricate platters and plates of fruits, cheese and home-baked bread.

In time, I returned to the bus station and waited for the coach to Wroclaw. I witnessed an older bus that was destined for a long drive to southern Serbia. The coach filled up with passengers and all sorts of baggage, including washing machines and other indescribable items, that reminded me of Indian or African bus lines. Once my bus arrived I found two seats to myself, placed headphones over my ears, and tried to sleep.

...

On Sunday morning, after deep and pleasant dreams, I was greeted by the comforting scent of a wood fire through a brick chimney. I sighted tall green trees and light blue sky shimmering through wooden windows. *Where am I?* Everything hit me at once: where I was, where I'd been, the David August concert, and what lay ahead. We were in the mountains, at a large lodge near a ski hill. Magia was in another bunk bed; she was chipper, and thrilled to start this wonderful new day and era together.

The lodge was at the end of a steep rocky road, near the top of a mountain. Dormant ski lifts sat idle, while lights and voices scattered from around the lodge. Entering the wooden foyer, a vast, organic central atrium awaited. With every piece of timber sourced from local forests, the structure comprised a gigantic woodwork masterpiece. Huge beams of trunks supported three levels of hand-carved rooms and corridors. A fireplace in the centre radiated light and warmth to every corner of the spacious lodge. Reception was an extension of a bar, that sprawled beside a long, deep kitchen. Tables filled with food and beer placated boisterous, happy Poles. Our dorm upstairs housed three wooden bunkbeds, but with no other occupants, we had the room to ourselves.

While sipping on honey beers, Magia and I chilled on a huge deck that overlooked a driveway and woods. At a nearby birthday party, around twenty Poles in their early thirties played guitar, told jokes I didn't understand and laughed.

"Polish humour!" Magia beamed.

The next satisfying morning, we drove home to Zielonki. We were greeted by Magia's two cats, Czupur and Xara. They acted like they'd similarly anticipated my return. I was overjoyed to be back, and wondered why I considered heading anywhere else. The realities of my pseudo-poverty revealed minus-$30 in my bank account, after the bus fares were deducted. Next week I had a debt to repay worth hundreds of dollars. Of course I was stressed how to solve this, but a lifetime of experience reassured that I'd find a way. And, somehow I did.

This lifestyle was just not going to cut it much longer. I was slaving away on work I increasingly detested, yet I remained perpetually broke. Twenty years ago I was homeless; I was an outcast on the streets, similarly surviving on a razor's edge with non-existent funds. It was unacceptable to comprehend that, after everything I'd learned and accomplished over two decades, I remained surviving day by day. It was time to break cycles. If I had to ditch technology and web work: so be it. This was always what I did to survive, and I wanted to thrive. If I was going to struggle, I might as well enjoy what I spent time on, such as immersing myself in music, arts and positive projects.

None of this mattered, right now. I was surrounded by unprecedented love from all directions, while growing into a new home, city and culture. Work hard, treat people well, and things would shake themselves out.

Chapter 16

Dobra Atmosfera

The remainder of autumn flowed like a mountain creek in the first rains of spring, sweeping through like a powerful tide of well-travelled waves. I settled into domestic life, warmed by the love of two sincere cats, and a special woman who was proud to share her world and home. Foraging for food in the Krakowian village of Zielonki included regular visits to next-door "Scary Shop", staffed by unsmiling old Polish women, who were surely amused at my communication anxieties. The local Gospoda served fresh, piping-hot pierogi and zupa, while Magia frequently feasted on fish. Larger supermarkets sold cloud-soft gnocchi, basil or capsicum pestos, and halloumi, that became staples for my inspired reconnection of cooking in a quality kitchen. I practiced and mastered Hollandaise and Halloumi Eggs Benedict: our Saturday morning tradition, complemented with oversized "buckets" of coffee, creamed and sweetened by coconut milk. Wake and bake-fuelled creative weekends further chilled out the already zen cats, Czupur and Xara. Big, black Czupur particularly felt like a kindred spirit. He was able to communicate using thought waves, and was highly receptive to human emotions. I relaxed into domestication, and manifested a cosy routine with no pressure, demands or inclinations to head anywhere. I had everything.

Slowing down afforded an opportunity to take a closer look at the world, and my place in it. Ingrained characteristics sought to flee; I was inexplicably stressed by the very notion of settling anywhere, or the unfamiliarity of having one place where to reliably return. Years of constant moving planted seeds of doubt about stability. My resistance to accepting the comforts of the Zielonki home caused occasional ripples, but Magia was patient, accommodating and optimistic.

"Dobra Atmosfera" in Polish translates to "Good Atmosphere". A major part of Magia's vision with Dobra Atmosfera was to counsel people in need, particularly women suffering from domestic violence. Magia believed that instilling principles of authentic "dobra atmosfera" was essential for improved energy in homes, workplaces and social environments. Her bigger dream was to craft a retreat on private land, with an animal shelter, and tranquil, inspiring surrounds for people to become immersed in nature. Magia's ideal space would be in the mountains or lakeside in a forest; it sounded wholly compatible with my personal dreams of future homes.

The more I settled into my new environs, the more I unwound. I took particular care to slow down. I studied new concepts, and allowed the undercurrent of inspiration from years of travels to rise to the surface, and solidify. It activated one of the great intellectual and enlightened periods of my life. Meanwhile, there was no shortage of new adventures.

Road Trips and Concerts

The final weekend of September was greeted by warm sunshine, beset by crisp, chilling breeze. Magia and I drove from Krakow to Warsaw, to attend a short-notice Maribou State concert at T-Mobile Festival. We resided at a quaint ground-floor Polish apartment, in the southern Warsawian suburb of Mokotow. The homely flat featured a handmade wooden bunkbed and single bed, with a wardrobe and small table. Our first evening took us to the riverside Planetarium, for a spectacular, full-peripheral broadcast of the galaxy. Hand in hand, walking riverside and through parks, or across Warszawian streets, the destiny of the universe led me here with Magia.

The concert was in an affluent area of Warsaw, hosted at a huge private functions space, that appeared understated from the outside. A large courtyard led to an ultra-modern building: pristine and white inside. A square atrium held various bars, where a hundred people milled about. The spacious, rectangular concert room was filled with a huge soundsystem, lighting rig and black curtains that covered the walls. Maribou State performed rehearsed new material from their latest album, Kingdoms in Colour, ahead of a world tour.

A few days earlier Magia had referred to me as a "Can of Ham".

To my befuddled expression, she explained that, like a tin of ineloquently processed meat, I bore an expiry date.

"It's because of your lifestyle," Magia murmured, bereft of much emotion. "I have the feeling you will be gone; maybe in weeks, or months, but I know it's true."

Magia compared herself to a "bus stop" on my journey: one leg towards a destination that was murky at best. I looked back at her with a flicker of sadness. Magia's perceptivity and humble acceptance lent me further respect for her. In many ways, Magia was my ideal match: my intellectual equal, my harmonious counter-balance. We were on similar paths, with complementary wants and needs; most crucially, at this same moment in time. This was a big reason that we became best friends nearly instantly. I sure found it hard to believe that what I had right now was anything more than a passing trend. Hence, as Magia accurately reflected – in conversations and through her writing – that I was merely stopping through: "Can of ham".

In my infinite dreams – the ones I'm with somebody – my love and I voyage through the universe. Single life afforded a daily roulette for love and magic, every time we stepped outside. Yet, it rarely actualised, making those moments it actually happened, extraordinarily special. We cannot take love and adventure for granted, and by now we know we cannot force magic. We can only put ourselves in the best positions to manifest our desires.

Whomever I'd travel with through this lifetime would be an adventurer, and a compatible travel mate. I undoubtedly realised this last year. While many girls were up for fun adventures, few held my vital prerequisites for harmonious co-existence: Lowkey, self-reliant, apt decision maker, truthful, communicative, modest, patient, peaceful, cool. Service might be slow. Sanitation be shit. Food be bland, or not exactly what was ordered. Bed be small. Room be hot. Water be cold. Rats in bathroom. Wait be long: No need to complain. Take each experience as they came, good or bad. Stay calm, be respectful, and everything will work out: usually and eventually.

Magia was certainly up for adventure. She crafted escapades of her own, like the wooden lodge in the mountains. One of her dreams was to cycle through the USA, culminating at her first Burning Man: the solo journey of a lifetime. Magia appreciated the plans I suggested, and often enhanced them. She paved the way for expeditions, like leading Sandino's Jack and Jill up the hills of Zakopane. The four of us strode through Polish mountains, riding a shuttle bus to a summit when winds were too extreme for ski lifts. At the top, we drank warm mulled wine and peered at majestic valleys below. Magia's car was a unique benefit I'd not previously enjoyed, with the oddity of none of my past girlfriends driving. Our road trips were fun. Magia enjoyed long treks through cities or forests, and was open to new food and experiences. She never really complained about anything, appreciating whatever budget accommodation I reserved.

This is not to say it was easy. By constantly living and traveling together, through numerous challenges, fatigue, inebriates and social pressures, tension was bound to arise. I maintained plentiful open wounds and triggers, that would send me spiralling into brooding behavioural patterns. Dating a psychotherapist who'd survived a battalion of her own life struggles, lent understanding, insight and compassion. Here was a woman who'd endured a childhood of physical and mental abuse, trapped in Catholic escapist and apologist thinking; first in communist society, then transitioning through the plastic facade of democracy and rampant capitalism. Magia overcame fifteen years of anorexia. She sensed that there was something seriously wrong with the modern world, but remained appreciative of the lifestyle she earned today. Her experiences meant she had her own spectrum of raw emotional triggers, particularly in response to male anger and attitude.

Cracks in our relationship occasionally surfaced; some at home, others on the road. Longer car trips always seemed to bring out stress and unhappiness in both of us. One November dawn we woke up in Krakow, with the first snow of the season coating the ground, ahead of a lengthy road trip to Cologne. An inexplicably muted drive led to reminiscing about Titanic in Bialystok, the last time our relationship felt like it was sinking. Fittingly, our terse night came upon a ship in Dresden: a converted boat hotel that supplied our quarters for the evening. We strolled around the generally-deserted old part of the historic city, mostly in silence. A freeing chat in the morning brought everything back on course, and inspired a jovial voyage ahead. Later we learned that long family car rides had been generally tense and unpleasant in both of our childhoods.

The next day we arrived in Cologne around sunset. Magia met old friends of mine for the first time: Jono and Miri. The four of us spent a couple of days deliberating on our smattering of personal endeavours. Magia introduced Dobra Atmosfera. Jono and I brainstormed the technological ideology for Memtell, that proposed a conscious rebuke to today's morally-suspect, privacy-spying tech behemoths. Magia's excellent Memtell suggestion proposed interlinking people's memories. We visited a community arts and wellness centre, that featured everything from yoga, meditation, open talks and music nights. Jono and Miri extended us invitations to their July wedding.

In Berlin, Magia and I booked lodging near Tempelhof; the rooms spanned a block of converted cubic shipping containers. As these little boxes were particularly frigid in plummeting temperatures, we affectionately referred to them as "Ice Cubes". From our little ice cube we explored majestic Tempelhof Airport, loitered on the bleachers of the Berlin Bears baseball field, and imagined twentieth century life in the middle of war. Tempelhof had been the pride of the Nazi party, having spawned countless aerial bombardments and missions. Thousands of casual visitors lingered around the vast runways; many were on bikes, skateboards or roller blades, while others flew kites. Magia and I strolled along the runway and alongside Tempelhof's vast deserted terminal halls. A sizeable and fairly-luxurious asylum for refugees was built out of shipping containers, near the police headquarters that was integrated with the remaining airport facilities.

The latest David August concert was performed at historic Columbiahalle, in its old aircraft hanger. Inside, we weaved our way through packed crowds, and settled in the front row. Magia and I became lost in music and embrace, while the bonafide artist David August sculpted layers of sonic textures, from a plethora of synthesizers and analog drum machines.

The next day I toured Magia around Berlin. At Brandenburg Gate we drove too far, into a square packed with hundreds of milling tourists; fortunately the police barely noticed us. After a few minutes of green-induced paranoia and calming myself, I navigated the car slowly, Playa-style with flashing dual blinkers, through the thick of the meandering masses, and past police. I toured Magia around haunts of my past Berlin times. We rolled through Kreuzberg, later pulled alongside the shuttered metal gates of Sandino World Improvement Network, then zipped to the landmark Dong Xuan Centre. We treated ourselves to heaping bowls of perfectly spiced noodles, and stocked up on exotic supplies from a Vietnamese supermarket.

With the Sun having fallen, Magia dozed in the passenger seat, while I navigated the car across the German autobahn under night lights. There was one guilty flash of a speeding camera, before we crossed into Poland. Within a few hours of whisking along the highway we revisited the comforts of Zielonki.

Bold new adventures were on the horizon, with Magia's first voyage to India two months away. This was our window together: right here, right now. Knowing that nothing lasts forever, and few nubile relationships last long at all, we must cherish every moment possible. Now, some work to do.

Self-Experimentation

"The Road Less Travelled" suggests that objectively observing our personal behaviour was a critical precursor to valuable lessons and insights. While on the cusp of uncovering deeper inner-secrets about a lot of things, I acknowledged that alcohol, particularly in abundance, was not healthy for me. That alcohol was such a rampant blight on society and health, was another blatant indication. The night I'd jealously and furiously smashed up a hotel in Seoul remained my last bout of binge-drinking, and the final colossal storm of my anger, although I was yet to eradicate drinking or anger altogether.

Each week I drank no more than a few bottled honey, cherry or coconut beers with Magia at home. Even on nights out, at festivals or unplanned city jaunts, I consumed minimal drinks, smoked a couple of joints, and all was under control. I knew that alcohol was neither the sole nor pivotal factor behind my angst. As a depressant, alcohol agitates moods like guitar amplifier saturation. For troubled souls it can provide early veils of comfort, before layered multitudes of the liquid drug's downer effects begin to overwhelm. I knew alcohol was a major downer; this is why after breakups, instead of drinking myself to oblivion, I countered with detoxes. Yet, for years before I'd ever touched alcohol, since a perplexed child, my anger raged along.

The comforts of Zielonki afforded me a quantum, cerebral leap into exploring my lifelong issues. I was in a controlled, peaceful environment, with an intimate, emotionally-resolute partner, who bore little inclination of cruelty or disrespect. Earlier in our relationship, every few weeks I erupted with bouts of frustration, purging sharp verbal tenacity. Like a beggar being beaten, I recoiled at each lashing, hissing and seething like an angry snake. Except, the beating was coming from within.

Considering the applicable factors, it wasn't alcohol, although alcohol didn't help. These events similarly transpired after I smoked Indica blend: the downer cousin of Sativa. Sometimes Indica stoked inspired bursts of creative energy, before the effects faded, and frustration unwittingly boiled over, simply by trying to communicate. Not merely simplifying English for a Polish native, but I was frustrated having to speak at all. This wasn't only Magia: it harked back to every past girlfriend, housemates, many friendships, certain work projects, and even pets. It might occur while I was cooking, alone in the kitchen, lost in deep thoughts, or typing away. Once somebody disrupted my cerebral momentum, particularly repetitively, I'd often snap back at the intrusion. Whenever my mind warmed up to its computational peak – such as while web programming – every little thing became a distraction. This was a big reason I tried to swear off computer programming for many years.

A further decline of my emotional frailty sometimes brought flashes of urges to be single and left alone, even if that meant shivering under a cardboard box in the cold. It was nobody else's fault: It was me. If other energies were disrupting my headspace, I preferred solitude.

After discussing my patterns with Magia, we better understood the symptoms, and various factors that contributed to my rage. At the end of the apartment's hallway there was a small cluttered spare room with a chair and desk – simply named "Last Room". Sometimes I brought my laptop to Last Room to write, or to craft my art and music. Whenever I felt stressed or tense, I departed the living room: a step that brought noticeable improvement. Creating space within our home and relationship was welcomingly effective.

This tweak helped, but it didn't solve everything. Upon noticing accelerating inner-tension ahead of Christmas – typically an annual pain point for me – I resumed Vipassana meditation every morning. Magia sometimes accompanied me, but I'd steadfastly practice without her. Regular Vipassana made a noticeable impact, with the inherent benefit of other factors not mattering so much at all. Even my minor gripes and common stresses felt less important. However, meditation was an aid, and not the ultimate elixir. We must diligently continue self-observation, and even experiment on the self – determining what works, what doesn't, and what might.

My recent purge of social media, and a nearly complete avoidance of news, greatly aided my progress. Eliminating Facebook from my life, save for a couple of weekly posts on the GASHE and Digital Nomad pages, led to less distractions from misguided social feeds and messaging, while bolstering my productivity. I spent less time on news sites, limiting myself to The Guardian, BBC and Positive.News – eventually eradicating news altogether. Earlier in the year, I quit my biggest waste of time: Fantasy baseball. It consumed countless hours every day, where I'd study baseball reports and advanced statistics to craft pointless but addictive future baseball lineups.

Having been online since 1994, I'd become tired of the wasteland of the modern Internet, manipulated search engine results, unrelenting ads, pop-ups, algorithms, tracking, government spying and ideological censorship. I felt a warm karma upon making more ethical tech decisions, even simply by considering alternatives, like researching self-built Linux systems and open source solutions. But it wasn't easy – there was a handful of powerful, state-sanctioned enterprises, that dominated every nook and cranny of the Internet and our lives. In this modern corporatocracy it wasn't by coincidence, but rather from decades of ingenious US military design, coupled with mass-societal psychology, through all-reaching media propaganda. The weak, manipulated and distracted mass populace could be convinced to believe just about anything.

I wondered about the impetus of my anguish: Was it the farcical, artificial state of the world, or its unjust corruption of power? Lingering scars of my homelessness two decades earlier? Lack of attentive parenting or family? Something deep down untrue I'd lived with unknowingly – like how my bubble-wrapped niece must wonder about the unsettling truth of her existence? Perhaps each aspect contributed, in parts and accumulated. These things I couldn't change, but I *could* alter my habits and reactions.

Inner peace does not randomly appear. There is no plateau. It is a journey to the end. We are constantly acknowledging and improving, learning and growing, and rising, falling and rebirthing. Mustering the courage to honestly assess ourselves is the beginning, and then we must come to terms with whatever the truth might be. Move forward.

Elevating Mental Consciousness

On the day I cancelled my scheduled autumn trip to the UK, I made substantial strides with Nomadic.Cloud development. Coincidentally, my bank balance rose from $2 to over $800. Perhaps the old Sea would have justified this banking bonanza to set out on a business-and-pleasure jaunt to the UK, but I was determined to make the most of the opportunity to settle down.

Money is a distraction, and an artificial carrot on a masked puppet master's stick. Money forces us to think about doing something with it: spending it, investing it, putting it aside, worrying about it, or over-complexly evading tax authorities when privileged with outlandish amounts – that the rich and powerful execute quite expertly. Tax dollars are needed to overpay for politician salaries and, inexplicably, their luxurious expenses. Having a lot of money ensures a lust for more, opening the mind to perverse gratification – of power, luxury, sex, revenge – that manifests misery in the absolute present. Sometimes it's easier to have just enough money to cover what's important: food, shelter, transport, communications and a little fun. I wouldn't wish blind inheritance or lottery winning on anybody, as no authentic happiness seems to come from it.

Yet, I strove to figure out a formula that could assure me

greater financial stability, instead of surviving daily and weekly. One such tonic came from avoiding expensive societies, such as Melbourne. Instead, I based myself in more affordable and inspiring regions, like the developing world. Minimising money stress makes a kingdom of difference for the psyche, and we can build on it from there.

My financial incompetence wasn't for a lack of hard work, intelligence, or bold ideas – but perhaps too many. Short-lived passion regularly inspired promising new concepts; I'd burrow down one rabbit hole, and out another. For twenty years I'd often reach the very end of a journey, with websites and plans ready to enact (see: Nomadic.Cloud), then lose faith, or discover a fatal flaw. Sometimes I realised I didn't really care about the project at all. I found it difficult to be driven by profit; instead I preferred the knowledge and experience that came from embarking upon any particular journey.

Intrigued by the potential of newer technologies such as blockchain, AI robotics and quantum computing, I was particularly enamoured of Holochain: a disruptive post-blockchain platform. The creators of Holo vowed to right the wrongs of the corrupted corporatocracy, through code. For a few weeks, programming returned as my main focus, although internally I was repulsed. I detested staring everlastingly at screens, attenuating an unnatural frequency of the brain that was fine-tuned for programmatical problem-solving. *For what?* Self-learning machines with legit artificial intelligence will soon devise far more powerful, efficient and secure programming algorithms. *Was dedicating my life to programming my legacy?* Surely it wasn't. Running a hosting and domain company was a serious obstacle for me. I was fed up with wasting time coding, or supporting mundane solutions like WordPress and email hosting, and I desperately sought a way out.

I still completed the Holo course, and became a Certified Holochain Developer. With this knowledge. I could recruit programmers to build more socially-transformative concepts. I'd long envisioned free education and secure communications in places like Malawi and across Africa, ethical computers comprised of recycled materials, self-defence robots and gadgets, a more transparent economic system yet eliminating income tax, immutable democracy, and helping people save and preserve their memories forever (a.k.a. Memtell).

I took every available opportunity to learn. Books were a welcome distraction from the computer screen, and I delved into everything from Stephen Hawking through Yuval Noah Harari. I learned about the history and future of our universe, planet and species. Hawking argued that there may be infinite universes, each with their own probability of reality, and this shaped my personal theories on applying quantum possibilities to our lives. Harari's "Sapiens" taught the evolution of humans over millions of years, and where modern society went wrong (e.g. the onset of the agricultural era, and private land / people ownership). "Homo Deus" forecast where humans are headed. Ominously, Harari warned of a looming global crisis, where citizens would soon be forced to decide between Privacy or Health. Every intellectual stimulation of the brain helped stoke it, keeping it active, healthy and exercised. I acknowledged that the brain was far more essential to longevity than the body, for we have the minds long after our bodies break down.

From my various experiments, I learned a few consistent lessons. More than a couple of drinks of alcohol was unwise. One coffee a day was sufficient. Indica weed or hash were not suited for me; Sativa or CBD were superior. My most peaceful and productive days began with meditation and writing, without Internet. I preferred a complete avoidance of social media and news. Long walks in fresh air helped unleash my creative brain. Tasty, healthy food and plentiful loving cuddles were essential. And, the stability of a safe and comfortable home provided an anchor, from which we can accomplish great things.

Polish Christmas and Musical New Year

My first proper Polish Christmas came at Magia's family house. For the first time, I met her mother, two brothers, their wives, two sweet and curious nieces and a little dog. I'd long considered Christmas awkward and uncomfortable, *particularly* with my family. Stepping inside Magia's mother's home was uncannily familiar, alike the longtime home of my Canadian-Lithuanian-Polish grandparents. The Dziewic house was adorned with faded photographs in wooden frames, religious ornaments, special silverware and abundant Christmas decorations. The main difference from my grandparents' home in Canada, was a complete lack of English.

A unique Polish tradition was the embarrassing "wishes" ceremony, where everybody individually bestowed wishes upon one another. In limited English, each of Magia's family members shyly offered hopes about my life, to which I replied with similar positive affirmations. Awkwardness subsided in time for a tasty dinner, with heaping plates of turkey, fish and potatoes. Afterwards featured Polish Christmas carols, where the entire family sang along. Embarrassed, I stared blankly at long, alien words, with lots of z's and w's. Within a few hours, amidst a joyful and accomplished buzz, Christmas was over.

With no other plans for New Years, we were invited to Magia's eldest brother's place. His house, steps from the mother's, stood in a small countryside village. Inside was modern and spacious, with high ceilings in a bright, open living space. The creative and free-thinking Jaromir maintained a music studio through a hallway, adorned with music equipment, synthesizers, drum machines and computer gadgets. Occasionally we disappeared into the studio and jammed. In the living room, I was invited by the two younger girls to play a dancing video game, where we rhythmically flailed away to popular commercial hits. It was so embarrassing that I concentrated extra hard. Even though this was my first time, I surprisingly won both rounds, to the delight of the youngest: sweet little Róża. At midnight, the six humans and little dog stepped into the zero degree night to watch fireworks from a hill. Magia and I held hands and kissed, with frosty breath and happy hearts.

Then arrived the biggest surprise of all, when Magia coordinated her keen family to sit around the living room, while I was to demonstrate examples of my music. As somebody who'd barely shared any of my creations, let alone to multiple intimate listeners at once, this was a new challenge. I acknowledged the safe environment, and that it could trigger positive momentum for my musically-intended year ahead. I presented a selection of my personal, unreleased classics since 2002, through to a draft of Arising and Passing. The entire family was authentically impressed. The karma of this New Year musical performance premeditated the year ahead, when I'd finally start shifting focus towards daily immersion in music study and production.

...

On New Year's Day 2019, Magia and I spent the day in bed. We were comfortably lazy, with coffee and late breakfast, watched films, dined on a tasty pesto gnocchi dinner, and indulged in delightful things that couples generally do in bed. This was the happiest holidays I could remember; maybe my best ever.

When I finally emerged back into reality, on the second day of the year, I caught up on several days of unread emails. Sitting in my inbox was a stunning surprise: Holiday greetings from Boogie. She'd written at 8am on January 1st, 2019.

"Dear Sea, I hope you are doing great, living your life happily, passionately, without regrets or fear. :) I wish you an amazing year filled with adventure and love. Hugs, Boogie"

Attached was a link to a Ted Talk: How to Live Passionately No Matter Your Age. This was the first time I'd heard from Boogie in eight months, and it predictably stirred emotions. I didn't know how to respond: *Was she calling me old?* Could she feel I was void of authentic passion in my life? Whatever her intent, it caused much contemplation, something I would deal with, or not, at a later time. At this point, Boogie continued to reside in a small but open part of my heart, that Magia was slowly and surely consuming.

With a loving start, and an unexpected peace offering from The Past, 2019 was underway. I had myriad issues to resolve – including what to do with Mother.Domains. I had no further desire to program websites or support hosting clients, and felt a growing yearning to spend the rest of my life on my true passions: music and art. Even despite barely checking the news, I could sense that something major and sinister was looming. All inclinations urged me to enjoy 2019 as much as possible, before the world changed forever.

Chapter 17
Year of the Pig

Each of the twelve years of the Chinese lunar calendar is represented by an animal. According to ancient Chinese fables, each animal's place was determined by The Great Race, overseen by the Jade Emperor. The first twelve animals to finish the race would earn years named in their honour. Over mountains, valleys and seas, impassioned animal competitors struggled through difficult conditions and challenging terrain. Eventually, the race was won by the clever Rat, who craftily snuck past the finish line, after graciously being carried across the water by second-placed Ox. Next came: Tiger, Rabbit, Dragon, Snake, Horse, Goat (or Sheep), Monkey and Rooster (or Cock). The playful and lazy Dog finished eleventh, ahead of the twelfth and final place, earned by the Pig. After the Pig, the cycle repeats. The honoured animals are celebrated at the commencement of each Chinese Lunar New Year.

In the year 2019, less than a century had passed since scientific revolutions assured the unlikeliness of an all-empowering monotheist God. If anything, humans have convinced each other that *humans* are gods: the most important beings on the planet. Future technological advances in biochemical augmentation, robotic prosthetics and infinite lifespans have nudged us towards manmade godliness. Humans frequently play God in the lives of other humans and creatures – deciding what's "best" for others.

Modern humans' track records with animals are abysmal – but what if animals had a say? What if each of the twelve animals of the Great Race examined their relationship with humans over the course of their year, and voted whether to keep humans around? How many would vouch for mankind? Pigs – smart, cute and curious – could not possibly approve of their species' routine genocide. Dogs are not treated altogether universally gently, even in the West. Tigers? Horses? Rats?

Inevitably, nature will intervene against humanity's destruction, whether through unstoppable viruses, mutations of immortal killer mosquitoes, or seismic and nautical events that wipe out everybody. Selfishness and righteousness are slowly killing humans off. The daily mass-pumping of gas, coal, plastic, industrial overflow, jet fuel, toxic fires and other garbage spewed into the elements, affects entire life cycles and food chains. The polluted air filters rain, that flows into water supplies, contaminating already-troubled water, dirtied by centuries of industrial filth and continent-sized patches of plastic and garbage. Human recklessness is killing fish, birds, smaller mammals and flora, and it's unsurprising that we're at the onset of the next Great Mass Extinction: this time, manufactured and sponsored by Man, Inc.

Capitalism, by its laws, foretells a shadowy future, dictated by autonomous armed robot corporations, in a society where machines rule and most humans are the pigs of tomorrow. One could argue that we're already there: perhaps disguised as free range products, and dressed up in fancy clothes, with the same plastic goods, faces and personalities.

Look around in any mega-supermarket, of which there are countless thousands. Tall shelves are packed with unlimited goods, laden with expiry dates. Because of consumerism's inherent oversupply, a huge proportion of these goods will never be used. Countless millions of animal lives are needlessly tortured and sacrificed every year, so that supermarket shelves appear full. Consider the vast amount of power and waste generated into every sliver of packaging, from manufacturing through transportation to our homes. We open each package, chuck out the garbage, consume whatever – then, repeat. The waste must also be transported and processed: more energy. Where does this garbage go? For years, rich countries shipped their waste to developing countries. Out of sight, out of mind; most humans don't see or truly care about the result of our collective habits. It's why naïve citizens are more likely to blame China or Islam for the world's problems, when we all have a hand in our collaboratively radical self-destruction.

Television is a blight: Thousands of channels, none of which are truly important. Blaring news and financial headlines, sports news, infinite hot-headed opinion, so-called entertainment, and pauses sponsored by pharmaceuticals. The vast amount of money, time and resources wasted on television exhibits humans for what they largely are: lazy, under-intellectual and misguided. The Media frightens us about health, and stoke fears, before people cure themselves with popular placebo medicines, shopping therapy, unhealthy indulgences and mindless TV.

Planet Karma is coming. Environmental and medical catastrophes are one human-stoked disaster or maniacal ego trip away from wiping out entire populations. War is coming; we're in a new Cold War now, and civil wars are on the brink. The latest financial crash will be a catastrophe, particularly for the poor: the Greater Depression, a hundred years later.

This is the Year of the Pig: A final year of human gluttony and excess, before the next cycle of animals resumes. Perhaps a dozen years, to enact progressive change for mankind and the rest of the planet, or death do us part. The old ways are coming to an end, violently or not, in sickness or in health.

A Living Taste of India

On the final, frosty morning of January 2019, Magia and I rode to Krakow's John-Paul Baptice airport, dispatched by Magia's mother and sister-in-law. LOT flew us on a small jet from Krakow to Warsaw, where we shivered on a transfer bus in sub-zero degree snow. After a five-hour layover in Helsinki's modern airport, then an overnight flight to Delhi, we arrived in India's smoggy and bustling capital at dawn. We rode a black & yellow taxi towards the heart of the noisy megacity.

For Magia's introduction to India, I booked a plush budget hotel in Paharganj: combustible, hectic and a controlled-chaotic unleashing of five senses. My sentiment was that, after several days in Paharganj learning to navigate traffic and street hawkers, she'd be well-prepared for nearly anything India could throw her way. And, Magia enjoyed it. During our first walk from Aura Hotel, uncertain of directions, we plunged through bustling and noisy streets, filled with motorbikes, cows and dogs. We vaguely gravitated towards Paharganj's narrow main convergence of rooftop restaurants and shops. At the top floor of a Nepalese restaurant overlooking the bustle of Paharganj, Magia feasted on her first authentic Indian cooking: palak paneer, jeera rice, mango lassi and butter garlic roti.

Aftereffects of jetlag rendered us confined to our hotel room for an unexpected fifteen-hour sleep, as our comfortable but windowless room obscured the Sun's clock. Complementary buffet breakfast was served upstairs, and we dined on room service in a big soft bed, while flicking through countless Indian movie and TV channels.

Sunday was our solitary touristic day. We commissioned a noble Hindu driver, who commandeered our city-wide tour from morning to evening. We visited Old Delhi mosques, Red Fort, Humayun's Tomb, dined on paneer lunch at a popular, shabby eatery, sauntered around Lotus Temple and concluded at a serene Hindu temple. The next morning, debilitating sickness rendered me immobile; we extended our stay by a night. We missed out on a drive to Agra, and a prospective sunrise visit to the Taj Mahal, but Magia wasn't bothered.

After the rugged assimilation in boisterous Paharganj, our home for the next week was a rooftop apartment in Mehrauli Village. Our veritable penthouse overlooked the historic Qutub Minar monument, a foresty area underneath dull-grey smoggy sky, rickety streets and creaky buildings. One over-intense spicy palak paneer rendered Magia ill, with side-effects of her first "Delhi Belly" lasting most of the year.

Despite my own nausea, I fulfilled an invitation to visit Karnal, specifically the Haryana School of Internet Marketing, run by GameX co-captain Navn Gupta. Joining me was the kind and devoted Govind, my GameX bedmate. The bespectacled domain prodigy braved hours on the bus to meet me outside Delhi's Interstate Bus Terminal, near Kashmiri Gate. Govind treated me to a delectable breakfast of dosas, curry and chai, before we rode through torrential rain on a long, bumpy ride north.

At HSIM's HQ I was royally greeted by a warm reception, and a whiteboard that announced my arrival. Smiling staff respectfully rose to their feet, before a smart-dressed Navn invited me into his office. Over pleasantries, platters of snacks were presented; I was so stuffed, I believed this must be lunch.

"Ah, no!" chuckled Navn. "Lunch is served soon."

Indeed, lunch was a special occasion. Each staff member had prepared a personal dish from their ancestry of family recipes. A dozen people sat around tables filled with heaping curries, breads, rice, and several unusual dishes I'd not previously tried. It was my duty to taste each and every one of them, with eyes curiously observing my reaction as I devoured each delight. Fortunately, everything genuinely tasted marvellous, although my belt was bursting, even before the dessert round of gulab jamun donuts soaked in syrup.

Proceedings shifted to a roundtable workshop. I introduced myself, and shared stories and wisdom from my two decades of Internet work. I answered questions on topics ranging from career advice through the future of technology. At its conclusion I was presented a special gift: a wrapped copy of the legendary Hindu text, Bhagavad Gita – "As It Is".

Although I'd already eaten enough for days, one of the sisters and her husband arrived, and they escorted me to their house. I was chaperoned by Govind, my careful minder. This excursion involved more snacks, sandwiches and drinks, that we downed at a modern, large white house. Euphoria from overeating offered a new and unusual high, but I could not further fit anything in my stomach. After rounds of selfies, I returned to the office, and bid farewell to Navn, Govind and HSIM staff.

Up the road, I splashed through puddles to jump upon an onrushing metal bus. Dozens of stunned faces were clearly impressed at a foreigner appearing like magic. A trio of young men towards the back took particular interest in me. The one sitting beside me benevolently bought my bus ticket, before the usual rounds of curious questions: *Where are you from? What do you do? Do you like India?* After they disembarked, it granted me an opportunity to prepare for tomorrow's BlogX national blogger conference. The bus roared through night, rain and traffic. Eventually I made my way home to the Mehrauli rooftop, where a cuddly and recovering Magia awaited me.

The morning's BlogX began casually, if not nervously. I was to present the morning's topic of podcasting, with esteemed broadcaster Bijay Gautum. My podcasting experience dated back to UMFM Radio, that I founded in 2001. UMFM maintained an unexpectedly popular directory of diverse music radio stations, and we produced cult-like in-house shows for years. Well-regarded drum & bass Knowledge Magazine published that I was "a pioneer of Internet Radio", and various world media over the years interviewed me as some sort of visionary. Since then, I wasn't much involved with podcasting.

The conference started slowly, with an energy that balanced the typical anxiety of organisers, and a laid-back, late-arriving crowd. The start was delayed, then came a smattering of technical issues. The void of vibe concerned me, in that our session was rapidly approaching, yet the audience wasn't warmed up. I knew our session had to be high energy.

After the ceremonial proceedings and keynote speech, I was called up to stage. The crowd of a few hundred bloggers politely applauded as I peered into the spotlight, towards video cameras pointing my way. Co-host Bijay was introduced. I gripped the mic like my MC Spence rap days, and welcomed Bijay.

"It feels like we're a hip-hop act." I turned to Bijay, surveyed the audience, then beatboxed: "Boom ba-ba KA, ba-BOOM ba-ba KA!"

This relaxed the crowd. I mostly asked Bijay questions about modern podcasting. Our presentation was informative, and apparently inspiring. A loud ovation filled the auditorium as we departed the stage, and a lively BlogX was underway.

Upon the lunch break, I remained so stuffed from yesterday's Haryana feasts that I barely ate much. Magia's stomach hadn't recovered to enjoy the lavish, four-star hotel buffet. Feeling mutually wretched, after the conference Magia and I returned to our rooftop apartment for necessary rest.

A shy female blogger invited us to Sunday's traveller picnic at Delhi's Central Park in Connaught Place. On a sunny afternoon, in front of a hundred youngsters I introduced myself, and summarised Plan Sea and my nomadic career. Speaking from experience, I assured onlookers: "Work at dreams: They can come true." A nervous Magia spoke after me; she mentioned this was her first visit to India, and previewed her Dobra Atmosfera blog. Afterward, the shy blogger and her friends escorted us around Connaught Place, treating us to juice and snacks.

Our fortnight Delhi visit concluded in the hip southern suburb of Saket, where we visited Nalin, his partner Ritu, and cute little dog, Cookie. Magia and I paused at Hauz Khas village for a few hours before our flight to Mumbai. Maybe spending two weeks in smoggy and noisy Delhi was excessive, but it was a productive time, and was certainly a strong introduction to India for Magia.

Loops in Goa

Mumbai was instantly pleasant upon landing, particularly its warm, tropical air. After declining a dodgy offer from a toothless cabby outside the airport, sparse traffic expedited our legit taxi's journey to the southern district of Colaba. Check-in was breezy at the budget but well-situated Carlton Hotel. Colaba was famous from classic novel Shantaram, particularly Leopold's Cafe. There was the landmark police station, across from which Magia absent-mindedly bought weed from an old Indian hippie. The area featured vintage British Empire-styled Victorian streets and courtyards, with a posh, security-guarded Starbucks in the core. Oversaturated with fancy restaurants and overpriced shops, there remained bargains to be found, particularly with sketchy diners serving some of the tastiest paneer of the trip. The hotel manager sneakily sold us whisky under the counter. Magia and I wandered around, passing naval installations and the Gateway of India.

While unable to book an overnight train from Mumbai to Goa, we managed to acquire early Saturday morning train tickets for the fifteen-hour ride. The friendly Mandovi Express in underrated third class prompted chats with nearby families, who shared digital books and homemade spiced snacks. Sometimes we lay on a metal bunk, listened to music or ventured nearer the train's exits, peering at passing trees and villages, as the train rumbled onwards. From Pernem station, a taxi van whisked us to Mandrem's Sunset Hotel, perfectly in time for sunset. The glorious orange ball fell beneath grey-blue sea, while green leaves blew in warm breeze. Opening our balcony door afforded ocean views. A short skip led to Sunset's tasty restaurant, and its comfortable upstairs shanti lounge that faced the beach.

...

After two revitalising, sunburn-recovering nights at Sunset, we made our way north along the beach to Arambol. Magia snoozed at Love Temple's shanti lounge, while I typed away. My inspired writing was complemented by fruit lassis, chai and snacks. Whatever confident and relaxed energy we emitted was a curiosity to others: initially an American traveller and a bikini-clad German. We were invited by a young French man to join a "donation only" Kundalini session: a style of sound healing meditation, definitely not to be confused with cunnilingus. In a yoga hall with a thatched roof and walls, our small group was led by the French's mother, who was allegedly a qualified teacher. Lying on a mat with our eyes closed, we relaxed to drone-like chanting, as various instruments harmonized, and occasional hands brushed against our skin. While we'd consented to respectful touching, nobody agreed to being filmed – an awkwardly perverse moment after the session, that the voyeuristic French mother and son sheepishly shrugged off.

Eventually, Magia and I arrived at La Cayden: our home for the week. A recent change in ownership reduced the hotel's previously impressive amenities. La Cayden's once-lively rooftop was no longer an Arambol hotspot. Still, Magia rapidly delighted in the locale: minutes away from the beach.

A few days later we toddled back from Love Temple, where we'd worked from breakfast to sunset. Magia and I strolled along the beach, revelling in the sights and sounds of waves, under ash-coloured sky. We could have walked at any other pace, lingered in other destinations or headed elsewhere – but decided on returning home to drop off our bags and chill. At the base of Arambol's main incline, past restaurants and countless mirrors of shops selling the same bargain souvenirs, we detoured to fetch a bottle of white wine and several king-sized beers. Directly across from La Cayden's staircase entrance, we paused for traffic. I monitored each scooter driver's eyes for their intentions. One motorist's brown hair flowed in the air, while a babe sat on the back; the driver stared into my face.

"Sea!!"

He stopped the bike while numerous others whizzed by. His beard threw me off, coupled with my lack-of-recognition psychosis. My first impression guessed he was Hash, from last year's "Goa on Acid". But this was somebody special from farther back on my journey: Harlequin, the young enlightened Belgian from Chiang Mai. Weeks earlier we were aware of our mutual

Indian presence, but locations and routes didn't seem compatible, and we didn't coordinate anything. Yet here he was, appearing directly in front of the entrance to our unannounced guest house, at the exact moment following our lengthy walk home. Conveniently, we now had wine and beer for all of us.

Our quartet headed to La Cayden's rooftop for snacks and frolicking mosquitos, while we caught up on our past fifteen months of journeys. Harlequin's return home to Belgium, following his inspiring stint in India, had been tough on his psyche. He'd observed friends, family and society in different ways, that generated stress and frustration. Consciousness nagged him about better uses of time and energy, rather that dispassionately scheming income for travels. He met Apu, his committed partner, during his past India trip; she was a talented illustrator and artist. Apu's golden-tanned skin and sandy blonde hair made her look European, although she was Indian.

This latest example of Grace was a reminder of many unexplained coincidences and mysteries. Compatible energies seem to magnetise together, even for a while. People come, go, and reconnect as needed. With Harlequin – another worldly and spiritual soul – it once more felt like: "See you again".

...

My favourite place in Arambol is This Is It. There were few better spots from which to write with calming views of the sea. This Is It was consistently graced by expert service, luscious food and drink, and an authentically friendly vibe. One could hang at This Is It all day with no pressure. Coconut lassis were a tangible dream, and coconut rice with baked peanuts: another heaven. Magia and I spent several days at This Is It, dreaming and writing from breakfast through sundown.

As it dawned on me that Connection is what make places special, this was certainly true with This Is It. Once, the staff trustingly handed us keys to their scooter for our drive to the ATM, that was otherwise a half-hour walk away. This was Magia's first-ever scooter experience: in India with no helmet. She was delighted to hold on from the back, while I navigated through narrow crevices and people-littered pavements. There was a short line at the main ATM, and the nearby alternative was shuttered. News reports announced that police arrested three

Russian men, who were carrying drugs and had detonated explosives at that very ATM, yesterday evening. For the purpose of relevancy, the news also detailed tension building between India and Pakistan. Recent terror bombings were responded by Indian air strikes on the Pakistani border. Deeper down on the streets of Goa, I could feel tension; it wasn't the happiest time in the country, region or world.

...

After a cruisy week at La Cayden, Magia and I headed south to Mandrem. We weaved through backstreets to Hotel Casa Grande: tranquil, spacious and flush with birds. This was our home of four nights, to commemorate Magia's fortieth birthday, and perhaps our nicest accommodation of the trip. The large room featured a discrete balcony that looked into the jungle, a soft queen bed, desk and dresser, and subtle but colourful artwork that adorned the walls. Simple, complimentary break-fast was prepared on the rooftop daily, served by a pregnant Russian, who was married to a Hyderabadian, while their young child played. The building was welcomingly peaceful, and was empty beyond another Russian couple.

On a friend's tip, we visited best-kept secret Ashwem Beach, nestled between southern Mandrem and Morjim. At comfortable Vayuu and their blissful upstairs lounge, we watched the ocean, a vacated sandy beach, and the setting Sun. Good fortune from random Americans uncovered an impressive goodie bag for Magia's birthday, that led to her first LSD trip.

Days later, after a triumphant and adventurous weekend for Magia's birthday, the acid's effects wore off, while we pondered our recent awakening. Sitting on the beach - which one doesn't matter, because it's all of them – we listened to the tide, and watched the stars in the sky. I sat back, breathed in, and passed her the joint.

Serving Demons At Vipassana

After a brief, bland stopover in Bangalore, we rode a rickety local bus to Tiruvannamalai. We spent a night at a good-value, humble guesthouse, and dined at the acclaimed Dreaming Tree cafe. In the morning we motored along the highway, before bouncing upon dusty, rocky streets, reaching the humble gate of Dhamma Arunachala. I'd be lost in service for twelve days, while Magia headed towards Auroville. Her Vipassana application was oddly not received by the centre, and now the course was fully booked. Kartik – Dhamma Arunachala's resident monk – relocated me to the same quarters as last year; coincidentally, the very adjacent bed. As guests solemnly filtered in during registration, I assisted with collecting rupees for handmade biodegradable soap, shampoo and toothpaste. Before the start of the evening's introductory session, I wandered around, observing how the centre had developed. Dhamma Arunachala featured more nubile trees, rock gardens, and foundations of modest new facilities that were under construction.

After dusk the course began; servers sat beside the teacher. Over sixty practitioners, mostly first-timers, faced the front. Long and slow, the opening few days of Anapana breathing practice were underway. I witnessed certain personalities emerge and develop. There was the spoiled arrogance of Price, an Israeli, who indignantly waved his hand to silence the respectable teacher, after questioning the ages-old technique.

"Suffering? I thought life was some happiness, some sadness, but not suffering."

Renny, a bespectacled blonde German in his thirties, was clearly physically suffering from hours of meditating. Day by day, breath by breath, ego dissolved from everybody.

The course's head teacher was a disciple of legendary Goenka: MA Subramanian, who was learned, and sometimes grumpy. He was assisted by a Canadian teacher, Ruth – one of the late Goenka's trusted aides – and trainee Stasick: a tall, stoic Ethiopian-Russian.

An unexpected benefit of serving, was eating full meals at dinner. Not merely a snack, as for other meditators, or only tea – as for previous students. Otherwise, the days were long and hard: Awake by 4am and assisting until 10pm, through teacher discussions. We served breakfast, lunch and dinner snacks, and sat beside teachers during question periods with frustrated students. An unforeseen drawback was a complete lack of personal meditation time. We remained on call to satisfy the regular needs of teachers and students. Lacking the opportunity

to deeply meditate, stoked violent thoughts. I envisioned plenty
of fiery revenge, and imagined defending myself against attacks
from anonymous strangers, before brutally and unrelentingly
retaliating. The upcoming wedding in Sri Lanka featured all
sorts of hypothetical negative scenarios, from those who were
once friends. Mother.Domains, Bower, and web work were a
headache. Boogie disappointingly revisited my psyche. All of
these storms pounded down on me; they bubbled to the surface,
and I couldn't release them. My moods were further agitated by
certain delicate or brash personalities. Renny became rude and
ungrateful at times, complaining about pain. He was seemingly
on the verge of quitting, but he persevered. I witnessed Price
briefly packing and leaving, before he returned and battled
through. In contrast to my original course, where one-third of
people quit early, there was only a handful of resignations: one
couple left because of the wife's grandfather dying.

A fellow server nicknamed Wolfman was spooky, like a
gravedigger or undertaker. He had the blackest skin of all,
contrasted by the same bleached white shirt and pants.
Wolfman lurched oddly and uncomfortably as stared out
maniacally to everybody. He rang the morning bells like a fire
alarm from hell; a contrast from last year's elegant smattering of
chimes. Sometimes he'd walk into the meditation hall, and
immediately fall into a deep trance, while standing awkwardly.
Towards his premature end, he began convulsing and hyper-
ventilating. Against instructions, he was mixing meditation techniques, and hence not practicing properly; this led to physical
and mental problems. Wolfman quit on the seventh day, leaving
two male servers: myself and the noble Muthy. There was only
one female server: a lovely Himalayan girl.

After the sixth night's teachers and servers recap session,
Ruth observed my exhaustion; perhaps she noticed the rage
bubbling up to my frustrated surface. Ruth suggested I sleep in,
that resulted in my deepest sleep of the course, and my only
recollection of dreams. I recalled a modern, inner-city skyscraper complex, one of those self-contained luxury buildings,
with an atrium, shops and restaurants. The roof of one building
led to a skyscraper, that soared very high in the air. Its walkway
was covered in shiny and polished black granite, almost like

marble. It was wide enough, perhaps a few metres, but any misstep or being blown off would ensure plummeting hundreds of metres to death. I was nervous walking in the wind, but the guide assured I was safe. Inside, elevator signs touted a restaurant with "Prices from 1200 or 1500". Rupees? Dollars? The elevator descended, before opening its silver doors to a shiny, sprawling lobby.

The second part of the dream came at a luxury resort's hotel room. A black woman with curly hair, in her late twenties, perhaps Ethiopian, shared her noble project. Her brother, who looked like Robert – a shaved-headed veteran Polish student at this Vipassana course – was meticulously editing a music video. Their parents sat alongside. The woman curiously had an A5 piece of paper with notes on it, but stashed it away. They seemed intrigued about my work. After a subsequent conversation, I went to grab a blue jacket, but it was hers.

"That's my jacket," she insisted.

I was confused. "Looks just like mine." This changed the tone, with a little noticeable disappointment from the family. The piece of A5 paper was in the pocket and could not be seen. I demonstrated an example of my work, a radio recording. "From the United Nations." Except it was not fully true: it was not the UN, but perhaps an auditorium at the World Trade Centre. The recording began, and paused; I distinctly heard my deep radio voice introducing: "Enough of this nonsense... Next up..." My voice introduced somebody, to which hundreds in the audience slowly applauded and cheered, then louder. I was proud.

In the final part of the dream, I ascended from a concrete stairwell or submerged elevator, reaching the beach level. Outside was a magnificent, lush tropical forest, with palm trees and deep greens. The beach and ocean were exquisite. The same woman and her parents stood on the shore. We exchanged glances, not awkwardly, but not over-welcomingly. I wanted to leave them alone. I wasn't sure if I'd insulted them because of the jacket mistake. As the dream faded out, I walked towards the forest. I had no idea what any of this meant.

On this seventh morning, Wolfman quit. I continued to absorb the energies of everybody. Without personal meditation time, I couldn't release the energy boiling within me. There was one pleasant but greedy kid who always took two, three, sometimes five helpings of dessert; I glowered at him. Contrastingly, Metta Bhana sessions were useful – generating love and compassion for anybody who popped into our minds, adversaries included. I was stressed and fatigued up to the end of the ninth day.

Day ten, when students could break their noble silence, was peaceful and relaxing. I was graciously thanked by several meditators for my service. The greedy kid and I chatted amicably. The experience overall felt very worthwhile. In the evening I turned on my phone to update Magia. She was "in the middle of nowhere. So much has happened." I was happy for her adventures. I wasn't suffering by missing her; no clinging, wondering or jealousy. Whenever I thought about her, there was a persistent, comfortable warmth in my heart, that offered me confidence and trust. The "open" relationship meant that even if something happened, it wasn't important anyway. I felt nothing but love and pride for Magia.

While different than expected, serving was revelationary by its end. I figured out a lot. I theorised that the roots of my rage might be a lifetime of one-sided bullying, and repressing other people's bad behaviour, that I was invariably blamed for. This started with a spoiled and selfish sister from an early age, who was constantly getting me in trouble. I resolved to cut down on "friends": No more friend collecting, and to trim away the dead weight. With a clearer insight into Mother.Domains, I leaned towards winding down the company. All of these were repressed inside me without resolution. Next time I served, I'd request a private pagoda cell to ensure personal meditation, while being more humble and less judgemental.

The journey from Dhamma Arunachala involved a hectic transfer onto local buses from Tiruvannamalai towards Auroville. As fate had it, Price and his fellow Israeli friend joined me on the bus. Many people are different than how we might originally perceive, and Vipassana had tamed and inspired both of them. Catching up with news, I was shocked to learn about the New Zealand mosque shooting, where hundreds died from racist rage. I couldn't believe a New Zealander was capable of such violent hatred, but I was unsurprised that the culprit was a 28-year-old Australian white supremacist: another misguided

byproduct of the nation. My New Zealander father had driven by
that very mosque in Christchurch, hours before the attacks.

At the very end, I envisioned myself alone. I'd almost always
been alone; most of the time I preferred it. Other people seemed
to drag me down. The rage remained within me, bubbling and
boiling, even in a clean and detoxed body, and I had no means of
releasing it. In Auroville, I steadfastly required peace and quiet.

Lost in Auroville

My coveting of tranquility was contrasted by Magia, who'd made
numerous friends at Green's Hostel near Auroville, and was part
of an intimate party crew. Although Magia's first LSD experience
came weeks earlier at her fortieth birthday, she was more of an
acid veteran by the next time we met. For my return, she
booked a few nights in an overpriced but comfortable private
room at Green's. For her it was a bonus, after a fortnight
sleeping on a mosquito-infested, rickety bunkbed.

The situation became awkward, in that I wanted no part of
parties or socialising. I was disappointed that Magia neglected
to book a house. Before I left for Vipassana, I presented her a
shortlist of attractive guesthouses I'd painstakingly coordinated
visits to, hoping I'd return to a peaceful place in nature. This
oversight sent me further tumbling down the vortex of misery.
Still, I admired the shift in Magia's energy. She appeared happy,
relaxed, and even more beautiful, clad in comfortable clothes
and dangling, soulful earrings. There was a smile on her face as
she expertly navigated her scooter. Her hair blew in the wind
when I toured her around other parts of Auroville.

After Green's, we booked a spacious room at Boomivalar for
five nights. Boomivalar was a large, white Aurovillian
guesthouse, with a huge balcony that afforded privacy and
shade amidst trees. Magia balanced socialising with friends, and
spending time with me. I was pleased she did her own thing. My
tense headspace caused a few arguments, that would linger and
fester for months to come. I sought solitude, and for people to
leave me alone, although sometimes I participated in group
activities. One night we visited a moonlight pop-up cinema
beside African Pavilion. It was presented by a French crew,

who'd driven from Europe through the Middle East to India, living and creating from a large converted van. Technical problems ended their journey's documentary halfway through. Instead, they screened part of "The Gods Must Be Crazy" - before a power outage cut it short.

One afternoon, we braved Tamil Nadu highway traffic to ride into big city Pondicherry. I'd never been so careful and alert while driving, with other motorists zipping along and approaching from all directions, irrespective of traffic lights. After weaving through compact, busy streets, we parked the bike and strolled around a commercial shopping area. Inside the popular multi-story department store, Pothys, I sourced a yellow kurta for the forthcoming wedding in Sri Lanka, and Magia bought several tantalising garments of her own.

The highlight of our Auroville stay was the final Sunday, when we entered the parks and gardens of spherical Matrimandir. We dropped mild acid, before becoming lost in the shadows of the spiritual centrepiece, under the watchful gaze of Moon and stars. We temporarily lost each other at dusk. I floated through a winding garden of flowers and plants. Eventually, Magia and I solemnly reunited at the central stoic pond – the landing place of sunbeams – under the giant golden ball of the Matrimandir. As we departed, alien-looking meditators ascended the ramp into the spaceship structure; one alien paused to peer at me, while a lady on a chair kept watch. I wondered what crazy things happened in the Matrimandir after dark: UFO contact? Tea parties? Orgies? Sacrifice?

Despite recent tensions, the tranquil, trippy day brought us closer. Holding hands, Magia and I exited the Matrimandir, hopped on our scooter, and returned to Boomivalar, ready for new voyages.

Tempers in Kochi

Monday was a challenging travel day, punctuated by the supreme inefficiency of the Auroville Post Office. After an hour of strife with disinterested clerks, Magia mailed a taped-up box of excess items to Poland, but it's abject appearance lent doubts about it returning home. I ignored nagging premonitions, and our scooter ran out of petrol outside the Matrimandir. While Magia sheltered under trees, I hiked for kilometres under the blazing Sun, to and from the closest bike shop. Forty minutes later, a dangerously rapid tuk tuk whisked us to Pondicherry bus terminal. The local bus to Chennai was blighted by a perverse old man in the back row. He first tried to touch Magia, then me. My post-Vipassana patience ensured the man would not be punched in the throat and pushed out of the speeding bus; instead, alerting the conductor put the pervert on notice. In Chennai we immediately hired a tuk tuk, that raced like a champion to the domestic terminal, in time for our flight.

Aswin graciously picked us up at Kochi's airport. The first stop was his parents' home for dinner. We resided at a remarkable budget hotel, Kenz Residency, a short walk from Aswin's downtown Ernakulem office. Kenz Residency was approximately $10 a night, for a very comfortable, modern room. Aswin's father's unfortunate hospitalisation ensured we'd stay closer to central Kochi for the week, instead of explore more of Kerala.

In the hotel room, Magia and I were frequently terse with each other. I wasn't coping well post-Vipassana, and Kochi was a big, intense city. I felt growing trepidation about the wedding. Sometimes tempers boiled over; both of us said nasty things, although my words often hurt others more. It wasn't a nice vibe, despite whatever brave face we tried to project in public.

Aswin and Navaneeth were at their hospitality best. They led shopping mall group expeditions, attended by most of their office. The four of us visited an insightful Fort Kochi art exhibition, near the sea. After four nights in Kochi, we left with an open invitation to Aswin's wedding in July. Although I was wary of such a rapid return to India, I certainly mulled the possibility. First, we had the matter of a month in Sri Lanka, and facing my ghosts of the past.

Chapter 18
A Wedding in Sri Lanka

Upon a warm, tropical Saturday afternoon in Sri Lanka's affluent coastal suburb of Mount Lavinia, Seshanka married Cassie, creating an everlasting union of Samarajiwas and Ringwalds. The ceremony was ordained at Mount Lavinia's Methodist Church, honouring the religion of Shank's Sri Lankan-Australian family. Dozens of guests cheered as the newlywed couple exchanged vows, kissed and triumphantly marched through the church. Most headed straight to the open bar. A cavalcade of colourful tuk tuks whisked each guest to the luxurious Mount Lavinia Hotel, where old friends partied responsibly into the night.

...

A short swift flight from Kochi landed in Colombo, capital of the island-nation of Sri Lanka. Our compact taxi zipped through Colombo's manicured neighbourhoods, showcasing British colonial-era architecture and courtyards, with a smattering of typical Western fast food outlets and billboards. Public buses roared past maniacally, and colourfully-dressed and business-attired locals went about their formalities. Most of the coast was obscured by railways and commercial buildings.

We checked in at our guesthouse near Mount Lavinia, scrubbed up and set out to explore; it was the evening before the wedding. The huge, prestigious Mount Lavinia Hotel was perched on the shore's edge. Down and around the monstrous structure led to a narrow but lengthy stretch of beachfront, where lights of a half-dozen restaurants shone into the sky. We treated ourselves to dinner at an overpriced beachside restaurant; Magia was infinitely impressed by a heaping platter of perfectly grilled seafood. We downed our lavish plates with cocktails, lifting the mood on what had been a tense couple of weeks. The change of scenery was a useful remedy.

After a hearty dinner and drinks, where we feasted on scrumptious seafood, we headed along the shadowy beach. We were approached by a tall rasta fisherman: Did we want weed? He fetched a sample while we loitered on the hull of his boat. At a nearby shack, a family sat on a floor watching a small TV, curiously glancing at us. Due to the Sri Lankan government's strict crackdown on drugs, everything had to stay discrete.

During my travel career, I'd largely avoided rip-offs. In South America, I had several scary moments in Buenos Aires, killer parts of Brazil, a barber in La Paz who cut me then uncompromisingly overcharged, dodgy Mancora in Peru, and much of Colombia kept me on guard. Intense concentration was demanded while living in Cape Town or stopping through violent Johannesburg. Somehow, I managed to stay low-key and out of trouble. Yet, in Sri Lanka's Mount Lavinia, I was a target.

On the wedding day, I returned home from breakfast with a fresh shave, while Magia remained at the hairdresser. A polite-enough young man paced beside me. "Silver," his name sounded like: the name of my former best friend Danny Silver, who I hadn't heard from in years. Close to my Villa Two Residence, having earned my reasonable entrustment, the dodgy Silver coaxed me out of Rs1500, promising to return with two small bags of green. He scuttled down the alley, never to be seen again, while I stood in searing sunshine waiting like a fool.

A muscular man politely approached me. He'd earlier observed me walking with the fraudster, and had sought to warn me. I cautiously recounted the story; the man was gravely disappointed, and more so when I shared the perpetrator's apparent name. For "Silva" was not the perpetrator, but the respectable longtime family name of this beach neighbourhood. The imposter ripped off a tourist while betraying the Silva family. I was promised he'd be "punched" and brought to me. Surprisingly, I felt neither slivers of rage nor disappointment; only patience, tolerance and compassion. The muscular man escorted me over the railway tracks to a nearby shack, where we fetched a generous bag of the medicinal herb.

From that point, locals recognised me everywhere. Men came out of their way, even on otherwise-deserted beach fronts, to apologise for the imposter's behaviour. On our final evening in Mount Lavinia, Magia and I were invited to Buba, a family restaurant on the beach. There, a waiter also apologised. Their generation – around the same age as us – were raised on this beach, growing up with tourists "like us". They believed in looking after us, and were repulsed by anybody who took advantage. I told the waiter I hoped the fake Silva would learn his lesson peacefully, although I sensed the imposter was due for pain and suffering, if not sparking a family war. We appreciated the warmth from the true Silva family, while heeding their warnings to be careful in the south.

...

With arms linked, the gorgeous Magia and I strolled under sunny skies, through the backstreets of dignified Mount Lavinia. My pre-wedding anxiety, about reuniting with potentially hostile acquaintances, was momentarily justified upon arrival. I was greeted by scattered smirks, and more than a few guests intentionally turned their backs to me. Still, well-tanned in my stylish yellow kurta, white kurta pants and light brown scarf, with mysterious Slavic Magia beside me, we were exotic curiosities. Some were genuinely overjoyed to see me again. Several refused to greet me, although everybody politely warmed up in time.

My most pleasant surprise was the presence of the real Danny Silver: my faithful best friend and DJ partner for many years. Danny was shy and contemplative at first, but the air gradually lifted. Danny was the wedding DJ, and punctuated the moment of my arrival with his touching, olive-branch audio selection, that reminisced of happier times. Of the thousands of songs we'd played together, "You Wish" by Nightmares on Wax, was the most memorable. One random LSD night, in Wazza's hotel suite at Melbourne's Crown Casino, we accidentally looped the song on repeat, many, many dozens of times – before anybody noticed! At the wedding, when the song started playing, I knew Danny was deliberately making a friendly gesture. Wazza did too, but his expression transformed to mortal embarrassment when I began explaining the story's origins.

"Shhh!" Wazza pleaded, looking around uneasily. "Don't tell my wife!"

The Methodist ceremony itself was far quieter than the elaborate Sri Lankan bonanza I'd anticipated. It was a low-key affair, with a few dozen attendees, including more foreign

308

guests than Sri Lankans. By ceremony's end, as decreed by the priest-in-training at his first-ever wedding ordination, Shanks was legally, contractually and religiously bound to monogamous infinity with Cassie, or suffer eternity in Hell.

After the ceremony, over a smattering of beer, wine and soft drinks, I cordially caught up with even the most contrite of my former friends. Dozens of pre-arranged tuk tuks whisked us to the extraordinarily fancy Mount Lavinia Hotel. Most of the guests could afford a pricey room here, although several of us stayed elsewhere. A huge group photo in front of the ritzy entrance fountain, brought together well-dressed guests, uniformed staff of the top-class hotel, and several tuk tuks. During an interval, Magia and I discovered the majestic rooftop, complete with shisha pipes, swimming pools and a panorama of the crashing blue ocean.

A while later, the reception commenced beside the golden beach, a short stroll from the hotel foyer. The risky open bar and enticing buffet placated any lingering anxieties, and we gratefully feasted at the table of Shanks' Sri Lankan relatives. Shanks, Cassie and several friends made impassioned speeches. Danny Silver spun tunes into the night. It was a wonderful reunion of old friends, who danced on the sand to old music classics that had defined much of our circle over the years.

The sound turned off around midnight, and most drunken guests staggered to their suites. I sat beside Danny Silver, his new girlfriend, and Magia on the shadowy sand, sharing a joint that had been risky to acquire. This felt a classy resolution of something that had saddened me for years. A few years earlier, in the midst of my regular Melbourne comings and goings, during my annual five-month world trips, Danny demanded more stability from his closest buddy. While it's sad being rejected, I wholly respected his decision: we must curate the energies we want around in our lives.

Despite my long-held trepidations, the wedding was fun and refreshing. I was able to say hello, and goodbye, to many. As I shared with Shanks, shortly after his reception speech:

"Shanks, no matter where in the world I was, no matter what was happening in my life, I was always going to be here for your wedding."

Shanks' brown eyes filled with pride; he smiled broadly and embraced me. Shanks was a true friend, even if years separated our visits. These were the friendships I greatly valued in my life: the ones that lasted beyond goodbyes.

Rat House

Our early impressions of Sri Lanka were edgy; the country was dramatically unlike our vague expectations of a smaller, chilled-out India. Perhaps this trickled down from government, where the Prime Minister and President waged ego-fuelled hostilities, that distracted from their purported purpose of faithfully serving their people and nation. The brothers of politicians were awarded prestigious land and casino developments, at the sake of coastlines and local communities. This corruption contributed to the increasingly unstable and unsafe civil situation brewing around the streets, churches and mosques of Sri Lanka. Furthermore, the President waged a brutal war on drugs and those who supplied them, where even simple, healthful amenities like marijuana were strictly illegal and highly punishable. We suffered constant rip-offs from touts, train offices and tuk tuk drivers. One night Magia was followed home by a strange man. Sri Lanka was not off to a particularly strong start. This was agitated by persistent tension between Magia and I, that was unrelenting since Auroville.

Our Unawatuna guesthouse, White House, was the epitome of "budget". White House appealed for its promise of "authentic local experience". €6 a night earned us a private bedroom and bathroom. Two single beds were pushed together to form a double bed under a mosquito net. Outside was a spacious, shared balcony, sometimes occupied by a creepy older resident tourist. The wily old grandmother was an ace shot with her monkey catapult. Several desperate puppies were tied on ropes. There was pair of scrawny cats – one with a broken forepaw. Countless bedraggled chickens, early-rising roosters, occasional monkeys, many birds and bugs. One distressed cow was usually tied in place. Rats were evident from daily fresh piles of poo in the bathroom, that was not seemingly cleaned for our visit. The toilet was "Not working". I uncovered a used condom under a filthy cabinet. Otherwise, the house was extremely sweet and lovely, in a small village surrounded by jungle, 200m from the sea. We affectionately referred to the place as Rat House.

Our culinary cravings were satisfied by Halloumi Eggs Benedict at Skinny Tom's, a welcomingly Australia-styled hipster cafe, that notably served coconut milk cappuccinos. We worked from Skinny Tom's back courtyard, on long benches shaded by trees. Under pre-monsoon humidity, my laptop struggled in the heat, and with other personal distractions I could not attain much working or writing momentum. I remained particularly furious at CoinTree, a scammy Australian cryptocurrency exchange, who botched a transaction and refused to reimburse me. Their indifference cost me around $400, and I reluctantly borrowed money off Magia in Goa.

After one morning's breakfast, Magia and I ascended boulders on Unawatuna's western point, above crashing waves, behind a Buddhist sanctuary. The ocean gushed with teal water, blue sky and white foam, that streamed towards a golden sandy beach. A cliffside of large grey rocks lay upon the coastline, where garbage was littered everywhere. Magia elaborated on the coldness she felt from me; she guessed I might prefer traveling on my own. Attributing multiple factors for my anxiety, my remedy was to source a peaceful location, with ocean views, undisturbed by touts or tourists.

I projected unpleasant residue from former friends, who were in the area following the wedding, and I waited for social plans that never materialised. I harboured ongoing money stress, and frustrations about Mother.Domains. I occasionally wondered about The Past. *Why did she contact me on New Year's Day?* Recent Vipassana exhibited deeper roots of my anger; its acknowledgement alone was beneficial, but there remained incomplete answers. Was I miserable because of touristic places I loathed? Of my latest money woes? Lack of independence? Disdain to remain in this relationship? I confided with Magia that I believed her jealousy would one day doom us.

For historical perspective, we were in an infamous part of Sri Lanka, that suffered from a catastrophic tsunami in December 2004. The killer tsunami torched the eastern coast, but there were lingering residual effects, with much widespread damage throughout the south, including Unawatuna. The beach felt like a soulless popup tourist trap, emboldened by the garish, titanic concrete slab of a forthcoming luxury hotel, purportedly developed by the President's brother. The hotel's construction loomed over neighbouring family guesthouses, obscuring sunset from the eastern side of the beach. The town was about to become further populated by visitors. Commercial developments would soon swallow humble family properties, such as The White House. An elder European resident, whose longtime home sat in the shadows of the nearby concrete monstrosity, shook her head and sighed.

"It's happening, whether we like it or not. There is nothing anybody can do about it. This is capitalism."

...

Our time in Unawatuna was an unmitigated disaster, with rat-dropping infestation at a supremely low-budget guesthouse, tension of old friendships fading away, and serious relationship strain. Our stomachs were knotted, while we overheated beneath a humid Sun. We were constantly bothered by street peddlers, pesky tuk tuk driver, and the cold distant glares of unfriendly tourists. I took out my frustrations on Magia, with sharp, curt criticisms of my pent-up irritations. I was further annoyed of not being wholly understood by her in English. None of these were her fault – she was the present trigger for my resurfacing of anger.

The situation became so acrimonious that, after our third and mercifully final night at Rat House, a restless Magia resolved to resume travels on her own. She bore a different face, one that was hurt and determined, and she was clearly fed up with my pollutive energy. Wearily, I scrambled to arrange backup plans of my own. There were good reasons to take a break. I desperately coveted Sea Time, that had eluded me for much of the trip, and certainly since wound-opening Vipassana. Time for ourselves could be refreshing and beneficial. I was wary of Magia's safety on a dodgy tourist island, particularly upon hearing stories about dangerous encounters for European women. Surely there were alternatives, for us to continue traveling together while creating space, starting with me improving my mood and treating her better.

Still, Magia resolved to travel alone. With no other restaurants open, we returned to Skinny Tom's, becoming tired of Halloumi Eggs Benedict four days in a row. While I caught up on emails, Magia researched her pathway into Sri Lanka's mountains, and navigated to the booking confirmation page of a week's hostel stay. Meanwhile, I'd reserved two nights at the little-known but highly-acclaimed beach village of Hiriketiya. Chatting outside in the empty back area of Skinny Tom's, I asked what Magia truly desired. It wasn't that she wanted to travel alone, but she believed in its necessity. Her preference was simply that I'd be nicer to her. Whatever she decided – travel alone or try again – I would accept. As we were both initially heading in the same direction, I made my pitch.

"Hiriketiya is a small, peaceful beach on the way to the mountains. How about we depart Unawatuna together, enjoy a couple of calm and positive days down the coast, and you can move on from there if you still desire?"

I resolved to improve my moods and behaviour. I wasn't happy taking out frustrations on my only close friend around: somebody who'd done so much for me. Yet, like many in my past, I was also pushing her away. After a while, Magia agreed to accompany me, and we set forth on one of the best adventures of our lives. Familiar with legit tuk tuk prices, we successfully negotiated an acceptable fare to the bus stop. The driver chuckled – he'd asked for three times as much! Catching bus 32 towards Dikwella, we boarded and gripped hard, as the metal rhinoceros bounced and weaved along the single-lane highway. As we distanced further from Unawatuna, our moods and the splendorous coastline improved. We passed numerous beaches: less people, more deep-blue water, yellow sands, and bliss.

Little Paradise

A tuk tuk dispatched us through narrow streets, up a hill and down another, with a sense we were approaching somewhere hidden and special. Stunning Hiriketiya's little turquoise bay featured 100m of golden sand, while dozens of surfers patiently awaited waves near mirrored left and right breaks. Lush, plush greens of tropical jungle were dotted by small boulders on its edges. Several small beachfront restaurants served juice and cocktails. We paused at a rundown beach shack for a fresh coconut, underneath an umbrella beside rocks and sea.

Our first guesthouse was Hasnal House, 150m from the beach and sea. Hasnal House was luxury compared to Rat House. The bathroom was bright, blue, spacious and clean. A comfortable, large bed with four posts had a white mosquito net assembled around its perimeter. We returned to Hiriketiya's beach, and climbed boulders around the coastline. We wandered along rocks halfway up the bay, inline with awaiting surfers. We took turns swimming in the warm, blue sea; neither the current nor waves were overly strong. A girl paddling nearby me was hit in the head by a surfboard; fortunately she was okay. This was my primary trepidation about surfing – not sharks or even cold – but the danger of other humans. Dinner at Peter's Surf Restaurant, on a secluded corner of the beach, was delightful. We feasted on fresh fish and chips, seafood with fried rice, and creamy mango and papaya juices. Magia fulfilled her aspiration of drinking a proper Pina Colada, with fresh coconut and pineapple juices. We slept and dreamed, long and well.

...

In Hiriketiya, we found solace by the sea, writing in warm breeze. Magia and I were back in harmony again. We're supposed to work at relationships, but why force things, particularly when gut instincts warn us? This was a sadness of life: The impermanence of everything, even the most magical, comfortable and real. Magia and I held a legit chance at Forever: Home, family, helping people and animals, driving home-converted buses, and even flying planes. Life together could be calm and loving the rest of the way. This seemed to be what I always dreamed. *Then why did I constantly feel pangs to set her free? Why did I crave solo journeys?* I questioned whether long-term, essentially-monogamous relationships were for me. I confided to Magia that I believed she deserved somebody more emotionally and financially stable: two traits that had reliably escaped me.

If I had money, what would I do? I'd certainly accomplish Van Sea in Europe, splurge on my musical ambitions, drive through Africa, and ultimately visit Antarctica and the Moon. In Sri

Lanka, with a bigger budget I'd set forth on my own, and Magia could do her own thing, as she desired. Maybe it would be together. The difference was, with both van and trip, I would not be reliant on her for Home. Then, Love would decide: Not the Money God.

Space was few and far between. It wasn't easy, intimately sharing an intense three-month trip through challenging foreign lands. We needed time apart to think; to become lost in nature, to feel where next. We often don't fully appreciate what we have, until it's gone.

...

Upon settling into Hiriketiya, the warming of weather and tropical vibes made a considerably positive impact on our psyche. We stumbled upon a sweet, secluded spot at the sea, called Screw-Pine Villa. The heart of Hiriketiya remained a short stroll away, but at Screw-Pine we were completely isolated. Magia and I wrote side by side, every morning and evening, often meditating together amidst the rumble of the ocean. We were best friends again, sharing every adventure and meal. Excursions to supermarkets, to load up on fresh fruit and snacks, were a boon. Juice was cheap, fresh and tasty, and there were enough decent restaurants around Hiriketiya for variety. Many nights we sat atop the Screw-Pine roof, eyeing the stars, Moon and sea, occasionally dozing. I inspiredly created music on the rooftop, to a beaming Moon and an audience of stars. Magia regularly frequently the roof alone; once she rushed down during a lightning storm.

The wonders of Screw-Pine helped assimilate us into a welcomed world of chill. This was everything we ever sought from a place. We were steps from a rocky, secluded beach, thunderous waves crashed against boulders, crabs scurried and paused, in-heat peacocks scuttled in droves, and little squirrels sketchily sprinted. Within moments passing through Screw-Pine's small back gate, the sea was before us. We had a cove unto ourselves. There was a natural spa surrounded by boulders; a calm pond with rock-filtered waves, and curious colourful fish that danced around us.

Screw-Pine's owner showcased an enviable demonstration of world-class hospitality. Breakfast was served daily, at our requested time of 9am, surprising us with different local variations of "hoppers", fruit, curries and juice. Although the owner's English was limited, his professionalism and care shone through. This was evident from his daily watering of plentiful exotic plants, attention to detail, and by lending us his scooter for weekend adventures. His service reiterated that it's the little things that make experiences enjoyable and memorable. Our corner room faced sunrise, with ample light, modern amenities and priceless views of the sky and sea. We paid Rs3000 a night for it all – less than €8 each.

Magia excitedly took her first surfing lessons on successive mornings. This facilitated sunrise starts, ahead of long and fulfilling days. We rode the scooter through dawn, alongside the sea and brightening jungle greens. While Magia surfed, I retreated to the top floor of Dots Cafe to write, undisturbed. There were many riveting excursions, particularly with the scooter. One sunny afternoon we drove to a gorge at Hummanaya blowhole. In a nook between boulders, darts of ocean water shot high in the air. During the ride, we passed new beaches, fishing villages and humble local neighbourhoods

One evening, we enjoyed a sunset on boulders that touched Ranlakshmi Paradise Beach. The orange Sun lusciously plummeted across the blue-greys of dusky water and rocks. Feeling famished, we randomly discovered Moon River, a super-chill restaurant situated beside an even more secluded beach, near the little village of Unakuruwa. For a couple of days, Moon River became our favoured hangout. We could have stayed there longer, but Magia remained keen on visiting the mountains, and it felt like time for change.

This was our slice of Little Paradise, abbreviated in twelve sensational days. We lived in the moment, accepted that the pleasurable would eventually pass, and made the most of it. Most importantly, I had my best friend back, and she was happy.

To Mountains From Sea

For our final evening in Hiriketiya, we embarked upon a sunset stroll, intended towards Peter's Place for dinner. Along the way, we were unexpectedly invited into the villa owner's Sinhalese-

Buddhist family house. We were served heaping piles of rice, curry and fish, and a proudly-presented bottle of whisky, that was poured into glasses with lemon soda. Magia and I sat on a carved wooden bench, while shy members of the family welcomed us. The proud owner maintained his professional front, but for the first time we saw a glimpse of his family side, when he smiled at his playful children, eyes alight. These were the authentic local experiences that money couldn't buy.

On our final morning, shortly after sunrise, down by ocean and rocks, we meditated. Breakfast was served: hoppers, curry, papaya, pineapple and curry. The owner's brother transported us by tuk tuk to Moon River. After a final swim, surf and smoke in the restaurant's perfectly tranquil confines, we ventured into the mountains. The day-long journey continued with a local bus to Tangalle, before a coach dispatched us at Wellawaya after dusk. There were no further buses running. An awaiting, slickly-dressed man pointed to a plush SUV, and encouraged us to hop in. My gut instinct warned they might be undercover cops. Irrespectively, we didn't have budget for fancy taxis, but we did have a bag of weed. Instead, we hopped in a tuk tuk, that ambitiously roared up twisting, hilly roads. We paused momentarily outside a gigantic waterfall that gushed from the sky, and eventually we arrived in Ella. Now well into the evening, Ella's short main strip was littered with tourists, while loud and bright billboards touted overflowing restaurants and bars. Ella otherwise held a comfortable, relaxed vibe.

Our home for the weekend was Enthral House in Kithalella. This was located up a steep hill that overlooked valleys and thick green forests, encircled by a pleasantly swirling breeze. The lodging was in the middle of a hamlet, where the noises of roads and schoolchildren ricocheted around the valley. There was much to see in Ella: Waterfalls, nine-arch bridges, temples, tea factories, peaks to climb and forests for wandering. One scooter exploration delivered us to a Buddhist monastery, that was under construction on the top of a mountain. We meditated inside the large golden dome while holidaying families sang hymns; Magia prayed in honour of her late grandmother.

We zipped around waterfalls, and cruised around green forests and tea plantations. One of the most majestic and dangerous roads I'd ever traversed across was the route to our Enthral House guesthouse. A steep incline led to a soaring peak, with a sharp turnaround at a wretched angle. It was the highest point of the mountainous area, and any little slip or distraction could plunge vehicles a thousand metres over the edge.

After the secluded splendours of Hiriketiya, Ella was too touristy for us. During one of our scooter expeditions we found a picturesque lodge, on the same mountain as the Buddhist temple. Ornate View offered two levels of balconies, facing a mirroring mountain. Inside featured a stone and wooden interior, spacious rooms, a large bathtub and TV. The place was nearly perfect for writing and chilling, but a little expensive at our bargained Rs4500 a night. Still, Ornate View became our choice for our final Sri Lankan splurge. We informed the owner we'd check-in tomorrow.

...

Arising the next morning, we felt unsettled, like a storm was coming. Magia and I shared an unspoken inclination to move away from Ella, and forfeit our luxurious mountain lodge. Instead, we rode a busy, rustic train to a mountain town called Haputale. Its local area featured appreciably few if any tourists, and Haputale was close to vast national parks. This particular morning was a famously bloody day in Sri Lankan civil history. Few knew what was about to transpire throughout the country, or that tourist areas like Ella were plausible targets. During the middle of our innocent train journey, violent terror started erupting across Sri Lanka.

Upon our check-in at Il Villino, its helpful, well-educated owner detailed the island's multiple terrorist attacks. Islamic militant groups had bombed churches and fancy hotels in Colombo and other locations across the country, killing scores of people. Warning signs were ignored, during the endless bickering of Presidents and Prime Ministers. Sri Lanka decreed a complete social media blockade; while we received occasional incoming notifications, we could neither open them nor reply. Friends were worried; Shanks dispatched numerous messages to his contacts, seeking to ensure our safety. We were completely cut off from the world – physically and digitally. The mystical power of premonition had seemingly led us away from

Ella this bloody morning. Haputale was perhaps the safest part of the country: high in the mountains, blanketed by military training and police academies, and no tourists around. There was a mosque beside Il Villino, that usually blared prayers every few hours, but was silent in the wake of the carnage.

Without news, nearby tensions or Internet distractions, our tenure in Haputale was welcomingly serene. With a backdrop of valleys beyond a 1400m slope, we wrote among clouds that fumed out of mountain crevices and green terrain. Storm patterns converged, merged and battled; drums of thunder, and walls of lightning, glittered by rain. There were abundant lakes in the distance, visible from our room's ceiling-high windows, or the curved little Roman-style balcony. We received kind service from Il Villino's smiling grandfather assistant, although the food was perhaps the poorest on an island of underwhelming meals. One particularly undercooked chicken resulted in multiple guests vomiting, including a fresh round of sickness for Magia. The thin walls of the three-room guesthouse ensured we could hear everybody else's undesirable movements.

Magia and I returned from an afternoon's rainy walk through a nearby national park, to discover bleeding cuts on our feet. A leech was biting Magia's foot, and sucking out blood. These non-native leeches were imported for military training: to teach recruits to be mindful while camping. After crossing a small waterfall, Magia had paused to refill her LifeStraw with the creek's fresh water. Fortunately, Il Villino had the remedy for leeches: a jar of salt water, a swab of which painlessly disabled the leech from Magia's foot.

Sir Thomas Lipton was famous for his Lipton Tea company, and the original source of his quality tea came from Haputale's nearby plantations. We reached the adjacent mountain's peak called Lipton's Seat, that featured stunning 360-degree views of surrounding mountains, and a plethora of tea plantations. Monkeys posed for photographs, eyed our phones and eagerly accepted bananas.

An early wake-up the next morning afforded our sunrise scooter voyage to 2300m-high Horton National Park. We didn't enter due to its excessive Rs4000 entry fee. Instead, we cruised around surrounding forests, and drifted along secluded jungle paths, on a mountain's edge. We rode down a deep, steep hill, into a grim, isolated village, whose sole road led past a house with an eerie, life-sized voodoo doll, of a European chained on its roof. At the end of the street was a small run-down Hindu temple, where a dodgy, pudgy boy stood with a stick.

"Loot," the boy repeated, mimicking a pirate, possibly contemplating robbing us. We rapidly reversed the scooter, and whisked back through the deathly village, up the lengthy hill.

...

Before dawn on our final morning in Haputale, we scooted down the mountain, and revelled in a sunrise breakfast on a waterfall. Perched on boulders lining the steep Diyaluma Waterfall, with nobody around, we savoured snacks and sandwiches, pre-prepared from Il Villino's kitchen. We raced back up the slippery mountain, in time for a scenic train to Kandy. The mountain city was the former Sri Lankan capital, during an era of ancient kings. On the surface, there was seemingly nothing remarkable about Kandy: it was a fairly big, noisy city. We weren't able to explore, because of a strictly-enforced curfew due to the national security situation. Our final night in Sri Lanka came at the modern Perfect Getaways hostel, on the most comfortable bed of the trip. We were too tired to venture out for much more than dinner. A small argument revealed that Magia and I were exhaustedly longing for home. Every time the relationship took a downturn, I thought about collecting my belongings in Zielonki, and moving on.

There was one particularly deep dream over the entire trip I remembered vividly. I was in a desert, in an underground network of caves, that suggested Arizona, although I'd not been there. Beyond intricate textures of caves, the colours were fluid pastels. Randomly, I met Boogie, who was later in her twenties, and emboldened with a strong, independent headspace. The vibe between us was friendly, but she was completely dedicated to the sole cause of earning her driver's license. There was nobody else in the dream, beyond a few random friends: no boyfriend or partner, and nothing of the sort was mentioned. There was no romance between us: only amicable and positive interaction. The girl from my dreams had returned; what this meant, I did not know.

Lady and Amman

After a Kandy breakfast, we waited a couple of hours for a gruelling afternoon bus, then rode through sapping heat to Negombo, near Colombo's airport. After a brief stop at Container Beach Restaurant, we spent hours slow-drinking surprisingly affordable, quality ice wine at a top hotel restaurant: IceBear. This was a few blocks away from the recently-bombed church. The neighbourhood was well under lockdown, and unsurprisingly had a hushed tension about it.

Because of the curfew, we had to exit the district and head to the airport early, while taxis remained available. This meant an eight-hour wait at the airport. The taxi couldn't drop us at the terminal because Colombo Airport was under complete military takeover. Vehicles lined up for miles to undergo rigorous security checks by well-armed military personnel. Those of us riding taxis and public transport were summoned for searches and brief questioning, on a guarded path. Officers verified our flight tickets, before we were waved through to an awaiting air-conditioned shuttle. The serious atmosphere was offset by the relaxed yet procedural nature of the young, co-ed Sri Lankan cadets; the buzz was exciting.

Entering the terminal, past further checks, I witnessed the biggest gun I'd ever seen up close. The officer stood between the waiting lounge and check-in counters. He had one arm on the gun's barrel, with his other hand near the trigger. He looked around continuously, exhausted like he'd been concentrating non-stop for days, yet he remained cool, and even suave.

We were extraordinarily fortunate to find two seats at the hall's only table, near the gun-toting guard and other rotating soldiers. Hundreds of passengers sat tiredly on the floor. There were very many hours of passing time; Magia and I took turns for short walks and toilet breaks. Everything felt awkward but safe, under florescent lights.

Eventually, check-in opened for our flight to Amman. Now past midnight, we'd technically overstayed our visa by a few hours, through my miscalculation of official visa days. The friendly officer bore no reaction, and stamped our passport with yesterday's date. The nondescript flight led to becoming lost in

Abu Dhabi's hectic airport, but the journey was otherwise smooth. The cheap flights I'd found to Krakow via Amman, were offset by Jordan's outlandish visa costs, that we had to pay regardless of our abbreviated 24-hour transit. A bus and taxi shuttled us along a rapid highway to our hotel. We passed consistently white and cream-coloured architecture, of mostly low-rise buildings. Jordan seemed relatively progressive, and was clearly under Western influence, with its billboards and advertising of mainstream brands and styles.

At the hotel, our originally-booked room was under maintenance, due to a broken pipe. Their staff escorted us to the nearby, more-expensive New Park Inn, but our original price was respectfully honoured. After another argument, Magia ventured out by herself, while I watched frustrating Manchester United flail their way through another horrific display. The hushed headspace was welcome, but I should have taken the opportunity to explore a new city. Magia enjoyed her night out: she walked around and found a friendly restaurant.

In the morning we wandered through Amman's contrast of ancient yet modern streets, and weaved around the city's distinctly creamy-white architecture. Up a hill to the Citadel, we peered around the valley of a historic capital that blended old wisdom and new ideas. It felt like a whole other world. Following a polite and efficient taxi to Amman's airport, a smooth check-in and short flight, we landed in Krakow. A friendly, talkative Polish taxi driver whisked us to Zielonki. We opened the doors to our home, greeted by two shocked but relieved, ratty rasta cats.

"Meow," a hoarse-throated silver Xara tried to coax, on several attempts. Shy, dreadlocked Czupur customarily hid in a corner, watching and waiting with his big contemplative eyes. Our family was blissfully reunited. We'd survived three months of global travel: a real relationship achievement.

Chapter 19
Himalayan Heights

Returning to the wondrous comforts of home in Zielonki lent a productive and contented routine. The cats, Czupur and Xara, were particularly thrilled; they'd looked ragged and had lost their voices in our absence. I deployed my wave of post-trip inspiration and a sense of mid-term stability to carve away at my ambitions. Van Sea felt closer to fruition, possibly through the dual problem-solver of wrapping up Mother.Domains.

My musical dreams, that lingered since childhood, reignited their long-repressed flame. Instead of whacking away on miniature plastic keyboards on an ancient laptop and broken headphones, I envisaged a more serious attempt at modern music production and performance. I obsessively researched MIDI keyboards, synthesizers, audio interfaces, reference monitor speakers, power conditioners and overpriced software. At some point, I needed a lighter, more powerful laptop. Suddenly I was committing to thousands of dollars in endless gear investments. I held an ethical dilemma of purchasing new vs. second-hand, and strived to put conscious thought into every decision. *What if a new item cost less than the best used alternative? Was shipping a second-hand item across the world more pollutive than locally purchasing a new one?* Disappointingly, I felt myself becoming sucked in by the caffeine of consumerism. Further fuelling my anguish was a complete lack of cash, or prospects to make any of these happen, yet I was stuck in a trap of my impulses and cravings. Gone was the splendour and pacifism of the moment.

After a period of tranquility, tension resumed when Magia tallied the remaining debts I owed her. This included the cash I borrowed in India after the Cointree rip off, and the flights home from Sri Lanka. Moments after I proudly paid her back for the flights, I was dismayed when Magia presented an additional figure, surpassing 150% of my expectations. Here I was focused on MIDI keyboards and discerning finer technical specifications between mundane power line conditioners, while Magia's frustrations grew about when, or if, her debt would be paid.

It wasn't the best-handled affair; during the momentary stress I melodramatically packed up my belongings. Magia, unimpressed, urged me to leave quickly. Rain poured outside; oddly, I received an unprecedented SMS weather warning, in English, from an unknown system that knew my precise location in Poland. Inclement weather and honest talking earned me another night's stay, but the next day Magia firmly insisted on needing time alone to compose herself. We'd had no space since returning from our trip.

My options included bunking in downtown Krakow, or a green mission to Copenhagen. Allured by the prospect of a useful Memtell planning session, I dispatched Jono a message. He was visiting Berlin for the weekend. This sealed it, and a €20 night bus from Krakow enabled my impromptu trip to Berlin. Hostel research uncovered Jetpak, located in a large lush forest in the southwest of Berlin. Jetpak was powered by renewable energy and promoted other sustainable practices. It sounded ideal: peaceful and out of the city, but close enough for downtown missions. I booked three nights, and left my return trip open.

My bus arrived in Berlin, as early frost hung in the air and the orange Sun slowly ascended. I entered the tall, thick trees guarding Grünewald forest, and reached humble Jetpak hostel before most others stirred. I was treated to breakfast, before I napped on a wooden bunk.

Awake and refreshed, I strode vaguely towards the centre of Berlin, without navigation. After the first three therapeutic hours, I paused for a water break at a library. On the street, a drink brand's promo staff handed me two mini bottles of fruity apple cider: a welcomed surprise, that earned my first smiles of this trip. With renewed spirit, I headed to the awesome Just Music store, and played on synthesizers without bother. I was overwhelmed and intimidated at the vast, costly tools available to musicians. On my way to Görlitzer Park to score green, I was amicably diverted to a friend's house near Tempelhof, for music and supplies. Later, I exhaustedly returned to silent, pitch-black Grünewald Forest, having hiked 25km – or 32,444 steps.

On Friday, I rented a bike and cycled to St. Oberholz, to meet Jono and Miri. Jono was slowly on the right track with Meintell, despite his rising, self-induced pressures related to a potential six figures of Euro investment. He remained in a rut composing a business plan for the platform. Jono sought to craft a creative consulting role for me, that would relievedly excuse me from hands-on technological participation.

In the evening, I jammed with another aspiring electronic music producer, in between chilling with the Jetpak crew around a fire, mostly my listening to German. The next morning I cheerfully departed Jetpak, and strolled through Grünewald Forest. I passed an abandoned railway station, that had been respectfully left for the forest to grow over. Notations were etched along its platforms, that during World War II many thousands of Jews boarded trains to their brutal fates from this station. This was another solemn reminder of the long, violent history of atrocities humans have regularly – and recently – committed. The warning was that, in some form or another, more will surely come.

A Wedding in Cologne

Having mutually regained some personal freedom, Zielonki life was generally happy and peaceful, for the next few weeks. For my 42nd birthday, we road-tripped to an open air festival in the Czech Republic, on the invitation of Klima. It was rainy, and I spent most of my time sleeping in the tent, while Magia wandered around the festival and nearby forest. The ride back was tense because of my slothfulness.

On my way to India was the matter of Jono and Miri's wedding. Magia and I booked super-cheap flights, that required a 3am wakeup, and a 100km drive to the city of Katowice. A couple of ghost trains from Dortmund led us to energetic Wuppertal, with its mesmerising retro art deco vibe, and uniquely elevated train. A bus to Mettmann brought us to the excellent Hotel Alte Fabrik, where we stayed in a detached two-floor loft. In the morning after a generous buffet breakfast, we rode a train to Cologne; the city was packed for the annual Pride parade. Everything was fully booked up.

Jono and Miri's wedding was a stellar affair, hosted riverside on a mid-summer's evening. An extraordinarily proud Jono beamed at his gorgeous bride as Miri strolled along the aisle. The crowd cheered after the newlywed couple exchanged their vows and kissed. The ceremony was followed by the customarily risky open bar, that was served from a lengthy reception hall. Further seats and tables stood under temporary shelters, alongside the historic Rhine river.

A big surprise was the appearance of Kim Thompson, my longtime friend and colleague from running Heavyweight TV. Kim – Shanks' ex-girlfriend – flew from Australia with her recent husband to attend. Another welcomed revelation was the presence of Ronald, from that awkward Cologne meeting over a year ago. I spent much of the evening reconnecting with him.

"I wanted to apologise for my behaviour that day," Ronald shared sincerely, to my astonishment. Peace was made.

The predictable combination of too much alcohol and not eating enough led to escalating haziness; much of the wedding became a blur. A friend of Miri graciously provided keys to her nearby apartment, useful for several hours of drunken sleep.

...

With a morning hangover, Magia and I made our way to Köln HBF. We shared big hugs and a teary goodbye, before Magia's train to Dortmund pulled away, through the flickering illuminations of the Sun. Seeking solace from the mass crowds, who were streaming towards the rainbow parade, I began my extended seventeen-hour venture to Budapest. The extraordinarily long and uncomfortable bus from Cologne Airport paused in Vienna, where I was one of four passengers "randomly" searched by police in the middle of the night.

The bus pulled into Budapest before morning rush hour. On an hour-long walk from Negliget bus station, I passed curiously vibrant old architecture nearer the heart of Budapest, crossed a sprawling bridge, and cruised through neighbourhoods. Eventually, I arrived at serene Shantee Hostel, and remained local for my sole evening in Hungary's capital. A late-night chess match between myself and a Dutch guest was interrupted by a power outage, that took us an hour to solve it. I barely slept during a restless few hours in the hostel's giant outdoor yurt, before my alarms sounded. A Mongolian woman gifted me a wake-and-bake, before I groggily rode a tram, then a bus, to the airport. I didn't see much of Budapest, but it seemed to be an intriguing, pretty city, with diverse architecture and culture.

A Wedding in Kerala

After a seven-hour layover in Kiev, I landed at Cochin International Airport: the world's first fully solar-powered airport. Aswin's colleagues kindly dispatched me to his village. Dozens of guests loitered around Aswin's house, that sported a canvas tent covering a long dining table. Aswin's father greeted me with the first of a hundred handshakes. His Malayalam words were met by my English; neither of us truly understood each other, but it was friendly all the same. Aswin looked fit and happy, and his skin appeared to be a little creamier.

After the RunCloud car rolled in after 11pm, we tucked into finger-eating of curries, rice, fried breads and chutneys. Unfortunately, the late time and an unknown rental curfew meant I couldn't return to Mayflower Mansion, the guesthouse I'd booked and pre-paid. Close to 1am, after some negotiating for his own complicated check-in, Navaneeth was granted keys to a hotel room, and we shared a king-sized bed.

Three hours of sleep later, the first alarm sounded. Navaneeth and I jolted up, and quickly readied ourselves for the wedding. We picked up the RunCloud guys at their villa and raced towards Vagamon. The wedding ceremony was politely delayed for our arrival. Eventually, we reached the auditorium, where hundreds of guests milled around. The stage was filled with red and orange colours, with Ganesh at the rear.

The ceremony commenced with a hypnotically monotonic chant from the Hindu priest, echoed by his assistant. Blessings rained down on Aswin and Sree, who were enveloped by their families. After encircling the stage, the couple came forward and were blessed – they were now married. This began a procession of greetings and wishes from guests, who intermittently paused for hundreds of official photographs with the newlyweds. Food was served on several long rows of tables and chairs: heaping curries, chutneys, pickled vegetables and rice, upon plates made from banana leaves, mixed and eaten with our fingers.

Afterward, our RunCloud crew and local guides drove to nearby Vagamon mountain. The peak afforded sky-high views, down gaping gorges up to rolling hills with offline zip lines, and a small lake for kayaks. We spent a couple of hours walking around in fresh air, amidst cloud-touching hilltops.

On Friday, RunCloud and I visited Aswin's GetMyAdmin office. Eight of us sat around Aswin's desk, chatting about service improvements and future business. Arif – RunCloud's CEO – vigorously shook my hand, thanking me for introducing them to Aswin during my prior visit to their Johor Bahru office. Over the weekend, we visited the majestic Athirappilly Falls, before stopping at a beach in the very south of the country. Sunday evening's reception concluded the wedding. We arrived to dual buffets of mostly non-veg food, miniature glasses of fresh grape and lime juices, vanilla ice cream, butter popcorn stands and candy. Hearty handshakes and offers of brandy came from Aswin's father. There was a plethora of further photographs and selfies, on stage and off. I spent time with foxy Jozy – a former GetMyAdmin employee – and together we downed plentiful more ice cream. I bid goodbye to the handsome, newly-extended family of Aswin and Sree, before I was graciously driven home by their friends.

In my cosy bed at Mayflower Mansion, I tuned into the cricket World Cup final, pitting underdogs New Zealand against England. This became one of the greatest cricket matches of all time. New Zealand could have won, after their fielder caught the ball, but he mistakenly stepped on the boundary. This resulted in six runs, instead of a valuable wicket (out). The match went to extra time, and actually finished in a draw, but England prevailed through another mundane technicality.

A Day at Dhamma Setu

Following a packed Kochi to Chennai overnight semi-sleeper bus, I disembarked near Tambaran Railway Station at sunrise. I walked fifteen minutes through already-bustling and noisy streets, to a new budget hotel, Jai Palace. After an early check-in and nap, I wandered around Tambaran in scorching and drenching midsummer monsoon heat, before returning to the room, and falling asleep in sticky sweat.

At 6am the next morning, I jumped from bed, ate idly sambar at a nearby diner, and rode a tuk tuk to the meditation centre. Dhamma Setu was one of the oldest and largest Vipassana meditation centres in the world. Nestled between a busy road, major highway and nearby construction, Setu was unlike the tranquility of Tiruvannamalai's Dhamma Arunachala. The Chennai centre attempted to muffle the outside world with thickets of tall trees and stone pathways.

The one-day course was entirely casual: students were permitted to bring turned-off phones and belongings into the hall, and one man wore shorts. The session commenced a little after 9am, with a recorded preface from Goenka.

"Laziness prevents you from practicing an hour morning and night," was the gist of Goenka's opening message. Around sixty students were coached through an hour of Anapana. A second session of breathing practice preceded the first hour of guided Vipassana. The same culprits behind my recent rage resurfaced, but I remained calm, under control and forgiving.

A simple lunch of rice, curry and chapati provided a nourishing intermission, before two separate hours of Vipassana. The course concluded shortly after 4pm, with a shorter session dedicated to Metta Bhana: the process of emitting love and compassion to whoever enters one's consciousness – even those previously vilified. I made neither friendships nor connections, but the process leant valuable motivation to resume practicing Vipassana daily.

...

After another restless sleep, I was awake by 5am. I reached Tambaran Railway Station in time for a local "Unreserved" train to Pondicherry. Only Rs35 netted me a ticket for a four-hour train, south through Tamil Nadu. I was curious about local trains, having heard horror tales of mass-packed bodies into carriages. I held tense recollections of my first-ever Indian train in Mumbai: it was dangerously jam-packed, with people hanging off outside, and jumping out of doors.

This train was fine. I stood for most of the journey in the second-last carriage. At the back, a leper sprawled over the dusty steel floor, with lacerations and open sores visible on his skinny legs. He presented a mild hindrance to passengers, who stepped over him near the carriage's exit. The countryside was impressive: lakes, mountains and forests. Yet these were offset by multiple tons of plastic and litter, dumped alongside the tracks. My brain ached for solutions to rectify a clearly worsening problem, that was furthered by deteriorating human habits, and the unrepentant manufacturing of single-use plastic.

Nearing the final hour, I was pleased to sit alone in silence, before a group of eight young Tamil men bundled into the adjacent bench seats. At first came customary stares, before a tall Tamil beside me accumulated confidence for his question.

"You from England?" he asked.

"Born England. Father, New Zealand," I replied, to their delight. Most of the men pantomimed cricket moves, referring to the recent England-New Zealand World Cup final.

They mustered enough collective English to piece together a basic conversation, then presented an animated app on one of their phones.

"You play games?" one man asked.

I paused, pondering briefly. "Life is a game," I answered. They loved it, hollering their new mantra.

Topics touched on why I didn't have a wife at 42. At some point, the tall ringleader pointed out each of his friends with an imaginary, lethal disease, including HIV. Chuffing, they pointed back at him, circling forefingers around their heads.

"Mental problems?" I suggested. Again they rollicked in delight, regularly repeating the phrase. By the journey's end, I was invited to the birthday party of one man's mother, but I realised I'd be nothing but a novelty in an awkward situation.

Auroville, Revisited

On a hot and balmy afternoon I located Light & Bliss, my latest Auroville home. I met the personable Krishna: a Ukrainian who'd married a Korean Aurovillian. Light & Bliss was like a lighthouse: white and curved, with rooms embedded within miniature towers. It was nestled in the midst of lush green and brown trees; many were adorned with cheerful pink or red flowers.

Auroville featured evermore new restaurants, cafes and shops near the main road, while fresh luxury condos had been erected near the Solar Kitchen. At African Pavilion, a big new dormitory had been built, with its peculiar attribute of a giant roof installed diagonally, as if it gracefully fell off. I rode past Youth Centre, beyond the upside-down car near Transformation, around the Solar Kitchen roundabout, and up a little side road to the dosa hut. After dinner, I returned to African Pavilion. I chanted with the circle, while a large group of young Indians uproariously encircled the fire. Bright bolts of lightning struck from around the sky, as distant thunder boomed. In the little lighthouse, I fell asleep surrounded by forest, the thick fragrance of flowers, high-pitched chattering insects and rustling breeze of leaves.

...

On my final night in Auroville, four of us from Light & Bliss dined at Tanto Pizzeria. Krishna was to fly to Korea the next day, for an extended stay. We were accompanied by Bob, a middle-aged but youthful American, whose first Auroville visit came twenty years earlier, and Patricia – a Belgian researcher. Topics included the looming world crisis and Auroville. Becoming an Aurovillian sounded overly complicated, while the benefits of regularly visiting, as Bob or myself did, were similar but freer. *Why did we have to officially belong to anywhere?*

On my way to Pondicherry the next afternoon, a car pulled up beside me. A respectable Tamil driver asked me a few questions, then waved me in. The journey dropped me near Pondicherry's bus terminal. He desired no payment, and even my offer of a tea or juice was politely refused. After dinner, and a stroll around the oceanside promenade, I reached the bus terminal, ahead of a sleepless overnight coach to Bangalore.

The next evening I met up with my former St. Kilda Beach housemate, Harry Gill, at Church Street Social. We caught up over cocktails, and occasionally smoked tasty but potent clove cigarettes. Harry was from Kolkatta, and had originally proposed meeting in Kasol, but his mother was sick and Bangalore was our compromise. Harry was definitely into parties. On a whim, we headed to a nightclub called Sugar Factory. The first warning was its placement within the Marriott Hotel, predicating the forthcoming expense. The stern and stressed faces of several youthful promoters reminded me of unsuccessful events I'd produced. Still, Harry offered to cover the exorbitant cover. Inside the sparse, virtually-deserted Sugar Factory, commercial dance music echoed around the walls of the gloomy chamber. Drink prices began at such astronomical rates, that we could only muster a double vodka and some finger food. The lifeless club ensured our rapid but upbeat departure. Harry wasn't concerned in the least, and we laughed about it for a while.

The Ferocious Parvati River

Much of my travel in this book was well-researched and intentionally organised. Other than Rat House or the occasional stale dwelling, most of my chosen guesthouses were exemplary. Yet, something felt intriguing about rocking up without reservations. My first visit to the Himalayas was to practice the art of spontaneity: not pre-booking or pre-planning anything.

The flight landed at Chandigarh airport in pouring rain. The pilot informed us that photography at the airport was prohibited, and all window shades must be closed. With many hours to kill before a probable night bus, I made myself comfortable at the airport arrival hall. A friendly off-duty security guard chatted amicably about literature and his beloved Himachal Pradesh. He urged that I save his phone number, "in case of any trouble" while in the Himalayas. At the time, I didn't realise this was precisely the help I might need.

Shuttling from the airport, towards the general vicinity of the supposed bus terminal, of which Chandigarh had several, I headed towards one of the wrong locations. Upon disembarking at a random intersection, I noticed an unusual smell, akin to fresh marijuana. Sure enough, there were thousands of green cannabis plants flourishing everywhere: beside the road, in parks and forests, even across from the hefty police station.

I trudged through trickling rain to Chandigarh Interstate Bus Terminal: a very local, concrete bus interchange. Ticket counters were packed with boisterous punters. There was a small row of refreshment stands, several public toilets, and an inner atrium of transport offices. While strolling cautiously around the facilities, I was offered a shared taxi from a sketchy driver with red, puffy eyes, who suspiciously made little eye contact. He asked for a high price, that would lower if he found other passengers. My gut: It did not feel like safe travel.

Beside dozens of awaiting bus bays and ticket counters, a couple of young men generously assisted me. Half an hour later, my ticket stall opened, and plenty of men heaved forward to capture an attendant's attention. My young guides pushed to the front and demanded assistance for their foreigner. The elder manager looked sternly in my eyes, while all of our ears strained to better hear. There were two options: A lavish, comfortable tourist coach, or an earlier, much cheaper local bus. Up for trying the native experience, I opted for the latter.

Hours of waiting later, the ride to Bhuntar boarded, ahead of the most maniacal, crazy bus of all. Even seasoned passengers were astonished at this particular driver. The old steel bus zipped past slow, heavy construction trucks, regularly passing them at warp speed, swerving moments before onrushing trucks and cars. I couldn't sleep from the bus' constant jerking, winding, sudden halts and jolts. The only respite came from a pair of tea and toilet breaks.

Nine wild hours later, we arrived in Bhuntar, in pitch black around 5am. I was greatly fatigued, barely able to keep my eyes open. A driver with two other passengers offered me a ride for a reduced rate, and the four of us rode along a bumpy and narrow road. We travelled higher through hills, surrounded by truly huge mountains during the very first sunbeams of the day. Along the way, we stopped at the driver's modest restaurant. Its flat concrete rooftop afforded my initial wondrous impressions of the picturesque and powerful Himalayas. There were solid, thick mountains, with slopes so steep that few animals and no humans could climb. The passengers impressively collaborated at a pear tree. One climbed the tree while the other skilfully caught fruit, as wild pears were picked and shared.

We arrived at dusk in the empty centre of Kasol's village. I desperately needed rest, and sought a decent hostel with an early check-in. Walking through shadowy Kasol streets revealed many shabby dwellings, and I recognised only a handful of lodging from prior research. First, I stopped past Moustache Hostel. Nobody was awake when I arrived; bodies slept behind reception desks. After temporarily sitting in their outdoor chill lounge, I decided its vibe wasn't for me.

Next up was Whooper Hostel: a chore to reach and find. It required slipping down steep slopes, from a hill's road down to the raging Parvati River. One local with dreadlocks motioned at me to slow down: "Be careful." After an exhaustive wrong turn up another hill, I located riverside Whooper Hostel. With nobody around, I crashed on the cushions on reception's floor, blanketing myself in sarongs.

...

Three hours later, awake and rested, I met Whooper's curious host. After a welcomed breakfast, I slowly came to my senses, and revelled in my inspirational new confines. I made a new acquaintance: a 22-year-old from a strict family in Mumbai. He was living under discriminating Hindu caste regulations, that controversially dictated who he could and couldn't marry. Bowing to pressure from his family, he recently broke up with his beloved – but lower-caste – longterm girlfriend. Presently enjoying his solo adventure, away from the expectations of family, the young man was wary of returning to the formalities of his default life.

"What I've learned from the world," I shared, from my insights gleaned through numerous similar conversations."Is that your family loves you, and they want the best for you. Sure, they might insist you become a doctor or lawyer. But, if you work hard and become a success, at whatever you have a passion for, your family will be greatly proud." His eyes softened, and a prolonged, calm smile revealed unspoken revelation.

As the hours gracefully passed on a lazy, rainy day, I fell deeper into relaxation. With Delhi pressures of my own life resuming next week, this was my final opportunity to truly chill, and make the most of these majestic surroundings. I revelled evermore in fresh air, beside the whooshing of a fiercely rushing river, lush trees and chirping birds.

...

Kasol was a grubby, lively town, centred around drug tourism. Most visitors were male Indians, and there were plenty of Israelis, hence Kasol's nickname: "Little Israel". Everybody appeared a little sketched out from the abundant hashish. I took solace at lovely Moon Dance Cafe, while most patrons rolled joints, sharing among themselves. After lunch I ambled around, correctly guessing that a prominent bong shop would be able to assist with personal smoking supplies. I definitely overpaid for something that was not the legendary Malana Cream hash, but it still looked and smelled nice. As a bonus, the owner gifted me a small pouch, curved like a grey and zippered penis.

Back at the hostel, a young Danny Silver-lookalike acted in French pantomime. I assumed he was a mime, but Argent was a deaf student from Paris, on his first trip to India. Argent was definitely a hash lover, chain-rolling and smoking at any given opportunity. He animatedly conducted conversations, that grew in complexity the more I practiced broken sign language.

On my third day, I sought to find the Jim Morrison Cafe. I became unintentionally lost for an hour. Increasingly large groups of Indian men stopped me for countless selfies, provoking the inclination: *I'm a novelty.* After directions from various passer-bys, I followed a narrow path, up a slippery hill behind Evergreen restaurant, where a small placard bore a graffiti stencil of Jim Morrison's recognisable face. Soon after, I encountered the first of two further groups of men who demanded selfies. Before I knew it, both groups followed me up a winding path through forest to Jim Morrison Cafe.

Inside the cafe was nothing particularly special: a rectangular room with cushioned floor booths, and several groups of noisy young Indians eating and smoking. The aggressive group of men ordered me to sit on a small cushion beside them. After the inevitable "Are you married?", one man asked to see photos of my girlfriend; I politely refused. The most gangsta one – overweight, crew cut, big round glasses, Yankees hat and faux gold chains – mocked me as a "foreigner". I stood up, bowed honourably in farewell, and departed. One of the nicer group's men disappointedly ran after me.

"Very unfriendly place," I told him in the doorway. He lowered his head, nodding in understanding. I strode down the mountain through the forest clearing. Two young men with short hair and moustaches jogged after me from the cafe's exit.

"Foreigner!" they yelled, with a sympathetic look, as if they were sorry for their brethren. Ignoring them, I power-walked, skipping down stones through trees. I remained calm, in the solitude of an impenetrable headspace, and sought somewhere familiar for the looming mountain downpour: Moon River Cafe.

Higher in the Himalayas

In the morning, I donated a chunk of hash to the deaf French traveller, departed Kasol and began walking to Manikaran. Rapidly, a car graciously picked me up for the drive. Manikaran was a frenzied holy Punjab town. It featured was a sizeable temple, beneath a complicated maze of stone steps, most through a multilevel concrete parking lot. At the bottom, a low bridge crossed the furious Parvati River. On the other side, a sun-stained building led down to a steamy catacomb and apparent hot pools. Scores of local men scanned me with fierce eyes, and I didn't dare venture down dark, wet steps, into the grey-grim dressing chamber. Back across the bridge at the temple, one hundred men bathed in outdoor pools. I navigated the parking lot labyrinth, and eventually reached the main road. I began an aimless hike up the mountain towards Tosh.

My bursting backpack, close to 9kg, was disappointing considering how light it started. Love was transporting 1kg of spirulina and moringa powders, gifts and frivolous accessories for your partner, while trekking through the Himalayas. Each heavy or superfluous item was a painful reminder for future minimalistic traveling. Power-walking with a bulky bag, 3000 metres above sea level, was further challenged by my recent lung-busting overindulgence of tobacco and hash.

Hours of uphill trudging led to higher, winding mountain roads. At one particular pinnacle, puffing and sweating, I took a well-deserved break on a boulder, that overlooked ribbons of distant road below. The storming Parvati river was shrouded by green hills. Far beyond I noticed a steel bus, grinding and bumping its way up the rocky road. Nobody in passing cars or vans had offered me a ride. I decided to try to flag the bus; if I was unsuccessful, I'd continue walking. By the bus' eventual grunting arrival, I was relieved when the growling steel beast clambered beside me, idling slowly enough for me to yank open the door and jump in.

"Barshaini?" I asked; the conductor nodded. I pushed through the aisle, to the vacant middle seat of the back row.

The young passengers beside me were friendly. In the distance, I noticed a barricade and police truck. With little hesitation, I hid the hash-filled grey-zippered pouch in my underwear, moments before officers halted the bus and hopped on. I knew I was the catch of the day; the trim-haired, thin-moustached drill sergeant almost held back his utter delight. He momentarily pretended to randomly harass other passengers, then gleefully skipped to dessert: Me. His colleague boarded the bus from the back; they both stood sternly to face me.

The thin-moustached officer patted me down, while I helped remove items from my many pockets. I tried to deflect attention from my secret bulge, and it nearly worked, as the colleague urged his partner to stop searching. The all-knowing Thin Moustache shook his head.

"What is this?" the gruff officer asked, feeling around my artificial lin. Sighing, I realised he knew, and I slowly pulled down my pants, in front of a captivated local bus. Apologetically, with a deep breath, I pulled out the grey pouch.

"Arrest!" it sounded like, from the colleague, in a serious tone. The rapid fire of police questions began, as both officers stepped discretely into intimate audible range.

"Where are you going? What do you want to pick up? Tell me now."

My answers were calm and consistent, and I revealed no threat. The hash wasn't a big amount, even though I'd overpaid for it, and I certainly didn't have more. At worst I'd pay a fine, but I had no idea how much. They searched my bag: every inch of it. Their eyes jolted extremely wide, as if they'd uncovered 1kg of cocaine, when the spirulina and moringa powders surfaced.

"Gift for girlfriend," I cooly explained. I had a little gift box, and my second passport was a particular curiosity, but they rightfully couldn't find any further contraband. Acknowledging I was clean, the search concluded.

"This is your warning," emphasised the drill sergeant, and they both departed. The bus' astonished passengers stared at me.

"I'm sorry everybody!" I apologised, and many of them laughed.

"It's okay man!" one young man smiled. "Did they take anything?"

The police had confiscated my pouch and hash. *I wish I'd given the French kid more.* Aside from rupturing my intricately-packed backpack, I felt lucky enough: No fine or jail time. I didn't even like hash anyway.

Two of the young men at the back, the closest witnesses, made polite conversation. They became intrigued upon learning of my complex roots and book. Both men – Anur and Saresh – were off-duty junior police cadets. Anur graciously invited me to stay at his brother's guesthouse. Apparently this was the final bus of the evening. It would have required at least four further hours of up-mountain hiking to Tosh, and there were no guesthouses along the way. I felt even luckier.

A while later, we arrived at Barshaini, near an under-construction hydroelectric dam, beside the furious Parvati river. I trekked behind the young men, up steep roads and rocks to Tosh. Anur was a part-time tour guide, and was keenly proud of his surroundings. Saresh - who looked like an Indian James Dean - was closer to my level (or lack) of fitness. Neither of us matched the pace and vigour of the experienced Anur, who effortlessly glided up rocks. A long half hour later, we surfaced at the base of Tosh, that required even higher ascending, up pathways usually only passable by animals.

Reaching our destination, Royal Himalayan Guest House, we sat outside around a circular table and sipped on chai. Facing us was a pitch-black wall of a mountain, while lights and signs from the small village glittered behind us. I locked my backpack in a bedroom, before Anur guided us around Tosh. We crossed delicate pathways, before stopping at a friend's very chill Shiva Cafe. Inside, four young men sang along with a guitar, while a trio of staff mingled. Anur, in Hindi, related the story of our meeting and my police encounter, to sympathetic murmurs. A slice of quality hash was presented as a gift, and Saresh rolled it up. Bowls of steaming red penne arrived with another round of milk tea, before several joints were shared. Back at Royal Himalayan, I was served a plate of butter paneer and fresh-made roti. A pear was plucked from a tree and tossed to me.

"What more would you like, Sir?" asked Anur.

"Nothing more, thank you! Everything is amazing!" I was

extremely grateful, especially about the double bedroom offered to me. Anur's brother also owned a campsite near the famous town of Malana, that I promised to visit next time I came here.

After Anur and Saresh departed for sleep, two new men entered. One intriguingly donned a NYY baseball cap and Western attire. Baba'd spent a big chunk of his life in Canada, near Toronto, where most of his family remained. He'd earned substantial money as a truck driver for years, before a bad accident ended his career. He was unable to maintain the hefty labour and long hours of industrial driving.

After sharing several joints, he transformed into a Baba. He was unconvinced by my answer to a simple question: *Do you have a wife?* My "year-long girlfriend" answer didn't placate him. He drilled deeper, and insisted on honesty; I was a little bewildered, as everything I answered was the truth. I remarked that I enjoyed my relationship with Magia, but Baba sensed there was more untold. I mentioned my dreamy three months in South Korea, with a much younger babe, our special connection, and its abrupt, long-distance ending. Solemnly, he turned to me.

"I am a Baba, okay? I speak the truth; I seek the truth. I see the truth." He paused. "You should write to her, and tell her she remains in your heart."

"The young one?" I responded; he nodded. I felt I'd quite admirably repressed my Boogie sentiments since her surprising New Year's Day message. Today was the day after this year's Borderland. Although my relationship with Magia was perfectly comfortable, I wondered if I still missed The Past. I realised it was probably overdue for a short, sweet letter to Boogie.

The Slippery Trek to Khir Ganga

After a refreshing sleep, meditation and breakfast, I hiked higher up Tosh. I had absolutely no plans, or any inclination beyond reaching higher peaks, and perhaps locating an affordable campsite. Huffing and puffing in altitude, ten minutes later my ambitions altered. For the first time in my life I doubted my fitness, to the point I questioned a potential fatality. My heaving chest warned of my heart attack scare a few years back. Instead, Snow View Dev Dhaba became my writing spot in the heavens.

Its little wooden loft was covered in carpet, and offered picturesque valley views under clouds. Randomly, Baba and his friend passed by and joined me for a while.

I telephoned the owner of a guesthouse in one of the lower regions, Kalgha, and felt inclined to head down the mountain. I crossed the huge dam construction, that was lofted precariously above the merciless Parvati river, and up a steep and hazardously slippery hill to Kalgha. The appropriately named "Lost and Found Galactic Friend's House" was concealed beyond plentiful narrow muddy paths, through trees and an abundance of fresh mint-like marijuana plants; many were four metres tall. Lost and Found's simple two-storey wood and concrete house faced a kitchen shack, built from sand and stone, with recycled glass bottles for insulation. A sizeable upstairs porch was the social centre, while a cosy indoor lounge was partially submerged. I cheerfully selected a double bedroom with jungle views for Rs400. The external bathroom and shower were a minute's walk through wet shrubbery and green weeds. A small group of thirty-year-old Indian men respectfully passed me a chillum, to smoke from a deceased artist's pipe. As rain fell, we moved to the balcony. Service was attentive and genuine; anything I wanted or needed, the crew provided.

In the morning, I opened my eyes to a mystical glimpse of dawn, through a forest beyond my window. Meditation and chai afforded a cruisy start to the day, but my intended departure to legendary Khir Ganga was becoming late. I was urged to hurriedly commence, and complete my journey before nightfall.

"Three hours there, bathe in hot springs, and come back," solemnly advised Butterfly, the tall, handsome, long-haired proprietor of Lost and Found. "You must return before dark. It is dangerous, and you will become lost."

Butterfly repeated important directions, particularly articulating one critical part of the return trip. Mistakenly crossing a certain bridge meant trekking on a different mountain, that would ensure a longer walk home. I donned my long-sleeved yellow kurta, green cargo shorts, worn-out Adidas trainers, and a blue fish sarong as a scarf. I squeezed a stainless steel water bottle in my back pocket. Ready, I set forth on one of the most remarkable journeys of my life.

I scaled the first steep hill of grass, rocks and mud. I realised that when a Himachal Pradeshian described a route as "flat", it still involved climbing and descending mountains. "Flat" to me was low-rolling countryside, or a minimal incline through the pavements of a metropolis. The path to Khir Ganga was nothing of the sort: thousands of metres above sea level, with foot-wide pathways that sliced dramatically around the mountain's edges.

Occasionally, I passed small clusters of trekkers; my progress needed only be faster than any group's weakest link. Fatigued individuals and groups headed in the opposite direction; some made eye contact and shared a nod, while others brimmed with fury in their eyes. I was regularly accompanied for short segments by an assortment of mountain dogs; they didn't guide in any meaningful way, but perhaps out of boredom they sympathetically tagged along. The higher I climbed, the slower my pace. After another ninety minutes, I stopped for the odd but tasty combination of watermelon-lemon juice.

"Thirty minutes away," offered one of the juice stop's patrons.

Slight, fresh rain fell, as languishing daylight increasingly became a concern. The sky was covered in grey clouds, and the slippery pathways challenged the limited traction of my old shoes. Every step higher up mountains induced increased effort, that was exacerbated by my hash and tobacco-saturated lungs.

Upon a curved, broad lower corner of a slope, a few dozen rocky steps lurched upwards. I saw a horizon filled with cafes, tents and the buzz of human inhabitants. The entire hill was covered in bright yellow canvas of restaurants and campsites, under specks of refreshing rain. Higher and steeper, cows grazed, local villagers meandered downhill, and the apparent top of the mountain pierced through the clouds.

While focusing for hours on hiking, I'd forgotten that the pinnacle of Khir Ganga was its balmy hot springs. I trudged upwards, through slivers of rain, sweaty, muddy and exhausted. The decadent hot springs featured steaming water in a blue square basin, beside a diminutive temple. The area was deserted. I slowly undressed, revealing swimming trunks I'd worn in lieu of underwear. Dipping my feet in forty-plus Celsius water was incredibly pleasurable. I sank into the bath, and submerged in soothing heat; all my pains and worries dissipated.

At the edge of the sky blue pool, I looked down at the plentitude of yellow tents, that stretched down as far as the eye could see, before they vanished into murky mist. The cool pattering of rain contrasted with the relaxingly-snug, piping-hot water. In the clouds, this was an absolute dream.

After fifteen minutes of hot springs pleasure, I felt clean, energised and reinvigorated. There was a bounce in my step upon descending the hill, as if my body disregarded the earlier hours of hiking. I was wet and hungry, and lounged on the cushioned floor of a large wooden restaurant with a warm fireplace. I devoured ginger lemon honey tea, paneer and rice. Rain fell more steadily, prompting the consideration of camping overnight, ahead of an early morning rush to Kalgha, then Delhi. A gut feeling urged otherwise, although heavier rain would complicate already slippery and dangerous paths.

A tad before 4:30pm, re-energised, I resumed the trek with urgency. Downhill was certainly quicker, but not necessarily easier, as my leg muscles constantly braked, further com-pounded by slipping in my aged running shoes. Rain endlessly intensified, with no sign of a Sun that would soon be setting. I assertively scrambled down muddy rocks, occasionally passing stoned canines along the way.

At the most critical moment, appeared a small plateau with an abundance of choices. With one particularly unhelpful dog on my heels, I headed up a narrow path towards bush. It was steep and slippery, above a ravenous waterfall that flowed out to the ruthless Parvati River. When the path disappeared into the mist ahead, I couldn't take the risk. One bad turn or slip assured the very stark possibility of falling to my death. The dog was a real hinderance; she didn't understand my insistence to turn around. The path was so dangerously narrow, I couldn't pass the confused canine. I gently prodded her while frantically pseudo-barking. The unimpressed dog rolled her eyes, and hopped onto an adjacent rock, that she delicately gripped with her paws.

Upon safely reaching the plateau, I heard another waterfall, spotted a bridge and crossed. Afterward, I realised this was the integral point Butterfly had specified, as I found myself on another, farther-away mountain, with nightfall approaching. The auxiliary benefit was this route presented greatly more otunning views, alongside a mountain's edge, instead of hidden in blackening, deadly jungle. There were plentiful steep inclines and declines, with extraordinarily slippery sections and narrow rocks, where looking down towards the Parvati River lent an elevated sense of life-dependent caution. Wild marijuana plants blossomed in abundance, by the thousands. There was one local village, accessible only by foot, with the closest road many kilometres of trekking away. The final descent through falling sun and rain was particularly enchanting: two huge, powerful rivers converged before the massive hydroelectric dam.

Down at the river basin, I crossed a rickety low-hanging bridge, while the fervent Jigrai Nallah gushed underneath. Sauntering up the trail on the Tosh side, across the powerful dam, I ascended to Kalgha. The most unhelpful dog of all took a fancy to my feet. The painfully slippery, sometimes falling, slow trek up a steep, slick hill was greatly inhibited by the dog, who playfully but forcefully chomped at my shoes the entire way.

Upon arriving at Kalgha, drenched and filthy, I trudged a kilometre through mud and grass, becoming Lost then Found. I was greeted with a warm, dry towel, a mug of lemon ginger honey tea, and a welcomed hash joint. I meditated and slept.

Every step of a dangerous solo trek literally impacts our life or death; there is nobody to help us. We rapidly, regularly practice critical decision-making. The narrow paths we choose dictate the struggle or ease required to reach our destinations, and help us navigate the bigger philosophical forks on our roads ahead.

Coming Down the Mountain

The decision to descend from Khir Ganga instead of stay the night, was particularly wise in that the storm never ceased. Rain slammed through the morning, and beyond the next afternoon. One of the staff informed me: "Rain was expected for days." An hour of leisurely packing in a thunderstorm was a useful means of spending time. I hoped for a break in rain, that never came, increasing the likelihood of sliding down a muddy, difficult hill. The ongoing downpour suggested I might not be able to leave Kalgha today; perhaps I'd miss DomainX altogether. And what about DomainX? I'd heard nothing from the organisers, other than vague potential participation. I preferred to remain in the Himalayas, instead of noisy, polluted Delhi. If not for my responsibility to Mother.Domains, I'd have stayed in nature.

With neither a break in rain nor respite in sight, I strove to make a soaking wet and muddy attempt at leaving. I was informed of an alternate, more accessible route down Kalgha. I bid warm wishes to the Lost and Found crew, and ventured in the general vicinity of their seemingly straightforward directions. Immediately, I became lost, soaked and grimy. After a slippery wrong turn, I found a small travel agency on a corner, opposite an A-frame that promoted Himalayan Nomads buses to Delhi. Stepping out of the rain, covered in mud, I took shelter in the agency's reception area. The diligent clerk discovered an available window seat on an earlier bus, that was departing from Kasol at 6:30pm. My new challenge became the matter of reaching Kasol on time, with the final local bus leaving Barshaini at 5pm. The present time was a regrettably smokeless 4:20. I still had to find the alternate downhill path from Kalgha, cross the dam and race to Barshaini. Still, I bought the bus ticket, while acknowledging the additional inherent stress. I felt the experiential reassurance that everything usually worked out.

The alternative route was certainly less steep. Its large rocks crafted an accessible, elderly-friendly staircase to the base of Kalgha. Slow and cautiously, step by step, with the support of a large stick, I safely and expeditiously descended. I speed-walked 1km to Barshaini, while debating the cost savings and slow speed of a local bus, versus paying for an expeditious taxi. I mistakenly marched through the entire town, that necessitated a slower trundle back up the mountain. Villagers pointed me towards an apparent taxi office. As I stepped in its doorway, I relayed my time constraints, and received the expected quote of Rs400. I was about to commit, when the local bus grunted into town, right on time. Thinking to use the bus to negotiate a better price, I turned to the taxi stand manager.

"Maybe I take the local bus?"

The men in the office, I'm not sure if they were posturing, shook their heads. "It could take two and a half hours," cautioned one man.

Having hiked from Manikaran up a big mountain road and

witnessed the slow, lumbering coach idle its way up, I knew time would be tight. I agreed to a taxi; they assigned me a senior Nepalese driver, who sped expertly yet cautiously down the mountain, passing every vehicle. We reached Moon Dance Cafe in Kasol a little before 6pm. I gobbled a channa masala dinner, with mango lassi and tea. By 6:20pm I was outside the supposed bus stand, beside other travellers awaiting the same route to Delhi. At that moment, the local bus from Barshaini pulled up, filled with foreigners I recognised from the mountain. If I'd taken this bus I *might* have arrived on time, but there wouldn't have been dinner or relaxing. There was no guarantee of light traffic, or had rain caused delays, or even landslides.

A little after 6:30pm, a small shuttle bus jammed nine of us for a lift to Bhuntar, in time to connect with the Himalayan Nomads coach to Delhi. The fifteen-hour journey was largely uneventful, but was entirely comfortable, with a reclining window seat and nobody beside me. It may have been the most enjoyable long-haul bus of my travel career, simply in comparison to the mad local bus up the Himalayas. Sometimes we have to personally experience the range of everything, to better appreciate the subjectivities of luxury and comfort.

Master of Domains

The whole reason I came to India the very first time in 2015 was because of the domain conference, DomainX. Their second edition was hosted in Bangalore in August 2015, and I'd recently started a domain business. Whatever my misgivings towards Mother.Domains and the domain industry, I owed a lot to my company, and India was one of those reasons. The DomainX crew graciously involved me in their conferences, helping me network and make invaluable connections. Hence, the DomainX conference was annually pencilled in my calendar.

DomainX 2019 was scheduled for the first weekend of August, at the Eros Hotel in Delhi's Nehru Place. I hosted a panel with the pre-assigned topic: "Why are domain names important?" Beside me at a front VIP table included the noble Nalin, live sound engineer "Mad" Oswin, a father-son from Mumbai, and many familiar faces from past events. During the final session, the audience was encouraged to gain feedback on the value of their domains, as reviewed by the stage's panel of pre-eminent experts. I nervously held my hand in the air, until I was granted the microphone for the very final domain of the session.

"Mother.Domains!" I wanted to yell, with a vague intent to sell. But, instead I called out the more sensible, "worldcup.blog", which didn't have much value as a generic, niche domain.

The DomainX afterparty was hosted at a loud, low-light nightclub in a shopping mall. There was a small buffet dished out under neon lights, and a risky open bar that poured me a plethora of double scotches. The dancefloor amusingly filled with domainers of all ages and social classes, who bounced to commercial Bollywood hits.

Oswin and I returned to the more sensible Delhi sector of Saket. The first bar demanded a whopping Rs2000 entry, but the second – a respectable-looking place called District – welcomed us for free. Inside I witnessed, for the first time in my previous Indian escapades, a nightclub packed with seemingly hot, mostly younger women. Oswin and I were escorted to a roped-off VIP area, and a stocky Nepalese barmaid sat us down.

"You want girls?" the barmaid asked. A gorgeous young Indian woman with long curly hair approached us; she politely and firmly clasped our hands. Oswin and I shook our heads: We only wanted beer! A waiter fetched two slim bottles of Kingfisher.

"Girls here are good," suggested the waiter. "Also, we have ladyboys."

"Ladyboys?"

"Yes!" he beamed. "Very good ones!"

Soon and mercifully enough, the house lights shone. The previously-gorgeous women were fully exposed in the sudden brightness. They were alike makeup-clad vampires, who promptly scattered and exited. I realised any of them, perhaps all, could be ladyboys.

...

DomainX's second day was highlighted by the bizarre actions of one young man, who bid outlandish amounts on literally every domain. It rendered the live-stream domain auction wholly frustrating, if not surreally entertaining, particularly upon the discovery that he used somebody else's credit card.

My lodging for my final nights in India was Hide-In Hostel in Saket, that featured an excellently chill rooftop. Nalin visited me on Sunday morning with his dog Cookie, and they toured me around a nearby park that was once an integral part of ancient kingdoms. We sauntered on old stone walls, that had previously comprised a fortress. I spent my final evening drinking whiskey at Nalin's apartment. We chatted about love and humanity, and watched impressive videos by talented Pakistani musicians.

My flight to Ukraine was smooth, before a night's stopover in Kiev: my first visit. Kiev was covered in concrete and uninspired old communist architecture, but it did feature pretty parks and gardens. I observed countless people keeping up appearances: plentiful model types donning designer brands, contrasted by bulky, scarred men, seemingly not far removed from battlefields. I roomed at The Tower Hostel: a huge, shiny, soulless megahostel, near a big park in a lively area. For dinner, I sourced a nearby African restaurant; I felt more comfortable with African brethren than at overpriced Ukrainian hipster bars. I provided advice, and apparently inspiration, to several young Africans, who'd ventured to Ukraine under the promise of the European dream; instead they discovered its cold, hard realities. At least there were African communities in Kiev – I'd noticed nothing of the sort in unabashedly white Poland.

The next morning featured a rapid flight to Budapest, from where Flixbus shuttled me along eight dull hours to Krakow, including an odd wrong turn, like the bus driver forgot the route. Along the way I met Mateuz: a friendly Slovakian who lived near Amsterdam. The bus was further delayed, upon being swapped onto a broken down bus without air conditioning; many passengers in the back removed their shirts.

My month overseas felt long in many ways, while rapid in others, but it was a lifetime apart from the world Magia and I shared. The warmth I felt in my heart, the embrace of my love and her two fluffy cats, in our apartment; life was beautiful. I'm coming home, baby.

Chapter 20

Homeless Where the Heart Is

Although we may wish for happy endings, life is not always so complicit. Often, our entire courses change forever from events outside of our control: such as war, or tyranny of others' ego, or sometimes through our own unintended actions, caught in the grog between living, dreams and sleep.

Upon my returning from the Himalayas, Magia, the cats and I enjoyed a revitalised and peaceful month in Zielonki. Magia observed positive changes in my behaviour, while I regained my drive and passion, even for mundane work objectives. We swiftly resumed our daily routine: waking early for buckets of coffee, hours of writing, then work. I meditated most days, usually by myself. I felt some confusion at the contrast between solo Himalayan journeys, versus the simplicity and responsibility of a home routine, where I barely left the house.

Everything appeared to be progressing swimmingly in our cute little home, although demons nagged at Magia, who was unable to sustain her happiness. She regularly fell into apathy, that included a lessened appetite, a defeatist reluctance to cook, demanding massages but not reciprocating, and a rudderless approach to establishing her Dobra Atmosfera blog. She'd not enjoyed space of her own in ages; while I was in India, she'd catered to her mother's demands, driving to and from their family cottage in Bulgaria. Moreover she constantly, testily demanded intimacy, that I was reluctant to fulfil, and this seemed to be the precursor for inevitable tension that would arise about anything.

"Open relationship," I reminded her. If she needed it, she was welcome to find physical gratification elsewhere. Naturally, I understood the imperativeness of romantic intimacy between partners, but I wasn't feeling it, and the constant pressure further lessened my attraction. My patience and resilience post-India remained high, but each burst of negativity from Magia oparked compartments of my brain, that suggested I leave my options open, such as where I'd head next, and when.

During several happy days at home, everything felt superb; life was fun and sweet, and our interactions were as cute as they could be. In evenings, after long days of computer work, I studied music production, and practiced with my newly-acquired second-hand Arturia Beatstep Pro. After music, or episodes of Game of Thrones, Magia and I regularly fell into deep sleeps together.

And then, everything changed, without consciously in control or aware. One night, slipping into slumber on the couch, with a nonplussed desire for everybody to leave me alone, I relocated to the bedroom. Drifting into sleep, entering the doorway of murky dreams I'd never recall, I fell further into a hole of seeking solitude. Magia, on her way from the bathroom, playfully bounded into bed; her hands were moist with cold water. During my semi-conscious fog, she grabbed me with her freezing hands. Startled, I heaved back at her, almost slapping away at the intrusion. For a moment, I wondered if I slapped too hard. I thought little of it, but when Magia departed to the couch, I realised I'd upset her.

...

The next day was a disaster, with Magia's fury not a secret. My actions triggered her lifespan of brutal memories: being beaten by her parents, and of every despicable male experience she'd known. She claimed I "hit" her, and we argued over semantics, including that I was barely awake, or that it was far from an actual "hit". I understood her reasonable request for me to find alternative accommodation for a few days of necessary space.

The situation further deteriorated, through full-blown arguments about every relationship grievance, including money and our lack of sex life. Increasingly unhelpful, was my suggestion that her jealousy moved her to spy on my online activities. Admittedly, it had never been much of a legitimate consideration, but it was among the various frustrated garbling I expressed, laced with my father's style of profanity. Magia's rage resulted in a violent reaction; my clothes were thrown from the drying rack, and I was ordered to leave immediately.

Things cooled enough to allow time to pack, while my boggled mind scraped for possibilities. I rapidly ruminated between staying at a hostel in Krakow, riding a night bus to Berlin, or mustering the courage to leave forever. Despite calm temporarily resuming enough to cuddle together on the couch, with visits by an aware and concerned Czupur, my late-night bus to Berlin was booked.

...

Extraordinarily early in the morning, I arrived at Berlin' ZOB bus terminal. Lugging my seldom-used bigger backpack, I reached a quaint cafe in the city's centre, for breakfast and work. A few hours later I met Flowa in Kreuzberg. Initially, I didn't recognise the thinner version of my soulful friend; he'd stopped taking his bloating anti-psychotic medication. I received a key to his Friedrichshain flat, where I appreciatively ventured for a nap. Following extended yet super-chill plans with DJ Andi at Greenhouse, I slept another eighteen hours.

Our few days apart were extended, after Magia asked if I wanted more time in Berlin. Flowa selflessly welcomed me to prolong my visit. One afternoon I strolled around the city, during Berlin Art Week. One power-walk took me to Tempelhof Airport. I smoked a joint under trees beside softball fields, and then made a first foray into the former Nazi airport hangar, that was presently a reception area for an overpriced art exhibition. Late one evening, as we discussed travel and hitchhiking, Flowa became inspired, and rapidly packed a bag. "I'm heading to Munich!" he declared, while bounding around the apartment. When I woke the next morning, he'd departed, leaving me alone in the flat for a welcomed few days.

Magia and I talked over a mobile app, seemingly clearing the air. She appreciated her Magia Time at home, although she was sad, as were the confused little cats. She insisted upon a few reasonable demands, and I promised to work harder at the relationship: pay a fairer share of bills, and put better effort into reviving our sex life. Missing home, I readily complied, and I intended to return to Krakow the following Monday. I spent the time writing, working and meditating. I cooked simple meals gleaned from budget supermarket ingredients. I skipped various events and parties; instead I remained homely and – other than Sativa and CBD oil – sober.

Over the weekend, Magia's tone reverted from renewed positivity to short, curt messages, that rekindled my wondering why I remained in this relationship. Extraordinarily early on Monday morning, I made my way through the cold, waiting for a bus that was thirty minutes late. I had an uneasy feeling, coaxed by the coldness in Magia's brief replies. The day was odd and surreal, grey and rainy, as the bus trundled through Poland, like the Sun was trying to shine but held back.

The bus rolled into grey Krakow shortly after 1pm, but Magia would not greet me at the terminal. A message: "Meet me upstairs." I made my way to the rooftop parking area, but I couldn't spot Magia's red Mazda. Instead, Magia stood near a stairwell, nervously finishing a cigarette, near a male friend I thought was somebody else. She walked towards me, and I warmly approached her, reaching for a hug. Without a trace of a smile, she pushed me away, frowning. She grimly launched into her practiced spiel.

"I've packed all your things. They are in the car. I have kept your music items at my house. You can have them back when you repay the money you owe me."

My blown mind took minutes to clear, boggled by the abruptness of the situation.

"Why didn't you tell me this before I spent my last money on buses? We spoke a few days ago, and everything sounded fine. We were going to work at things."

Magia shook her head. "Nothing was fine."

"You're throwing me out on the streets! With no money!"

She remained unflinching. My mind switched focus to solving this stark, sudden challenge, including where I'd stay tonight, and from where cash would appear for hotels and food.

After a short while, the chat warmed and became more civil. This was far from the first time I'd suddenly been tossed from my home, onto the street. I didn't begrudge her one bit, other than her waiting until I'd ridden a costly night bus to impose the news. In one sense, I was relieved the decision had been made. I owed her money, sure; I supposed it's reasonable she held my valuable items, even the Arturia. Later, I realised her actions mirrored my mother's: confiscating my beloved music equipment, packing my bags, and kicking me out of the house.

Manipulatively, to slow time down and gain an opportunity for reconsideration, I requested a dreaded cigarette; Magia eagerly withdrew one and lit it for me. We amicably chatted deeper about everything. At her car, the old blue Mazda, I removed everything unnecessary from the big backpack. She was holding several of my belongings anyway, so I could afford to grab everything later. I opted against bringing the tent, that would prove to be a noteworthy decision, but gathered the military-grade sleeping bag, in case I needed warmth, literally on the streets or under a bridge.

We sat, leaning against the open trunk of the car, while devouring further ultra-thin cigarettes. Betraying the severe circumstances, our body language was that of best friends, almost touching each other, speaking passionately.

"You'll hate me," Magia sputtered. "You'll be so mad at me."

I shook my head. I was not mad at her. She hadn't done anything unreasonable. Perhaps it was another instance of accepting whatever somebody else dictated at my detriment, that would simmer inside me for months, but I remained relaxed. Any urgency in my brain was about where I would sleep tonight, and how to muster funds to survive. Magia's first Vipassana course was to begin the next day. I realised that my returning to Zielonki wouldn't be an option, at least until after her ten days of Vipassana – if she was able to complete it. She seemed to pick up on this vibe, for she turned to me, with her eyes full of fear and love, restraining tears.

"I'm confused. It doesn't feel like it's over," Magia warbled. I nodded in agreement. She continued: "Please, let's chat again after Vipassana."

We embraced long and hard, before I gathered my backpack.

"I'm not mad at you, don't worry. You did nothing wrong." I paused, before quoting words from my dear Malawian friend, Henly. "This is not goodbye. It's see you again."

My eyes held back tears behind sunglasses, and with around 15kg of life on my back I slowly hobbled away, walking straight, not looking back. Steely determination consumed the entirety of my focus, to solve my latest mess: Where to sleep, how to eat, and prepare to move on.

Living Rough, Revisited

Magia Cafe in the historic old square was the first establishment I'd ever visited in Krakow. I sat in the cafe's inner courtyard, surrounded by my bags, while a trickle of cold rain fell from grey skies. I opened my usual smorgasbord of useful lodging websites, and researched over the intentional lengthiness of a large pot of flowering jasmine tea. Not wishing to retreat to Berlin so quickly, and with Magia in Zielonki for another night, I decided to stay longer in Krakow. A sliver of me hoped for an unrealistic invitation to look after Magia's apartment, or the delirious unlikelihood of rapidly raising $1000 to reacquire my musical equipment, then never return again.

Deciding on Atlantis Hostel, I had sufficient cash for a couple of night's accommodation and meals. I transferred $100 from my company account, for sanity and breathing space. I hauled my bags through rain to Atlantis Hostel; check-in was seamless, and I paid under €20 for two nights. I showered, changed and wrote from Atlantis' comfortable lounge, while downing a coconut beer. I put out subtle feelers to certain friends, and Flowa warmly invited me back to Berlin: "As long as I needed." Several other prospective opportunities were scattered across Europe.

When homeless, particularly with bleak prospects, it's highly useful to have milestones to aim towards. Mine included finding a way to India as soon as possible, after the Bonobo and David August gig in Amsterdam. Six months of an Indian visa would require arriving in India by November to depart before May. I sought to raise funds to repay Magia, and recover my beloved music gear. Forced survival mode opens one's mind to all possibilities. Life-dependent hustle for work and camaraderie, usually translates to food and shelter. I followed up with several past and present clients, although the dimming status of the Australian economy was increasingly prevalent. Another visit to India was an opportunity to cement Mother.Domains, and would be a business trip: the company could muster surplus funds for flights. $100 a week was enough to live adequately in India. My main challenge was to survive in Europe for another two months, then everything should be OK.

I needed to proactively spend time, and next week's Avant Art

Festival in Wroclaw was appealing. A prompt reply by the festival's PR representative, Kasia, offered free passes in exchange for media coverage. *Super!* The following week, the festival was to move to Warsaw, that could creatively consume another week's focus. Then only one week remained before Bonobo's Outlier in Amsterdam.

Plans evolved in Berlin. Old friend Heidi Heart was DJing at Sisyphos in Berlin, and strongly urged I join her. I liked Heidi – she was a gorgeous Australian traveller, radiant in mind and spirit, similarly a writer, deep thinker and romantic. She was somebody I'd been curious about for years, but we'd not had the opportunity to hang out and gauge any vibe. I heard from The Russian – the pseudo-flame from my epic 2016 trip – who invited me to the Ukraine for her birthday. Ana – the Serbian-Canadian whom meeting for Oregon Solar Eclipse was the impetus of my original 2017 trip (that instead led to Korea and Poland) – was living in Paris, and was curious about meeting up.

Suddenly, life didn't seem so bad. I had warm places to stay, enough to eat, access to festivals, and potential rendezvous with cool, beautiful women. What lingered was shock, through the sudden surrealness of my situation. Yet, I held a hardy mindset to battle through, one day at a time. It felt like the very beginning again; from that arose the inherent excitement that anything, anywhere and anyone could happen.

...

The next morning, I woke with the gut-wrenching, shock-subsided blow of reality. This two-plus-year trip had furnished a constant onslaught of disoriented and emotional wake-ups. Two years ago today, I willingly slept on the streets of Seoul, and the parallels of Korea were not lost on me. Magia and Boogie were two completely different souls, yet uncannily similar: psychotherapy careers and violent abuse histories included. They each represented my "dream" relationship: Boogie was my youthful male fantasy, and Magia warmly offered a loving home and family – perhaps what I coveted most. The ego inside provokes us to want more than we have, leading to inner torment, and inevitably losing everything we have. *"Gratitude is appreciating what we have; ego is the want for more." - Auroville.*

After a comfortable night's sleep in Atlantis, I worked over an oat cappuccino at the Cytat Cafe. A morning chat with Magia was upbeat, before she stoically rode to her first Vipassana course. If I needed emergency finances, I could sell off the miniscule crypto I held, albeit at poor and wasteful prices. I forwarded drafts of a Mother.Domains master strategy document to my business partners for feedback. My selfish option would be to sell our hosting division immediately. Its quick cash windfall would fund my winter in India, ensure a portable music studio, I'd put aside the remainder for a future van. Vitally, if I had a cheap van, I'd no longer have to worry about scrounging for places to stay, although autumn chill offered a warning about winter. The van did not make much sense at the moment, or perhaps ever, with infinite travels on the horizon.

...

The overnight bus from Krakow to Berlin afforded little more than fleeting restlessness. My overriding rumination was where to sleep tonight, as Flowa was out and would be home late, possibly beyond midday. I was loathe to stumble to Kit Kat Club, bedraggled and carrying oversized bags, to fetch his key. Stubbornly, I'd rather kill time elsewhere and meet him later. *Where to sleep?* My mind drifted to Tempelhof, the vast old airport, where there may be discrete corners offering sufficient respite from frigid winds. The dugout areas of the baseball field were an attractive possibility, if I could climb its fence. Under a dugout bench I could rig a comfortable, windless capsule, with my sleeping bag, sarongs, a towel and piles of clothes. Another option was finding a 24-hour cafe. I researched homeless shelters in Berlin, emergency housing and Buddhist temples, whose patrons would undoubtedly lend compassion if I was discovered. Had I brought the tent, there would be no such debate – I'd pitch it in Grünewald Forest, and hope to avoid detection from park rangers or astute neighbours.

When the bus lumbered into Berlin, I groggily scrambled to gather my items, and made my way to Messe Nord station. An S-Bahn south around the city barrelled towards the district between Tempelhof and Flowa's Friedrichshain residence. Flowa telephoned to urge that I find him, so I swallowed some pride and headed to Kit Kat Club. At the club's entrance, the bouncer took a bemused glance at me. Upon my determined insistence that my "naked friend" Flowa was awaiting me, I was permitted into the welcomed warmth of Kit Kat club. Numerous guests robed themselves for the outside world, collecting bags and jackets from the busy coat check. A girl fetched a huge backpack and several smaller bags of her own. Some astonishingly sexy women in little more than lingerie, men in underpants and various gothic styles, came and went, mostly leaving.

After waiting awkwardly for half an hour, I decided to make my way inside. I removed my jacket, shirt and phone, dispatching them at coat check, where I explained needing to find somebody for a key. Inside, Kit Kat became darker and louder; couples of all orientations kissed in corners, the grim, sweaty toilets were overpacked with guests, and the dancefloor raged with fifty dancers facing the DJ. At a couch downstairs, a muscled man in black leather undies picked up a medium-bodied woman wearing lingerie, placed her on the couch, and parted her legs to either side.

Around another corner, Flowa bounded at me with a broad smile. He was not naked, and his new weight-deflated appearance remained alien to me. With a fleeting surge of adrenaline, I considered remaining at Kit Kat, downing a few drinks and maybe enjoying some luck of my own. The realities of fatigue demanded otherwise. I fetched the key and bid farewell to Flowa, gathered my belongings from a different coat check girl – "You're the key guy!" – redressed, and returned through early morning Berlin sun to Flowa's apartment.

...

On Thursday evening, while Andi deejayed at Greenhouse, I met a chatty, drunken Colombian filmmaker. In little time, she wanted to marry me for a European visa. She seemed eager to commence with pre-marital sex, and kissed me.

"You're shy," she uttered. "Why you shy?"

I wasn't really into her like that, even newly single, in an open relationship to begin with. I confided that marrying for a UK passport might not be her most reliable means of accomplishing European residency, with Brexit looming.

Friday was the international Climate March. Many millions of people flooded the streets of Berlin and other cities around the world. Multiple converted trucks and vans blossomed into mobile sound stages. Not feeling like crowds or parties, I headed home, ahead of a calm weekend of meditation, sleep and writing. I missed making music.

After the weekend, I finally renewed acquaintances with longtime friend, Spikey Tee. We were supposed to meet in Berlin last year, before Flowa kidnapped me at Kit Kat Club. British-Jamaican Spikey Tee was a respected music producer, international DJ, and recording artist. Spikey was a vocalist for Sola Rosa, and appeared on Morcheeba's best-selling Big Calm album. Spikey lived a similarly transient and nomadic life. While drinking beers on couches outside his local Späti, Spikey relayed his respect and admiration for the "many inspiring" projects I'd conceived. It was surprising and humbling to hear. To me, it felt like a clutter of too many undertakings; most never fulfilled my lofty expectations.

"On the surface, it might look solid. But nobody sees that it's such a struggle behind this," I responded, lost in my eyes but proud.

"Of course it is," Spikey soothed. "It needs to be."

We chatted about love, life, happiness, making music, the coming economic collapse, and the plummeting state of the world. "Big changes are coming." Noting that there might be a desperate final attempt by rulers to impose ultimate control, we theorised about what conflicts the Powers That Be would invent, to further distract, divide and distance society. Perhaps a health crisis or war?

...

For the first time since I can remember, I nearly pitied myself. After resurrecting myself countless times over the years and, despite all of my accomplishments, wisdom and experience, I was homeless, again. While I was shivering on night buses, and gauging which dugout of an outdoor baseball field to sleep under, my immediate family received collective inheritance and house sale windfalls worth millions of dollars – but not a penny for me. My newly-millionaire Canadian aunt was faffing about on beaches in Florida, yet was "too busy" to complete her legal role of will executor, in the wake of my grandmother's death. Hence, I never received the Canadian Savings Bond my grandmother put aside for me, while I was living on the streets decades earlier. My father, in the wake of his wife's death to longterm illnesses, boasted about buying a "powerful new car", and spoiling his step-grandkids rotten, but not a sliver of anything for his son. My mother crafted tales about being excluded from inheritance, causing more dramas for her.

Friends reneged on agreements, past acquaintances and adversaries lied about me, and certain business partners didn't communicate necessary information. Spoiled prima-donna clients whined about truly inconsequential issues, angrily making threats – while paying scraps. There was no doubt that I was on my own: my decisions and my consequences. I felt a growing bitterness, having been thrust out in the cold by my mother, or old housemates, or the girlfriend I loved, and felt a lack of authentic connections with friends and family.

Inversely, there were selfless, giving souls like Flowa. He understood the "traveller life", graciously offered me a crash pad any time I needed, and a safe space to store my belongings. There is an entire spectrum of quantum possibilities of humans: the good, bad, conscious and misguided. The altruistic, selfish, caring, loathing, asexual and perverse. With every characteristic available, we hold the power to become anybody. Actions speak louder than words or social posts.

Avant Art Festival in Wroclaw

A little after sunrise, I awoke on a bus from Berlin to Wroclaw; outside was ominously grey and dull. My heartstrings were tugged upon viewing Polish-adorned billboards, as memories of my sweet Pole flooded in. I missed her cute pride and joyous enthusiasm, our warm apartment and the cats. My home of the next five nights was historic Hostel Mleczarnia, in the centre of Wroclaw. My budget room included a dodgy, dark complex-ioned roommate, who neither said hello nor responded to such, with his lack of eye contact reminding me of thieves or other miscreants. A temporary German roommate joked: "ISIS?" On closer review, his suspicious behaviour was concerning; he certainly *could* be a terrorist. The thin young man nervously paced around, wearing the exact same clothes everyday, speaking to no-one. He guarded a removable USB drive, while maniacally monitoring the stock or crypto markets, making sure nobody could see.

The opening evenings of Avant Art Festival were sit-down affairs; the first from an auditorium, the next from a large theatre. The performances were creative and unusual. Japanese sound design artists manipulated bird and nature sounds, and tinkered with vintage analog gear, like cassette tapes, and gongs amplified by microphones. Industrial, instrumental hip-hop by Dälek, then modular synthesis from Zonal, scattered across Impart's theatre.

The showcase Friday evening came at Stary Klasznow, an old cathedral. First I had to find the place, that led me through murky courtyards, shadowy parks and alongside the church's Dominik residence for priests. Eventually, I located a flower-adorned entrance leading to the "Stary Klasznow Pub", while cheesy Foreigner or Survivor played on lo-fi speakers. *Was this part of the art?* I laughed, and encircled the block to a more concert-like entrance. A hundred people milled around, drinking and smoking. Soundcheck's big shattering bass rumbled from the adjacent church, while strobe lights flashed. Lost downstairs in a dungeon, I searched for an entrance that was not yet open, while drizzle scattered across the awaiting crowd outside. It pleasantly reminded me of my exhilarating first rave in the late 1990s, at an old Hamilton, Ontario church.

The doors soon opened, and I navigated to the very front and centre of the stage. There were pretty Polish women everywhere, yet plenty of odd Polish men. One in particular attempted to ruin Aisha Devi's performance, by loudly singing along, while the occasional Pole frowned, and requested he stop.

"I don't care! Blah blah blah," he sang over and over, his mental illness apparent. Otherwise, the concert was brilliant – particularly the goddess Aisha Devi.

Meditation, Compassion and Forgiveness

I woke Saturday morning to Magia's inspired, proud messages: she successfully completed ten days of Vipassana. She apologised for her past behaviour, hinting at the newfound enlightenment I'd anticipated. My two postcard gifts to her were discovered; the first was a scooter from Delhi that I'd stealthily clipped on the fridge, and another was sent more recently from Berlin, during our first split. Unfortunately, decisions were made; I'd deliberated over two weeks of my own reflections, and leaned towards returning on a solo path. Proceeding from here had to begin with mutually-improved communication.

The day I departed Wroclaw, the weather was viciously windy, although neither freezing nor wet. Magia wanted to meet this evening, but I was non-committal; I was fully on my path. My intent was to continue to Warsaw for the conclusion of Avant Art. As my bus pulled into Krakow Główny, Magia awaited. The warmest and longest embrace at the bus stop melted away all fears and reservations. It reassured that everything was going to be okay, amplified from the newfound enlightenment in Magia's eyes. We sat in her nearby car and chatted. Magia depicted her preliminary Vipassana revelations. She'd been endlessly sad since we said goodbye, and battled to finish the course. While the gruelling opening few days of Vipassana were a struggle, she overcame the challenge and basked in the experience. She even dreamed of Boogie: "forgiving" and accepting her. Apologising for her actions, Magia aspired to resuming a life together.

After a tasty Indian dinner, with our arms linked we wandered around the perimeter of Krakow's old wall. We located a bench in a dim, isolated corner, to light a joint she'd prepared. I withdrew a small bag of CBD I'd acquired from a shop in Wroclaw. I humorously shared having discovered a secret pocket this very morning – eighteen months after buying the jacket in Bangalore! I placed the CBD inside this pocket. Magia presented me a ziplock bag filled with wrapped-up ginger, and other helpful remedies for my recent cough and cold.

At the same time, a van pulled up: it was a police vehicle. It was unhelpful that I was holding a fist-sized chunk of something wrapped in aluminium foil. We chucked the joint behind the bench. Moments later, two young police officers marched towards us, wholly smelling the joint's potent Indica. I was a clear target, weary with my long hippie hair and track pants, yet I was extraordinarily chill and polite. The officers preferred conversing in Polish with Magia. In the wake of Vipassana, she handled it very calmly.

While emptying my pockets, I was more worried about explaining the peculiar lump of foil-wrapped ginger, but the officers immediately realised what it was. One cop patted me down, while the other scoured behind the bench, searching for the discarded joint. I shared a photo of the CBD container I'd purchased in Wroclaw. While CBD was recently legal in Poland, the nation's strict police exercised the right to confiscate anything for testing, while often imprisoning suspects for days. Good thing for my hidden pocket!

"I prefer CBD," I cooed. The main cop nodded at me emphatically, as though I was a naïve but harmless foreigner. The cops departed towards their awaiting van.

Relieved and delighted, Magia and I exited. We headed to Magia Cafe for a pot of jasmine pearl tea, and chatted in its dungeon-like basement, until it closed. Afterward, Magia started driving towards the hostel I'd booked, despite the time being after 1am; my heart sank.

"Let's go home," I suggested; Magia's eyes lit up.

The cats were enthralled upon our reunion, and both Czupur and Xara greeted me with warm affection. Despite fatigue after a long and harrowing day, we conducted an hour's Vipassana, before falling asleep in each other's arms. Everything felt back to normal. Love and optimism returned, as we continued sharing a path through the universe, for a while.

Avant Art in Warsaw

My first few days back in Zielonki were like I'd barely departed. The main difference was twice-daily meditation sessions, that started at 4am or 6am, and were repeated in the evening. Magia's dedication pushed me to work harder at Vipassana, enabling a deeply relaxed home and internal zen. The cats meditated (or slept) nearby for much of the hour-long sessions.

Colour and warmth returned to what had been a cold and dreary period. My month trudging around Berlin or Wroclaw, in the grunt of the day-at-a-time struggle, was drenched in grey and monochrome. Did I prefer the month alone? Lugging my life on my back, jilted in sadness and stoic determination, despite true independence? Or a warm home filled with cats, plants and love? In that sense, of lonely homelessness versus loving home, there was no contest. Yet, confusion flooded my subconscious.

On the weekend, Magia and I travelled to Warsaw for Avant Art. Our meditative mindset ensured the most peaceful of our extended drives together. Upon arriving in Warsaw, we checked in at the well-situated Lulu Hostel. The hostel sat beside the city's impressive national stadium, and was a thirty minute walk along a large bridge to the centre of Warsaw. The calm setting on tree-lined streets was five minutes from the Vistula River.

For Friday night's concert, Magia was officially my "photographer". Magia wore a black top and jeans, while I adorned my long yellow kurta and light brown scarf. The venue was a huge rectangular space, packed with several hundred guests. We made our way to the front for Greek Goddess Abyss X, who adorned a long black dress and veil, reminiscent of a funeral. We took a break while Coucou Chloe jumped around on stage, then returned to the very front and centre for Magia's hero, Aisha Devi. The lights came down, strobes flickered and ambient sirens blared. The diminutive, high-energy Aisha bounded around the stage, hammering at keyboards and manipulating effects. Aisha often grabbed the microphone and tunefully bellowed.

The weekend's magic began when I was left on my own, while Magia visited the bathroom. As I sat on a stairwell, a short blonde Pole made conversation, before inviting me to join her social circle. On our way outside, Coucou Chloe met her fans, joked about showing her tits, then peeled off half her shirt, revealing a rounded breast and dark brown nipple. Outside, a joint was welcomingly shared. A tall, confident woman with shortly-trimmed light-blonde hair, turned to me.

"Does anybody here speak English?" she asked, full-well knowing I did. "Do you have a lighter?" I fetched one from a nearby man.

Francesca was from London's Middlesex (where I was born), and was heavily involved in festivals and music events, including the legendary Boiler Room. Particularly captivating to me, was that she played clarinet. I recounted my primary musical ambitions, that required a flute or a reed for several songs. I noted my winter aspirations of heading to Goa, finding a house near the water, and enlisting a small band for a musical project. Francesca spent much time in India, particularly in Goa. All this while, the musical empress Aisha Devi stood near us, chatting with a circle of her own, yet inching closer. She seemed curious of our conversation about Goa and experimental music projects, or perhaps she was intrigued by my flamboyant Indian clothing. I noticed Francesca had a lighter all along.

Magia and I moved inside, with our heads buzzing from the joint, and stood near the bar. Again, Aisha Devi appeared beside us. I became nervous, overthinking what to say, with the opportunity to meet somebody I admired only one cool, casual opener away.

"Maybe it's a body double?" I joked to Magia.

Minutes later Aisha was beside me, chatting with another group, one of whom asked her: "So... You grew up in Switzerland?" Perhaps seeking to change the subject from her similarly-complex answer to "*Where are you from?*", Aisha stumbled into me. Not enough for my need to catch her, but she definitely captured my attention. Everything was okay, but I shyly smiled, said nothing, and there vanished my opportunity to meet Aisha Devi that evening – or ever. Upstairs, Magia and I returned to the front of the stage for the final act – Finland's Amnesia Scanner; ironically, I don't remember it.

Irrespective of the outcome of my post-Vipassana reunion with Magia, I'd still have been here in Warsaw. In a parallel world, I'd have been single, a fragment more recovered from heartbreak, and open to progressing new encounters. I'd most likely have conversed with Aisha, about music, meditation and the world, and maybe have hung out more with Francesca. *Where would life head then?* The incomparable benefit of true independence, was that the answer could be: Anywhere. Home is where the heart is; homeless, the heart leads everywhere. My instinctive gut and over-thinking brain attempted to solve what I truly wanted. The vibrant colours of love, home and family? Or the greyness of long days alone, with occasional rainbows into magical new terrain?

RIP Gabrielle Ansley

On the morning of Tuesday October 15th, after meditation and a few hours of writing, I opened my email to discover a short, sad message from my father: "Gabrielle passed away this morning." They'd been married for nearly three decades, with most of their time around Melbourne, a few years in Sydney, and their "family" cottage in Brittany, France. Tears streamed down my face. Magia immediately comforted me. We lay in silence together on the couch, while she held my forehead. Wise Czupur gripped my hand with his furry black paw.

Gabrielle was strong and brave to the end, greatly outliving doctors' predictions. For many years she suffered from the lethal combination of lymphoma and motor neuron disease. Gabrielle and I were not close, but I was grateful for her assistance to my father in the wake of my parents' divorce. She helped ensure my expensive Singapore education, while providing my dad a steady best friend and companion.

Not long after, I learned another past acquaintance, Nikky Wheatley, took her life last Christmas. In this sadness, arrived another reminder that life was short, and to make the most of the rare experiences we share with others. Time shouldn't be wasted fighting, or festering divisions or conflict.

Tripping in Amsterdam

Amsterdam Dance Event featured Bonobo's Outlier gig, that also billed David August, Jon Hopkins and the Black Madonna. This was Magia's first visit to Amsterdam. Calculating time and petrol costs, on top of ridiculously-overpriced Amsterdam lodging, replaced our road trip plan with a more budget approach. The low-cost flight from Krakow to Eindhoven went smoothly. Our first BlaBla packed us in a small car with four hot, smart girls, two of whom were to participate in Amsterdam's marathon. Magia and I were dropped near Zuid station on a sunny afternoon. We each brought a small backpack, although her choice of hiking boots became a hinderance. We inspiredly strolled north, ambling through the city's promenades, eventually pausing riverside for a sandwich and rest.

Our first coffeeshop was 1e Hulp on Marnixstraat. To initiate proceedings, we acquired a pre-roll of strong Sativa, taking it upstairs to a sketchy, smoky den. Its packed space was filled with unfriendly, brooding stoners. We hiked a mile to Kashmir Coffeeshop, where we comfortably lounged on an oriental couch, and rolled joints from a bag of blissful Lemon Haze. Shortly after, we briefly met up with Vanilla, one of the Dutch from Nowhere; Anders was home, caring for their recent love child. Vanilla toured us around her old neighbourhood: the busy heart of Amsterdam's Red Light district. Scantily-clad girls underneath masks of makeup were separated by windows from juvenile, drunken and disorderly tourists.

Before ferrying across the river, Magia and I loaded up on supplies, acquiring overpriced but potent magic mushrooms from a small shop with a mushroom sign. Gathering joints from Voyagers coffeeshop, we boarded the ferry to NDSM, the city's creative, former-industrial harbour. Entering the spacious, giant old factory, presented the typical onslaught of food, drink and merchandise stands. We gratefully stuffed our bags and jackets in lockers. The venue offered two stages: one was a concrete arena with symmetrical steps lining its sides, and the larger hall was reserved for the main acts. I covertly observed that the main stage's right speaker hid a corner that offered unfettered access to a prime spot in front of the stage. By David August's set, we were absolute front and centre.

David August's myriad synthesizers harmonized lush sonic textures, building up into his opening, that sounded unnaturally loud and distorted. This resulted in the first of consecutive, prolonged power outages. Eventually, with lighting effects minimised to lessen the power load, David proceeded with his set: essentially the same setlist he'd performed for a year. I'd hoped for a cutting-edge DJ set, that would adequately set up Bonobo's. Still, in an era where many artists relied on laptops and automation software to drive their shows, David's expert coordination of analog gear was commendable. Contrastingly, Bonobo rocked the house on simple DJ gear, performing his classic tracks with spirit and enthusiasm. The secluded little corner behind the stage's speaker remained unfathomably empty, keeping us front row for the duration of Bonobo's energetic two-hour set.

Once Jon Hopkins' DJ set began, his avid fans elbowed forward for their rightful central places. Closing the show was the Black Madonna: a white, short-haired Catholic lesbian. She coaxed the on-stage VIP section to dance along awkwardly to cheesy dance-pop, before settling into a deeper set. We watched from steps at the very back of the cavernous, boomy warehouse. Fatigued, with the time approaching 6am, we retrieved our bags, and ferried across the river to Amsterdam.

Thus began Magia's introduction to the homeless lifestyle. We had nowhere to stay in exorbitantly expensive Amsterdam, with no certainty of lodging until Cologne a few days later. Predictably exhausted from a massive Saturday of travel, city hiking and dancing, anywhere warm and safe was appreciated. At Centraal Station we found a secluded corner, and snuggled. An hour later, Starbucks opened its doors, and we crafted a cosy nook on reasonably comfortable couches. With sufficient warmth, overpriced coffees, and wifi to pass a few hours, we smashed through the barrier of fatigue, ready for a sunny Sunday in Amsterdam.

We became lost in Amsterdam's myriad of canals and similarly-styled old buildings. Oddly, we did not encounter any parks, thwarting the idea of finding a tree under which to nap. After further hours of aimless ambling, we returned to Centraal. At an isolated spot beside the river, we divided our bag of Dragon Dynamite magic mushrooms, and munched them. Upon boarding a ferry to NDSM, the mushrooms started to hit me. It was difficult to stand; I wobbled around on the ferry's deck, while my stomach gurgled. Magia, beginning her first proper mushroom trip, wasn't sure she felt them, yet.

Upon landing at NDSM, the mushrooms were in full force. We gingerly disembarked, and meandered towards the festival. Upon sitting, the combination of extreme fatigue and gravity of hallucinogens began anchoring us in place. To resist inevitable sloth-like immobilisation, I pulled Magia up, seeking a more serene and inspiring locale. We moseyed into a deserted parking lot, to a corner surrounded by the river. Sitting on a concrete slab, we faced the water and a dock, that was splashed with trippy graffiti of splendid patterns and colours. Magia, clearly delighted at her new experience, occasionally laughed uncontrollably, at nothing in particular. The graffiti throbbed, boats bobbed, and breathing was felt everywhere throughout us.

Hours later, we prematurely killed the almighty buzz, by downing cold sweetened coffee. The comedown fast-tracked the onset of exhaustion, not having slept in thirty-five hours. We composed ourselves, and trudged into the closing party for Amsterdam Dance Event. We passed under a shipping yard crane, then through a popup market. We were thwarted while attempting to fill our water bottle ("Sorry sir, you need to buy tokens, and then water costs three tokens"). There were other examples of the drudge of money-over-art at this commercial festival, that was littered with sponsors. Meanwhile, a ginormous wall near the venue was adorned with conscious graffiti: Make Art, Not €.

A few circuits of the venue revealed no vibe, and we wearily walked to nearby Nooderlicht Cafe: an artistically converted barn. While sipping on tea, I researched available rooms, hoping to uncover last-minute deals, and the hunch paid off. One such deal was Botel, a large ship converted into a floating hotel, that greeted each arriving ferry at NDSM. It cost a tad under €60 – unquestionably cheap for Amsterdam. The best part, was that Botel was only a few minutes walk away.

We finished our tea, and strode with newfound exuberance. After checking in at Botel, we warmed into our room, taking appreciatively hot showers. The room sported a river-level view of the adjacent ferry terminal, with Amsterdam in the distance. As the Sun fell into darkness, the boom of the festival's closing party ricocheted over the water. Magia and I made love in the shadows, and we fell into a superbly deep and deserved sleep.

...

As sunrise flooded over the river, we meditated from our room on the ship. We sipped on a large coffee from the ship's bright restaurant, while I attended to frustrating work. After crossing the river, we enjoyed tasty, wholesome breakfast at Greenwoods Cafe, then picked up additional mushrooms for later. At Hunter's coffeeshop, Magia rummaged up confidence to ask the clerk about their strains of available Sativa. The rude Parisian mocked her, insulting her intelligence by monotonously recounting trivial differences between Sativa and Indica. I was not in the best mood, stressed from work issues that surfaced to start the week, and I unleashed on him.

"We know that. We were hoping for a deeper answer." I glared at him. "Why don't you serve these other people, while we reconsider doing business in this establishment."

The comment hit hard, as the clerk rapidly realised he was not best-representing his workplace. His demeanour became more professional as he served the next customer.

"Do you want to leave?" Magia asked.

"It's up to you – this is your purchase."

Magia ordered a gram of bio Amnesia, that the clerk respectfully supplied with humility.

"I'm really sorry about that," he apologised.

I smiled. "It's okay, man. It looks busy and stressful."

Slowly we travelled to Alphen aan den Rijn, after a regional train from Centraal. I was still grumpy, coming down from the weekend and yearning for Sea Time. There was a man sitting on the train, maybe in his early fifties, a little overweight, with a round face and mid-length grey hair, possibly homeless.

"Are you okay?" the man asked, looking me up and down.

Surprised, I nodded my head. "Fine."

It's like he sensed I needed space. "Just go do your own thing!" I wasn't sure I heard him right, as I passed him.

After a pause, I replied. "Exactly."

"I know!" the intuitive man replied, as if he heard my thoughts.

The hour-long train helped soothe my frustrations. I appreciated the opportunity to discover more of the Nether-lands. Compared to Amsterdam, Alphen aan den Rijn was a hushed ghost town by contrast, with minimal people on the street. We stocked up on a final Sativa sample from the Dutch Gold coffeeshop, then headed to Mateuz's humble apartment. We'd met on the post-Himalayas bus from Budapest. Mateuz graciously welcomed us, spearheaded a hefty pasta dinner and shared stories from his travels. We drank wine and rum, smoked from his air-less bathroom, and Magia and I crashed on the couch's pull-out bed.

...

On Tuesday morning, Magia and I rode a bus to Cologne, arriving in the late afternoon. We were greeted by Jono and

Miri. The newlywed couple had recently settled into their vast new apartment, a few blocks from their previous dwelling. Memtell was being finalised as a company, with its first major shareholders on board, including a well-established greeting card distributor. Jono had a late afternoon business flight to London, cutting short this catchup, but he left much to consider, particularly about trialling a Memory Book concept for Plan Sea. I treated Magia to all-you-can-eat Sushi. We arrived at the restaurant on the cusp of it closing, but the time limit ensured we ate far more sushi than normal, satisfyingly leaving many empty plates stacked high.

On Thursday morning, a BlaBla Bus delivered us from Cologne Airport to Berlin. Day buses were usually a drain of a day, but in this instance it was necessary; at €12, it was easily the cheapest option. Occasionally catching uncomfortable sleep, at one stop Magia departed to buy coffee.

"If the bus leaves without you, I'll see you in Berlin!" I joked. She was not impressed.

Upon returning with coffee and a snack, Magia was in a sour mood; she pushed my arm off her and swatted me hard. Her gloom deepened, itching for an argument, and she was clearly researching buses from Berlin to Krakow. I calmly realised that if she made any such rash decision, I'd end the relationship. The backup part of my mind began processing alternate plans, including definitely hanging out with Heidi Heart this weekend, and expeditiously making my way to India.

After nine hours on the bus, we arrived at Berlin ZOB. At Flowa's Friedrichshain apartment, the gentle giant greeted us graciously, meeting Magia for the first time. He served a dinner of tasty cooked vegetables and fluffy eggs, and together we prepared ginger juice. Magia and I strolled in spring-like weather alongside the river to Görlitzer Park, before immersing ourselves at Just Music, where Magia delightedly fiddled with modern synthesizers. On Saturday morning, we watched the Rugby World Cup semi-final at a packed Belushi's Sports Bar. An inspired England team overwhelmed the double-defending champions New Zealand All-Blacks. For lunch, we visited huge Vietnamese complex Dong Xuan for tasty coconut and mango curries, before stocking up on Asian condiments, like chilli sauces and ginger snacks, but not shrimp paste or "Ambitious" cans of crab.

After a nap I felt only like sleeping, even skipping a home-cooked Indian dinner with a few of Flowa's friends. Around midnight, Magia was determined to head out. I'd not heard from Heidi Hart; out of respect to Magia, I didn't follow up. I preferred to rest, and was perfectly content with Magia enjoying a night to herself. She ventured to the city with Flowa's two male Indian friends, and she soon met a pair of Norwegians, who were in Berlin for the weekend, armed with sufficient party supplies. I woke around 6am, to a recent message: "I'm okay. Just walking around." Then: "I am safe, slowly walking home." She'd taken half an ecstasy – the second of her life – and was intimidated by long lines at clubs, including Kit Kat Club. In the end, Magia enjoyed the morning by herself. I was impressed by her very Sea-like adventure, and it didn't really matter to me what she did, or who she was with. This underscored the premise of the "open relationship" – we could enjoy anything without worries. "I'm loyal," she'd assure me later, although Kit Kat Club certainly would have tested that!

Unleashing The Angry Snake

A very early bus and delays eventually led home, where the adoring cats greeted us. While slowly falling asleep on the couch, I confided in being overwhelmed by my short-term work demands, but Magia's sabbatical-like attitude was consistently: "Don't worry, don't stress."

"If I can't be productive in Zielonki, I'm not going to remain in Zielonki," I curtly replied. Everything changed, again. Magia was perturbed, just like on the bus to Berlin. When I headed to the king-sized bed, she remained on the couch.

"I can't sleep," she said. I knew something was up, again. Lying in bed, unable to fully doze, I wondered: *What now?*

In the morning, Magia barely spoke. She didn't brew me coffee, and worked from her bed while I typed away in the kitchen. For the second time in a matter of days, I reconsidered my devotion to her, and out-of-the-way life in Zielonki. I didn't want brooding energy in my home, or to be further ignored without communication – it felt like my mother's tense house all over again. I'd warned Magia that the biggest pitfall of ecstasy was its brutal comedown days later, and she seemed submerged in it. Ecstasy comedowns were new to her, and she was unable to acknowledge it – multiplied by a poor diet, exhaustion from travel, pain from lugging her backpack in heavy hiking shoes, sleeping on all sorts of random beds or floors, and breaking the vital double-daily Vipassana meditation rhythm. I realised all of these, and intended to let her recover on her own time, but for now I needed space and silence. Yet, even after she intentionally finished off all the remaining food, she had the audacity to enter the bedroom, after I retreated there with an emergency popcorn dinner.

"I'm tired of these games," Magia began, and I lost it.

"My games?!"

I swore at her, and told her we'd chat after my food. I'd remained calm all day, but I'd had enough of her mood swings. The pattern was evident: We couldn't live a few weeks without her acting to doom things. Later, Magia acknowledged this and apologised. Not the least of my many frustrations, was knowing from recent experience that she maintained the power to kick me out of the house, back onto sub-zero freezing streets. Next time, there would be no return.

During our fiery conversation, I was rabid, seething like an angry snake. For all the many people I'd let walk over me, with them distortedly asserting their righteousness, playing victim then blaming me, this would not happen again. Magia, as closest to me, was the first to absorb a taste of my newfound transformation. At one point she screamed back, and I braced, waiting for her to kick me out, but she didn't. Black, fluffy Czupur settled in between us, as if to serve as a furry barrier and mediator.

In a more subdued moment, I explained that at different points in relationships, participants held altering views, and sometimes we needed to be told what others observed. In this case, as her elder, and the one not coming down from ecstasy or skipping meditation, she needed to ponder her behaviour and overreactions. I hinted how close the relationship was to being over, with one foot out the door, and if she had any respect for me or our time together, she would listen. It took a while, but the conversation eventually settled down; her body language revealed sadness and defensiveness, and overtones became more amenable. Talking more openly led to a stiff hug, and an evening of awkward but accepting peace.

The next morning unfolded with an hour's meditation, together. The woman I loved, with her ego and insecurities knocked down, again became jovial and optimistic. The day blossomed into the dream home environment we both yearned for. We were a tight circle of four kindred souls, there was love in the air, and all felt back to normal. It took a strong conversation, and my firmly asserting my rights, with maturity from both sides to listen and reflect.

The Answer to Everything

As cannabis-based products and CBD medicines become globally available, even in strict places like Singapore, the next wave of natural remedies to gain mainstream acceptance, will surely be hallucinogens. The following weekend, Magia and I indulged in local, top quality, 100% clean mushrooms, from the comforts of our home. Through its effects, I revisited that all-knowing state unique to hallucinogens: a reconnection with the universe, a portal into the self, and revelations of our place in wider time and space. In my altered headspace, the splendid apartment revealed Magia's artistic mastery. The flat's fiery red wall was adorned with dozens of green, twisting plants, backlit strings of lights, and shadows that flickered across the ceiling. The cats became more playful and explorative as the afternoon unfolded. Xara temporarily overcame her extremely painful constipation, while Czupur unprecedentedly and confidently wandered out of the front door, to assess what life might look like on the other side. To Czupur, perhaps the universe consisted of infinite concrete stairs.

I looked at Magia, smiling and laughing, and regarded her youthful beauty in fresh light. My deep voice of universal reason shared how lucky I was to have her. Visions of our future streamed into my head: of life together, little children, more animals. *Sure, there will be challenges.*

On the business front, I motored forward, putting in the groundwork to sell the Mother.Hosting division. After receiving half a dozen strong offers, I narrowed down the options. I was particularly enamoured by the approach of Warwick from JetHostPRO. Warwick was confident, kind and understanding. To gain trust, he shared references from similar transactions, and outlined his honest blueprint. Warwick eased my trepidations about inconveniencing my longtime hosting clients. The week before Christmas we closed the sale – worth over $20,000. This brought the greatest achievement and relief of my professional career. Even the grumpy Bower seemed impressed at the sale. With its proceeds, we paid our first dividend, sorted most of our debts, and could concentrate on more fun aspects of Mother.Domains, like developing domains such as global legal weed supply, Deliver.Green.

During a paid work trip to Cologne, I met the entire Memtell team, including French multimedia developers, 12MVP, and Melbourne-based technical director, Kyle. It was an upbeat and optimistic time. I presented audio examples of memory-telling, narrating snippets from the Plan Sea story, atop photographs. Jono and Miri treated everybody to an Indian dinner.

...

Each evening and weekend, I bunkered in the Last Room, practicing and fiddling away with musical equipment. While learning sampling techniques, I rapidly pieced together complementary piano parts, crafting wondrous sequences of seductively lush tones. I'd spend the next few months bolstering a masterpiece, with each new touch complementing and enhancing the other parts. The song came together so magically, that there was only one possible name: Magical. After the hosting division sale, I upgraded to a "new" laptop – a lighter, second-hand 2014 MacBook Pro – and bought other used gear found at great deals. My musical ambitions were well underway. One of our road trips returned us to Wroclaw, for a classy Apparat concert at a lavish concert hall. I toured Magia around some of the excellent places I'd discovered in the city.

As 2019 came to a close, I enjoyed my second successive happy Polish Christmas at Magia's mother's house. This time, I sang along with Polish Christmas carols. The newly-born triplets were not present for health reasons. To celebrate New Years, Magia and I visited friends for well-behaved festivities. A guest shared his extremely potent homemade moonshine.

Here I was at 42, with the answers to all my big questions unfolding: Love, life, happiness, business, and freeing myself to focus on my creative passions. My inner resistance - the infinite traveller with no fixed address – was melting into grasping this rare window of love. Blossom it, nurture it and, with its stability, progress confidently in other aspects of life.

As I basked in unprecedented contentedness, I appreciated every step of the way, and of everybody I'd encountered. Each was a piece of a puzzle, that eventually revealed a complete portrait. Following my heart had resolvedly led to clarity, love and home. Life had been a struggle for too long; now it's time to enjoy it. For now, any remaining battles were in our minds, something we steadfastly possessed the power to control.

Everything was coming together: Dreams were being realised, and happiness was abundant. It seemed that little could stop it, other than ourselves. Unfortunately, as we waded into the optimism of the year 2020, sinister masked undercurrents, who pulled the strings of the world, were about to change life dramatically, for everybody.

Chapter 21

One Final Crazy Adventure

Upon departing Krakow on a freezing winter's day in late January 2020, I held little inclination that the world as we knew it was on the precipice of human-engineered catastrophe. Our trip felt like a simple but wondrous three-month break to India. Magia and I were to practice slower travel, mostly between Goa and Auroville: Live a little, learn a lot, and return home inspired. But, outside factors are often out of our control.

Continually striving to travel minimally, I packed a week's worth of summery clothes, with my "new" lighter laptop. A Seaboard keyboard and Apogee One audio interface, with an in-built microphone, would serve as my mobile recording studio. Altogether, my solitary, smaller new carry-on backpack weighed around 8kg. Before leaving, I hugged the cats goodbye. The all-knowing Czupur brooded on his throne, refusing to look at us; we were abandoning them, again.

"Czupi," I promised, orally and through mental frequencies. "Yes, this trip is long – the same as last year. But, this time you will have a friend living here, looking after you! I'll see you soon."

Czupur continued to stare intently in the opposite direction. Magia had arranged one of her longterm friends, a house painter, to look after the apartment in our absence, primarily to keep the cats company. With a fleeting glance at our comfortable Zielonki apartment, it didn't occur to me that it could be the final time I saw the flat or the cats again.

A brisk, budget flight delivered us to Oslo's northern Gardeomon Airport, where we waited all day for our international connection. From a cosy cafe corner, I put the finishing touches on my song Magical, and triumphantly uploaded it to the LANDR online mastering service, readying it for release. The overnight Norwegian Airlines flight to Dubai was uncomfortable, with cold air and stiff seats. The traveller beside me shared his sad story, six months after an unfortunate breakup. He was a firefighter and paramedic, who'd recently travelled to sixteen countries with his ex. One morning after a friend's party, he woke up groggy, drugged, and beside another girl. Baffled but honest, he confided the error with his girlfriend, and she ended the relationship. Months later, he learned that friends had playfully spiked his drink. Despite holding resentment towards drugs – and those friends – he was curious nonetheless about mind-openers like LSD.

At Dubai's ultra-modern airport we lounged at a high-end chocolate coffeeshop, before our flight to India. Upon landing in the reasonably-deserted terminal at Mumbai's airport, I noticed a strange official sign, well-framed and intentionally visible. It announced a health warning, about a new contagious "Corona" virus, specifically attributed to "Wuhan City, China", and to be aware of relatively flu-like symptoms. It sounded like another American anti-China crusade. The matter gnawed at me temporarily, but, as I'd steadfastly not followed news for months, I didn't hear anything else about it for a while.

Falling Off a Speeding Train

Our airport taxi dispatched us to our hostel, that was perched in solitude among the chaotic madness of Andheri East. Zostel was home for our first four decompressing nights of this trip. Zostel featured a large semi-outdoor courtyard, with long bench seats and a couple of "shanti" spaces. An on-demand kitchen served tasty snacks and drinks.

After a couple of days of re-assimilation into Indian life, Magia and I headed to the Global Vipassana Pagoda, featuring the world's biggest freestanding dome. Reaching Gorai's northwest corner of sprawling Mumbai was an hour-long affair, beginning with walking through boisterous traffic, then riding a packed Metro train to Andheri Station. After lining at the ticket counter, we bought a pair of one-way tickets to Borivali. The steel Western Express train hurtled through packed local neighbour-hoods, picking up and dispatching hundreds of passengers along the way. Many people dangerously jumped off the moving train onto platforms, while others hopped on. Occasionally, there were mild collisions, when eager jumpers leapt into impatient passengers, who'd huddled closely near entrances. Nobody appeared seriously injured, today; it was normal, daily life in Mumbai.

At Borivali, we hopped in a tuk tuk for a short drive to the small ferry terminal at Gorai Jetty. Two ferries awaited passengers: one northward into local villages, while the tourist ferry to Esselworld and Water Kingdom landed a short stroll from the Vipassana Pagoda. We were fortunate to sit on the packed wooden boat, while local families stood and chattered away; some curiously stared at us. After the refreshing motorboat ride across pretty Manori Creek, we arrived at the Esselworld Jetty. The giant golden dome of the Global Pagoda and its subsequent touristic experience were alike a theme park. The security officer verified our return ferry token, before warmly welcoming us to Vipassana-Land. A slight incline weaved through lush trees, botanical plants and flocks of happy birds, as the Sun beamed over the Pagoda's golden orb. Blue skies soared atop golden Buddhas, with an elephant statue that bowed towards actual relics of the former living Buddha, that were respectfully stashed near the top of the dome. Statues and monuments adorned parks and gardens around the perimeter. There was a small food court brimming with simple Indian delicacies, notably thali and fresh-squeezed juices.

Entering the cavernous dome, I marvelled at its spaciousness and unique sonic tones. Gender-separated by a small circular podium in the very centre of the Pagoda, Magia and I meditated for an hour inside the giant structure. Almost immutable silence was ironically contrasted by simultaneous absolute loudness. Soundwaves reverberated from outside – like pedestrian steps, kids playing or birds singing – that reflected across opposite curving walls, bouncing for infinitum. Magia and I were wholly rejuvenated and grounded after an hour inside the Pagoda. In enlightened headspace, we filled up our water bottle from the filtered tap, perused the heroic statues outside the golden dome, and exited the complex through the only way out: via the Vipassana book and gift shop.

After crossing the river on the ferry, a tuk tuk whisked us expeditiously towards Borivali Station. So far in Mumbai we'd been unable to source Indian mobile numbers, and were hence unable to book a ride share. We couldn't connect to public wifi: access required a One Time Password (OTP), that was unhelpfully sent to mobile numbers. With regular taxis twice the price, we decided to return the way we came: Western Express down to Andheri, then a Metro or taxi from there.

We purchased two tickets at the Borivali ticket counter, and were advised that our train was due from Platform 5 or 6. Pushing through packed crowds, we approached the top of Platform 5, and noticed our train was arriving. We raced down the stairs and, observing that the first carriage was fairly crowded, continued striding beside the tracks. The next carriage had several large drums near its entrance. I reckoned there was insufficient space, so we kept walking.

The Western Express train, without sounding any horn or announcement, slowly began pulling away; we picked up our pace. Magia hopped on the next carriage as the train began to move more briskly, and I jumped on behind her. Looking around, I embarrassedly realised this was the Female-Only carriage. Women stared back at us, and I felt disrespectful standing there, so I leapt off the rolling train. Magia took a fleeting glance, and vanished. Without mobile numbers or wifi we had no way of communicating, and I realised she didn't know the address of the hostel in this mammoth megacity. I had to hop on.

The train accelerated past. It didn't appear to be traveling too briskly. As the doorway of an onrushing carriage approached, defying inner and outer warnings, I leapt on, grabbing the iron pole of the carriage. I landed forcefully on the edge of the train's outer metal step, but grossly disregarded the physics of jumping on a speeding train, or the momentum of opposing movement. Grabbing onto the pole with my stronger right arm, I swung into the train. I realised I didn't have much control, and considered attempting rolling further into the speeding carriage, despite the sharp metal tracks below. My left shoulder slammed against the pole with considerable force; I bounced the opposite way. My grip on the pole let loose, and I tumbled down at such a speed that it toppled me from the train altogether. I fell hard onto the concrete platform.

In a hazily surreal instant, seeing railway tracks and the onrushing of slicing steel wheels, a stark inner warning roared:

ROLL AWAY ROLL AWAY. Instinctively, I executed a commando roll away from the train. Dozens of horrified local passengers gasped. I tumbled considerably further, and lay motionless. I wondered if I'd broken anything, or worse. I'd hit my head, and I could feel pain somewhere, but adrenaline masked artefacts from the accident.

"I'm okay!" I smiled embarrassedly, but upon trying to move I knew not everything was okay.

Surrounded by a wall of worried passengers, four station security officers pushed through the crowd, each holding bamboo sticks. They were gravely concerned. I hobbled to my feet; my white kurta pants were sprayed with blood. I realised my left ankle was in particularly bad shape; the other leg was cut and bruised. My shoulder ached, and my sore head had taken a knock, that explained the mild blurriness. I'd lost my sunglasses, that broke, and one of my sandals; both items were gratefully returned to me. A young man politely offered a chug from his water bottle. I tried to smile and present that all was fine, although I was deep in shock, with infinitely repeating flashbacks. ROLL AWAY.

Escorted by kind station police, I hobbled along to the station's 24/7 emergency clinic, where several medics attended to me. They sympathetically patched up my wounds and applied yellow anti-septic. I had a bruised and bloody right hand. Most of the blood stains on my pants emanated from a badly swollen and scraped left ankle. Mostly, I worried about Magia. She'd have no idea what happened, and we couldn't contact each other. I had faith in her intelligence, and I wondered how she'd handle it. I hoped she found the hostel safely.

After I came to my senses, the senior officer escorted me to a platform, to await the next train to Borivali. The officer let me hotspot his phone so I could dispatch a message. I'd have taxied back to the hostel, but I had to check if Magia was waiting in Andheri for me. At Andheri Station, after gingerly disembarking from the Western Express, I limped though thousands of frenetic passengers during rush hour. There was no sign of Magia. I trudged to the nearby Metro, and boarded a packed carriage. My intended exit at Marol Naka station was prohibited by an older man with suitcases; it was impossible to push through. At the next stop, I forcibly exerted departure, then limped down the stairs. Even more dangerous was attempting to cross the hectic road; one person died on the street that night.

Instead of hobbling the distance to Zostel, I splurged on a tuk tuk. Even for notoriously horrid Mumbai traffic, this evening was particularly chaotic, with swarms of honking vehicles from all directions. We encountered the most immobile traffic jam I'd seen, on a narrow road that stuck trucks couldn't pass. After an hour to pierce traffic, the driver couldn't find Zostel, and we looped in circles around the maze-like neighbourhood.

Soaked, blood-stained and sweaty, eventually I limped into Zostel's reception, then to the back lounge. A scared and relieved Magia was overjoyed to see me. She chanted Polish spells, that sounded like "Goodness Gracious". While sipping a juice, I slowly recounted the story. Eavesdroppers were fascinated, but were rightfully concerned: Mumbai trains had a deadly reputation. There were plenty of daily accidents, and thousands of people died each year from similar incidents. Furthermore, there were no announcements on platforms that trains were departing – a common complaint from locals.

Magia braced my one-legged hopping until we found a nearby hospital. The staff was caring, concerned and friendly, and the doctor was professional, courteous and articulate; he offered his personal number should any complications arise. I was stitched up, and a tetanus shot was injected into my buttocks.

For many days and nights I encountered vivid flashbacks. There was a consistent freeze of the railway tracks hurtling towards me: ROLL AWAY. It appeared the universe kept me alive, for a little longer anyway: perhaps to witness the coming global madness.

Lurking Anger Rising

We caught a late-night bus from a hectic area of Andheri East, ahead of a sixteen-hour ride. The coach cut around cities and carved through mountains. Magia and I succumbed to a flu-like illness during the trip – perhaps from the bus' air conditioning. I was greatly aided by hearty doses of antibiotics to heal my train accident wounds; I held a strong immunity and recovered quickly.

Arriving in Goa lent a natural remedy, stepping into warm sunshine and tropical breeze. For our opening nights in Arambol, we lodged at Magic Park: a yoga-centric assortment of basic but overpriced huts. Our room promised "sea views", although the water was obscured by a fence. Magic Park featured a spacious, shaded outdoor lounge, that hosted group activities like yoga and acoustic concerts. Shanti tables served tasty organic and vegan food from the kitchen.

Arambol had noticeably improved in its cleanliness, and also sported a happier, friendlier vibe. We returned to This Is It, renewing our pleasant habit of writing with inspiring views and expert hospitality. We discovered Arambol Breeze, a condo building undergoing renovations, above Black Pearl Coffee. Arambol Breeze became our affordable, well-positioned home for the month. The hotel-like room included a small balcony, a square table, and one of the most comfortable beds I've slept on. The price plummeted the longer we stayed. In the heart of Arambol's main strip, we were a few minutes walk from the beach, and ten minutes from This Is It.

Despite the outward happiness of Arambol's visitors, under the surface lurked tensions from gang wars, police busts, and muzzled sentiments of the rising global health scare. Locals seemed less friendly and more aggressive. Goan gangs had grown wary of foreign rivals, including Israeli, Russian, and even French gangs. Police shut down the Nigerian gang in November. One morning downstairs at Black Pearl Coffee, I witnessed the collection of "tax". Local gangs rustled up rupees from each shop. The only place they dared not broach was Russian co-working guesthouse, No Name. Local merchants were already dejected from an already rock-bottom tourist season, largely fostered by the collapse of Thomas Cook Inc. There were plentiful signs that the global economy was in rotten shape.

Around the corner from Arambol Breeze was a reggae-oriented restaurant and concert space, Twice in Nature. On our first visit we randomly crossed paths with Z-Angel, the laidback Bombay socialite who was part of my original Roadhouse Hostel crew. Z-Angel welcomed us to sit with her friends, some of whom were DJs and part of touring soundsystems. Twice in Nature was not immune from rising tensions, and even propagated some of it. Late one otherwise innocuous evening, we witnessed a full-scale brawl, and a serious pummelling. With everybody casually minding their own business, an indignant, privileged and possibly suicidal Indian, with a long black beard and fancy clothes, marched in and criticised a skinhead from the reggae crew. The skinhead happened to be the manager of Twice in Nature. Black Beard stood right beside me, and after repeating numerous derogatory insults, he made his final patience-exhausting remark.

"You are shit to me," Black Beard chided the skinhead, repeating it enough times to provoke an aggressive reaction.

The burly skin-headed manager charged at Black Beard, and tackled him, that involved barreling through me. Momentum pushed Black Beard away from the floor-cushioned lounge, and he tumbled into the concrete courtyard, gracefully falling to the ground. The owner jabbed several fast punches to the chatterbox's head, before they were separated by chilled-out reggae types. From a distance they stuttered nonsense back and forth, declining into farce. While seemingly friendlier and jovial, violence occasionally re-escalated.

The mood seemed to improve, until another unrelenting wave of the chatterbox's annoying taunting. This was the last straw for others around. In burst a fierce, furious, muscular Nepalese or Vietnamese cook, who raced through the courtyard, and pushed a path through the crowd. Gravely concerning, was when a half-dozen other men – cooks and randoms – kicked the bearded fool senseless while he writhed on the ground.

At this point, somebody's life was in danger. Despite my injured wrapped-up ankle, I leapt up and limped forward to intervene. Others pulled Black Beard into safety. Unperturbed, the chef terminator unrelentingly pounded and barrelled away, reminiscent of prime Mike Tyson. He ran after the Beard, fighting through a dozen strong but pacifistic men, to unleash further blows.

In a moment of calm, I slowly made my way to the epicentre. I stood between both men as a peacekeeper, searching the depths of two sets of furious yet listlessly blank, brown eyes. I noted a twinge of pain and fear in the Beard, but only concentrated hatred from the Terminator.

"He's not worth it," I urged; Terminator pondered, then nodded. He talked to a friend, trying to relax, while glaring at his nemesis.

Yet, the Beard kept yapping – impressive for somebody who'd taken countless blows to the head. His indignant selfishness suggested suicidal tendencies. Maybe he believed the police were coming to help him, or that he was entitled to stay. During a lull in tension, Terminator escorted several women to safety. My gut instinct fetched Magia for departure; it was late anyway.

At the corner of a shadowy backstreet, we passed a half-dozen well-dressed but frowning young Hindi men, with their sleeves pulled up, purposefully striding towards Twice in Nature. Perhaps the Beard hadn't called police as he'd threatened, but instead rounded up the boys. Tonight's battle might be seven rich boys, against a dozen sedated reggae heavyweights and angst-filled Nepalese cooks.

For four successive days we witnessed brawls, fights and escalating tension in Arambol. Meanwhile, others were blissfully oblivious, a holiday's escape from reality – perhaps the final such jaunt for many.

Living Ghosts of the Past

By our second week in Arambol, we'd settled into a pleasant and stimulating routine. On weekday mornings I rose early, meditated, then headed to This Is It for breakfast and work. Magia caught up with me later, often after exploring the beach. Her main project was preparing her Dobra Atmosfera blog for launch. Many days we worked from the relaxed, seaside confines of Shri Sai, a serene and well-priced restaurant around Arambol's cliffside corner, towards Sweet Lake. After a rest and shower, we'd find a nice place for dinner, sharing heaping platters of paneer and rice, accompanied by creamy lassis, fresh-squeezed juice and masala chai.

One evening we returned to Twice is Nature, the week after the brawl, and sat in a corner beyond the dancefloor. Everything felt wonderful. Magia was happy and smiling, although my bandaged, still-throbbing ankle restricted my dancing. We enjoyed tokes of strong hash, and beats from the all-star reggae soundsystem crew. This was their final night in Arambol, before they'd head to perform at VH1 Supersonic festival.

Magia and I hopped up to dance; she more adventurously waded into the centre of the dancefloor. While I stood at the back, bobbing on one leg, I spotted an uncanny resemblance: Boogie. I dismissed it as another wave of self-inflicted psychosis. The clone was almost identical: angelic face, long brown hair, skinny, medium height, a carefree demeanour, and Borderland-like rose-tinted glasses. She was with a tall blonde male, who had slightly curly hair, and wore glasses; he also looked familiar. Boogie hadn't spent much time in my recent psyche; yet here in Arambol was her living doppelgänger. An exuberant Magia noticed I stopped dancing, and then observed the shocked expression on my face. I hesitated before telling her.

"That girl looks exactly like Boogie. The guy looks familiar too."

This killed the vibe for Magia. She sized up the free-spirited Boogie lookalike, and felt threatened. I wish I hadn't said anything, but I shared another controversial update.

"I'm sorry you can't handle this stuff. I have to let you know, there's a chance we'll cross paths with somebody else."

"Who??"

"The Russian."

Magia wasn't impressed, whatsoever. I'd recently heard from a former short-lived flame, The Russian. She was a fiery, outspoken brunette, with whom I shared a whirlwind post-Afrikaburn South African road trip in 2016. After an intense, acrimonious goodbye, we met up in Moscow, months later. This again ended coldly and dramatically. We cut off communication for years, until The Russian sent me a hugely-surprising, upbeat email on New Year's. Just like Boogie did.

During a rare recent message, I learned The Russian was planning to visit a love interest in Arambol. My alternative was saying nothing to Magia, but truth is important to me. There was a good chance The Russian didn't even make it to Goa. I assured Magia that if *she* ever became an ex, I'd greatly value reconnecting with her, irrespective of what any partner might think. In future conversations about the same topic, Magia insisted: "I don't reconnect with ex's. The past is the past; I move on." We'd later learn this was not altogether true.

I deeply regretted the timing of it all: it spoiled an otherwise wonderful night. I didn't intend to coordinate any plans with The Russian: the universe would have to make it happen. We all braced for a random encounter.

...

The day after Valentine's, feeling a need for Sea Time, an inner voice entered my dreams. It asked whether Magia was the longterm partner for me. I loved Magia infinitely: she was the sweetest soul I'd known. Magia was unprecedentedly easy to live and travel with, and was a positive, reliable complement to every adventure. With Magia I could envision a legitimate future together, at our self-built home in nature. Still, the relationship lacked physical chemistry. I was unable to be fully honest conversing about everything that bubbled within me, because of her jealousy. I wondered if other girls might be less demanding. I also questioned whether *any* relationship was for me.

Flaura, a vivacious French brunette I met at This Is It on 02.02.2020 – the evening I officially released "Magical" – was surely alluring. On Flaura's final night in Arambol, Magia, Flaura, Swiss-German Klara and I headed to a rave, in a quarry near Ashwem. The party was excellent, with quality Berlin-style techno from a Russian crew. There was a moment when Magia and Klara disappeared into the shadows. Flaura, excited and affectionate, with her wide brown eyes looking into mine, seemingly leaned in for a passionate kiss. Whatever relationship openness I couldn't. The "open" part of the relationship had a far deeper connotation to me than condoning intimate interactions with others. It was more about freedom to live and grow. "Freedom" would not detract from the respect and loyalty I held for my beloved, sensitive partner – whatever my internal conflicts. Especially, if she was there.

As days passed, Magia noticeably and admirably worked at coming to terms with The Past, and prepared herself for a prospective encounter with The Russian. This regularly impressed me about Magia – she was intelligent and sensitive, acknowledged her lessons, and strove to improve. How Magia handled The Past would determine our relationship's chances – *if* she even wanted it.

Return of The Russian

After several travel delays, The Russian verifiably arrived in Arambol, but we were yet to cross paths. We preferred for it to manifest organically. All of us knew it was inevitable – perhaps she'd pop out of nowhere.

I caught up with several friends from the past, including a Canadian Burner friend from Melbourne – Colleen – and her brother Riley. I reunited with Melbourne house DJ Jedgie. We'd spun together at regular events in Fitzroy, including Baxter's Lot. Magia and I picked up the big fella outside his hostel in Anjuna, and crammed three of us on our scooter. Jedgie noticed a police check ahead, and I ignored my own premonitions. We were pulled over by astonished Anjuna police, and "fined" Rs500.

On a casual evening at This Is It, Magia and I met an intellectual young man: Akash from Guragaon. Akash was the down-to-earth son of a national builder; a humble millionaire. Akash invited us to his family's new house, and one afternoon Magia and I chilled at the sizeable but modest estate in Anjuna. We stepped across thick green grass, and around stoic fruit and nut trees, that surrounded the old colonial-style house. Samosas and homemade dhal, roti and tea were graciously prepared. Akash was well-educated and enlightened, stoking chatting deeply about future societies. We shared altering perspectives on the world, psychology and relationships. We learned about the future of Goa, specifically the new airport being built in the north. The airport would inevitably bring hoards of new visitors to lower Maharashtra, and accordingly filter through Arambol. It was another reminder to enjoy the present. Everything changes.

...

Police were active in Arambol across the entire season, beginning with arresting long-established Nigerian gangs in November. On numerous occasions Goan Police busted venues, infiltrated parades, and swarmed the entire beach. One tranquil evening, while Magia, Jedgie and I lounged on Arambol Beach, a "shady" guy wearing a baseball cap approached us.

"Want any weed?" the guy asked, slyly.

"Ah, we're good for that, thanks," I replied.

"Want coke? Opium?" he persisted. I politely refused.

His crew of a half-dozen probable officers sat nearby, blasting traditional Indian folk music from their little boombox, while trying to act like renegade partiers. As a consequence of the season-long police presence, nobody had offered us any drugs the entire three weeks we'd been in Arambol. Then a sketchy guy from an inauthentic group approaches, straight up asking about cocaine and opium? Waiter friends had updated us about regular police busts in Arambol, and this appeared to be one such operation.

...

An odd flashback came in a sober moment of clarity. It revisited an incident as a young boy in Singapore; maybe I was nine. My mother, a devout Roman Catholic, shuttled us to church every Sunday, and we were imposed into weekly Catechism classes, that propagated the wonders and myths of Catholicism. At some point, my mother broached the idea of my possibly becoming an altar boy. I recalled the introductory alter boy training session, at our family's St. Ignatius church in Singapore. I remember shyly arriving at the familiar church. After being toured around, I was handed a robe to cover my clothes. The kind old priest, who was seemingly a good man, coached me through various rituals, ensuring my bending over, kneeling down, serving hosts and wine. I was naïve at the time, but there was something awkward and unsettling. Having since learned about the widespread, constant abuse of children throughout the Catholic Church – most of which is buried in the news and covered up by complicit politicians – it further felt creepy in its possibilities. Somehow I repressed it for over thirty years, and it popped out while dancing at a carefree house music party, on the beach outside Sunjay's Sun Tribe.

...

On a mid-week evening, after a lovely dinner at a beachside restaurant, Magia headed out to ecstatic dance with friends. While I was happily making music at the apartment, an incoming message from The Russian arrived. She'd been in Arambol for a fortnight, and we still hadn't crossed paths. With our time ticking down in Goa, we had to jumpstart the process, so we made plans to meet.

I left a note for Magia: "I shouldn't be home too late. I love you."

At Shanti Gossip Tree, The Russian and I renewed acquaintances, for the first time since Moscow over three years earlier. The Russian – Masha – maintained an impressively calm, zen aura. Masha's curvy body was layered in hippie clothing, and she wore dangling earrings that fell from behind her long brown hair. We'd barely spoken over the years, but it felt like our friendship had endured. We chattily strolled around Arambol's cliffside, past restaurants and shuttered shops, before settling at Sweet Lake. We lounged on tanning chairs facing the sea. Over the first bottle of red wine, we shared our tales of loves and life. Masha was similarly a doer and traveller, with many freelance projects. Presently she was representing a dildo company, and spent much time in blissful Siberia. Masha was a regular participant in Burning Man Russia.

After an hour, we rode through Arambol to a house on Pernem Road. I met Misha – a Russian international Burner and sculptor, and his much younger girlfriend; together they raised a baby. Misha was planning a small beach burn, that might happen on Sunday: Magia's birthday. We were cordially invited. Some of their Russian friends arrived at the house next door. The night lasted far longer than I anticipated, into the early morning. There was much drinking and smoking, while I listened to Russian conversations. I was invited to crash at either Russian house, but I worried for Magia's psyche. After staggering forty minutes home, through virtually-deserted and wholly shuttered Arambol, I knocked on the apartment door a few times. Eventually, a sleepy Magia opened it. She was grumpy in the morning, but was relieved I returned home safely.

...

On February 29 – Leap Year – I formally launched Plan Sea to the world, by releasing weekly chapters in an eBook series. The special event was hosted at This Is It, where we were granted permission to takeover the stage. The day happened to be the hottest and muggiest of the year, with electricity brownouts across Arambol, and it was too energy-sapping for people to be outside. This ensured small and slow-arriving guests, while we suffered technical difficulties throughout: frequent power cuts, and sound equipment didn't work. I played music from a playlist curated over the course of writing Plan Sea.

It was wholly surreal sitting on stage between Magia and The Russian – two of the most impactful souls of my life. Masha was more social and personable, while Magia sat tense and contemplatively. Other Russians arrived, as did a few other friends, like Jedgie, and Baba – a kind soul from Delhi.

As the afternoon led to the evening, This Is It filled up, and an excited crowd gathered for the nightly dinner and concert. We had the best seat in the house for the one-man reggae act, and we'd set up the night's electric energy. Several others, including Magia and Baba, insisted on visiting Twice in Nature. I disappointedly succumbed to group mentality, and we departed in the middle of the packed and lively concert.

...

Magia's 41st birthday transpired in Arambol. This time around was more contentious. The Russian crew's burn was confirmed for sunset on the same evening. I wanted to satisfy everybody – bring Magia for a lovely picnic and sculpture burn at Sweet Lake, then head to Riva for dancing. However, Magia preferred to spend the entire evening at Riva, bringing Z-Angel and Klara.

I decided to head to Sweet Lake earlier, then race to Riva afterward. This was likely the last time I'd see Masha, as I was heading south in a few days. Misha sculpted a fire girl out of wood, that stood several metres high. Russian pancakes and other snacks were served, with abundant bottles of wine. Ten people attended: several Russians, Baba from Delhi, and a random older American lady. As night fell, each of us lit a corner of the sculpture, and flames flickered high into the sky. We watched the embers of spirits fly away into the nether.

To rush to Riva, I hired a motorbike taxi. Riva's admission charge was hefty for an hour's stay, so I loitered outside Riva's beach entrance, observing its security and door operations. I randomly made friends with more Russians, who were similarly waiting to enter. We scoured the sand for discarded wristbands, finding one – but we needed several more for everybody. At a certain interval, security vacated their post, and we dashed in. Riva was packed, with hundreds of drunken and stoned revellers dancing to ragga drum & bass. From a comparably uncongested area behind the DJ booth, I scoured the crowd, and spotted Magia with her crew. I pierced through dancing bodies to say hello, but Magia was cold, and her friends initially ignored me. Magia'd told everybody I went "on a date" with an ex-girlfriend.

When the beats finished, a sweaty, inebriated Magia found me, and we sauntered up to Riva's back lawn. Along the way, Magia paused to smoke hash with Klara and some friends. This onset a massive head rush and sickness. On the grass, I held Magia while she occasionally vomited. She'd been treated to many drinks and smokes. Riva closed, while I nursed Magia and constantly fetched her water. At some point we mustered enough strength to slowly trudge out of the venue, and ambled along the beach. I looked after her, and she appreciated it.

Another Little Paradise

After a productive and eventful month in Arambol, we sought to explore the south of Goa. We desired a tranquil place overlooking the sea, from which to create and meditate. I filtered through hundreds of online reviews, searching for subtle references that hinted at picturesque seclusion, similar to Sri Lanka's Hiriketiya or Moon River. "Surf beaches", "hidden gems", "chilled out places" and alike helped gather candidates for consideration. Colva or Palolem were likely overcrowded, but two smaller beaches – Agonda and Patnem - sounded perfect, and received praise from hippies, creatives and waiter friends alike. Agonda felt like a good place to start.

Along the way from Arambol, we stopped in Morjim for a prospective ping pong tournament. We were invited to participate by a recent Russian-Israeli acquaintance, Papa Bolshoi. He was a publisher and curator of intriguing products, like teas and atomic gold. For our solitary evening in Morjim, we rented a humble room in a guesthouse, a ten-minute stroll from Morjim Beach. Bora Bora was overpriced, and attracted a well-heeled if not egocentric crowd. A DJ spun quality Berlin techno to an empty dancefloor. While Magia hoped to play in the ping pong tournament, this particular evening featured little more than warmup matches.

With the actual tournament days away, we continued our journey. While we waited for bus in sapping midday heat, Magia wandered about the nearby shops. I stood on the main road, near a haphazard temporary wall of rock bricks. A 20kg boulder slipped onto my left ankle, that was still swollen and recovering from the Mumbai train accident. Blood and bruises ensued, as well as a dizzying need to catch my breath beside the road. Eventually, a local bus from Morjim delivered us to Mapusa, then another to Goa's capital, onwards to Madgaon, and a final shuttle to Palolem. Buses and transfers were efficient; we didn't wait more than ten minutes before each departure. The cost was around Rs100 each for the five-hour journey.

At the entrance to Palolem, we hopped in a scenic tuk tuk to Agonda Beach, that felt like rediscovering paradise. Arriving before sunset, we checked into acclaimed Saturn Jungle Huts. This stellar property was situated riverside, off Agonda's calm main street that ran parallel to the water, and 80m from the Arabian Sea. A sandy pathway led between chilled-out Love Bites and pricey Agonda Diva guesthouse. We emerged onto soft sand, into a panorama of deep blue sea. The golden beach was lined by coconut trees, restaurants and guesthouses. Happy cows lingered, and carefree dogs strode around, while hundreds of birds – mostly eagle-like Brahmani kites and crows – chattered excitedly. The sea was the warmest and most pleasant temperature I'd encountered in decades, probably since Hawaii.

Agonda Beach was another little paradise. The quality of cafes and restaurants was impressive, and the abundance of happy animals felt like a fairy tale. Saturn's owner was an impassioned Vipassana practitioner, who often travelled the world to meditate. His ultra-chill, honest service, and that of his noble assistant, were of the highest standard. Our little yellow jungle hut was accessible down stone steps that led to the river. Outside each hut featured a pair of chairs around a circular wooden table, with privacy and shade assured by plants and trees. In the surrounding trees were the nests of hundreds of birds. The spot was a melting pot for hungry jungle mosquitoes, and we heard an unrelenting symphony of nature sounds. Coconut trees swirled overhead, with netting to protect from deadly falling shells.

We loved Agonda, and extended our stay another week. This sliver of paradise was what we lived for. I preferred not to move anywhere for a while, although Magia harboured ambitions to visit Kerala and its mountains. I had a forthcoming three-day Vipassana course in Tiruvannamalai. In Auroville, I hoped to spawn a garbage initiative for its neighbouring villages. I sought to present a Sun Moon Sea peace orchestra concert. We were to visit self-sustaining farms and rainforests, to learn renewable methods of gardening for herbs and crops. I made an appointment at holistic-oriented Auroville Dental Clinic to extract my four painful wisdom teeth. The final week of our trip was intended in the Himalayas, near Dharamshala, home to the Dalai Lama, and then we'd fly from Delhi to Krakow. It was best to relax while we could.

Occasionally, we rented a scooter to explore the wider surrounds. One sunrise we visited Cotigao Wildlife Sanctuary, although there weren't many animals around. One of the routes led to a treehouse near a waterhole, cloaked in tranquility among mostly unspoiled nature. On another morning, we ventured through small mountains to the Savri waterfall. Trekking thirty minutes down a steep slope, led to a cliffside waterfall that roared over a large pond at its base. Magia braved the freezing cold, and waded into the water, swimming towards the waterfall, where pure water crashed upon her head. Monkeys observed from nearby, and were certainly appreciative of banana peels we tossed towards them. On the way back, we ran out of petrol, a short walk from Mangaal Farmstay. Over stimulating conversation, we were treated to organic watermelon-mint juice, buckwheat pancakes, and the tastiest carrot cake. Afterwards, they helped refill our petrol.

Nearby Butterfly Beach required a risky ride, down rocky slopes through jungle, before hiking the remaining fifteen minutes to its cove. While fairly isolated, the beach was littered with tons of plastic, further propagated by lazy guests of the adjacent commercial nightclub, Leopard Valley. With rising temperatures, and rampant pollution across the planet, it felt that Nature would surely strike back.

Reality Check

Each morning we woke riverside at our jungle paradise. Six o'clock bells rang from the beachside church. Meditation within the hut's mosquito net proceeded early morning sunrises, that slowly cascaded through the jungle's trees. Writing over breakfast and coffee led to afternoons of deep blue skies. Magia loved the warm sea, swimming like a dolphin or a frog through the waves. Friendly beach dogs became our buddies. Magia named the leader of our favoured trio, "Van Halen" - because he loved to jump on us. "Lil Tofu" reminded me of Auroville's Tofu. The gang's third member was a ratty little black and white dog, Magia named "Scarpetta", Polish for "sock". Scarpetta was bullied by the slightly older dogs, but they banded together when their territory was broached by other canines or wayward cows. Everything was beautiful, suspended in extended moments of perfection. Magia and I were once again living in harmony, in paradise, enjoying nature, warm weather and slowing life down, even for a while.

As time wore on, I experienced bouts of depression. I felt an increasing sense of irrelevance. I was no longer an active part of communities, and terse online societies were awash with brainwash, naïvety and conflicts. My relationship with Magia felt more of a friendship, with its end feeling ominous and inevitable. Meanwhile, I had no other close friends around.

Furthermore, in these present near-perfect comforts, I debated the need to travel at all. Remain in an inexpensive tropical paradise, or move for the sake of it? Increasingly, it felt like Auroville wouldn't happen, and I questioned my intentions or purpose altogether. What lay ahead in Europe and Poland upon returning "home"? What would I do there? What did I truly care about? It sure wasn't web development, web hosting or the phony, soulless business game - but how else was I going to make a living? How was the van going to happen?

Adding to my stress, was regularly smoking strong Indica, dwindling finances and four piercing wisdom teeth. The lack of relationship space emanated from being confined in a little jungle hut, with a stir-crazy partner who demanded more attention than I could provide. My flexible life included compassionately catering to preferences of others, and so I adjusted for Magia. With less people around and no social functions, she and I were inherently, unbreakably unified.

Despite my avoiding news and most social media, there was increasingly widespread concern about the global pandemic. People were increasingly, visibly stressed, and jabbered about the darned virus, whether we liked it or not. People who were hooked on the poisonous intravenous of mainstream news were particularly draining.

Our Kochi visit was postponed, after Aswin messaged about local complications related to "Corona". The cancellation of my Vipassana course soon followed, citing "maintenance". I interpreted these as clues to stay put, and further settle in Agonda. When we learned we couldn't visit legendary Gokarna - not far away in neighbouring state Karnataka - and needed to remain where we were, the realities of lockdown - whatever that might entail - became apparent. One fateful evening at Love Bites, we overheard guests blasting "facts" and opinions about the dire state of the world. I realised we could no longer escape it. It was time to read the news.

Chapter 22

Lockdown in Paradise

During one big dose of the Uncertainty Principle, in March 2020 the world was placed under collective house arrest. With a perfect storm in place, global control was mass-coordinated and imposed upon the citizens of Earth, tantamount to a state of war. Cities were sealed under lockdown, previously-open borders were shut to outsiders, food supplies were cut, every school was closed, international transportation – flights, freight, buses, trains and metros – universally halted, monitoring and surveillance intensified, and questionable emergency laws were rushed into legislation.

The culprit was the so-called COVID-19, a strain of Coronavirus similar to the flu. Whatever the truth behind it, this was a masterclass implementation of "hyper-normalisation" - a recent political strategy of manifesting "fake reality" within its populace, to stoke confusion and division. It didn't really matter what anybody thought about Coronavirus, or their beliefs about its origins: lockdown was globally enforced irrespectively. We could entirely ignore the news, yet still absorb the crisis' encompassing energy. It affected everybody in today's inter-connected world.

Societies and classes reacted differently. Many rich and privileged, who'd never previously experienced strife or suffering, complained about their dire inconveniences: of losing money, or luxurious aspirations quashed, or thwarted property sales. Western customers frantically emptied supermarkets, notably hoarding toilet paper, to the bemusement of most other cultures. Elaborate festivals were cancelled, nightclubs were shuttered indefinitely before on-sold to churches and gentrifying developers, and group hangouts were prohibited, while masks and "social distancing" became new norms.

Most people were scared about the immediate ramifications on their personal health and safety. Many were unwilling to ask deeper questions, such as the roots behind the unrelenting assault of coordinated media information, or politically-convenient motives that stoked heavy-handed responses to the crisis. In one swift move, Coronavirus helped ease the climate change emergency, halt international drug and human trafficking, and cripple global terrorism.

Less-friendly characteristics of inherently-divided Western societies became intensified. Anti-foreigner and immigrant stances hardened. Legitimate citizens, who happened to be overseas, were warned to "stay away", in the midst of furore about potentially-contaminated expats returning home. Everybody was to be wary of one another.

With humans unable to interact physically, this was an ideal scenario for Big Data. Now, the vast majority of everybody's conversations were replicated on the servers of Google, Amazon, Microsoft and Facebook. Controversial legislation in numerous countries, including America and Australia, punitively mandated the collection and years-long storage of all citizens' online activity, messaging and data, with authorities granted rights to access it, whenever they deemed necessary. Every mobile, webcam, Alexa or Google Assistant became a consensual spy device in citizens' homes, offices and cars. Big Data analysed movements, reactions, conversations and trends, for further marketing, algorithmic manipulation and, inevitably, future pandemics. The world was firmly under totalitarian control, and not by accident or coincidence.

...

On Sunday March 22, 2020, the Indian coastal state of Goa initiated its first-ever curfew, aiming to restrict the spread of COVID-19. Rules prohibited public movement, particularly between towns or districts, and people were to be contained within their homes from 7am to 9pm. Magia and I spent the first day of lockdown at our riverside Saturn jungle hut. We wrote, sipped on masala chai, and ate pastries and fruit stocked from the previous day. One humble restaurant, Agonda Corner – that we affectionately referred to as "Trippy Dosa", for its nightly psychedelic illuminations – promised they would remain open and look after us. There were plentiful other visitors residing at guesthouses without kitchens or restaurants. That first night's dinner at Agonda Corner was tense. We had to eat discretely in the shadows. Other tourists were frantic, notably three bedraggled Italian lesbians, who looked starving and scared.

On Monday morning, the state's emergency control measures were extended by three further days. Following early morning meditation on the golden sands of Agonda Beach, we returned to Trippy Dosa: now closed indefinitely. Other resorts and cafes were only open for their guests. The Goan government initially overlooked the humanitarian necessity of maintaining food supplies, despite locking countless thousands inside. Lockdown was soon extended again, and food at restaurants and homes dwindled, accelerating grief, panic and fury.

The situation lent further encouragement for us to expedite finding alternate accommodation – somewhere with a fridge and kitchen – if not departing India entirely. Reluctantly, but out of necessity, Magia and I jumped into the rabbit hole of COVID-19 news for the first time. This unveiled a tsunami of emotional opinions from passionate friends and family, who were trying to help. It meant absorbing months of news and hysteria in one intense dose, and it naturally translated to considerable stress.

As I'd suspected, it wasn't the virus I was worried about, but globally-coordinated media spin. Coverage reminded me of past outbreaks, such as SARS in 2002 – not long after 9/11 – and Swine Flu in 2009 – following the Global Financial Crisis. Iran was somehow the only other country added to a "banned" list alongside China – even though numerous countries suffered far worse outbreaks. Few other news topics could be found. Generally-reliable sources such as The Guardian and BBC were awash with COVID commentary, featuring statistics tables of cases and deaths, reminiscent of Olympic medal tallies. Logging onto social media was a regrettable exercise, where floods of posts showcased unprecedented naïvety. People were either self-proclaimed experts, or petrified.

Magia and I worked together, diligently researching safe pathways out of India. On the insistence of Kiwis J-Man and Hannah, and the blessing of Magia's Polish mother for "anywhere but India", New Zealand rapidly became an appealing option. J-Man and Hannah graciously offered to host our fourteen-day quarantine in the comfortable upstairs loft of their house, in the tropical town of Whangerei, north of Auckland. Airfares were expensive, but I found the lowest possible fares for a shuttle from Goa to Bangalore, ahead of Singapore Airlines flights to Auckland. We'd depart one paradise for another! Magia had long desired to explore New Zealand, and as a Kiwi it made sense for me. In a moment of calm, we booked the flights, then closed the news, and savoured our surroundings.

...

When we woke the next morning, Magia and I expressed similar doubts about our hurried decision. We'd previously experienced parallel trepidations last year in Ella, Sri Lanka, when we followed instincts to move to the mountains, hours before learning of that morning's terrorist bombings.

"We rushed into it," we both concurred, questioning the need to leave Agonda at all.

Goa, despite the madness of the world and escalating cases within India, was comparably COVID-free. The handful of positive cases came from Caucasian foreigners, who'd arrived from risky countries, and they all recovered rapidly. Goa's consistently warm weather was not prone to flu. International flights became barred from arriving in India, and all planes would soon be blocked from leaving.

I held a litany of personal trepidations about rebuilding life from scratch in New Zealand. For whatever the country's impressive progress under Prime Minister Jacinda Ardern, the country was still part of America's Five Eyes intelligence gang. In numerous ways, New Zealand was similar to Australia, towards which I maintained a plethora of misgivings. I'd have to apply for tax numbers, enrol in government programs, open bank accounts and muster income in a suspect economy. New Zealand was remote for global travel, and prohibitively expensive for anybody living off $200 per week. If September's elections overturned the country's progressive movement, and installed an Australian or British-like neoconservative government, New Zealand wouldn't be attractive whatsoever.

By dinner time, Magia and I acknowledged that remaining in Agonda to wait out the crisis might be the safest and most sensible option. Our flights home to Poland were only a month away; I had no issue with enjoying our little paradise until then.

While Magia maintained a restless inclination to continue traveling, I knew in my heart we wouldn't be heading anywhere.

With Saturn's amenities unsuitable for lengthier survival scenarios, we needed to find somewhere self-sustaining, that included a kitchen and fridge. We could stock up on non-perishable food and other supplies, and ride it out – no matter how brutal or dire lockdown might become. We slept on it again, and in the morning we cancelled our New Zealand plans. Within days, New Zealand raised its alert to Level 4, shutting the border and restricting movement entirely. We felt no regrets by avoiding unsafe airports and mass crowds. There was a chance of being locked down along the way – such as in Bangalore or Singapore. After a fortnight's quarantine in New Zealand, we'd enter a new world, in an expensive, foreign land, in winter with one week of summer clothes, as far away as possible from Krakow. The safest decision was to stay put, whatever the short-term inconveniences.

Residential options included Khaama Kethna: a sustainable eco-estate nestled tranquilly in an Agondan jungle. The prospective two-floor wooden house featured a spacious balcony overlooking the jungle, and its isolated location promised silence. There was a huge on-site restaurant that housed the only wifi on the property, and we were keen to help replenish the centre's organic garden to grow food.

Outrage and pressure from locals, ensured Agonda eventually reestablished reliable supplies, initially through multiple restaurants and delivery services. Access to food made Saturn more attractive, and we now had the property to ourselves. Nature was immune to media. On numerous evenings, blue and green phosphate illuminated waves under twilight sky, while beach dogs playfully chased after scattering crabs, who burrowed in the sand. Other than occasional cows and dogs, Agonda was a veritable ghost town.

...

Waking up, I rubbed the dust from my eyes, and remnants of foggy dreams rapidly vanished. I remembered the here and now. *Disappointing.* Despite awakening in paradise to the sounds of crows and eagles, the dream world was superior to the actuality of Earthly existence. I preferred sleep. Another long day lay ahead: the same routine, killing time until the situation eased – whether it was days, weeks or months. Coconut and mango trees, the river, steps from golden sands and green-blue sea, made for an enviable backdrop, but we remained trapped in our minds, as well as our physical confines.

An announcement blared that Indian lockdown was further extended by twenty-one days. The mood of stranded Himalayan restaurant workers and tourists became evermore grim, such as at Sunset Restaurant for one evening's sombre dinner. Fatima Restaurant was a reliable option for takeaway, and a couple of shops remained open. The ATM generally functioned, but we stored an extra supply of cash, just in case. Sharp divisions formed between humans. Pale, privileged types fearfully locked themselves inside, with little more than news and social media. Freer souls asserted our right to venture into nature and swim, or acquire essential food, out of survival. Some locals glared at foreigners, wondering why we remained. Beach dogs scrapped for dwindling food, while cows panicked in hoards. Contrastingly, birds thrived, endlessly chirpy; mass murders of crows, eagle-like kites hovered over trees and sea, and smaller birds checked-in ahead of monsoon.

On the first Friday of lockdown, March 27, police arrived to scare. Paranoid locals had filed complaints with Goan police, about clusters of people frequenting Agonda Beach. Sunset was the solitary milestone of each locked-down day that many people looked forward to. Magia and I wandered south along the beach towards Sunset Point, for Friday's weekly acoustic performance. A Swedish guitarist and his audience would gather between boulders, with a backdrop of sea, sky and falling Sun.

Moments before we rounded the cove, a sharp whistle halted us; a police truck was parked 200m away. Three officers sporting long, thick bamboo sticks swarmed onto the beach, heading towards anybody in sight, angrily waving sticks and yelling. The combination of their angle and the narrow beach would ensure they'd cut us off before we could scoot past them. We were walking alongside an Australian lady, Rochelle, when she spotted a large piece of polystyrene that washed on shore. As a good Earth citizen, Rochelle fetched the litter, and headed to a bin to dispose it. Police threatened her with sticks, and

Rochelle scuttled away. The officers menacingly chased several slower tourists along the beach, including an older man, and a woman carrying a baby.

Magia and I ducked into nearby White Resort, our original plan for dinner. We hastily sat at a table in the sparkling, all-white open air restaurant, with one other guest and a half-dozen staff loitering. Furious stick-toting police appeared mere metres behind us. Yelling and screaming, the head policeman barked at a manager.

"What is this?!"

"Restaurant, sir."

Following evermore cursing, the police threatened the manager, who frantically signalled to staff to cut the lights. The other guest bolted for his room, while Magia and I scrambled through the resort to the main street, that was empty, eerie and hazy. For the first time in many years, I was scared, even though a beating wouldn't have been the worst scenario. As I would not accept unreasonable punishment, I harboured visions of fighting back, arming myself, hurtling rocks – whatever it took to defend myself and those around. Yet, we were wholly powerless, under police and political control of the world's new order.

You Cannot Force Magia

As calm and upbeat as I tried to present, the stress of the draconian situation toiled on all of us. Magia was particularly susceptible to pressures and experienced a handful of breakdowns. She drained my energy and demanded much attention. One afternoon while she was happily frolicking in the sea, I packed away my laptop, locked the jungle hut and headed to the beach. As I crossed the sand, Magia was sobbing uncontrollably; I thought something terrible happened.

"I lost my new sunglasses in the ocean," Magia wailed.

Replacing her previous pair had been quite an ordeal. A week or two earlier, we rode the scooter around nearby Canacona. She'd shortlisted several establishments, and we painstakingly visited one after another to find the precise, authentic pair she desired. Despite acknowledging the risks of swimming with sunglasses, they vanished in the ocean. While Magia bawled, I waded into the sea, trudging around the shallow waves where she'd been swimming. The tide was strong enough that plastic objects could be churned and pushed southwards with pace.

I realised Magia's uncontrollable crying wasn't altogether about sunglasses. It seemed a reasonable release of everything that had manifested over the previous months: Arambol, lockdown, the mystery of where next, and whether it would be with me. Still, there were further signs of her inability to cope with the stress of survival, during an emergency situation that could certainly deteriorate. I felt my primary mission was to return her safely to Zielonki, and then possibly move on myself. Magia acknowledged similar sentiments, and considered returning to Zielonki alone, mindful of the ramifications.

"We're buddies at everything," she sighed, on numerous occasions.

I'd lovingly referred to her as every type of buddy imaginable: Travel buddies, beach buddies, cuddle buddies, writing buddies. I regarded us predominantly as best friends – not that I believed this limited our long-term chances of building a home and family. I loved Magia very much. Yet it felt a compromise for both of us, about our desired, dream relationships, and what more we felt might be out there.

One of the next mornings, Magia badly hurt her back while awkwardly lugging a heavy watermelon across the road. Her moods worsened upon each chat with her worried mother, who Magia admitted was the root of much of her life's anguish. Susceptible to external pressures and stresses, Magia simply wanted to return home: to her apartment, cats and family.

I had no such luxury, as home for me the past two years was Magia's flat in Zielonki. Most of my belongings remained there: my clothes, gear, music equipment, tent and sleeping bag. Without Zielonki, I would be homeless – again. It was the same old loop: somebody else decided they wanted change, and I was thrust on my own. Where else could I head? New Zealand made sense, although it wasn't wholly ideal for my international aspirations, or the onset of winter during a flu pandemic. South East Asia was viable – excellent weather and affordable – although the world was on the cusp of locking up further. A karma bomb had exploded all over the broken United Kingdom, with a miserable population spawning increased crime and violence, and perhaps its worst government in a long line of political failures. Canada, in its close proximity to the USA, offered no reliably safe or captivating solution. Helping schools and communities in Malawi was a well-spirited idea, but Africa was a tough place, with its own brutal turmoil and conflicts. Even remote little African villages, with barely any connection to the outside world, were locked down, with its citizens forcibly ordered to don masks. The whole world was a mess.

…

Under intense urging from her family, and a convenient Goa to Warsaw flight, Magia booked emergency tickets home, alone. Seats were not accessible to other EU residents, such as on my UK passport, unless we were married or had I officially registered as a Polish resident. While I exerted no pressure whatsoever – it was her decision – a part of me hoped for an adventurous and romantic spark, that would bond us through surviving the crisis. This was a reason I liked the original New Zealand idea: it would ensure we'd stay together, at least a little longer. I didn't blame her for wanting to return home – if I had my own home and family I'd consider the same. But, I wouldn't leave her alone.

With Magia's flight days away, the clock ticked down on our relationship. Online chats with Jono balanced work with friendly perspectives. He and Miri had observed special magic between Magia and I, and they hoped we'd persevere.

"Please, Sea," Jono warmly offered. "Who knows what the future will bring? After necessary time and space apart, maybe you'll want to remain together. Don't rule anything out."

…

On Magia's final full day in Agonda, she restlessly rose before sunrise with a wild mind. Following the yawn of dawn, we meditated on the beach, despite the distraction of playful dogs, as light filled the sand. We strolled south around the shore, around a cove, into the jungle and up to Sunset Point, where huge boulders sat surrounded by sea. We watched a trio of silver dolphins swimming, while fisherman in wooden row boats lay nets for fish. After a nap, we ate Shahi paneer – Magia' new favourite – with lemon rice, green salad and coconut lassi.

The day was surreal, stoic and sad. Despite our precious fleeting moments together, emotions erupted during an otherwise tranquil sunset saunter along the coast. In bursts of anguish, Magia stormed away indignantly, in response to my innocent comment about being careful. She needed time to think; within twenty minutes of brooding on the beach, peace was made. In the evening we enjoyed a special grilled pomfret fish dinner, with salad, pulao rice and Corona beer. Nothing could mask the stark reality that our physical coexistence would soon be suspended indefinitely.

...

At 3am, the first alarm blared. We'd barely slept. Magia was alert, and diligently checked her pre-packed bags and vital documents. She left behind substantial medical supplies for me, "in case". In the grey grog of the very early morning, we calmly sipped on instant coffee with coconut milk. Sleepiness suspended reality, and every minute, as fast as each ticked away, felt vivid and important.

The pre-booked airport taxi arrived earlier than expected. I carried Magia's bags to the road, where three other evacuators awaited, including a Polish couple. The taxi driver wore a mask and gloves, maintaining his distance. Van Halen, the carefree jumping beach dog, wished Magia safe travels. After the mask-clad foreigners arranged themselves in the taxi, Magia and I stood outside the cab. We gazed at each other for the final time. We kissed passionately, long and hard, before the tightest of embraces; our last cuddle. Exchanging deep, mournful glances, Magia entered the ride towards her emergency evacuation. She waved from the window as she passed me; we almost touched each other's hands. The taxi vanished into sleeping dusk, and turned right, then away. Magia was gone.

Alone

I was a wreck. Instead of sleeping, I diverted energies into productive creativity. I sampled high-resolution sounds of the riverside jungle, mostly multiple species of birds, cicadas and occasional distant dogs. I filmed a time lapse of sunrise through coconut trees.

Magia and I exchanged several messages upon her arrival at Goa's virtually-deserted airport. She reported that hundreds of masked foreigners waited in queues for hours. A faulty seat earned her a upgrade to Business Class! While Magia flew home, I experienced the complete gamut of human emotions. Initially, relief. Intimate, daily relationships were demanding at the best of times. While her safety and contentment were my priority while together, now I could focus on my own litany of challenges. In worst-case or apocalyptic scenarios, I was free to make decisions, and move as necessary.

The other side of my bipolarity, was abjectly missing my closest friend and soulmate. Anguish arose from recounting memories of happier times: exploring, scooter missions, beach walks, home life, cats, and fading dreams of our hypothetically shared future. *Maybe we simply needed space?* After hours of fiddling around with music, I was tired of the computer, and missed Magia's companionship. I wondered how long I'd last before I'd seek to return to her side, despite the petty conflicts that frequently surfaced. A comforting reflection, was that the universe manifested these actualities, and rocketed us back upon our separate trajectories, as needed.

...

Magia felt trapped upon arriving home, under lockdown in cold Poland – in her apartment, but also within the nation's regressive, paranoid society. The Polish government mandated use of a controversial quarantine surveillance app. Upon receiving a daily SMS, users had to snap and share geolocation-tracked photographs, within twenty minutes. Data was saved and stored for up to six years. If Magia, or anybody, was labelled "as a threat to national security", they could be quarantined indefinitely. Instead, she turned off her phone for two weeks, waving to police from a balcony when they arrived each morning to check on her. Her afterglow of recent travels pushed her to complete tasks, and she prepared to return overseas.

"New Zealand? India?" Magia ruminated, during our inspired, whimsical conversations.

The tone of Magia's messages was inconsistent and mixed. It sounded like she accepted and was excited about new horizons, but I was confused as to whether her plans involved me. I knew customary phases of shock and inspiration would eventually lead to answers. I could not force her; she had to discover the truth herself. Yet, every morning I missed her, and felt the gut wrench of loss.

My moods habitually improved upon opening the jungle hut's door, and especially when stepping onto the sands of the sea. The shore of Agonda Beach began to recede from rising, raging tides. Soon there would be little reason being near the water, with monsoon season approaching. Dogs and cows scavenged the beach and streets for scraps of food. Some cows ate plastic. Certain dogs looked pleased to discover discarded baby diapers, for a delicious, pre-packed surprise.

...

When our original LOT flight to Poland was officially cancelled, it confirmed the obvious: I'd not be returning to Zielonki at the end of April. The next milestone was based around the expiration of my Indian visa. Despite the pleasantries of paradise, my routine became mundane. Seven days a week of work and music kept me busy. I was reliant on two open restaurants for takeaways, that cumulatively became expensive. Walking along Agonda's small main street to Fatima Restaurant passed blooming white flowers, brimming with fragrant scents, while noticeably increasing garbage littered the road and river.

On April 14, India's Prime Minister, Narendra Modi, broadcast an important national announcement. While waiting for food at Fatima's, I observed paranoid, entertainment-oriented Indian news with flashing red lights, a countdown, and stock-like tickers gratuitously tallying cases and deaths. Field reporters donned masks, speaking in hysterical raised-pitched voices. Modi's responsibility was to break the news to a frustrated nation, at the risk of fuelling a billion people's anger: towards the state, police and each other – foreigners included. Modi confirmed the expected: Lockdown was to be further extended.

Beyond Fatima, my other restaurant option was Omkar, towards the north of Agonda Beach. It's manager, Victor, consistently overcharged for simple meals. After I'd order a typical paneer, rice, garlic paratha and a lassi or juice, Victor'd pretend to check the menu, and input imaginary prices into a calculator. Sometimes bills were outlandish; he justified "rising food prices". One evening at Omkar, I met Irish Dan and a very pretty Canadian brunette, Sasha. Dan and I connected immediately – about travel, politics and truth. We hung out a few times from the sandy patio of their north beach hut. Any minuscule fragments of human interaction were greatly appreciated, in this era of social distancing.

From Saturn to Sunny

After seven weeks at Saturn Guesthouse, it was time for new horizons. I couldn't stay at Saturn indefinitely, as they were soon packing up for monsoon. The kind owner Pankay offered a place at his brother's property in Patnem, although it similarly had no kitchen or fridge.

On the evening before lockdown, Magia and I sat upstairs of Love Bites, enjoying sunset writing, sea views and scrumptious food. A couple entered; first I noticed the pretty blonde and her positive energy. Diva, a German, sat nearby us, joined by her long-haired Indian boyfriend. Sunny was peculiar, with a blankness in his eyes, as though he didn't trust us, or perhaps held secrets of his own. They'd resided for months in the jungle at Khaama Kethna, and were looking for a new apartment. Sunny was a DJ; Diva, a yoga practitioner. The next day, lockdown began and was indefinitely extended. The following weeks were intense and hectic, from booking New Zealand flights through to Magia's abrupt departure. Similarly, Diva soon returned to Germany under pressure from her mother. I was offered the spare room in Sunny's house, for less rent than at Saturn. Through my crisis confusion, I couldn't decipher my trepidations about moving in with Sunny. There was a voice urging my reconsideration, but it didn't offer answers. I assumed it was about sharing a residence, when I desired a place alone. Sunny's plan was to return home to Kolkatta in two weeks, and then I'd have the majestic place to myself. I decided to take the spare room.

The pretty two-bedroom apartment sprawled across the entire top floor of a large house, atop a remote hill that lent safety, even from a tsunami. There were sea views from any of the flat's three balconies, and seemingly constant breeze afforded respite from sapping pre-monsoon humidity. The place was charming and inspiring, and, because of the crisis, affordable. The normal price was Rs30,000 per month; my rent was Rs15,000. I knew Sunny paid less, but how little didn't concern me at this point.

While the apartment was gorgeous, the living situation was less than ideal. The house, particularly the kitchen, was filthy. Old garbage bags were discarded on the balcony, spawning multiple maggot infestations, including under a kitchen mat. I consistently paid for most of the groceries. Rent was suspicious: "Don't talk to the owner about money." I was grossly over-charged for whatever smokable supplies Sunny could muster. He typified the lazy, directionless stoner: a talker and taker. During a conversation about garbage, that we personally had to burn, I suggested not including plastic in the trash.

"Ah, the planet can handle it now. After Corona, the Earth has taken a break from pollution." Sunny was oblivious that nearby humans and animals breathed in toxic, burning plastic. He felt no inclination to clean up his own putrid garbage; meanwhile he condescendingly ordered me around the house: put garbage here, chop vegetables. Everything was on his watch, irrespective of what I might be working on. I could probably tolerate two weeks, but then the bombshell arrived: he'd likely stay until the middle of June: "Because of the situation." I deeply considered moving out. I needed time to myself, or I'd explode.

...

During a video conference with Magia, she looked radiant. Her eyes were electric, and she acted calm and cool. Czupi, the incredibly aware cat, could hear my voice, and looked around aimlessly for me. I missed home: they were my family. As time passed, Magia was similarly lonely and lost. She sent one lengthy, point-blank message that demanded my making certain commitments to our relationship. She was seemingly stuck in the past, rehashing our long-ago points of contention. But, even if I made promises to her, what about next time she booted me out of the house? I was presently more concerned about survival. For a few days, I couldn't reply. Days later, at Omkar for my first sit-down dinner in a month, I sent a lengthy message, expressing honest concerns about our longterm prospects.

"I can't hold you back from what you truly desire, and I hope that you're able to find what, and who, you're looking for," punctuated my response. Deep down, I was sad.

...

One evening, having enjoyed a colourful sunset on Agonda Beach, I headed home. Suddenly, police swarmed from the pathway. Two officers bolted towards the beach, whacking people, most of whom scattered and ran. One officer darted at me with a stick, then momentarily thought better of it. Instead, he turned to beat an Indian, a good man who'd shared numerous sunsets near me. I exaggerated limping from a groin I'd pulled while swimming, and slowly meandered past Agonda Diva, to the road. I nodded solemnly at a masked police officer, who gripped his stick beside the police car. A paranoid local had complained about groups enjoying themselves on the beach. Goa presently had zero Corona cases, and everybody had been locked up as veritable prisoners for a month, meaning no risk of infection. This suggested that this entire COVID-19 exercise wasn't really about health, but instead the imposition of domination and control, that certain humans with power corrupted into humiliation.

...

I witnessed multiple instances of cruelty against animals in Agonda, some by animals themselves. Territorial dogs, particularly large packs, often turned on weaker members. During my only time swimming in the serene and scenic north part of Agonda Beach, two dogs began fighting – a black and a tan-coloured dog. All of the black dogs ganged up on the tan dog. It was a wild, prolonged fight. The black dog entourage eventually overwhelmed the tan dog, and they all ferociously snarled. There was a foreigner family swimming nearby, who'd arrived with the pack of dogs. The olive-skinned, short-haired French man had a Caucasian wife and mixed-race baby. The man was never the friendliest: he wouldn't look others in the eye or say hello. He leapt from the water to protect the tan dog, separating it from the raging pack. When a particular black dog continued pouncing, the French man punched the black dog, Mike Tyson-style in the face. Then a few more brutal punches - releasing his lifetime of anger on an animal.

Another unfriendly man, whose house was across the street from Saturn, similarly never looked anybody in the eye or said hello. He was clearly full of rage and disdain for everything: animals, foreigners, and even his family. I frequently observed him, mask-clad, on the beach, with a heavy, sharp stick to scare dogs. One particular day, while I waited nearby his wall for a meeting with Saturn's owner, a herd of cows arrived near Agonda Diva's entrance. A cow strayed onto the man's property, proceeding to drink water from a foot bath, beneath an outdoor staircase. The man grabbed his stick and, like an expert baseball player or hoodlum, whacked the cow hard, and brutally. As the cow fled, the man violently hurtled his stick towards the poor animal. I stood in stunned disbelief – I considered warning the man that if I ever caught him again, he'd be the next to receive such a beating. But then I'd be watching my back the rest of my time, in an already tense, foreign village.

…

Relations at home gradually, temporarily thawed, lending a warmer domestic environment with Sunny. There was a realistic chance he'd have to stay longer, so we might as well make peace. My insistence upon keeping the kitchen tidy, and a couple of shared cleaning sessions, led to improved habits. I accepted he was who he was.

For Sunny's thirtieth birthday, his Palestinian and Dutch friends baked him a potent hash cake. We visited Viking's Jungle Huts, chomping on magic cake and downing beers with several Lebanese visitors, while beats scattered from portable soundsystems. The inherent heaviness of ingested Indica sapped much of my energy and optimism. Writing and work, I could usually find a way to power through, out of necessity. But whenever I lost motivation for music, I realised I was depressed about something, or was too drained from hash. And, what was the point of anything, anyway?

One Saturday, Sunny invited me to accompany him to Duck & Chill for a casual hangout, but I declined. Instead, for the first instance in three weeks, I had the place to myself. This did wonders for my psyche, and rejuvenated my passion for work, music and life. Irrespective of Magia, relationships or housemates: I needed Sea Time.

410

Feeling sympathy for Sunny's money woes, I crafted him a part time, hour-a-day job. This simple assignment would pay him Rs2000 per week – enough for his food and basic living expenses. The deal was simple: he'd have to emerge from bed before noon each weekday for a work briefing. Tasks were related to research for Deliver.Green – a global legal cannabis directory. Upon the completion of each week's tasks he'd be paid – and the deal would extend another week. Sunny appeared thrilled for the opportunity to earn legitimate cash, particularly from a topic that appealed to him.

The first Monday passed without him waking in time; instead he stumbled out of bed around 1:30pm. I insisted that he'd have to make a better effort – and we agreed on noon Tuesday.

"Knock on my door to wake me up!" Sunny requested.

I shook my head and frowned. "It's not up to me. If you want the job, it's up to you to wake up for it."

On Tuesday, noon passed; he clambered out of bed after 1pm.

"Sleepy! No electricity! No alarm clock was possible!"

"All excuses!" I sighed, balancing tough love and patience.

What more could I do? I'd presented him a useful opportunity to earn much-needed cash, instead of scrounging off friends. He didn't exemplify any of the skills or work ethic I'd typically hire for projects, and I couldn't offer him a glowing reference to my business partners. It was a dead-end situation.

The first week passed, and Sunny sufficiently accomplished his tasks 1 ½ of the 5 days. On top of my other duties, I was now consumed by trying to manage an unmotivated worker, for a role I created as a favour. My decision was aided the following week, when Sunny didn't surface on Monday, or on Tuesday when he stumbled out at 2:30pm. With cautious deliberation, I acted on impulses.

"Mate, it's too late now. This arrangement isn't working. It's finished."

Stunned, he turned around. "Whatever you feel is best," he muttered coldly, before proceeding to rant on the phone. The vibe between us drastically altered. He was no longer patient and polite.

...

As the second month approached, Sunny considered staying longer. I wondered why I was paying 100% of the rent and bills, to support somebody who had no interest in earning their keep. Sunny was a negative energy in many ways – leeching off his naïve German girlfriend, not being the most faithful boyfriend, or ripping off friends for spare cash.

Agonda Beach became increasingly unswimmable. Tides and currents made for difficult wading into the water, before being churned and chucked around by hostile waves. Garbage and slicks of oil drifted to shore from the storms. The rising heat before monsoon was nearly unbearable. For all the earlier optimism, of a dream house on a hill overlooking the sea, it was rapidly unfolding as unenjoyable, pointless exercise. I seriously considered Papa Bolshoi's offer about relocating to the North.

With regular storms rumbling through Agonda, power outages increased in frequency. The biggest blast occurred when lightning struck a nearby house, and the neighbourhood's power shut off. Upon nightfall, Sunny and I visited the house of Saffa, a Palestinian, and Sana, his Dutch girlfriend. They'd been in Agonda for six months, before the added months of lockdown, and Saffa was particularly eager to leave. We ate home-cooked lentil soup, while listening to Indian, Arabic and Pakistani music, curated by Sunny. When we returned home, the power and Internet remained out, up until the following afternoon. Confined to my small, hot room without use of the ceiling fan, I was forced to open my windows. I became a moist and tasty buffet for delighted jungle mosquitoes, but the worst part was the constant high-pitched buzzing.

…

An amazing Saturday night party started innocuously. Initially, it appeared to be little more than a few stoned guys sitting around at Viking's Jungle Huts. This changed upon the arrival of a soundsystem and multiple crates of beer. Slowly, new energies filtered in. Sunny and I erected the solitary loudspeaker. We could only stream online music. Guests included Roma – a vivacious French lady my age, and longtime Goan partier, Moony. There was humble and articulate British Nate, a curvy Canadian named Wendy, and pretty blonde German Pia; each comfortably assimilated into our growing, glowing circle.

Moments after most guests arrived, the flashing red, white and blue lights of a police truck illuminated the road. All of us, other than Viking and a guesthouse resident, ducked through darkness and hid in the jungle. Without my phone or shoes, I scuttled across a small murky bridge, and skulked behind a broad, shadowy banyan tree. The police interaction was brief, and soon their truck rumbled away. This unified the group, and the party was underway.

It was a simple affair; the first party since lockdown began months ago. It didn't matter that there was only a dozen of us, or a solitary speaker streaming pre-played sets, with occasional choppiness or pauses. People were on their best behaviour: humble, engaging and generous. Several danced; others sat on floor mattresses, eagerly chatting. Many mingled near the kitchen, gulping down Roma's homemade mango punch, that was potently laced with a bottle each of dark and white rums.

At sunrise, a large group of survivors trundled up the hill. Through the jungle, we meandered to the south shore of Agonda Beach. Two young puppies who'd been reared by Pia accompanied us, excitedly frolicking with their little legs, cautious and nervous, but asserting admirable bravery. Occasionally, people braved the calm crashing of waves, and entered the coolly-refreshing water. Later, Viking and I entered the sea in our undies.

After a few revitalising hours, the group began splintering away; some headed onward to furthermore afterparties. I braved the long solo walk home, while Sunny cycled ahead on his bicycle. I was overjoyed at the authenticity of togetherness. The captivating evening reiterated that one didn't need heaps of crowds, famous DJs, elaborate soundsystems or big budget facilities to engage in a rocking party. It's all about the people and the vibe.

...

A few evenings later, while I strolled along Agonda Beach on the rainy pre-monsoon day, I passed a pensive Viking, who was facing the waves. At the same time, police gathered around the southern corner of Agonda, gratefully without sticks, where dozens of people congregated near a turbulent cove. Viking and I ducked into nearby Rama Resort for a beer. He was struggling with his own long-distance relationship, with a Tahiti-based European. Lockdown forced the cancellation of his flights to Tahiti. Viking hadn't shared his troubles with anybody for months, and greatly appreciated plunging into deep conversations with an avid listener. We downed a couple of beers, then returned to my apartment, where the power was out. In candlelight, Viking cooked noodles for supper, before a noticeably anxious and subtly-complaining Sunny arrived with a friend. Sunny warbled several bizarre statements, including how much this flat normally cost, "before Sea came". He complained about Internet and electricity bills, that weren't previously requested by the owner, while I regarded it as fairly compensating a single mother of three kids. Why should she pay for our exorbitant Internet or electricity bills? Sunny was particularly stunned when I murmured that I might only stay two more weeks. This would mean that he'd also have to leave.

I was serious: if I didn't have the place to myself for my expected final month in Goa, I'd head elsewhere. I desperately needed space and solace, to figure out my life and next steps, without bad energy cluttering my surroundings. It's strange how unspoken intent often manifests change – so, be careful what we wish for.

The Falling Sun

Another party at Viking's Jungle Huts was scheduled for Thursday night, as a farewell to Viking before he returned home to Delhi. Everybody from last weekend's brilliant party was re-invited. We all knew how wonderful Saturday had been, and hence we held a certain level of expectation. With a realistic chance of hosting an afterparty, Sunny and I scrubbed our home for hours: bathroom, kitchen, balcony, floors, bedrooms. The place had never looked better.

In the early evening, we hastily decorated Viking's property for a bigger party. I spread coconut branches to dim strings of periphery lights. This week featured several DJs bringing their live controllers, including one "top" DJ from the Goan club circuit. The party rocked in terms of music, and there was triple the number of guests. However, while it was chill enough, and felt like a "proper" party, the vibe was less friendly. The same generous and selfless souls from Saturday exhibited traces of ego, and even hostility. With the world under lockdown, and while most of the global population was mortified about straying from social distancing, it was an odd energy: smiles on the surface, despite anguish lurking underneath. Drugs helped stoke this disparity, temporarily enhancing guests' artificial emotions, bracing for the comedown.

A combination of over-strong mango punch and small amounts of party favours ruined me. I was perpetually on the brink of nausea for hours. I remained pensive, and was not in the mood to make mindless conversation. I realised there were few souls here with whom I saw any future connection. Even the prettier females: I wasn't really into them, particularly with Magia still consuming my heart. The transparent unfriendliness of several guests, my stomach's ongoing queasiness, and a gloomy feeling about *something*, prompted my departure. After an hour's walk along the deserted main road, I crashed for several hours.

...

Waking on Friday morning, I felt too fragile to work. I was summoned for a conversation by the property's owner, Betty, who wanted to clarify a few issues. Her eldest daughter occasionally translated. It surfaced that Sunny had been dishonest about rent and bills. He'd separately instructed both Betty and myself to "not discuss money". She cited vague amounts and discrepancies. I informed her what I was paying – it was 100% of the rent she received – and that Sunny had never chipped in for bills. His laziness about changing the Internet plan, as he'd promised, cost us over Rs5000. As Sunny was not contributing much if anything financially, and had seemingly betrayed her trust, Betty would be asking him to vacate.

Despite this reasonable means of ensuring my own place, I felt absolutely zero joy at prospectively forcing anybody onto the street. I felt Sunny and I had come a long way; after bonding at the party I was proud he was my housemate. If he didn't have anywhere to go, I'd cover his rent, or I'd move out myself. Fortunately, Sunny had a standing offer to stay for free at Galaxy Jungle Huts. His plan was to return to his mother's home in

Kolkatta, although the region's recent cyclone and COVID-19 red zone didn't presently make Kolkatta safe or appealing. I didn't want to break the news to him immediately, and Sunny wasn't home yet anyway. Betty was insistent on a three-way meeting. When Sunny eventually returned from the party, worn out and coming down, I let him sleep, and we'd chat tomorrow.

...

The stress of the following morning ruined my typically serene and creative Saturday. I couldn't lock into focus with this unresolved situation. At 11:30am, Betty and her family waited patiently from the back garden. On their insistence, I begrudgingly knocked on Sunny's bedroom door a few times, before he finally ventured out.

"They can wait," was Sunny's first mistaken comment. "I'm going to make some tea first."

Following months of repressed frustrations, I erupted.

"Motherfucker! We have been waiting for you. Now!"

This hardly improved the vibe, and Sunny was tense and defensive from the outset. He casually clambered to the balcony, while the family watched from downstairs. I joined them outside. This supposed three-way conversation was nothing of the sort, as Sunny railed away non-stop in Hindi, jabbering and pleading incessantly. I waited with hand-written notes and questions on a scrap of cardboard, seeking to determine whether he'd misappropriated money, or perhaps there was a mistake in calculations.

At some point during Sunny's tirade, I finally lost patience.

"Sunny!" I yelled, to cease his rambling. "Be quiet!"

"You be quiet, Sea! This is between me and Betty."

"What? This concerns me too!" And, after he ignored me, I lost it further, screaming and yelling back up at him. "Shut up!"

"You shut up, Sea!" as Sunny turned to the family. "Sea is a former homeless person!" He sneered insultingly. The irony, was that now he was homeless.

Betty urged me to calm down, as she'd witnessed enough to make her decision. Despite his idle threats about informing the police, Sunny was requested to vacate, by a week from today.

...

Around the same time, Papa Bolshoi reiterated an invitation to visit his three-bedroom jungle house near Arambol. This made for a tempting prospect of change. The Agonda house was becoming an unnecessary stress and money pit, however lovely it was. The balcony view of the ocean would soon be covered by plastic, ahead of monsoon. What might the north of Goa offer?

A stormy Friday morning of neither power nor Internet ensured that I couldn't reach Ganesh, the driver dispatched to fetch me. Ganesh didn't know directions beyond my address, that wasn't findable on any map app. At 11am, I concernedly gathered my small backpack and headed towards the main road. All of the street's power was out. I stepped inside a stationary shop, seeking pens and a small notebook. The clerk graciously offered her phone as a hotspot; pinpointing my location enabled Ganesh to arrive in his car within minutes.

Ganesh was a well-spoken, switched-on young gentleman. We excitedly zipped along empty tropical highways and picturesque locales. While conversation was upbeat and intelligent, a sickening downer came when we passed a dead body, that lay beside a wrecked scooter, along the main road after the bridge from south to north. Her corpse lay with a large gash in her leg, and her face was covered by a small towel. Dozens of masked police and onlookers milled around. Ganesh and I didn't talk much after that.

The taxi crossed into familiar territory. I noticed that most of Mandrem's beach had washed away from storms, and a wild sea raged at higher tides. We arrived in an outer part of Arambol. I greeted Papa with a hearty handshake, while Ganesh prepared tasty egg rolls. Over our first of many chais, we chatted about the wider implications of global and local lockdowns, superpower geopolitics and mass-surveillance. My mind was blown about the state of the world, from the unique perspective of a Russian who was born into the KGB. I learned about Japan's possible influence on present-day events. We discussed the blatant, widespread anti-China campaign, not helped by the Chinese's predictably awkward and uncool reactions. America and its allies were always miles ahead.

The main impetus behind my Arambol visit was to gauge mutual interest in Papa's intriguing project: Nameless.

Subprojects or "tables" – whether media, arts, shops or social programmes – would share resources and revenues between participants. Nameless members were granted access to the group's collective assets, such as motorbikes, fancy cars, yachts and houses. Vast excursions to sensational global spots were proposed. This certainly made for an appealing, mind-opening proposition; albeit a drastic lifestyle shift. Papa held a bold and often ambiguous vision, that left many details unanswered. He originally needed my help with blog editing, masterminding blockchain strategies, and general counsel. He saw something else in me, but I wasn't sure precisely what.

During a break, we drove to Mandrem for simple grocery shopping. Unlike in the stricter south, north Goa locals didn't tolerate police or government meddling. Countless foreigners rode on bikes and wandered about their days. Other than a few masks, Arambol and Mandrem appeared normal. Papa had frequently urged me to experience the "freedom" of the north, and now I understood. With ongoing hassles at the house in Agonda, largely from Sunny's lazy and dishonest energy, it opened my mind to change.

...

The energy at the Agonda house instantly improved upon Sunny's departure. The broken fridge started working, occasionally. Vivid dreams became nightly and regular, albeit flashbacks to my earlier eras, such as baseball, certain tall brunette model friends, and other moments from my long-ago Melbourne days. It felt like I'd wasted time, and reiterated that life was extraordinarily short.

Sunny had emptied the house of all kitchenware; the upside was, by searching for new items, it had the pleasant aura of moving into my own place. I acquired an electric kettle, cutting board, a large and small knife, two forks, a spoon, frying pan, cooking pot, drinking glass and two pretty teacups. Furthering this liberating freshness, was relocating from the small, urine-smelling bedroom with an undersized bed, into the lush master bedroom. The bigger room afforded its own square balcony, and two walls of airy windows meant waking up each morning surrounded by trees and sky. My dreams and sleep further improved, particularly now that my feet fit on the bed.

Much of the first week was spent cleaning up Sunny's messes
literally and figuratively. The kitchen was a disaster; I removed
maggots and scrubbed every surface. Sunny's stale, smoky
bedroom had seemingly never been scrubbed. The fridge had
blown during a lightning storm and cost Rs3,500 to repair. I
wasted countless days of time and energy arguing with
frustrating, service-disoriented Internet provider BSNL, about
our insane Rs5000 Internet bill. I discovered that most of
charges had been accrued before I even moved in: meaning they
were Sunny's. BSNL teased us; they occasionally cut off the
Internet, thwarting my necessary work. My sentiments about
remaining in Agonda bounced around like a trampoline;
whenever the Internet reliably worked, I felt comfortable about
extending my stay.

I was offline most of the week and all of the weekend. By
Sunday afternoon, unable to bear the inability to update friends
and clients, I zipped around the ghost town of Agonda. Nowhere
I'd previously used wifi was open: not a signal anywhere. Tar-
smeared sands and bored dogs greeted me during a short stroll
on the beach. Heading north along the beachside road, I sidled
up to Cupid's Guesthouse. Their manager kindly allowed me use
of their wifi, and one man graciously fetched me a beer. After
apologising profusely to clients, I sent Sunny a message about
how his Internet bill had gravely inconvenienced me.

"I'm very sorry, Sea," Sunny replied. He promised he would
repay me, something.

Tuesday was also the day of the most torrential rain so far:
non-stop downpour, with floodwater accumulating around
neighbours' houses and nearby backstreets. Ferocious storms
lashed at the coast, while howling winds ripped against the
building. In the wake of the cyclonic storms, I couldn't visit the
ATM, pay the Internet bill or fetch vegetables from the market. I
sat and deliberated. How many more signs did I need to make
the bold move to depart for greener pastures? I was far too
worried about other people: for instance, the single mother
downstairs who relied on rental income. My whole life I'd tried
to appease others by staying silent, and tolerate their grief, at
my detriment. With Sunny, I reacted with patience and
tolerance. But, where do we draw the line of compassion?

A few days later, I was randomly in the centre of Agonda, stopping at the ATM. Sunny motored by on a scooter; he paused to stare at me, and considered his options. Then, he ignored me, and briskly pulled away. I never heard from him again.

The Question of Magia

The day I was preparing to inform Betty that I was leaving in two weeks, her kids summoned me from downstairs.

"Sea! Hello? Hello?" I thought they'd ask about my rent. Miraculously, they presented several containers filled with food. "Today is our little sister's birthday! We wanted you to have this."

This unexpected generosity touched me profoundly. The chicken curry with rice and noodles, and large home-baked brownies, were sumptuous. The gesture prompted renewing my tenure at the Agonda House for another month. After I sorted Sunny's hefty Internet bill, we cancelled BSNL and sourced a more reliable provider.

With the house decision confirmed, I made a first attempt at rebooking flights to Europe. I submitted a form through LOT Polish Airways to reschedule my original Delhi to Krakow flight, for Friday July 17. This was clearly predictive, as international flights remained suspended in India and Europe. Poland was closed to outsiders altogether, prompting widespread criticisms of the country that, like Hungary, Poland was reverting to dictatorial or communist control. Optimistic conversations with Magia reassured a mutual commitment to making the relationship work, whatever our doubts about its long-term chances. We felt unified as best friends and confidants.

...

I celebrated my 43rd birthday over a low-key dinner at Mickey's restaurant, on Patnem Beach. A large storm brewed, and the power shut off for the night – courtesy of a fallen coconut tree. While sitting in candle-flickered darkness, my sole guest arrived: Sasha, the Canadian girlfriend of Dan the Irish. I was thrilled that anybody came. I enjoyed a birthday dinner of paneer tikka masala, rice and beer. Sasha and I were the only customers the entire night. At around 11pm, Mickey's staff clearly wanted to leave. During a slight break in the downpour, a helpful man escorted us with an umbrella to our scooters. I briskly changed into my waterproof jacket and pants.

The tall man urged me: "Drive slow and carefully. Be aware of cows sleeping on the road."

Riding a scooter through torrential monsoon lightning storms was riveting. The raincoat kept me adequately protected, while I whisked on my scooter at a moderate pace. The epically-stunning highlight came under falling monsoon rain, amidst trees and mountains of paradise, when a herd of majestic grey water buffalo stood on the road, basking in the rain.

...

My routine, during unrelenting monsoon storms and lockdown realities, was simple and straightforward. I revelled in months of extended Sea Time, with few plans and no distractions. Each morning I woke from dreams, straight into meditation. I wrote over fruit, muesli and coffee, before coming online and diving into regular work – mostly helping Memtell. Some afternoons I'd ride the scooter through the jungle, to load up on supplies from shops, or brave the busier road to Chaudi market. With breaks in the rain, I'd reach Agonda or Patnem's mostly-deserted beaches, for a glimpse at grey, stormy seas. Sometimes Little Tofu and Scarpetta greeted me, but Van Halen had a big welt in his head, and followed other dogs around.

Evenings and weekends were all about music. I locked into studying music production, and practiced with varying concepts. I crafted several intricate tracks, releasing a few songs globally on major services. To take breaks from music, I cooked elaborate dinners – either pesto gnocchis or spicy paneer.

I accomplished all of this for months without smoking any weed. I did engage in a month's LSD microdose experiment. Around once a week I bought a bottle of red wine. There was an absence of social life – none of the people I knew in the area were particularly outgoing or friendly. Whatever occasional plans I made, others postponed. This was a time for solitude, and for concentrating on the self.

...

Despite occasional bouts of positivity, Magia's sentiments, moods and messages remained mixed, lost and occasionally grim. We both felt in perpetual limbo. When international flights resumed, I hoped to take the earliest available plane to Poland, although I might have to wait in Cologne or Berlin until entering Poland was possible. Our phone conversations were becoming a weekly habit. Magia's aspiration was to ride across Poland on one of her brother's custom-made eBikes, and camp at outdoor music festivals. I wholly encouraged her to pursue all dreams of adventures, festivals, and whatever necessary experiences she derived from them. I was very proud of her.

Tuesday June 30 marked the day of India's international flights announcements. India and China were physically at war, with fatal skirmishes near the northern Himalayan border. During a call with Magia, I confirmed that flights would not be resuming soon. When I mentioned being lonely and bored in deserted Agonda, and was considering moving north to Arambol, Magia became defensive. I asked her directly about specific festival dates for August. I'd be wholly pleased to bunk down in Zielonki, look after the cats and assemble my music studio, while she travelled. Magia hesitated, mirroring her recent non-committal answers about the topic.

"I plan to leave at the end of July, and I'll probably be away all of August," Magia said softly. An alarm in my brain sounded.

"Who will look after the cats?"

"Meehow and Miss Igga," Magia replied, and it clicked for me.

"It sounds like I don't have a home to come back to. Is this correct?" There was a long, contemplative moment of silence. I took a long breath. "I think it's time to end this relationship."

Magia paused, then calmly launched into her spiel.

"Look, we're friends, that's it, and it's fine. I want to be loved in a different way. I want to be the Boogie for somebody else, like she was to you. Exciting! Passionate!"

I didn't even feel like a friend to Magia at this point. Magia craved festivals, psychedelic experiences and romantic flings, while I was locked in a foreign land, that was at war with the planet's rising superpower. I'd been waiting to return to what I thought was home – our home.

"Of all the things in your life," she continued. "I'm down the list. Your music, your work, your travel... I'm down around number five. I want to be the most important thing to somebody."

Magia elaborated, cooly and clearly, in the confident voice and neutral tone that I admired about her. She reiterated her belief that I was still in love with The Past, even though it no longer felt true. She repeated that I was attracted to other women, that I wasn't planning to stay in Zielonki for long anyway, and that I didn't see a future with her. Admittedly, she hit a raw nerve with some truth behind her words. After Magia paraphrased numerous false concepts, as if they were my sentiments, my patience expired.

"Shut up!" I swore, at full velocity. "Stop telling me what I think about anything! You don't know how I feel! You are stuck in the past. The same old arguments. Your jealousy is out of control!"

With a yell, I forcibly hung up the phone. I had a fleeting thought about chucking it. I was devastated that Magia underestimated my love and commitment to her. Remorse hit me when I realised that might be the last time I'd hear Magia's voice. I certainly didn't want to hurt her. As my anger subsided, sadness filled my soul.

I dispatched Magia two messages over the remainder of the evening. One was short and sweet. The next was more detailed. I defended myself, and inquired if I was being treated like a friend. Both of my messages apologised for yelling, and reiterated the same theme:

"Good luck in life, love and new adventures."
Once again, I was on my own. Everywhere, and anyone, was possible. For Magia, and for me.

Chapter 23
Preparing for Sea Change

By now, you should have an intimate sense of my actual life, at least over these past three-plus years of travels. But what were my alternative, quantum life possibilities? This story could have led anywhere – and, I suppose, it did. I couldn't quite imagine that by the end of this book I'd be locked down in Goa – or any place, stranded in infinite limbo. The world in its present abject state, was far less of a surprise.

Let's hypothesise that South Korea never happened – perhaps I was unable to manifest the possibility, or the invitation never arrived. I'd have missed out on some of the most powerful times of my life. Not only the magic of Jeju, but also the soul-affirming journey that followed: through South East Asia, India, Vipassana, Berlin, Poland and Goa. I likely wouldn't have met Magia or many other incredible people; granted, I'd have ventured to alternate places, and encountered entirely different spirits.

Inarguably, there have been sacrifices. Quitting my Melbourne high school softball coaching job of eight years, was one that seemed huge at the time, but I accepted as necessary, and soon felt no regrets. I've lost touch with plentiful friendships and social circles. When we're not regularly around in people's lives, particularly those who are resigned to a static location in the monotony of The System, we drift away. Other travellers can wholly sympathise. Like us, they come and go, sometimes to cross paths again; but, usually not.

Change involves sacrifice, at least a little anguish, and waves of second-guessing. Sure, it can be scary to imagine the unknown: that murky nothingness, compared against the comforts with which we're familiar. Yet – whatever our circumstances – we'll always find a way to survive. When we're down and out, even at the last moment: a portal appears.

Waking up the first morning after any major shift can be highly disorienting. Dreams thin out into shards of sunlight; we yawn out of grog, and wipe our eyes into the present: *Where am I?* Then we remember yesterday's hectic move, surge with adrenaline about the day ahead, or drown in another sobering hangover from The Past. Wherever we came from, involved at least a handful of goodbyes – some, for the final time. There are new horizons to explore. We can look forward, more than behind. There is little we can do about the past, other than learn from it, and honour its memories and legacies through our future actions.

The longer we're alive, the better one realises how entirely short life is, and how much more rapidly time seems to pass. The journey is not the destination. The future is not assured. We must make the most of our time.

Living Dreams of the Sea

If I'd penned out everything I sought from life, today I seem to just about have it all. I'm in the tropics, surrounded by nature, a stroll away from the beach and sea. The temperature fluctuates in the realm of mid-to-high twenty degrees Celsius. I feel the pure love of a carefree puppy and kitty, as well as from a sizeable posse of neighbouring street dogs. My diet is ripe with fresh organic fruit and vegetables, sourced from nearby markets, while I linger somewhere in between vegan and vegetarian. Coconut trees grow in abundance; I prepare my own beloved coconut milk. I'm blessed with affection and companionship. The area brims with creative people and inspired projects, within a safe, upbeat bubble, while the outer world recovers from this year's chaos. I've been freed of my mundane corporate chores and most of my web work responsibilities. I can now fully focus on my passions. How could life get any better?

Yet, even after three years of exponential growth, I still don't have the answers to everything. I've not solved my anger and rage, or why I habitually, self-destructively push people away, even those trying to help or love me. I wish I could be a friendlier and happier person to those around, and to myself.

Enlightenment is a quest that lasts through our journeys to the end. The solutions may come at a later time, or perhaps they won't at all. But, we must keep working at things.

...

I blissfully remained at the Agonda house through July. My days encompassed sunrise wake-ups, meditation, writing, tropical scooter adventures during monsoon breaks, the big loyal dog (and the furry friend he constantly invited over for dinner!), and producing music into the night, interspersed with cooking and movie breaks. I so greatly enjoyed my productive and distraction-free routine, that it was difficult to pack and leave. With monsoon closer to ceasing, decadent weather was approaching. I'd soon be able to stroll to the shore, and swim in heavenly, warm sea; reunite with Lil Tofu, and write from chilled-out cafes.

However, as days dragged on, it felt like the right moment for change. Agonda was too quiet and lonely, and exciting new opportunities were brewing elsewhere. It's not like where I was heading was any less special – just more of an unknown.

Around midday on Saturday, August 1, 2020, my evacuation crew rolled up to the Agonda house. Ganesh was driving; a shaved-headed, muscular Russian named Dmitri sat in the front, and Papa Bolshoi rolled joints from the back seat. I bid farewell to Betty and her family, bundled my minimal bags and a box of kitchen supplies into the awaiting white car, and we rumbled north along the jungle road.

Upon arriving in Arambol, I was greeted by the bum-waggling of Chapa: the lovably-excitable resident puppy. I was granted a double bedroom, that had a desk and a small ground-level, Portuguese-style balcony. The single-floor house was in the middle of the jungle, beside a small river that flowed from the mountains. A big green gate led to one of Arambol's main roads, near the petrol station, market junction and ATM. Reaching the beach mandated a five-minute scooter ride, or a twenty-minute shortcut walk through nature.

Papa and I chatted over chillums and coffee. The handsome young live-in housekeeper, Sonu, arrived home with a bag of groceries, often playing with the animals. Kitu – the ginger-white kitten survivor – playfully taunted Chapa, distracting the puppy from chewing Sonu's shoe. Sometimes a Russian named Killer visited. He was a fighter and martial arts practitioner. Last year, Killer ran into bad luck with Goan police, and his life had suffered for it. Otherwise, he was a cool and caring guy.

As monsoon rumbled away, Nameless invested in professional gear, and we began assembling a music studio. I purchased an acoustic guitar, and started practicing regularly for the first time in years. There was a modern Pioneer DJ setup, with large club-grade speakers. Plans were to build a small geodesic dome on the house's roof, and convert it into a shanti chillout space. A projector and screen made for vibrant movies. An old fishing boat and several kayaks were available for expeditions along Chapora River. My rent, activities, and transportation – like the scooter – were covered, in exchange for my ongoing assistance of Nameless projects.

Arambol oozed vibe, that had been completely lacking in the south. Musicians, artists and writers complemented stranded visitors, many of whom had come to Goa for a couple of weeks holiday, before being indefinitely stranded in paradise. Arambol's most popular establishment was Cafe Food Planet, who opened its doors during lockdown and built up much goodwill. Food Planet was a daily hangout and meeting spot for sunsets, and the adjacent calm, clean sea made for scintillatingly refreshing swimming. Elsewhere, little cafes served homemade coconut milk coffee and exquisite vegan cakes, and the aroma of spices was abundant around dozens of Indian restaurants. This Is It slowly shook off its monsoon dust, and prepared for an inevitably challenging season ahead.

The global crisis lowered expectations for almost everybody, that lent a further serene atmosphere. People worked together and tried to make the most out of today's actualities. Many travellers had to stay put for a while, encouraging the building of more meaningful relationships. It was time for creative solutions to common problems, and to focus on more worthwhile aspects of life.

...

On the work front, I turned down several opportunities, preferring to keep my schedule as open as possible. There was one point where I was managing somebody's WordPress blog, building a tricky online shop, resurrecting a hosting brand, blueprinting a co-living and co-working hotel, blossoming a demanding new relationship, and sinking deeper into becoming a director in a new corporation. I had to stop myself. *What was I doing?* I hadn't spent years distancing myself from these unwanted elements, to suddenly regurgitate them in different forms. Instead of fully focusing on music, I'd again be stressing about needing to earn money from things that I didn't really want to do.

Up until November I continued to perform odd jobs for Memtell, on a month-by-month consultancy basis. The company's once-vast investment funds were rapidly drained by over-costly app development. For months I acknowledged that I could lose the contract – and my only source of income – at any time. Jono often looked like a bedraggled mess, spending long hours, seven days a week, under fire to generate huge sales on the cusp of a global economic meltdown. He struggled to manage his first major tech project, with team members spread across continents, high-level German investors, and the moral conflict of environmentalism versus mass-printing.

"Sea, you've seen Memtell grow from the beginning," Jono told me during one of our video conferences. "You've been a big part of it. I'm very grateful, in this chaotic time of the world, and with people everywhere losing their jobs and livelihoods, that I'm blessed with this opportunity. I'm living my dream, Sea."

For me, the very notion of developing and supporting old-era web apps, on top of massive, daily money stress and dreary corporate consequences, seemed more like a nightmare. It was a reminder to be careful what we dream for: there's always another side we can't quite imagine. It's like aspiring for a professional music or movie career, yet at the time we can't fathom the life-changing demands and deadly repercussions of fame and fortune. Still, I was greatly appreciative to Jono for finding a role for me during tough times, and I'll help him as he needs, when the time is right.

Even though I lost my only income stream, I was relieved. For at least a few months, I could live off my first-ever savings. In the coming season, I could dedicate full-time headspace to my music. I could begin crafting my film, *The Dogs Live On*. I'd find a way to sell books if I needed cash, and use my skills and experience to consult others. Somehow, I'd find a way to survive, again.

...

In the months since our split, Magia and I remained close friends, despite occasional challenges. Over the summer, Magia delightedly fulfilled her dreams of solo journeys, travelling around festivals throughout Poland (life surprisingly went on mostly as normal in Poland despite global and local paranoia). Following one festival, she lived in a teepee in the Polish mountains, while conducting workshops for Dobra Atmosfera ("good energy"). Magia and her crew began planning a festival for next year around Dobra Atmosfera's altruistic theme.

She moved on in some ways, with hints in photos and messages about other guys. Yet, I felt no twinges of jealousy. There's a reassuring power in my heart, and an overwhelming sense of pride I have for her, that is difficult to explain. What most pleased me was seeing her smiling face: She looked happy, refreshed and excited. This exemplified "true love", for the growth of the other person – with or without me.

Sure, I missed her. Of any part of my history I'd most wish to loop for eternity, I'd choose Zielonki with Magia. I loved our routine: Czupur, Xara, buckets of coffee, meditation, writing, music, gospoda lunches, national park treks, road trips, concerts, cuddles, lolec and honey beer. It was the greatest, most loving home I'd known, and what I miss the most since being stranded on my own. I was irrefutably blessed to share an extended sliver of this existence with her. Our experiences will live with me, in my heart and soul, until the day I die. For that, I will always love Magia.

Life is Short; Mending Bridges

I've never recalled life passing so quickly. Elders and family often exclaim: "Wait until you get older!" I'd observed this about routine: the more we manifest formulaic, even mundane consistency, the faster life and time seemingly pass by. Yet we can travel for three months, with every day different, full and exciting, and it feels like forever.

I've looked back to where I was ten years ago, and wonder what the coming decade will bring. I look further back to twenty years earlier, when I was emerging out of homelessness, and rebuilt myself as "Sea". This spanned epic years in Toronto through Melbourne, then major world trips for seven years and counting. Yet, much of it now seems like misspent energy. Twenty years from now I'll be in my sixties. This is a very limited window, within which to accomplish most I've ever set out to do. That's why it's time to progress my lifelong musical aspirations, and start thinking about a longterm home.

Life is particularly too short to waste on battling differences with other people, especially if they were once dear to us. Sure, space is essential, and sometimes we need years of time apart. There are some people that I'm not quite ready to embrace again, and maybe I won't ever be.

Everybody I've ever encountered has influenced my cumulative, present state of learnedness and being. The antagonists I may have despised at the time, still had a profound effect on me, just as those who supported me and patiently took me under their wings. *Everything and everyone is a lesson.*

Think back to your past: of all the far-distant souls, who once meant so much. Are there any to whom it might be time to reach out? A short, well-written, positive letter can be a wonderful surprise. There's a supreme chance that, from time to time over the years, they've similarly wondered about us. Perhaps they've harboured misgivings, and maybe it was over something we had no idea about. Opening the bridge of communication lifts a weight from our shoulders, and is one less piece of baggage we carry forward. Sometimes it can wholly rejuvenate old friendships. At very least, we come to peace with the past. And, it feels nice.

Time heals wounds. Through emanating understanding and compassion, forgive the distant past, if it's at all possible. Reach out to somebody who meant something, while any chance remains in this lifetime.

Quantum Imagination

We now know that everything is possible. Every little decision impacts our future: of who'll we meet, new opportunities, and even life or death itself. We can listen to premonition, or follow clues presented by unspoken powers, or decide to ignore everything altogether. This is our freedom to choose.

Maybe we resolve to change ourselves, through better health and meditation. Or we muster the courage to say sorry, embrace the love and the gifts we have, and try to be happy. Each and every decision shapes our future. But, whatever we choose, we must stand behind it, and move on. There will be plenty more decisions to come.

Plan Sea begins and ends by exploring the quantum possibilities of everything, and how any singularly-altered decision can lead us to other dimensions. Life is full of "what if's". One microsecond's difference in departure can determine whether or not we cross paths with somebody, or narrowly avoid disaster. Choices of where to go, eat, chill or party, can alter everything.

Let's reconsider how this book – and my life – could have changed, had I made different choices, or avoided them altogether. Some for better or for worse.

...

Imagine I didn't smoke my final joint, before a last lap around the quarry at Borderland; instead, I responsibly crashed in my tent. I'd never have met Boogie. Korea wouldn't have happened. It's possible I never wrote this book or learned Vipassana. Yet, magic still likely would have transpired at Borderland's Lighthouse afterparty. Where would I have headed after India?

...

What if Boogie and I had caught our original flight on Jeju Island, after the wild mushroom night on Mount Sanbangsan, or if I'd left in an emotional huff during intense times in Seoul? I'd likely have returned, defeated, to Melbourne.

...

What if I never took a Vipassana course? Perhaps the universe would have run out of patience with me, despite its many warnings and clues.

...

I made peace with Shami, and remained at Sandino in Berlin for the remainder of the 2018 summer. There was no Baltic Trip. I never met Magia, Czupur or Xara. I over-indulged in a wonderful weekend in Hamburg for David August, before returning to Sandino's end-of-summer party the following week. What next?

...

Had I not sculpted the Baltic Trip precisely in its actuality, slicing through Krakow at the start of that particular weekend, or if the Tinder algorithm changed, would I have met Magia? Would I have been part of Nameless? Probably not: I met Papa Bolshoi, who crafted my rescue mission from Agonda, through her.

...

What if I didn't make peace with Magia after being homeless in Berlin? I'd still have attended Avant Art in Warsaw, and likely chatted with Aisha Devi, who might be a friend by now. I'd stay with Flowa in Berlin afterward, then reach Amsterdam for Bonobo and David August. A few weeks later I planned to head to India. A six-month visa visit in India from October would have taken me through the end of March, when lockdown began. Same same, but different.

...

In September 2020, feeling a need to vacate India, I flew to Berlin and resided in the spare room at Flowa's flat. I progressed my music: I recorded an album and recruited a band. I enjoyed some of the naughtier pleasures of Berlin. One weekend I returned to Kit Kat Club, where all my inhibitions were swept away. My proximity to Krakow improved my friendship with Magia, while Memtell stepped up its role for me in Cologne.

...

From Goa (or Berlin), I flew to Portugal, initially sleeping on Heidi Heart's couch. Within a few weeks I mustered up funds for a cheap van, and together we travelled the coast. Heidi conducted sound healing to captive clients, while I studied organically ambient music, specifically the frequencies and tones of our planet, Moon and stars. After an intense and wholly satisfying time together, eventually us two space travellers resumed our solo travels through the universe.

Aftcr landing in Praguo, wo were transported to a glorious estate in the forest. Once all the Nameless crew arrived, we rode motorbikes and sports cars south through Italy, arriving at Sardinia for several refreshing weeks, residing in big houses by a beach. We filmed water sports for the blog, and reasserted old-school human connections around campfires. Collectively, our skills helped produce movies, boutiques, a music label and continental distribution networks for monoatomic gold.

Back in May 2017, depressed, anguished and broken in my humble bungalow in Melbourne's Brunswick West, what if I made the responsible decision to cancel my travel plans? I couldn't afford five weeks through Europe. Even though home wasn't the happiest or most supportive place – in large part to my moods – it was still home. I'd have picked up whatever web work I could find, including WordPress sites and low budget web maintenance jobs. I'd take on all the extra coaching and umpiring work available. I'd have drifted into new social circles.

Without the courage to change, I would be strictly locked down in Melbourne today. I didn't make a move, despite years of nagging and warnings. Stuck in the same old rut, and now trapped in a place I didn't want to be, under a worsening draconian government.

From the driver's seat, I peered around the coastline, agape at the sea and the surrounding mountains. *What an incredible week!* From the back, the puppy and kitten frolicked playfully, spilling sand across the floor; soon they'd doze for hours. The music equipment, having being recorded for the better part of days, was responsibly covered up.

The passenger door opened. Her eyes beamed from behind her colourful, round sunglasses.

"Are you ready?" I asked, dusting the sand off my shorts.

Our next destination was to find some land. I'd finally saved enough to afford something modest, and I'd uncovered plentiful hidden gems in nature that could be acquired for a bargain. We had enough wooden poles to craft a modest geodesic dome, to start. It was time to build a home.

"Ready!" she grinned. The door banged shut behind her.

Shifting into gear, our van pulled away from the coastline, and trundled towards the mountain road. The deep greens of trees waved in the wind, as an orange peel and violet crumble scraped across the sky. The red Sun fell into the backdrop of the horizon, greeting the evening's silver Moon, and both reflected upon the calm and spirited Sea.

...

If you had a crystal ball, what scenario would you choose for me? All of them were, or are, possible. At least one of them appears to be underway. Most would trigger a chain reaction of riveting new experiences, that would head in unforeseen directions. Yet, I wouldn't trade any of these for the path that I remain upon today.

And what path is that? Where am I heading next? What awaits me, after considerable time locked down in Goa? Visiting my mother and friends in Toronto? A return to Europe or Malawi? A smiling Magia in her Zielonki living room, with her two fluffy cats, a life of home and a reasonably stable future? Full focus on my music and art, irrespective of the struggle? A big opportunity related to my passions, that unwittingly emerges?Might I cross paths with another compatible soul, and fall deeply together into invigorating new adventures? Head overseas, into the unknown, with little money and no prospects, but open to any possibility? The mountains? The sea? Van Sea?

Now that we've come to the end of Plan Sea, I'll leave that up your imagination. Anything and everything is possible – in my life, and in yours.

Sea and Chapa, Arambol Beach, September 2020 (Photo by Sonu Kumar)

Gratitude

Special Thanks & Acknowledgements

Plan Sea wouldn't have been possible, if not for a lengthy succession of people along the way. Here's a partial list.

To my Family: Janice, Euan, Shannon, Sophie, Kathryn, uncles and aunties, Laura B and Becca. RIP Nanny & Grandpa Bernard. RIP Majerle, and all the dogs who live on

Very special thanks to my Zielonki Family: Magdalena Dziewic (Magia), Czupur, Xara, Panda and the Dziewic family

Editing help: Andrew Bock, Malina Douglas, Sarat Rao, Karen A.

Mother.Domains: Dougie Bell, Greg Bowering, Faren Harcourt

The NoName Family: Papach, Gauresh, Abhishek, Noriko, Buji, Sonu, Chapa, Kitu, and the extended Chapa street dog family

My Goa friends and crew: Brown Coconut, Linda, Dharmesh, Shekhar, This Is It, Amadis, Veronica and family, Kitty Masala, Kayzen, Sriram, Laxmi, Maria, Oscar, Danielle Pettee, Imogen, Naseer & LayerCake

Goa Roadhouse Crew: Jennifer, Adele, Kinjal, Pavitra, Ash, Kevin Gauge, Constantine

India: Aswin & Sree Mohanan, Nalin Savara, Navaneeth, Manmeet, Navn, Govind, GameX cricket team, Pratik, Joxy, BlogX, Noopur, Krinal, Sagar, Baba, Jai, DomainX

Auroville: Samata, Min, Delphine, Laurie, African Pavilion, Khrishna, Aurelio, Marc's Cafe, RIP Tofu

The Sandino crew: Micha, Claire, Jack, Emily, Roxanne & Maxine, Jonathan, Carsten, Pedro, Brian, Thijs

European friends: Tom Allen, Peter Czech, Jono & Miri, Laura (Aura), Flowa, Dani "Andi", Mashface, Spikey Tee, Wiki & Anna, Michael Woodman & Karen Powell, Yasmine Ameen, Bella Alta, Camilla & Sander, Annalou Oakland, Corinne "Cora", Jan Klima, Lenka, Daniel & Magdalena II, Cansu, Rachel Zhang, Laura Stra., MZ Wood, Chris Yardley, Dane & Kasia, Heinrich, Beth J, Tiago, Joao, Collaborate Krakow, Harrold, Andy Weisner, Camilla

Canadian / US friends and crew: Jim Goodale, Jess VanDusen, Martin Tan, Evren & Courteney, Marc & Hillary, Tim Vant, Dave McKay, Ana K, Dodd, Dim Borisov, Liz & Lesley, Don "Dawn", Julia & John Dimon, Kaylee, Ian B, Tony Baglino

Australian/NZ friends and crew: J-Man & Hannah, Bec & Jess Barnett, Shanks, Cassie, Ash Lar, Danny Silver, Harry Gill, Nicole, Lolly Belle, Lizette, Rob Sheather, Chris Mitchell (& family), Josh, Garrath Holt, Barry McCabe, Luke McD, Lady Erica, Jeff Halls, Kaye & Jimmy, Alex Schoeffel, Dan Eakin, Jason Snake Catcher, Jolz, Nik G, Al M, Adam Rap, Underdogs, J-Red, Katie Valentine, Jon Yau, Ladybug, Lisa Unicorn, Dr. Love, Will Wilde, Alfred Pek, Ailish, Maddock, Rachel B, Susie Norton, Eric Dorien, Jedgie, Tolli, Sage, Hegg, Alicia B, Alex V, Erin R, Jeremy Rice, Class A, Ben, Kjetil, Arty, Lumi, St. Kilda Baseball, Melb. Softball, Shelford, Bill & Gracia Wood, GentleFox, Adrienne Elks, Simone

Asia crew: Jason Vandal, Masia "One" Lim, Skinny Rogers, Joachin, RunCloud, Rajendra, Korean Tongyeong Family, Jeff Cenedella, Mark Dake, Dustin's, UWC SEA

African friends and crew: Henly (Kingfisher), Vincent/s, Winnie, Ben Schoeman, Tim Doyle, Nola S., Kyran, Wandile, Kaytee B

Goenka for giving hope to humanity through passing down Vipassana Buddha-Dhamma

And to the one who taught me that Thanks were unnecessary – that they should be felt, and hence could remain unspoken. Thank you for the incredible memories I forever hold dear to my heart. This story wouldn't have happened without you. ♥

Coming Soon
Other SEA projects and creations

THE DOGS LIVE ON (2030)

The sequel to *Onward Muttford* (1996) in immersive cinematic form, with certain shows complemented by a live orchestra. Set in a realistic dystopian future, the wasteland of the world is little more than a totalitarian playground for the rich and privileged. Meanwhile, utopian city-societies stealthily emerge in Antarctica.
https://thedogsliveon.com

NOBODY'S FRIEND (WORKING TITLE)

While Sea lived on the streets of Ontario from 1998-1999, he wrote about all of his experiences. His book – and computer backups – were stolen, and the writing was lost forever. One day, with the time and resources to revisit this era, the aim is to recreate this harsh but inspiring tale of survival and hope.

ANIMISM

Sea's underground music producer alias. Cinematic, orchestral, downtempo, atmospheric, jungle, world music, experimental, ambient, electronica and more. Album and live show to come.
https://animism.live / @animismworld

SUN MOON SEA

Global, non-profit peace orchestra striving to unite and inspire humanity in conflict and historical regions across the planet.
https://sunmoonsea.org

KINGFISHER MALAWI

Kingfisher is a campsite for volunteer teachers on the shores of stunning Lake Malawi, southern Africa. The project teaches local kids, sustains orphans, and builds schools. Contributions help buy bricks, school supplies and orphans' food / education.
https://kingfisher-sekanawo.net/

Plan A is our main path in life. Plan B: a backup that comes through. Plan Sea is to go with the flow.

Be ready for anything. And enjoy every moment along the way.

www.ingramcontent.com/pod-product-compliance
Lightning Source LLC
Chambersburg PA
CBHW021220060726
47590CB00005B/1576